This volume marks the one-year anniversary of the series.

Its contents are memorable to me too.

Who will Raku end up with?

I hope you'll keep following the story to find out.

Naoshi Komi

NAOSHI KOMI was born in Kochi Prefecture, Japan, on March 28, 1986. His first serialized work in *Weekly Shonen Jump* was the series *Double Arts*. His current series, *Nisekoi*, is serialized in *Weekly Shonen Jump*.

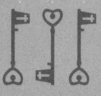

NISEKOI:
False Love
VOLUME 6
SHONEN JUMP Manga Edition

Story and Art by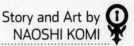
NAOSHI KOMI

Translation ⟋ Camellia Nieh
Touch-Up Art & Lettering ⟋ Stephen Dutro
Design ⟋ Fawn Lau
Shonen Jump Series Editor ⟋ John Bae
Graphic Novel Editor ⟋ Amy Yu

NISEKOI © 2011 by Naoshi Komi
All rights reserved.
First published in Japan in 2011
by SHUEISHA Inc., Tokyo.
English translation rights arranged
by SHUEISHA Inc.

The stories, characters and incidents mentioned
in this publication are entirely fictional.

Printed in the U.S.A.

Published by VIZ Media, LLC
P.O. Box 77010
San Francisco, CA 94107

10 9 8 7 6 5 3 4 2 1
First printing, November 2014

www.shonenjump.com

www.viz.com

NISEKOI
False Love
vol. 6: Showtime

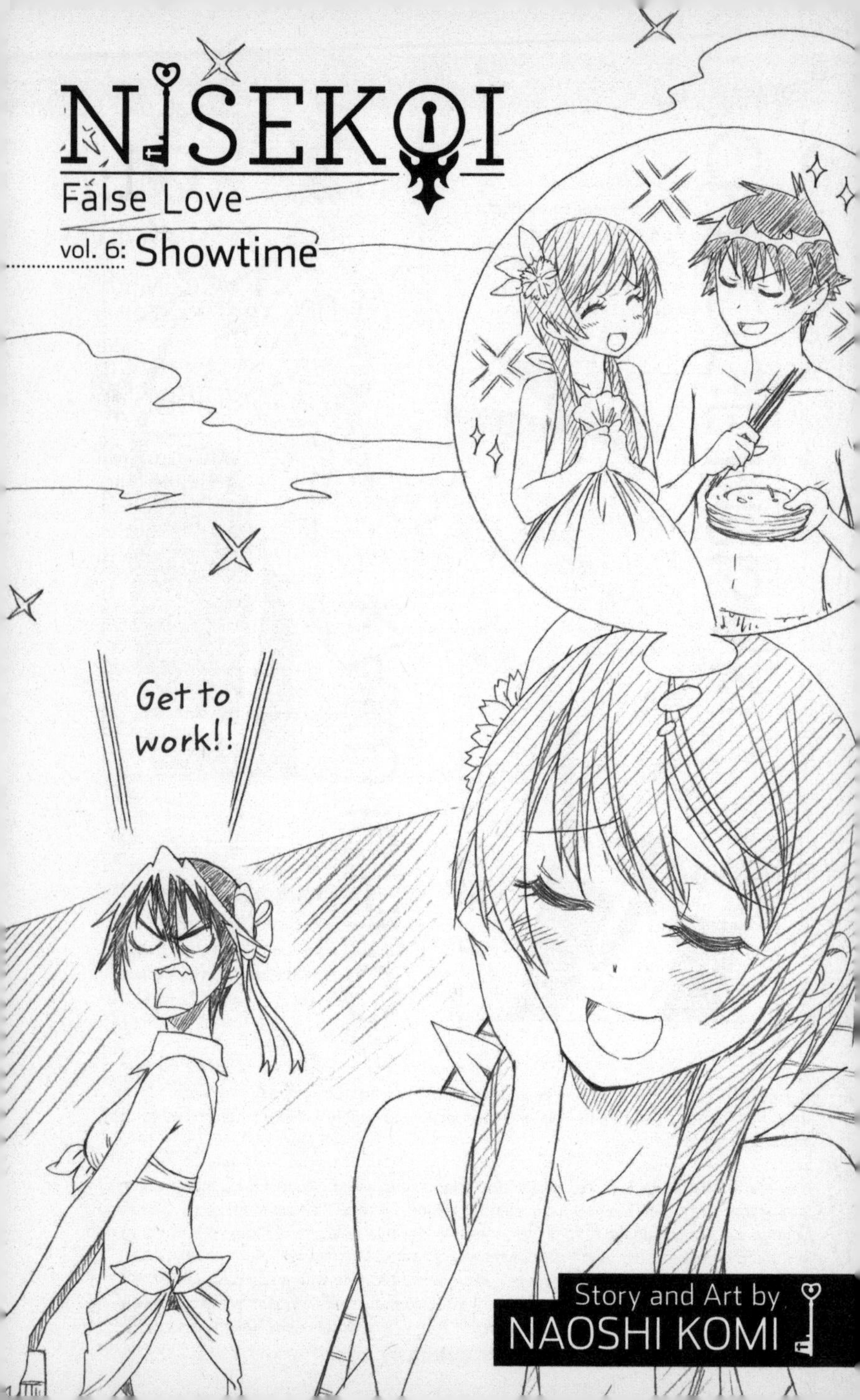
Get to work!!

Story and Art by
NAOSHI KOMI

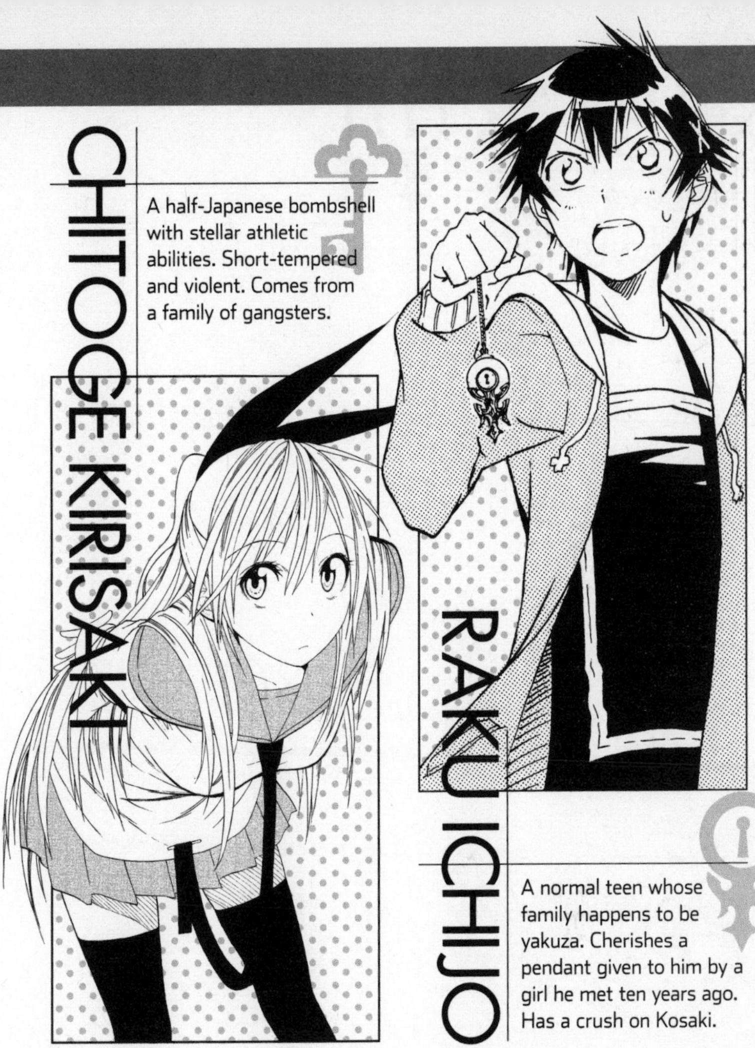

CHITOGE KIRISAKI

A half-Japanese bombshell with stellar athletic abilities. Short-tempered and violent. Comes from a family of gangsters.

RAKU ICHIJO

A normal teen whose family happens to be yakuza. Cherishes a pendant given to him by a girl he met ten years ago. Has a crush on Kosaki.

Raku Ichijo is an ordinary teen...who just happens to come from a family of yakuza! His most treasured item is a pendant he was given ten years ago by a girl whom he promised to meet again one day and marry.

It all starts when Raku is forced into a false relationship with Chitoge, the daughter of a rival gangster, to keep their families from shedding blood. Despite their constant spats, Raku and Chitoge somehow manage to fool everyone. The plot thickens when Chitoge discovers an old key and memories of her own first love ten years earlier! Meanwhile, Raku's crush, Kosaki, confesses to him that she also has a key and made a promise with a boy ten years ago. To complicate matters further, a new girl, Marika Tachibana, shows up claiming to be Raku's fiancée. The whole gang then goes on a beach trip, where Kosaki asks Raku to kiss her!

THE STORY THUS FAR

KOSAKI ONODERA

A girl Raku has a crush on. Beautiful and sweet, Kosaki has no shortage of admirers. She's a terrible cook but makes food that *looks* amazing.

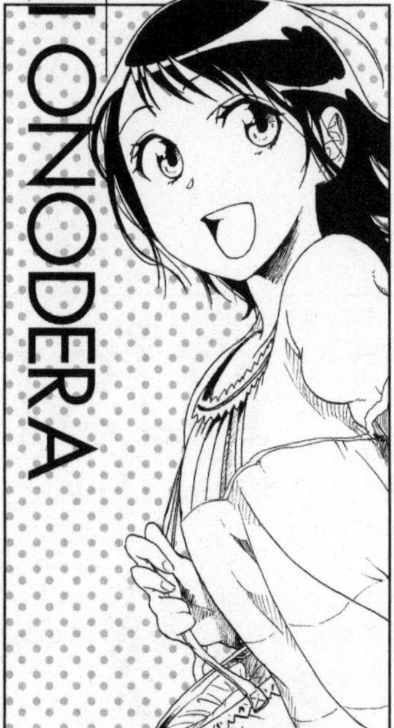

MARIKA TACHIBANA

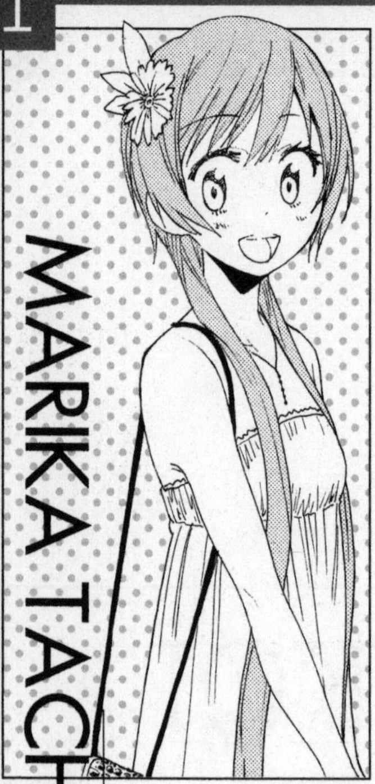

Daughter of the chief of police, Marika is Raku's fiancée, according to an agreement made by their fathers—an agreement Marika takes very seriously! Also has a key and remembers making a promise with Raku ten years ago.

SEISHIRO TSUGUMI

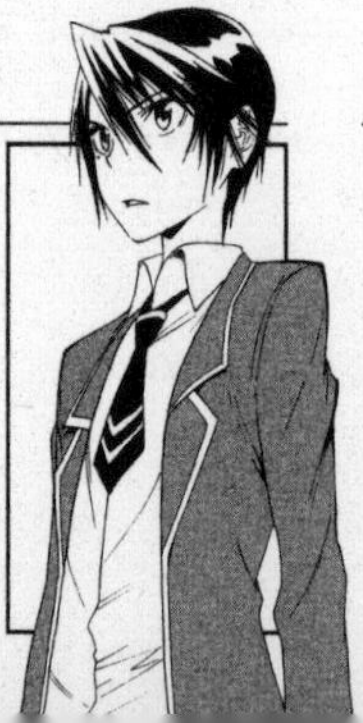

Adopted by Claude as a young child and raised as a top-notch assassin, Seishiro is 100% devoted to Chitoge. Often mistaken for a boy, Tsugumi's really a girl.

SHU MAIKO

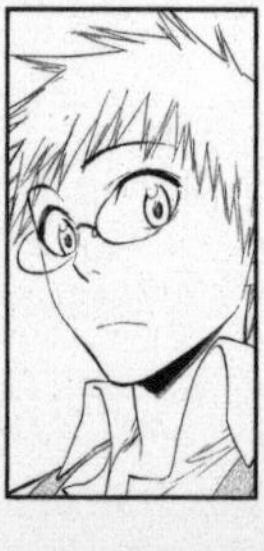

Raku's best friend. Outgoing and girl-crazy. Always tuned in to the latest gossip at school.

RURI MIYAMOTO

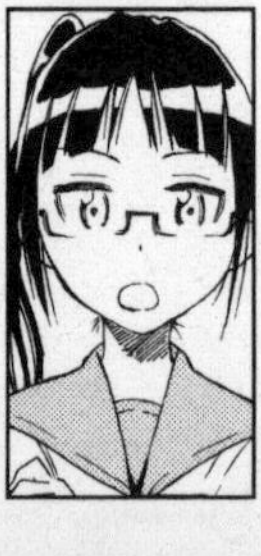

Kosaki's best gal pal. Comes off as aloof, but is actually a devoted and highly intuitive friend.

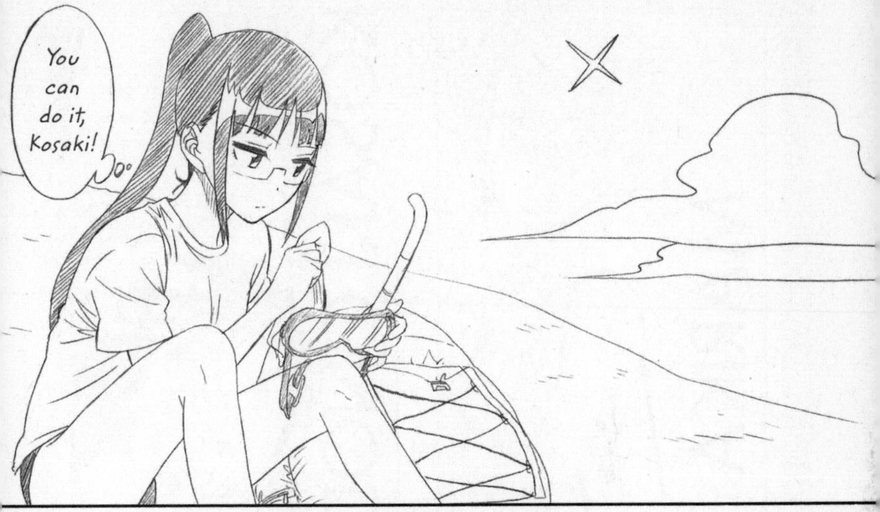
You can do it, Kosaki!

NISEKOI

False Love

vol. 6: Showtime

TABLE OF CONTENTS

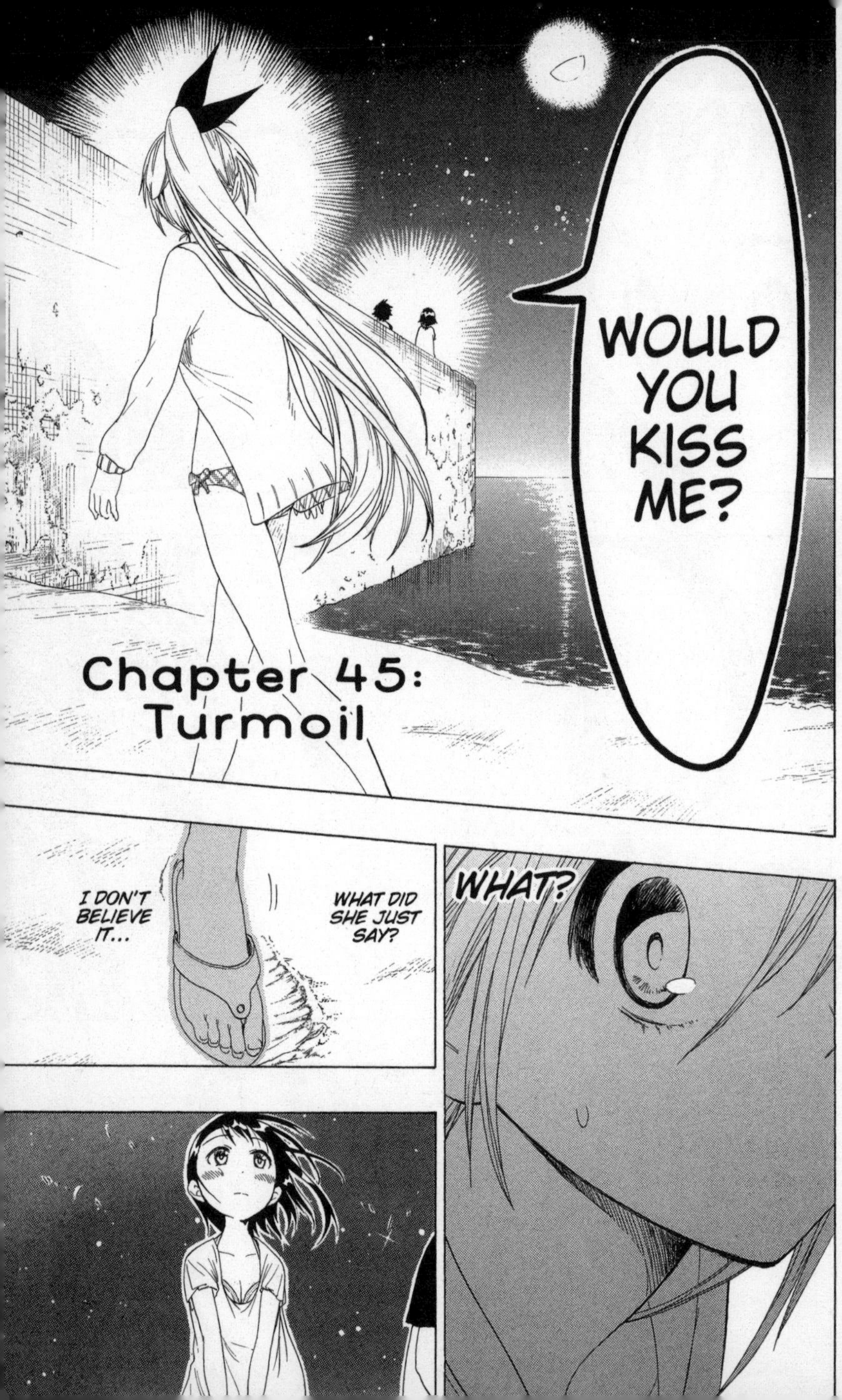
WOULD YOU KISS ME?
Chapter 45: Turmoil
WHAT?
WHAT DID SHE JUST SAY?
I DON'T BELIEVE IT...

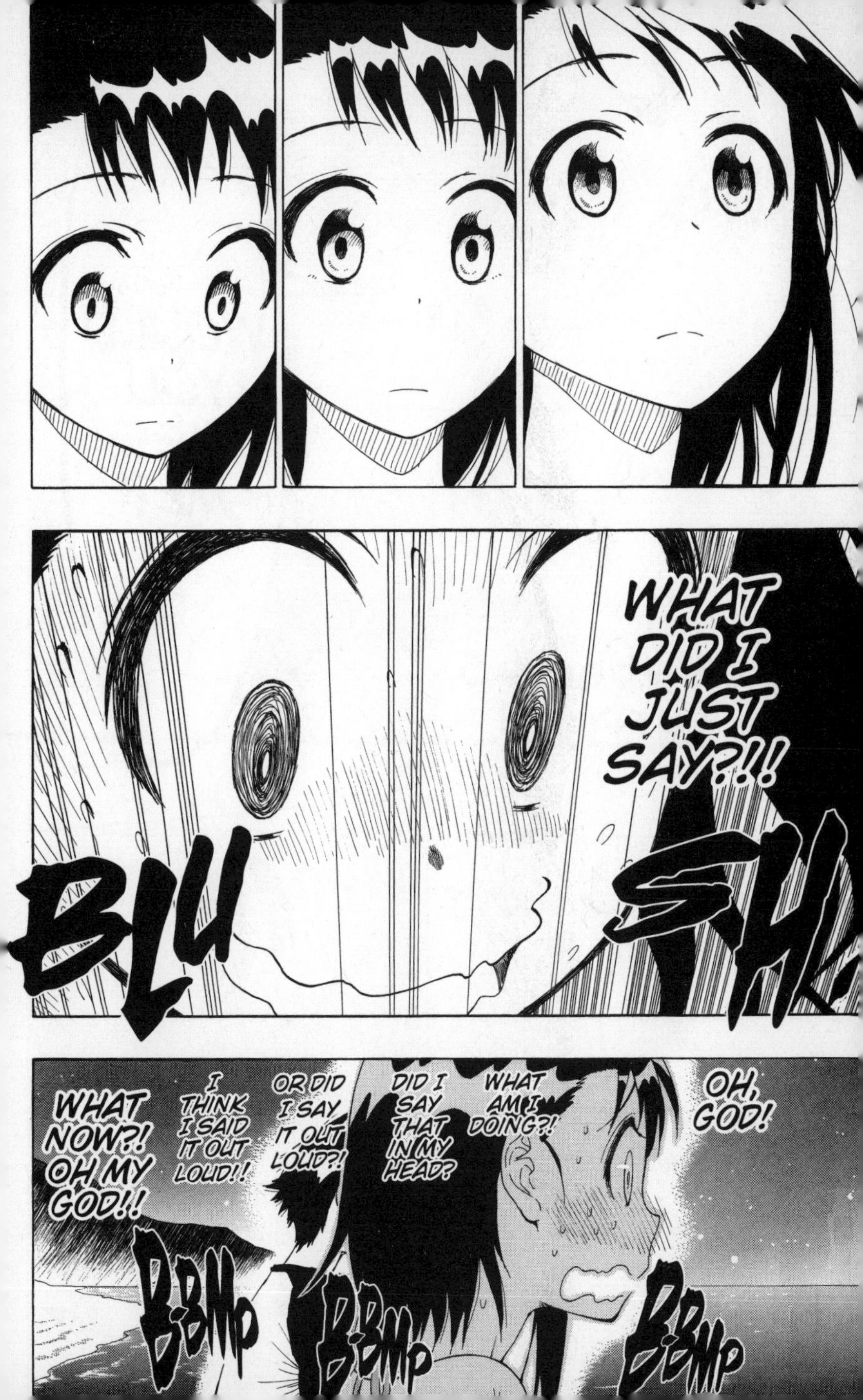
WHAT DID I JUST SAY?!!
BLUSH
OH, GOD!
WHAT AM I DOING?!
DID I SAY THAT IN MY HEAD?
OR DID I SAY IT OUT LOUD?!
I THINK I SAID IT OUT LOUD!!
WHAT NOW?! OH MY GOD!!
B-BMP
B-BMP
B-BMP

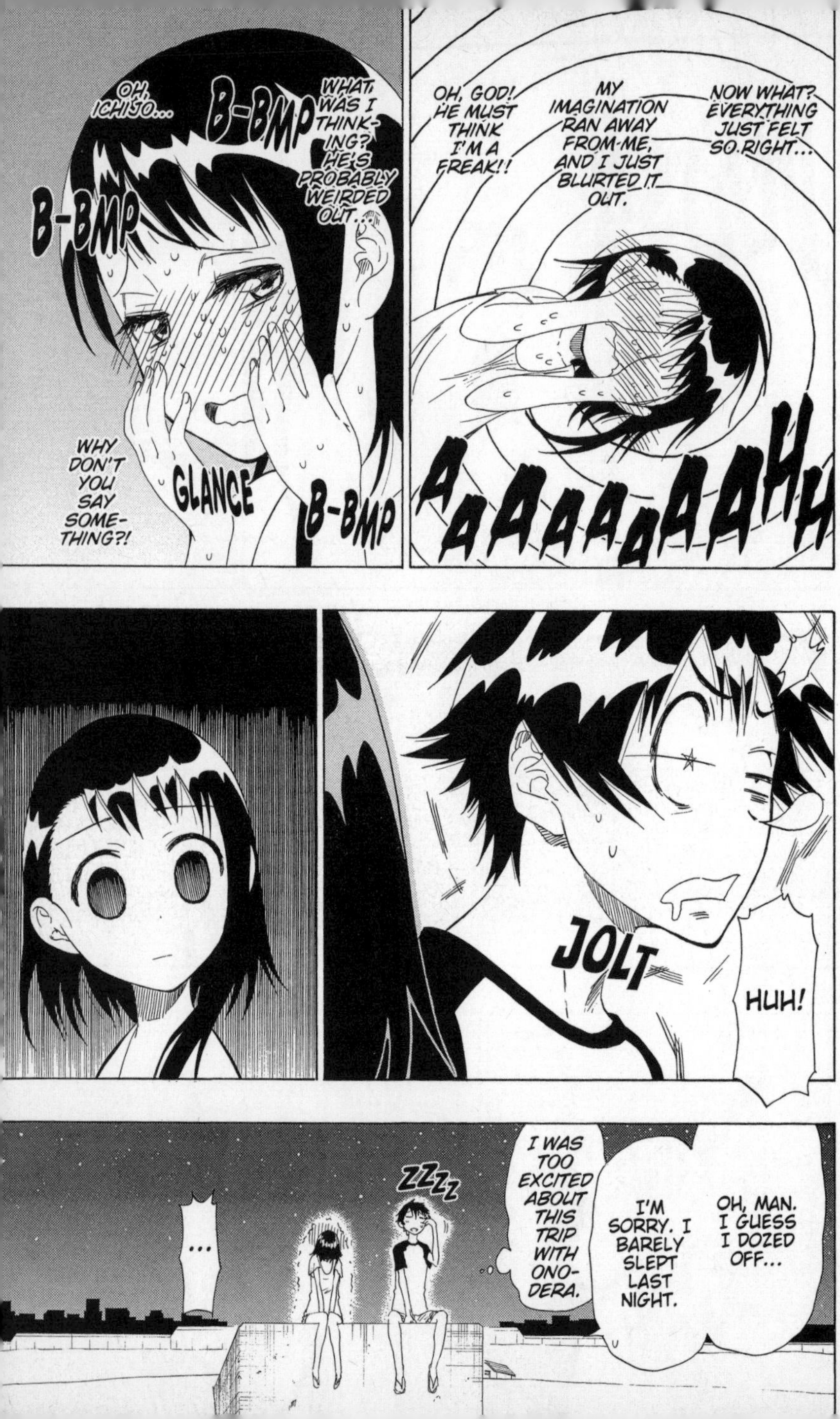
NOW WHAT? EVERYTHING JUST FELT SO RIGHT...
MY IMAGINATION RAN AWAY FROM ME, AND I JUST BLURTED IT OUT.
OH, GOD! HE MUST THINK I'M A FREAK!!
AAAAAAAAAAHH
WHAT WAS I THINKING? HE'S PROBABLY WEIRDED OUT...
B-BMP
OH, ICHIJO...
B-BMP
WHY DON'T YOU SAY SOMETHING?!
GLANCE
B-BMP
JOLT
HUH!
OH, MAN. I GUESS I DOZED OFF...
I'M SORRY. I BARELY SLEPT LAST NIGHT.
I WAS TOO EXCITED ABOUT THIS TRIP WITH ONODERA.
ZZZZ
...

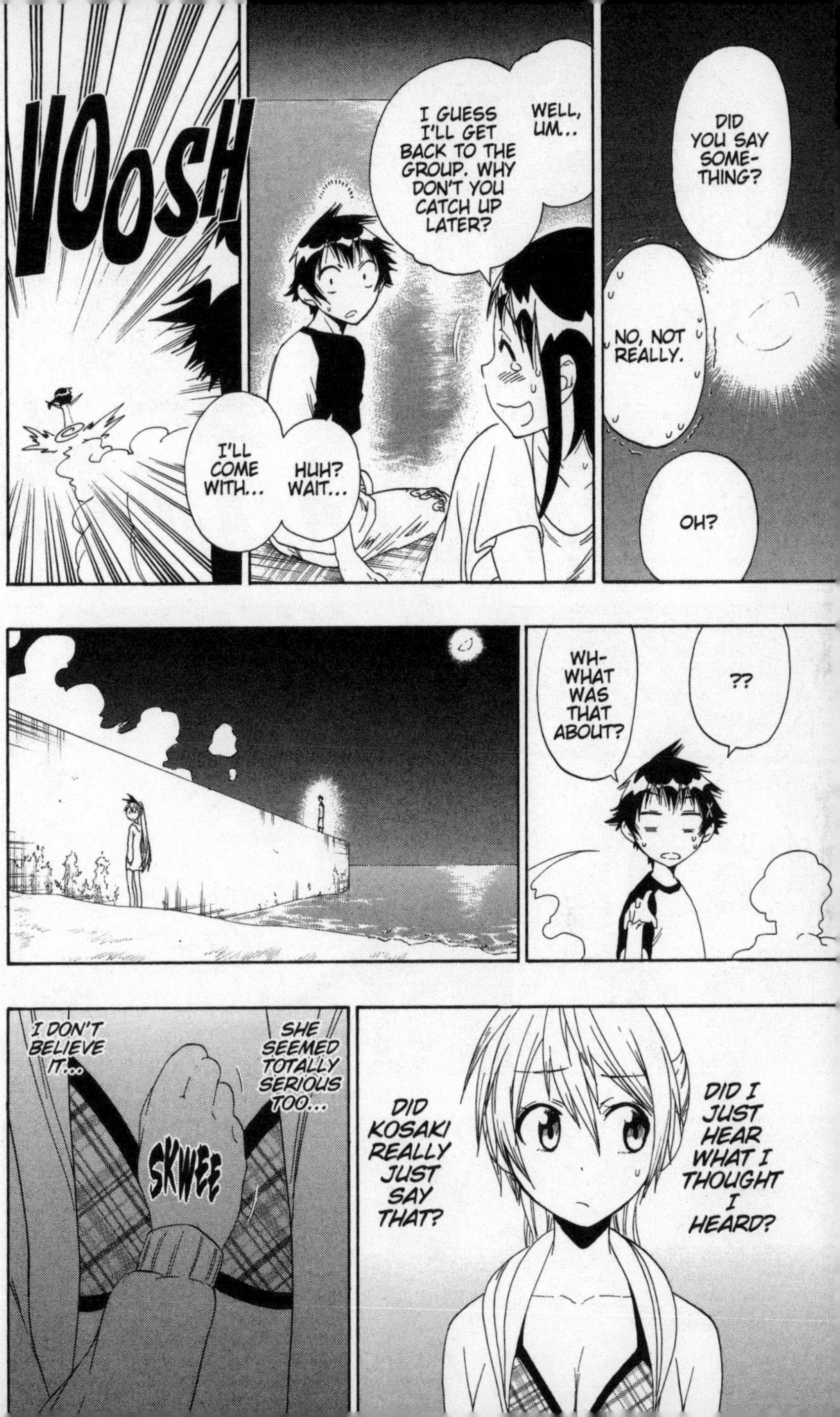
DID YOU SAY SOMETHING?
NO, NOT REALLY.
OH?
WELL, UM...
I GUESS I'LL GET BACK TO THE GROUP. WHY DON'T YOU CATCH UP LATER?
HUH? WAIT...
I'LL COME WITH...
VOOSH
??
WH-WHAT WAS THAT ABOUT?
DID I JUST HEAR WHAT I THOUGHT I HEARD?
DID KOSAKI REALLY JUST SAY THAT?
SHE SEEMED TOTALLY SERIOUS TOO...
I DON'T BELIEVE IT...
SKWEE

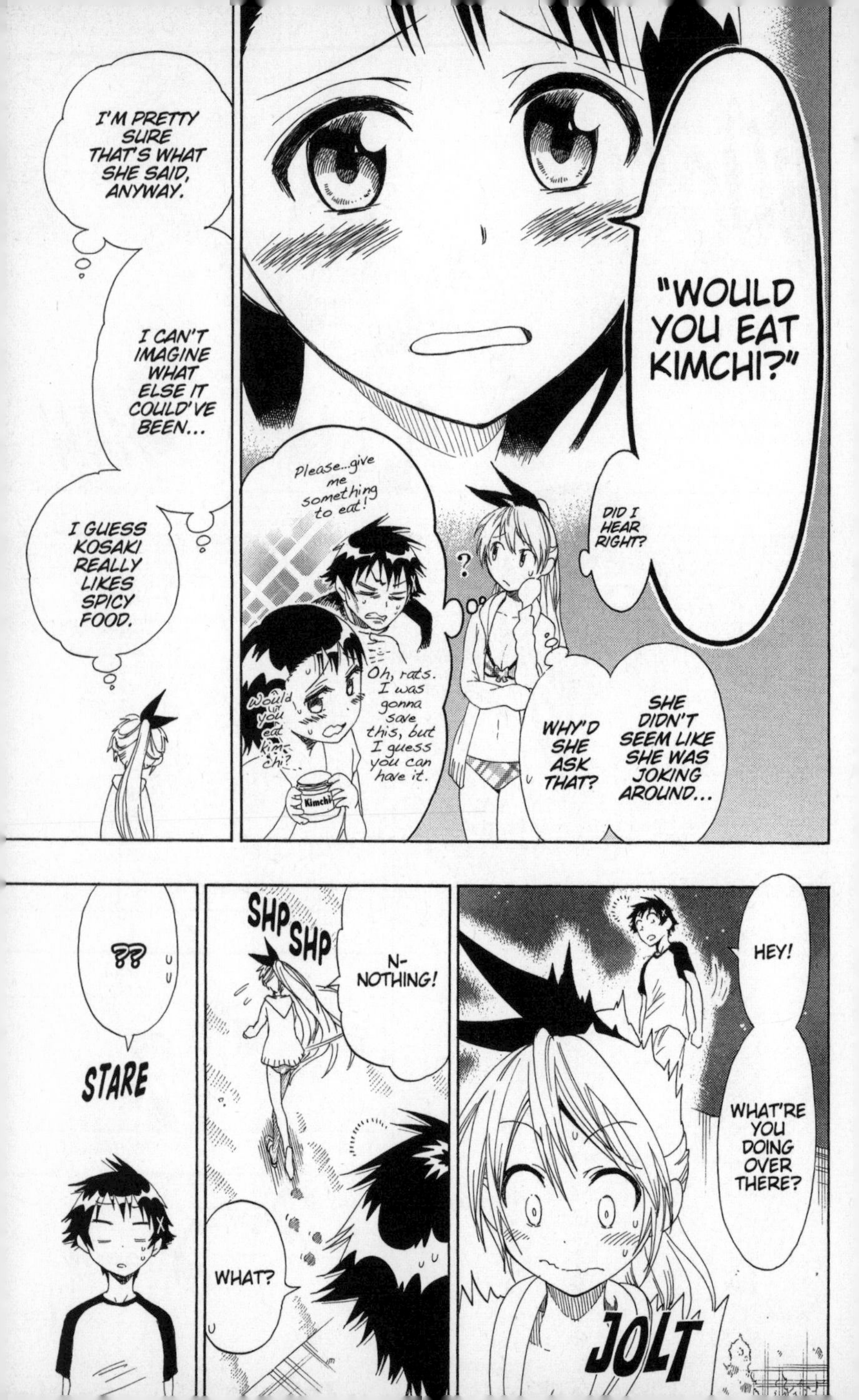
"WOULD YOU EAT KIMCHI?"
DID I HEAR RIGHT?
Please...give me something to eat!
Oh, rats. I was gonna save this, but I guess you can have it.
Would you eat kimchi?
Kimchi
SHE DIDN'T SEEM LIKE SHE WAS JOKING AROUND...
WHY'D SHE ASK THAT?
I'M PRETTY SURE THAT'S WHAT SHE SAID, ANYWAY.
I CAN'T IMAGINE WHAT ELSE IT COULD'VE BEEN...
I GUESS KOSAKI REALLY LIKES SPICY FOOD.
HEY!
WHAT'RE YOU DOING OVER THERE?
JOLT
N- NOTHING!
SHP SHP
WHAT?
??
STARE

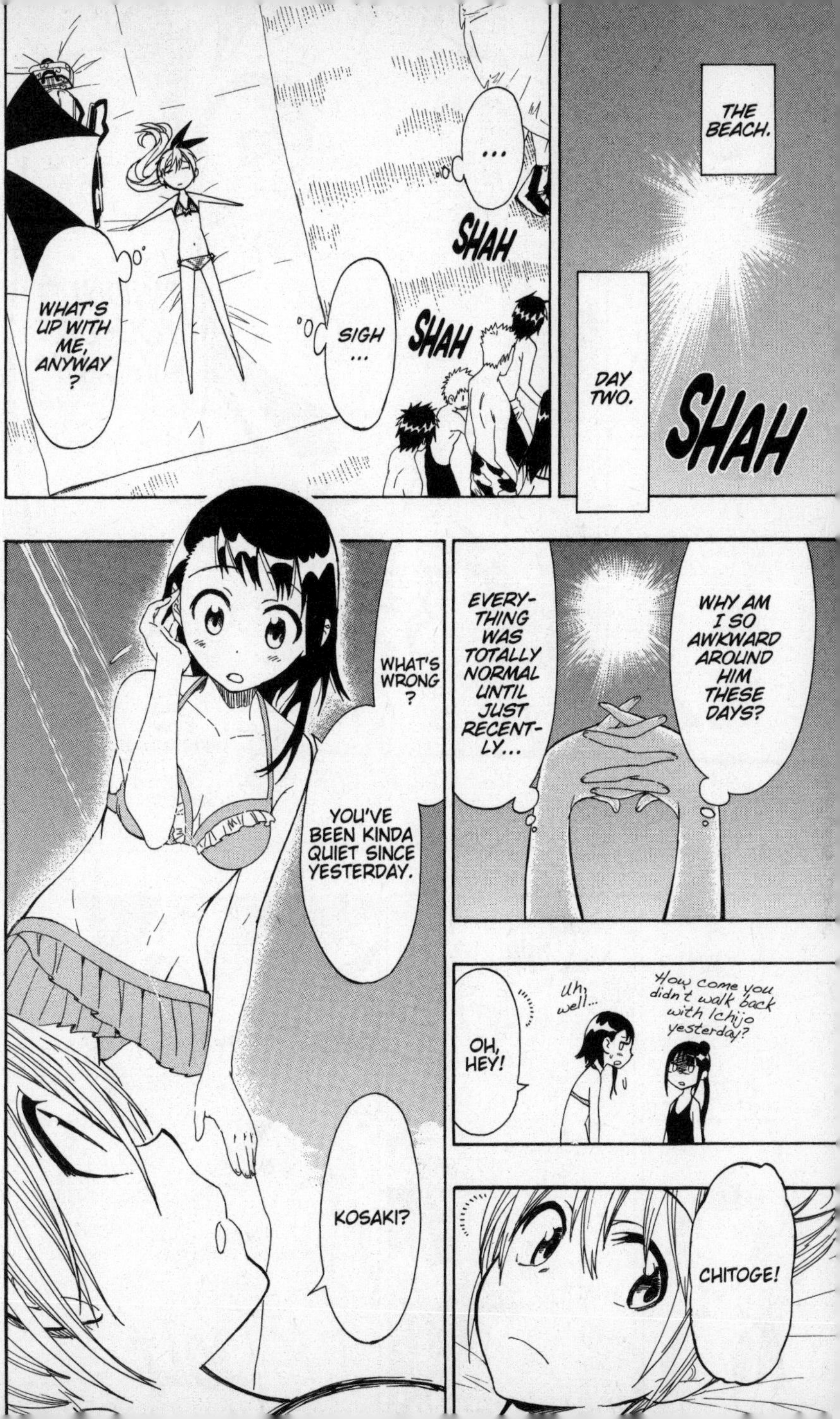
THE BEACH.
DAY TWO.
SHAH
...
SHAH
SHAH
SIGH ...
WHAT'S UP WITH ME, ANYWAY?
WHY AM I SO AWKWARD AROUND HIM THESE DAYS?
EVERYTHING WAS TOTALLY NORMAL UNTIL JUST RECENTLY...
How come you didn't walk back with Ichijo yesterday?
Uh, well...
OH, HEY!
CHITOGE!
WHAT'S WRONG?
YOU'VE BEEN KINDA QUIET SINCE YESTERDAY.
KOSAKI?

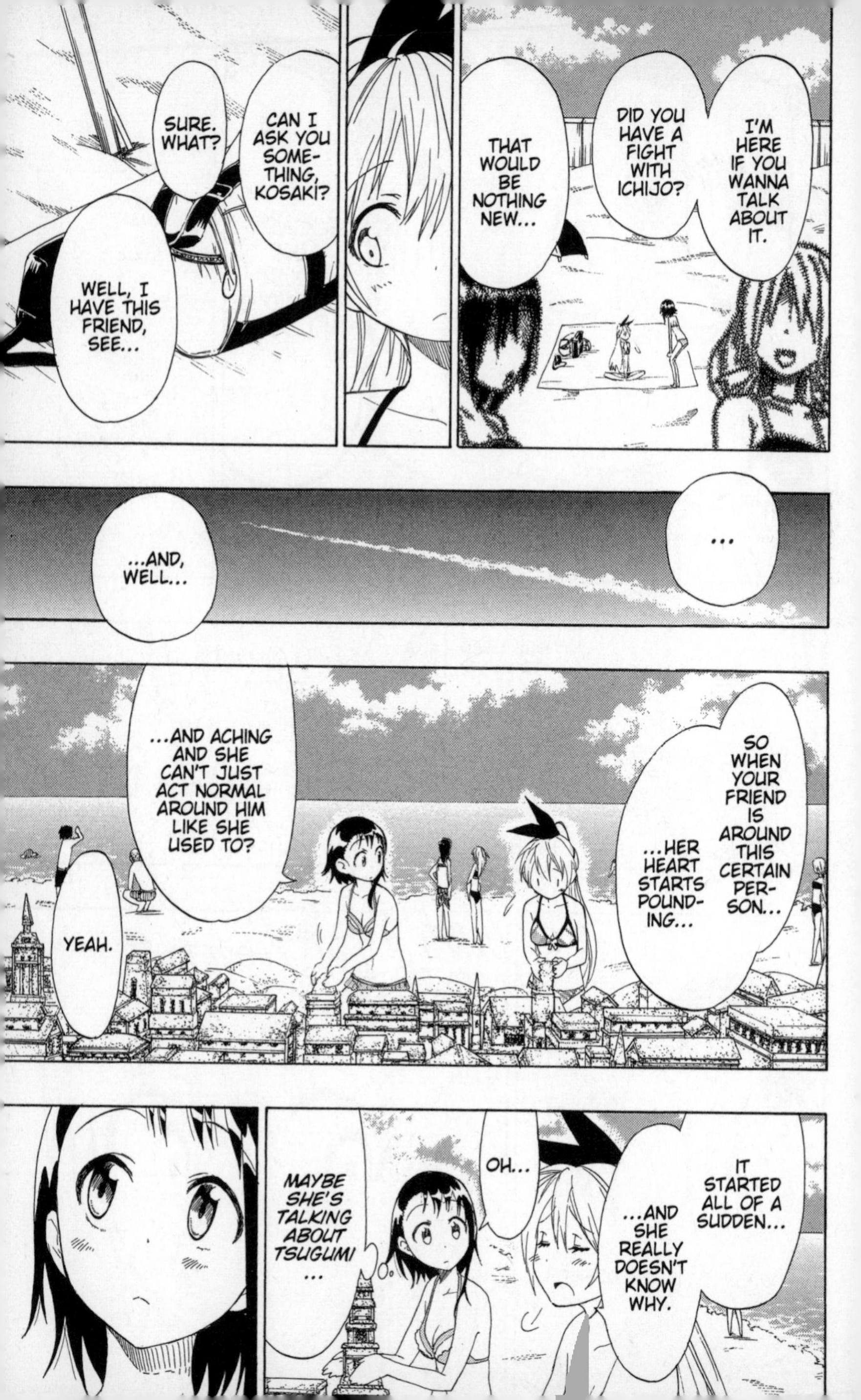
I'M HERE IF YOU WANNA TALK ABOUT IT.
DID YOU HAVE A FIGHT WITH ICHIJO?
THAT WOULD BE NOTHING NEW...
CAN I ASK YOU SOMETHING, KOSAKI?
SURE. WHAT?
WELL, I HAVE THIS FRIEND, SEE...
...
...AND, WELL...
SO WHEN YOUR FRIEND IS AROUND THIS CERTAIN PERSON...
...HER HEART STARTS POUNDING...
...AND ACHING AND SHE CAN'T JUST ACT NORMAL AROUND HIM LIKE SHE USED TO?
YEAH.
IT STARTED ALL OF A SUDDEN...
...AND SHE REALLY DOESN'T KNOW WHY.
OH...
MAYBE SHE'S TALKING ABOUT TSUGUMI...

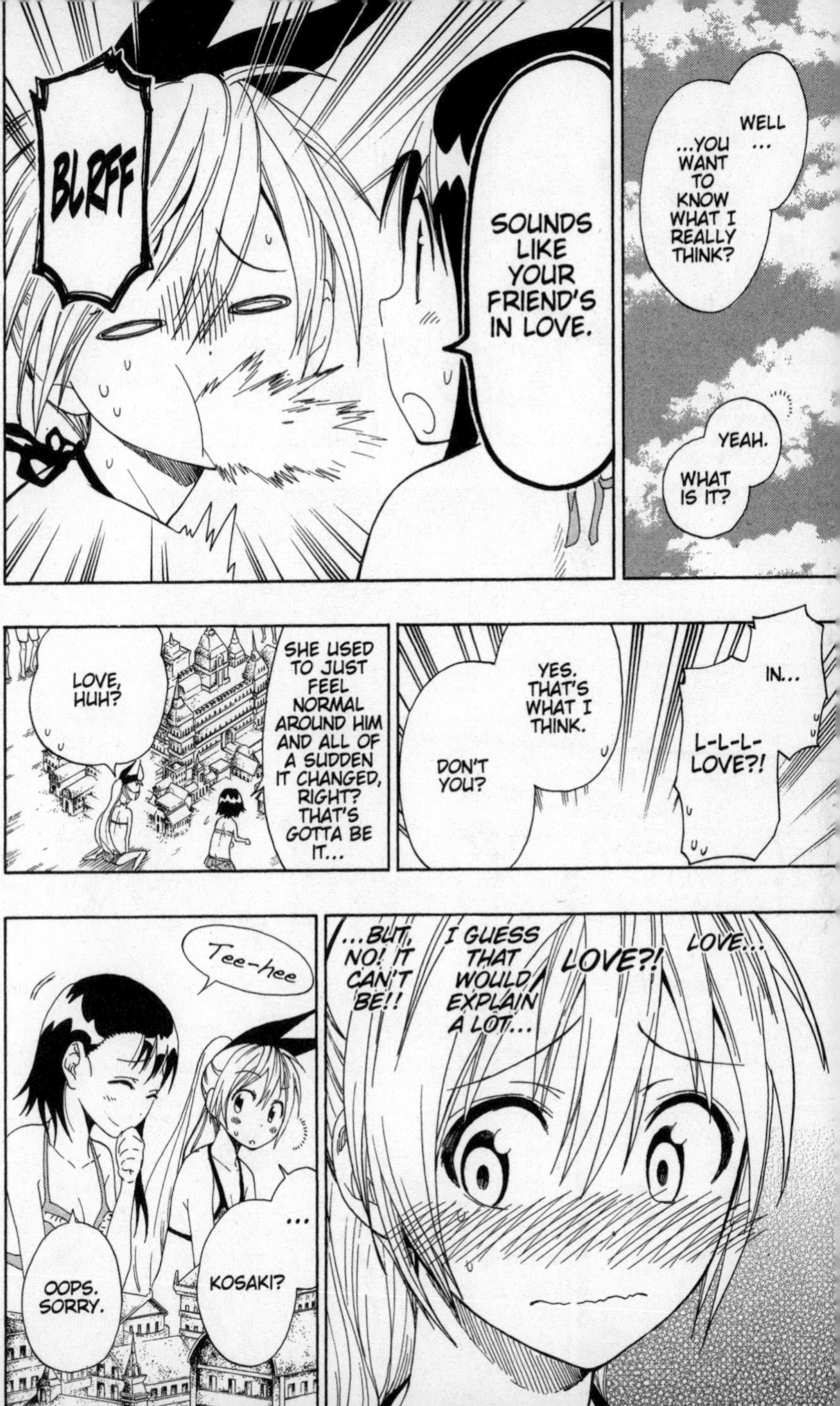
WELL ... ...YOU WANT TO KNOW WHAT I REALLY THINK?
YEAH. WHAT IS IT?
SOUNDS LIKE YOUR FRIEND'S IN LOVE.
BLRFF
IN... L-L-L-LOVE?!
YES. THAT'S WHAT I THINK.
DON'T YOU?
SHE USED TO JUST FEEL NORMAL AROUND HIM AND ALL OF A SUDDEN IT CHANGED, RIGHT? THAT'S GOTTA BE IT...
LOVE, HUH?
LOVE...
LOVE?!
I GUESS THAT WOULD EXPLAIN A LOT...
...BUT, NO! IT CAN'T BE!!
Tee-hee
...
KOSAKI?
OOPS. SORRY.

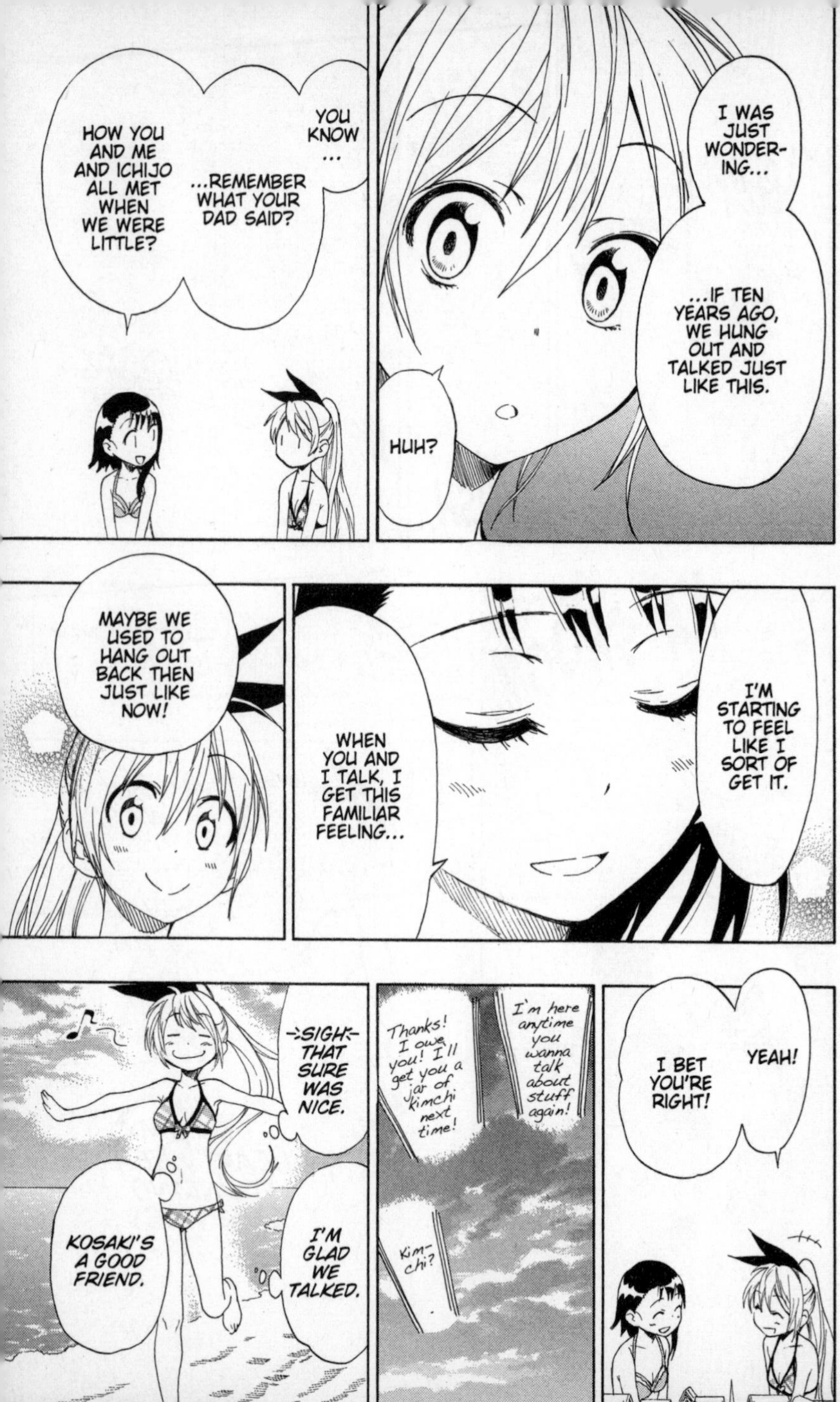
I WAS JUST WONDERING...
...IF TEN YEARS AGO, WE HUNG OUT AND TALKED JUST LIKE THIS.
HUH?
YOU KNOW...
...REMEMBER WHAT YOUR DAD SAID?
HOW YOU AND ME AND ICHIJO ALL MET WHEN WE WERE LITTLE?
I'M STARTING TO FEEL LIKE I SORT OF GET IT.
WHEN YOU AND I TALK, I GET THIS FAMILIAR FEELING...
MAYBE WE USED TO HANG OUT BACK THEN JUST LIKE NOW!
YEAH!
I BET YOU'RE RIGHT!
I'm here anytime you wanna talk about stuff again!
Thanks! I owe you! I'll get you a jar of kimchi next time!
Kim-chi?
-SIGH- THAT SURE WAS NICE.
I'M GLAD WE TALKED.
KOSAKI'S A GOOD FRIEND.

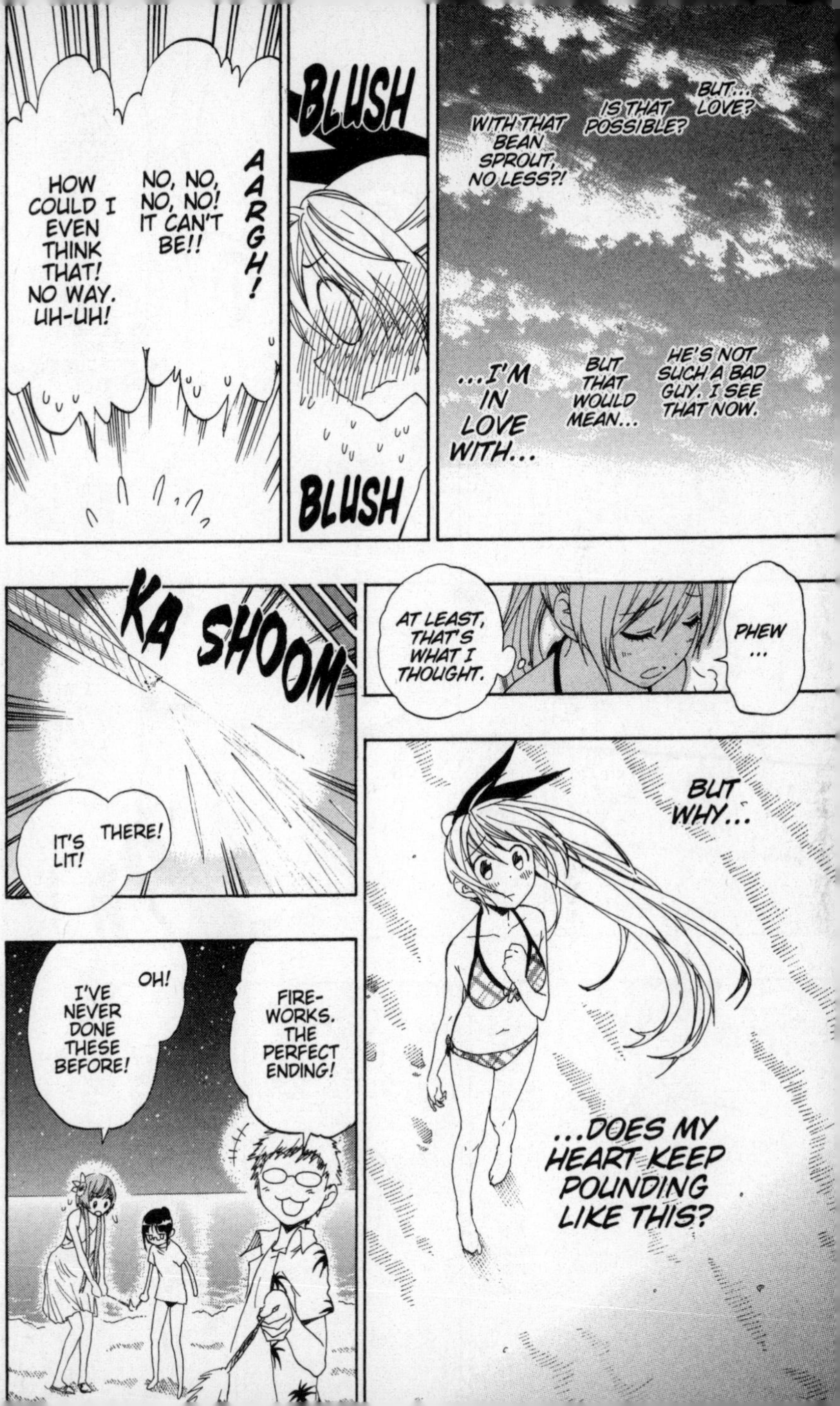
BUT... LOVE?
IS THAT POSSIBLE?
WITH THAT BEAN SPROUT, NO LESS?!
HE'S NOT SUCH A BAD GUY. I SEE THAT NOW.
BUT THAT WOULD MEAN...
...I'M IN LOVE WITH...
BLUSH
AARGH!
BLUSH
NO, NO, NO, NO! IT CAN'T BE!!
HOW COULD I EVEN THINK THAT! NO WAY. UH-UH!
PHEW...
AT LEAST, THAT'S WHAT I THOUGHT.
BUT WHY...
...DOES MY HEART KEEP POUNDING LIKE THIS?
KA SHOOM
THERE!
IT'S LIT!
FIRE-WORKS. THE PERFECT ENDING!
OH!
I'VE NEVER DONE THESE BEFORE!

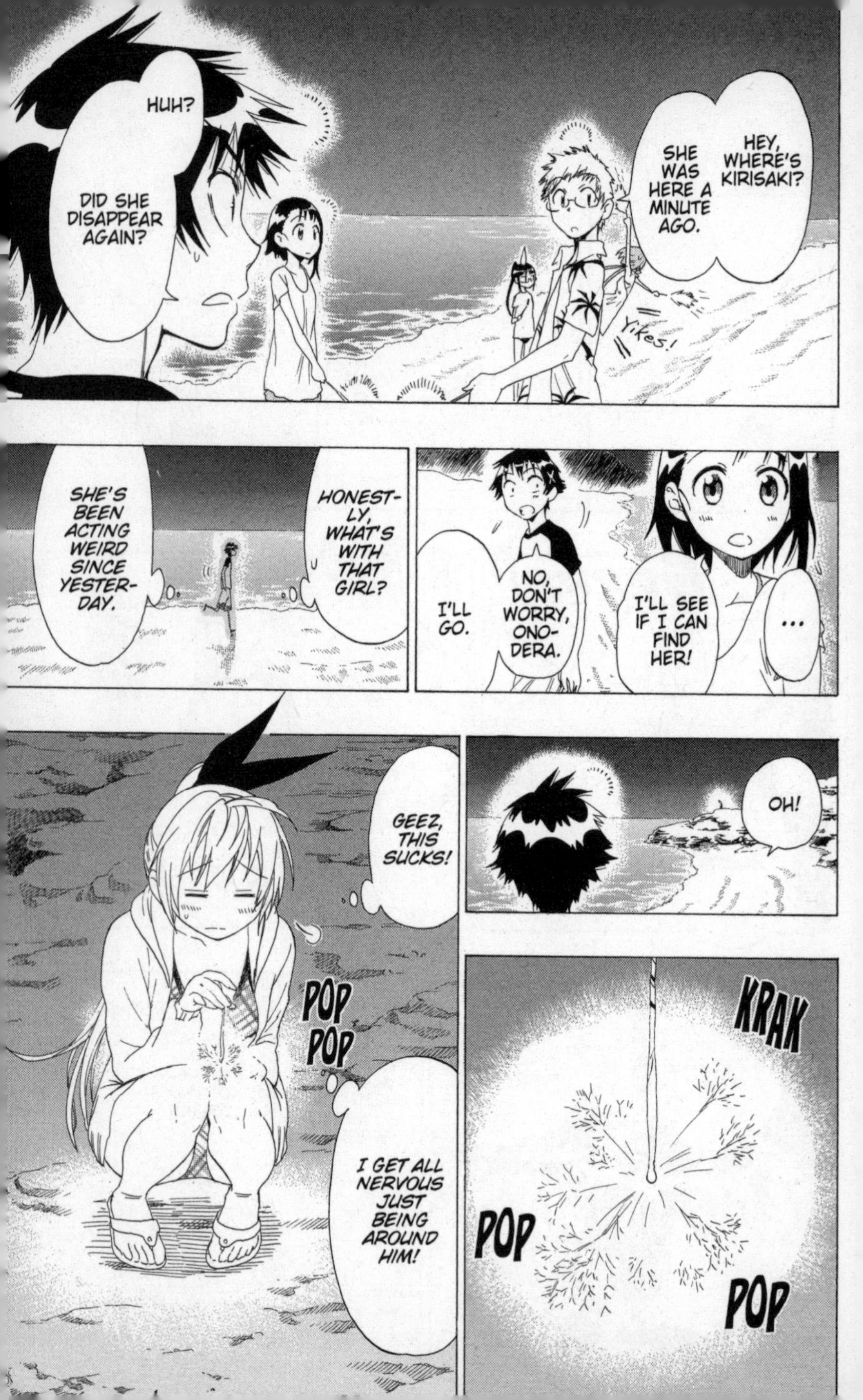
HEY, WHERE'S KIRISAKI?
SHE WAS HERE A MINUTE AGO.
Yikes!
HUH?
DID SHE DISAPPEAR AGAIN?
...
I'LL SEE IF I CAN FIND HER!
NO, DON'T WORRY, ONODERA.
I'LL GO.
HONESTLY, WHAT'S WITH THAT GIRL?
SHE'S BEEN ACTING WEIRD SINCE YESTERDAY.
OH!
KRAK
POP
POP
GEEZ, THIS SUCKS!
POP POP
I GET ALL NERVOUS JUST BEING AROUND HIM!

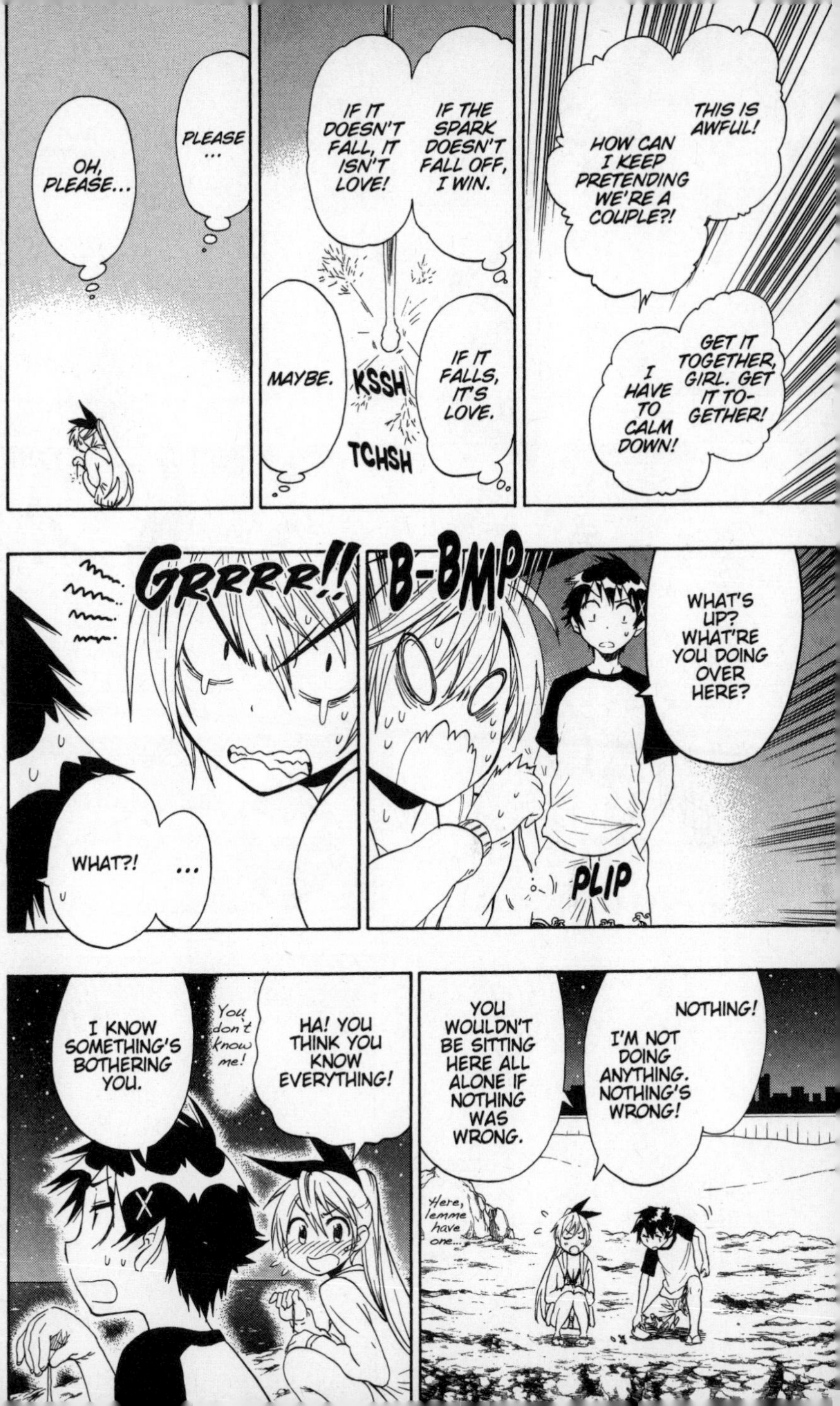
THIS IS AWFUL!
HOW CAN I KEEP PRETENDING WE'RE A COUPLE?!
GET IT TOGETHER, GIRL. GET IT TO-GETHER!
I HAVE TO CALM DOWN!
IF THE SPARK DOESN'T FALL OFF, I WIN.
IF IT DOESN'T FALL, IT ISN'T LOVE!
IF IT FALLS, IT'S LOVE.
KSSH
MAYBE.
TCHSH
PLEASE...
OH, PLEASE...
B-BMP
WHAT'S UP? WHAT'RE YOU DOING OVER HERE?
PLIP
GRRRRR!!
...
WHAT?!
NOTHING!
I'M NOT DOING ANYTHING. NOTHING'S WRONG!
YOU WOULDN'T BE SITTING HERE ALL ALONE IF NOTHING WAS WRONG.
Here, lemme have one...
HA! YOU THINK YOU KNOW EVERYTHING!
You don't know me!
I KNOW SOMETHING'S BOTHERING YOU.

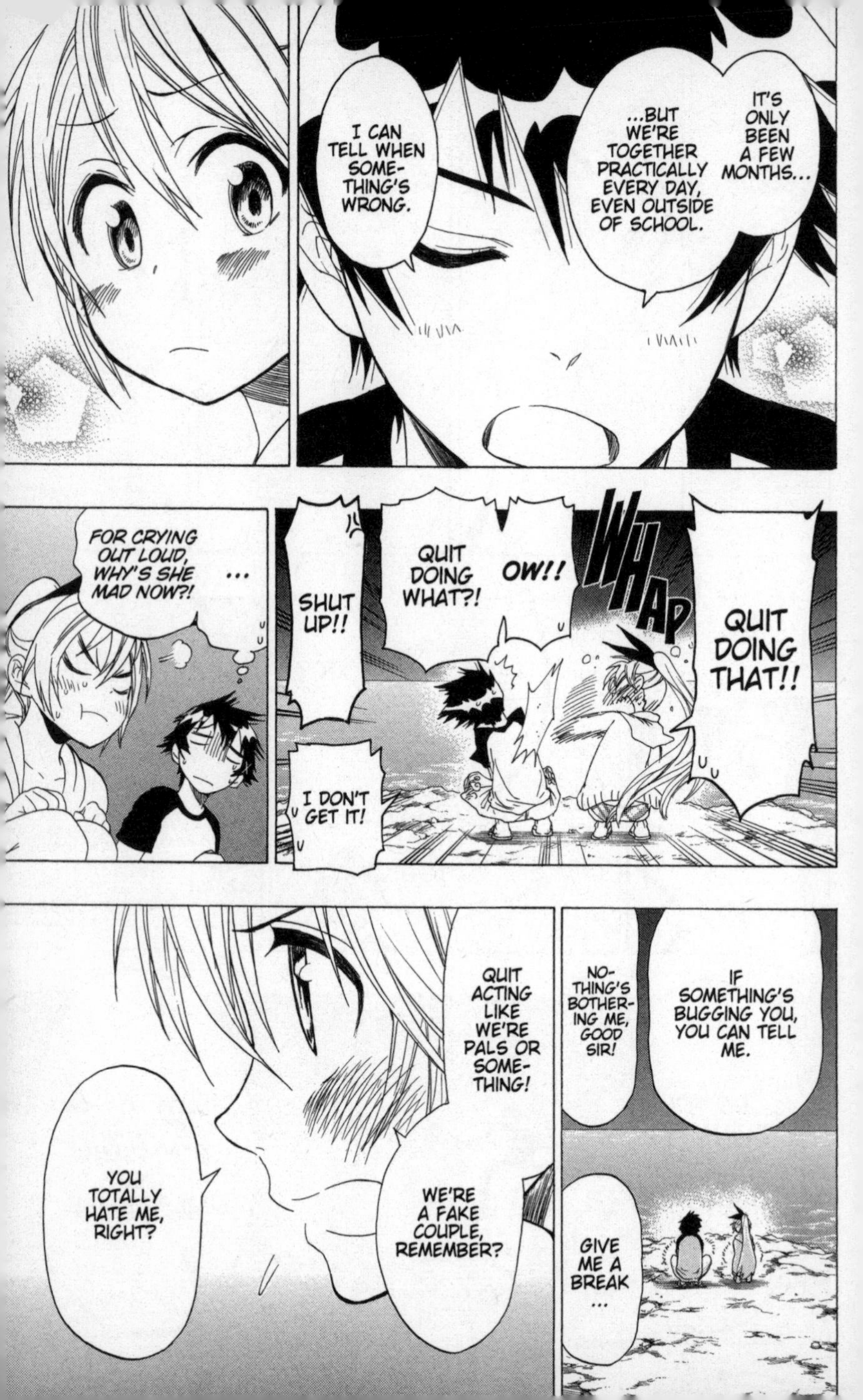
IT'S ONLY BEEN A FEW MONTHS...
...BUT WE'RE TOGETHER PRACTICALLY EVERY DAY, EVEN OUTSIDE OF SCHOOL.
I CAN TELL WHEN SOMETHING'S WRONG.
QUIT DOING THAT!!
WHAP
OW!!
QUIT DOING WHAT?!
SHUT UP!!
I DON'T GET IT!
...
FOR CRYING OUT LOUD, WHY'S SHE MAD NOW?!
IF SOMETHING'S BUGGING YOU, YOU CAN TELL ME.
NOTHING'S BOTHERING ME, GOOD SIR!
GIVE ME A BREAK...
QUIT ACTING LIKE WE'RE PALS OR SOMETHING!
WE'RE A FAKE COUPLE, REMEMBER?
YOU TOTALLY HATE ME, RIGHT?

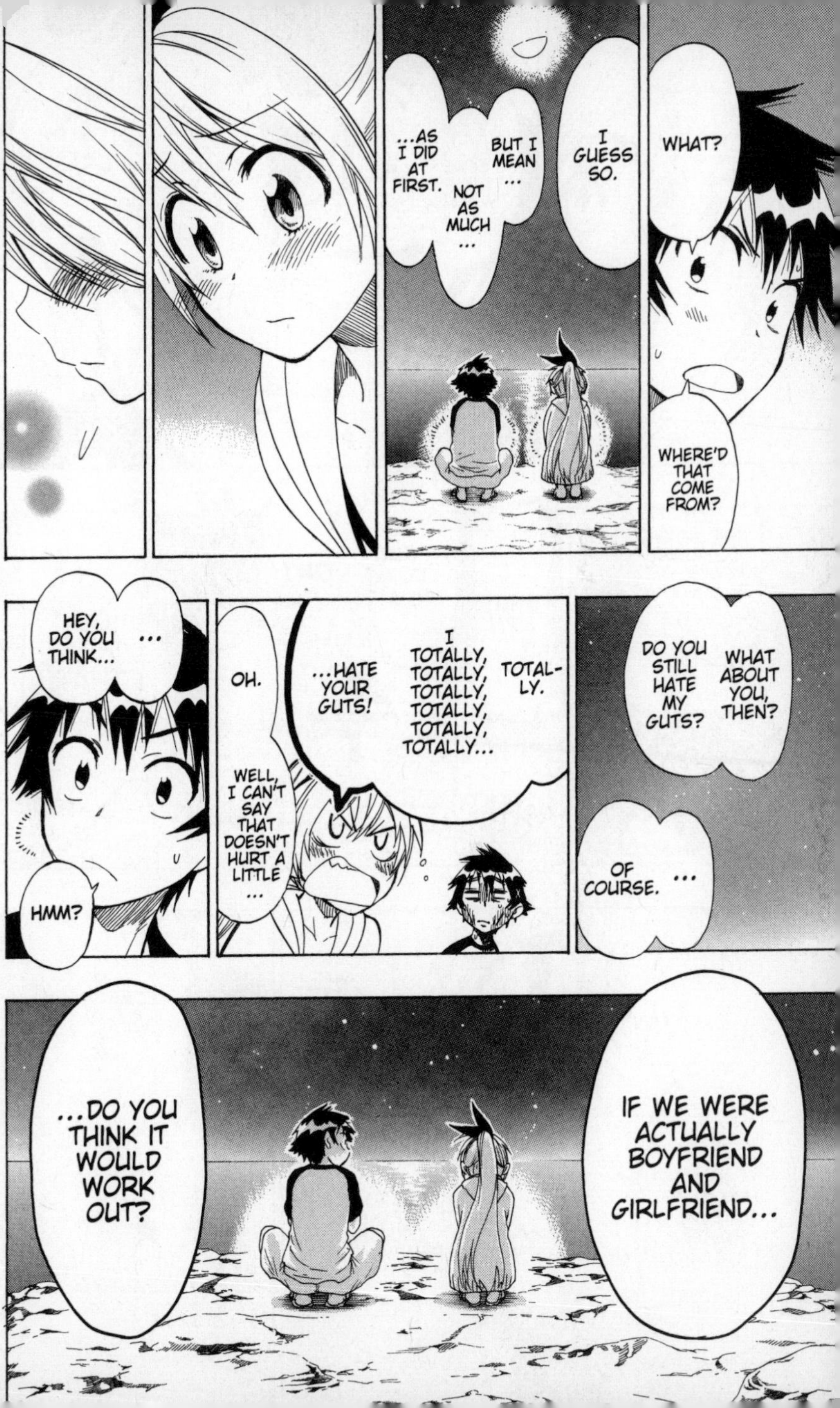
WHAT?
WHERE'D THAT COME FROM?
I GUESS SO.
BUT I MEAN ...
NOT AS MUCH ...
...AS I DID AT FIRST.
WHAT ABOUT YOU, THEN?
DO YOU STILL HATE MY GUTS?
OF COURSE. ...
TOTAL-LY.
I TOTALLY, TOTALLY, TOTALLY, TOTALLY, TOTALLY, TOTALLY...
...HATE YOUR GUTS!
OH.
WELL, I CAN'T SAY THAT DOESN'T HURT A LITTLE ...
HEY, DO YOU THINK... ...
HMM?
IF WE WERE ACTUALLY BOYFRIEND AND GIRLFRIEND...
...DO YOU THINK IT WOULD WORK OUT?

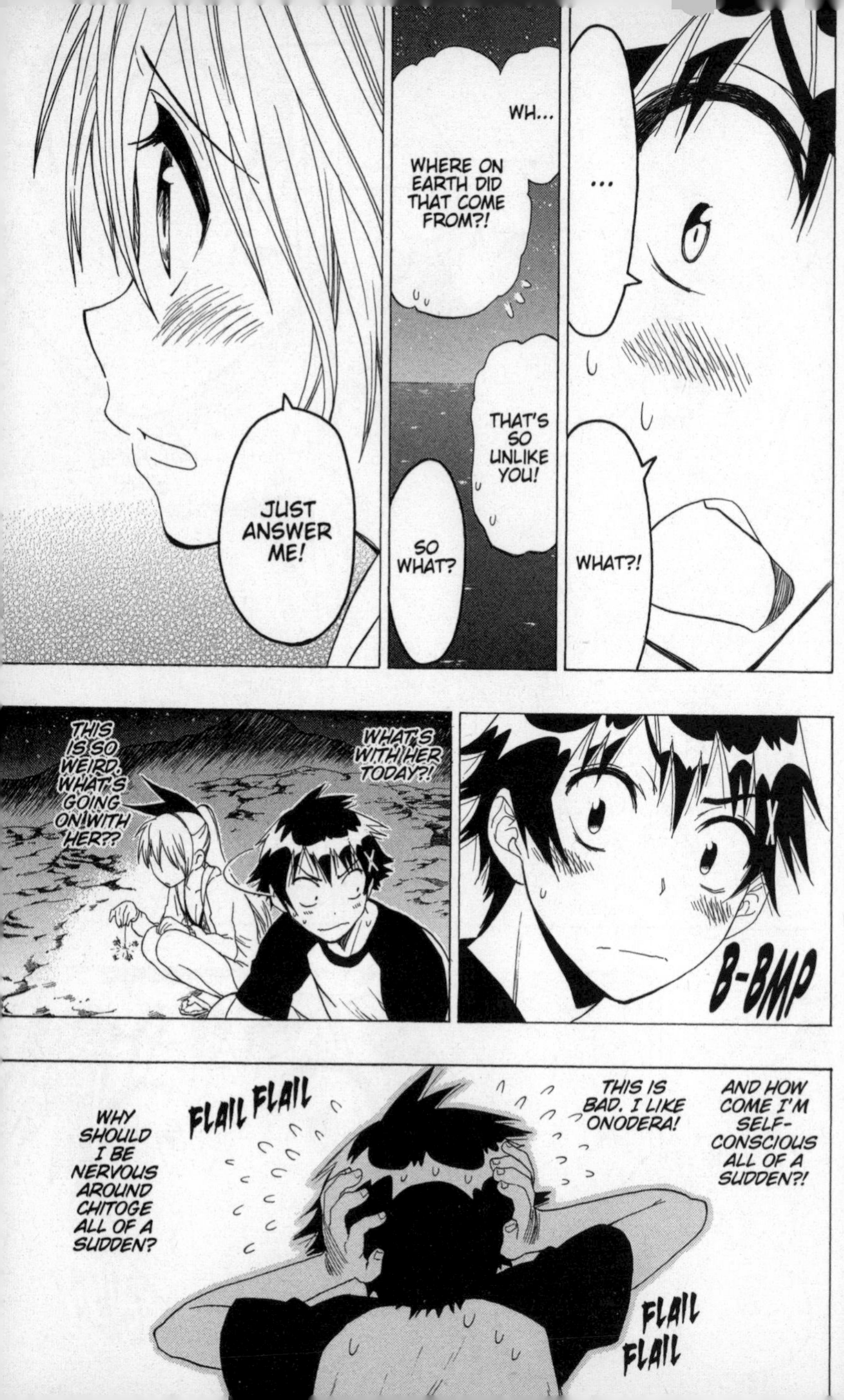
...
WHAT?!
WH...
WHERE ON EARTH DID THAT COME FROM?!
THAT'S SO UNLIKE YOU!
SO WHAT?
JUST ANSWER ME!
B-BMP
WHAT'S WITH HER TODAY?!
THIS IS SO WEIRD. WHAT'S GOING ON WITH HER??
AND HOW COME I'M SELF-CONSCIOUS ALL OF A SUDDEN?!
THIS IS BAD. I LIKE ONODERA!
FLAIL FLAIL
WHY SHOULD I BE NERVOUS AROUND CHITOGE ALL OF A SUDDEN?
FLAIL FLAIL

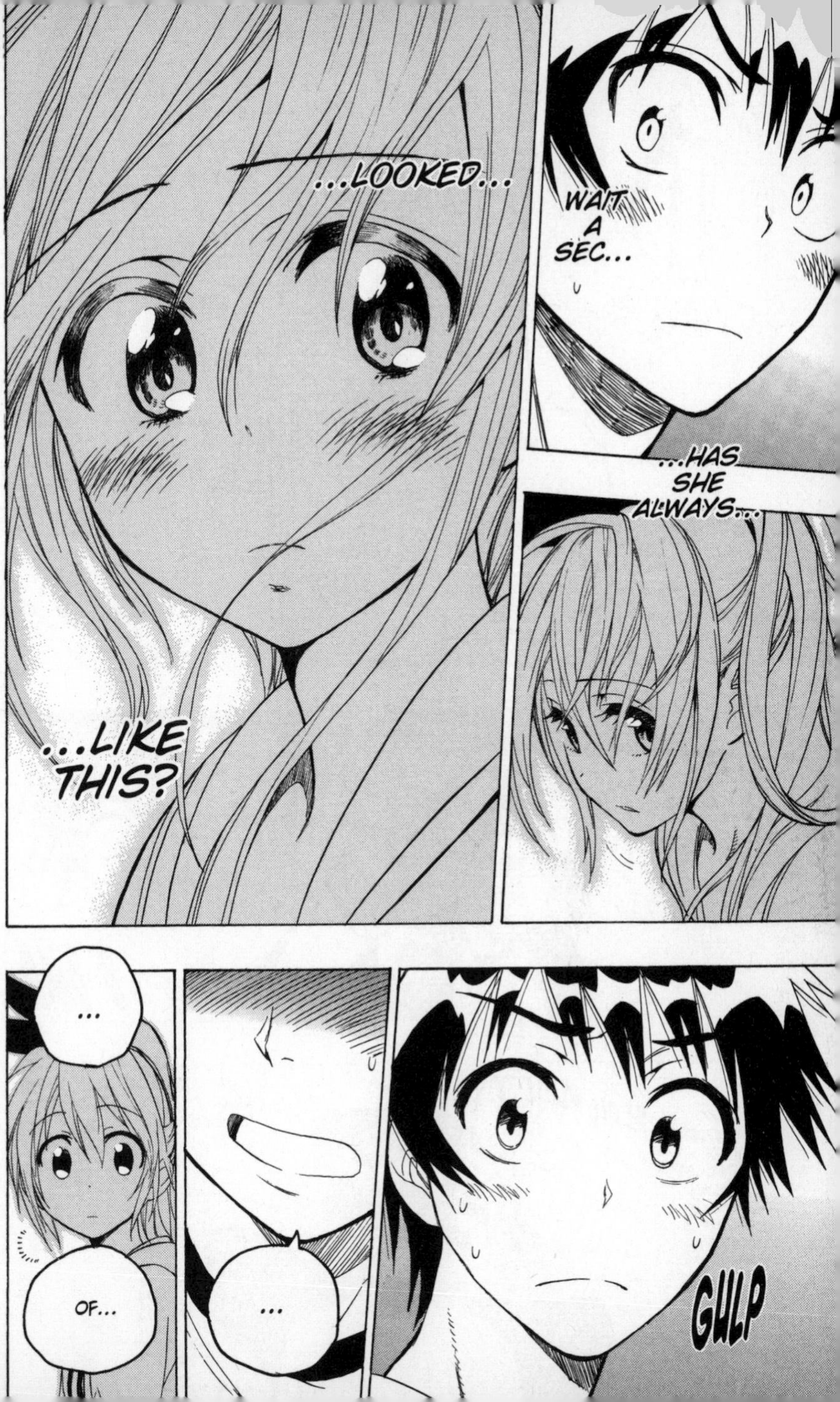
WAIT A SEC...
...HAS SHE ALWAYS...
...LOOKED...
...LIKE THIS?
GULP
...
...
OF...

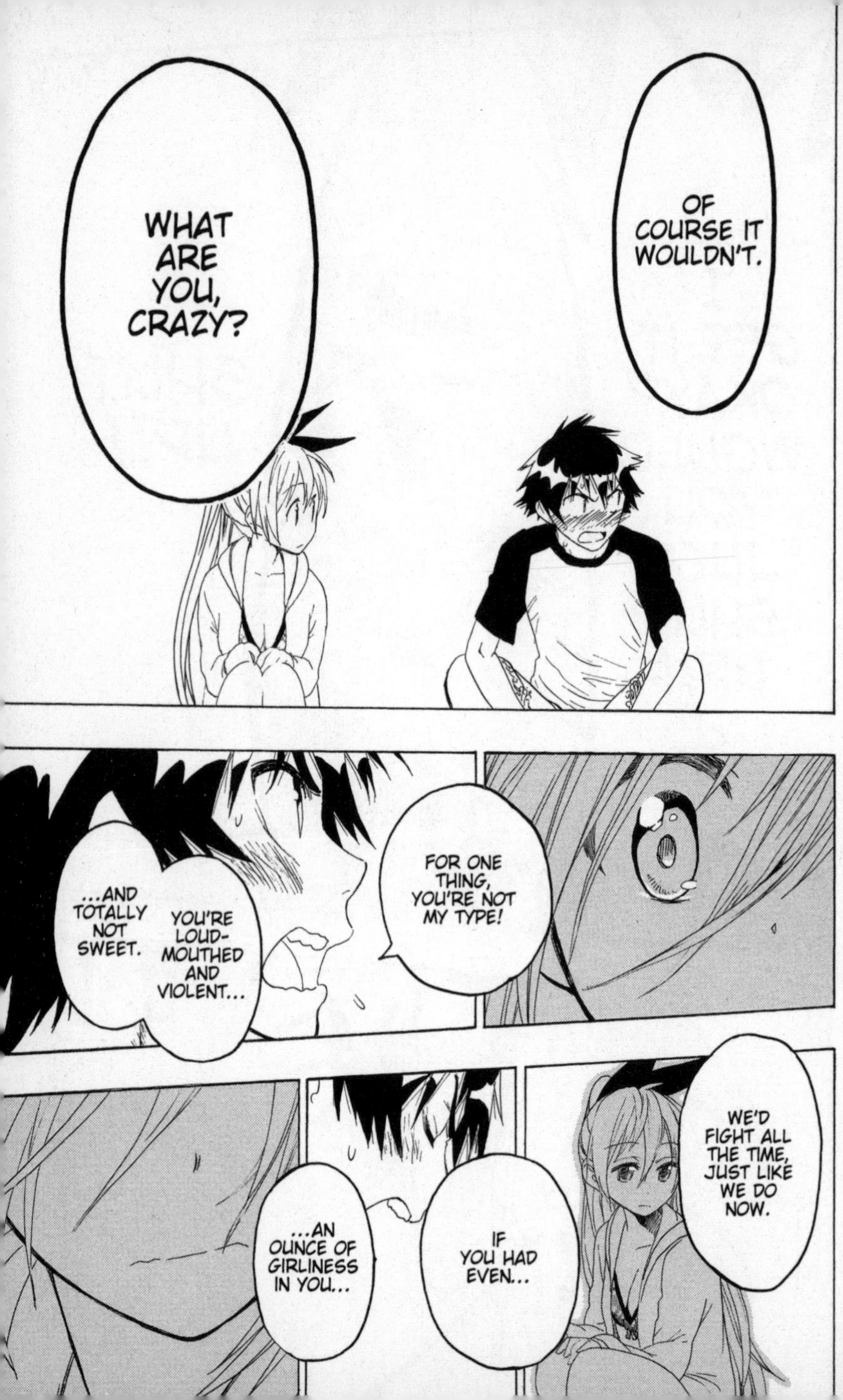
OF COURSE IT WOULDN'T.
WHAT ARE YOU, CRAZY?
FOR ONE THING, YOU'RE NOT MY TYPE!
YOU'RE LOUD-MOUTHED AND VIOLENT...
...AND TOTALLY NOT SWEET.
WE'D FIGHT ALL THE TIME, JUST LIKE WE DO NOW.
IF YOU HAD EVEN...
...AN OUNCE OF GIRLINESS IN YOU...

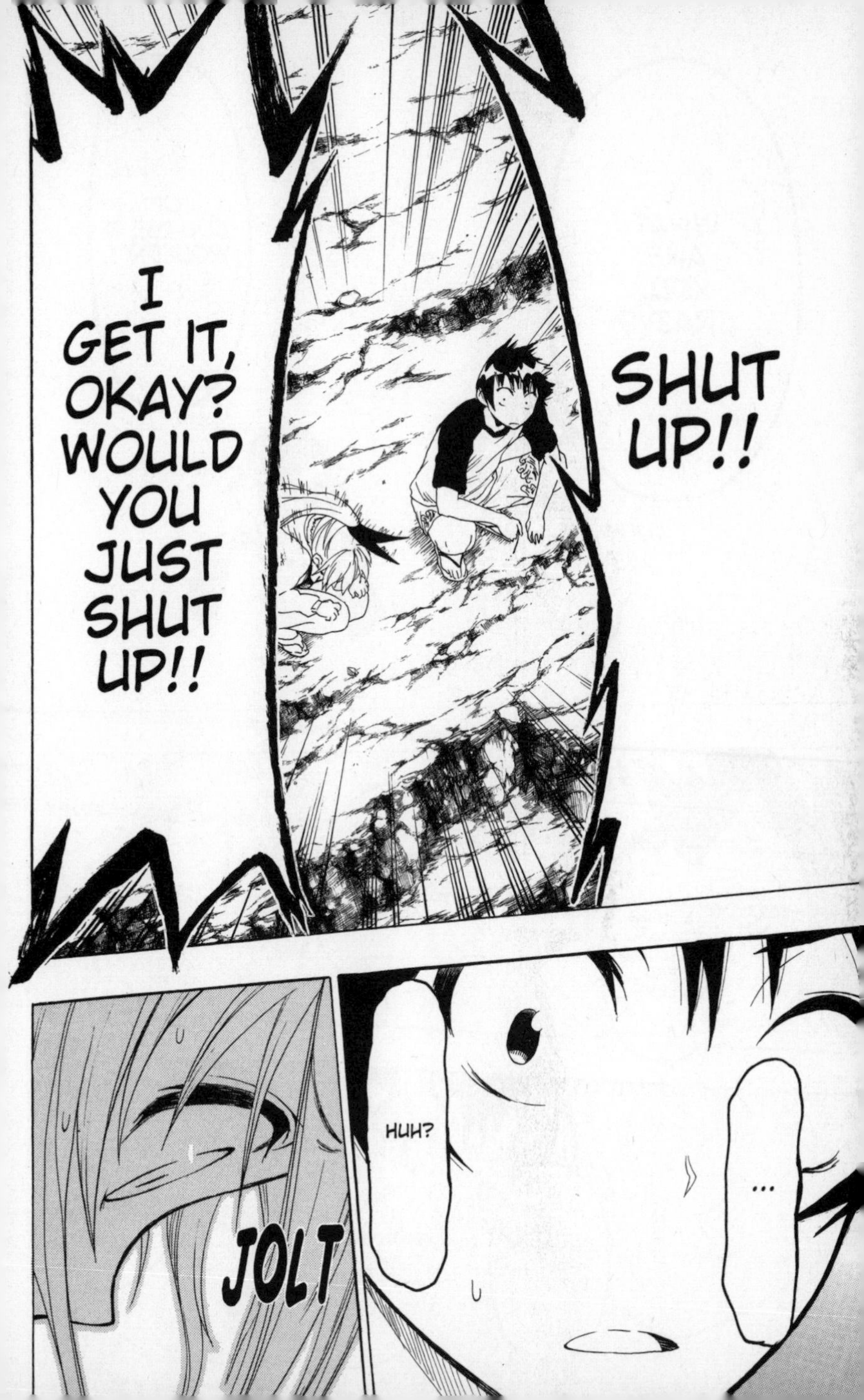
SHUT UP!!
I GET IT, OKAY? WOULD YOU JUST SHUT UP!!
...
HUH?
JOLT

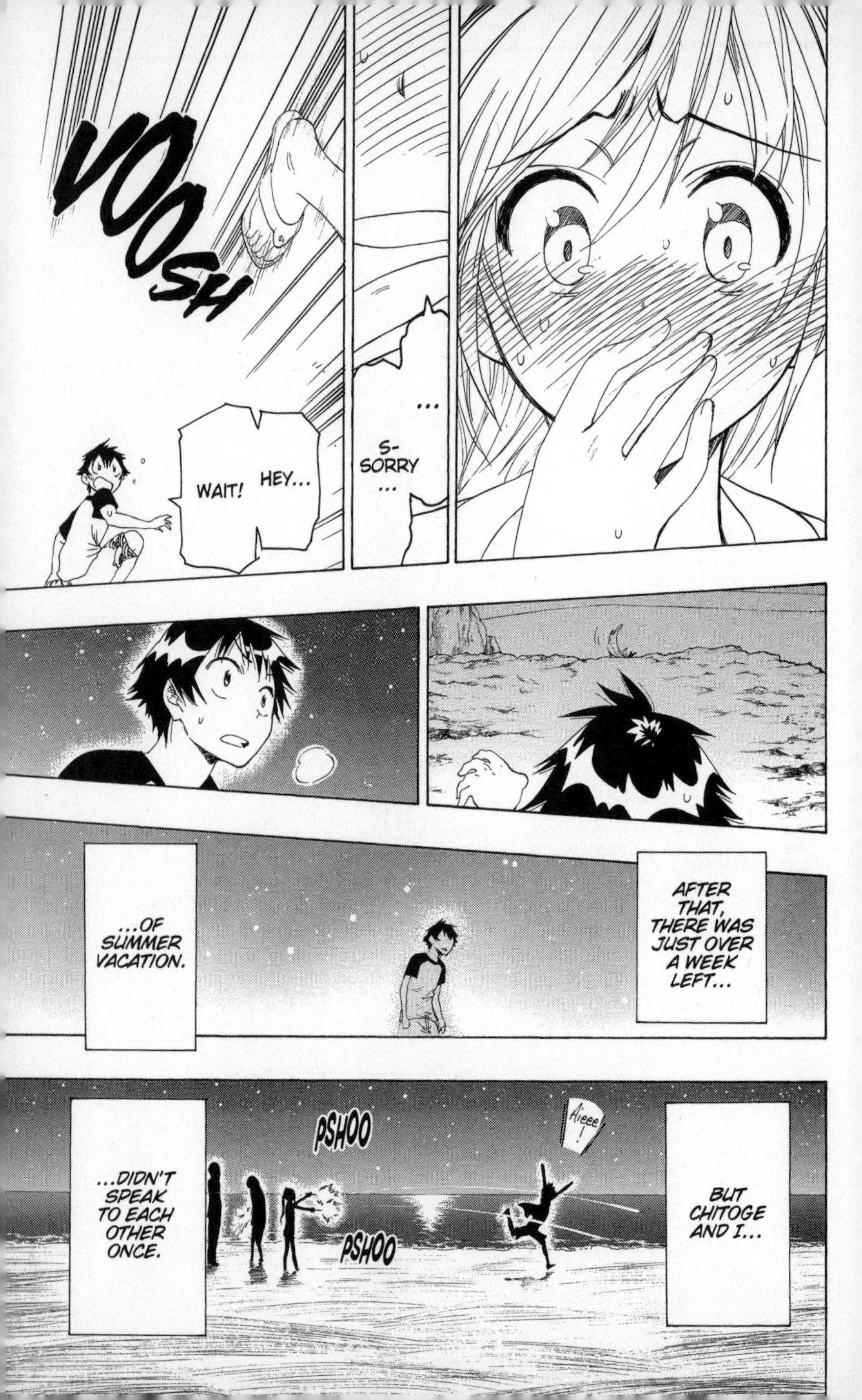
...
S-SORRY ...
VOOSH
HEY...
WAIT!
AFTER THAT, THERE WAS JUST OVER A WEEK LEFT...
...OF SUMMER VACATION.
BUT CHITOGE AND I...
Aieee!
PSHOO
PSHOO
...DIDN'T SPEAK TO EACH OTHER ONCE.

The reason Tsugumi wasn't in the fireworks scene.

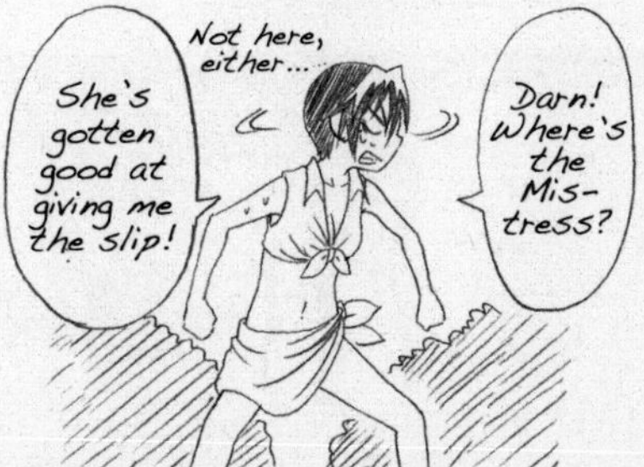
Not here, either...
Darn! Where's the Mistress?
She's gotten good at giving me the slip!

Chapter 46: The Play

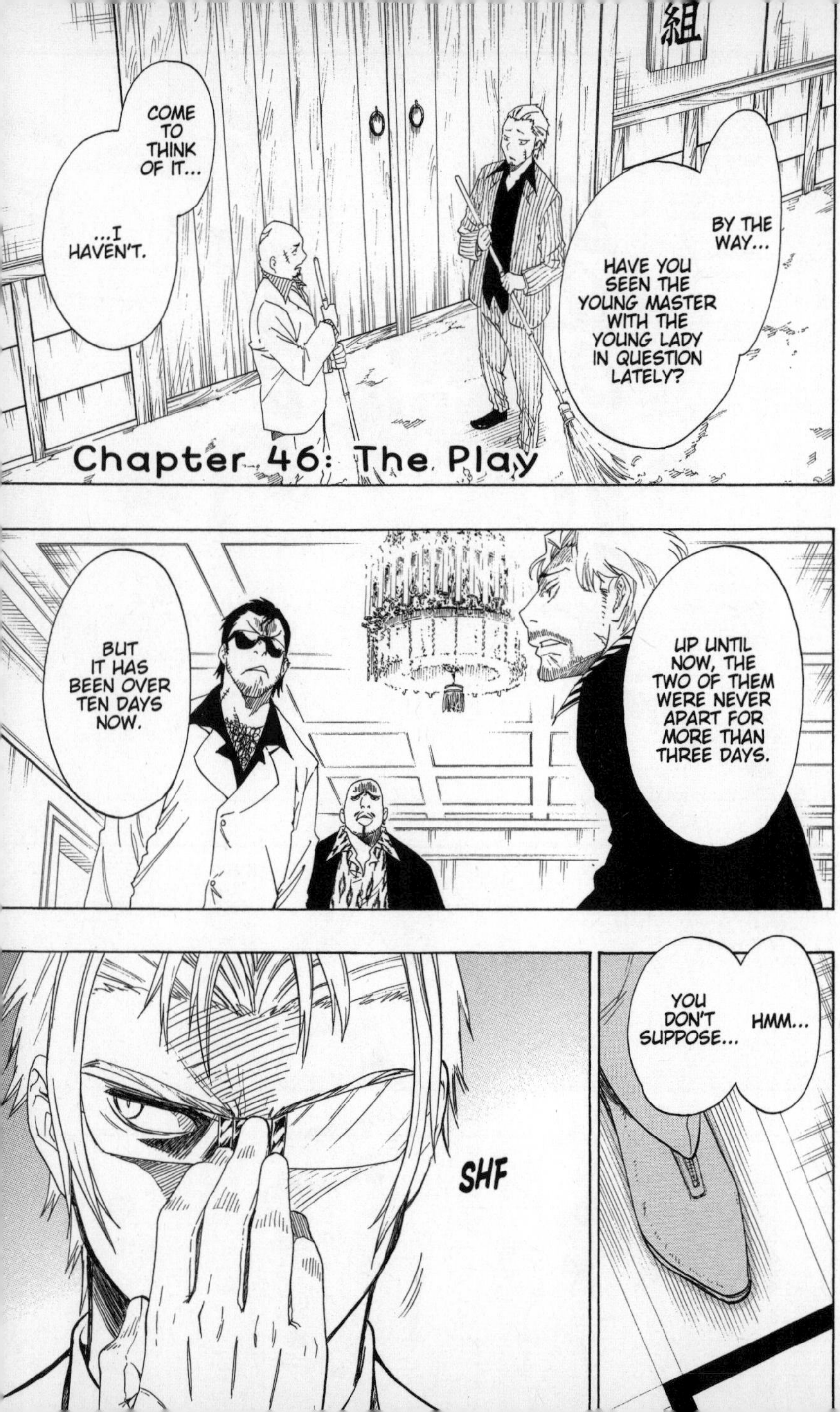
BY THE WAY...
HAVE YOU SEEN THE YOUNG MASTER WITH THE YOUNG LADY IN QUESTION LATELY?
COME TO THINK OF IT...
...I HAVEN'T.
UP UNTIL NOW, THE TWO OF THEM WERE NEVER APART FOR MORE THAN THREE DAYS.
BUT IT HAS BEEN OVER TEN DAYS NOW.
HMM...
YOU DON'T SUPPOSE...
SHF

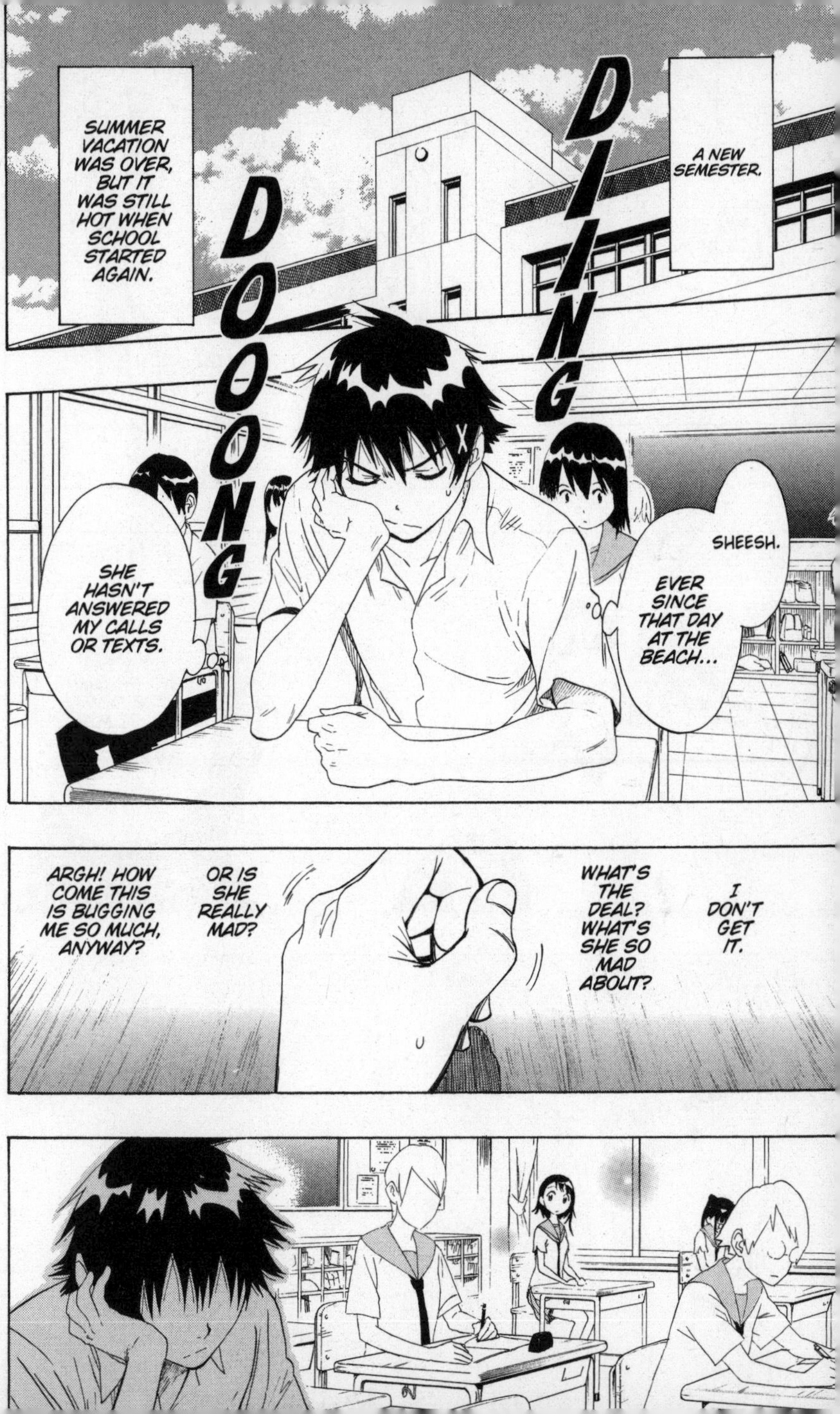
A NEW SEMESTER.
DING
DOOONG
SUMMER VACATION WAS OVER, BUT IT WAS STILL HOT WHEN SCHOOL STARTED AGAIN.
SHEESH.
EVER SINCE THAT DAY AT THE BEACH...
SHE HASN'T ANSWERED MY CALLS OR TEXTS.
I DON'T GET IT.
WHAT'S THE DEAL? WHAT'S SHE SO MAD ABOUT?
OR IS SHE REALLY MAD?
ARGH! HOW COME THIS IS BUGGING ME SO MUCH, ANYWAY?

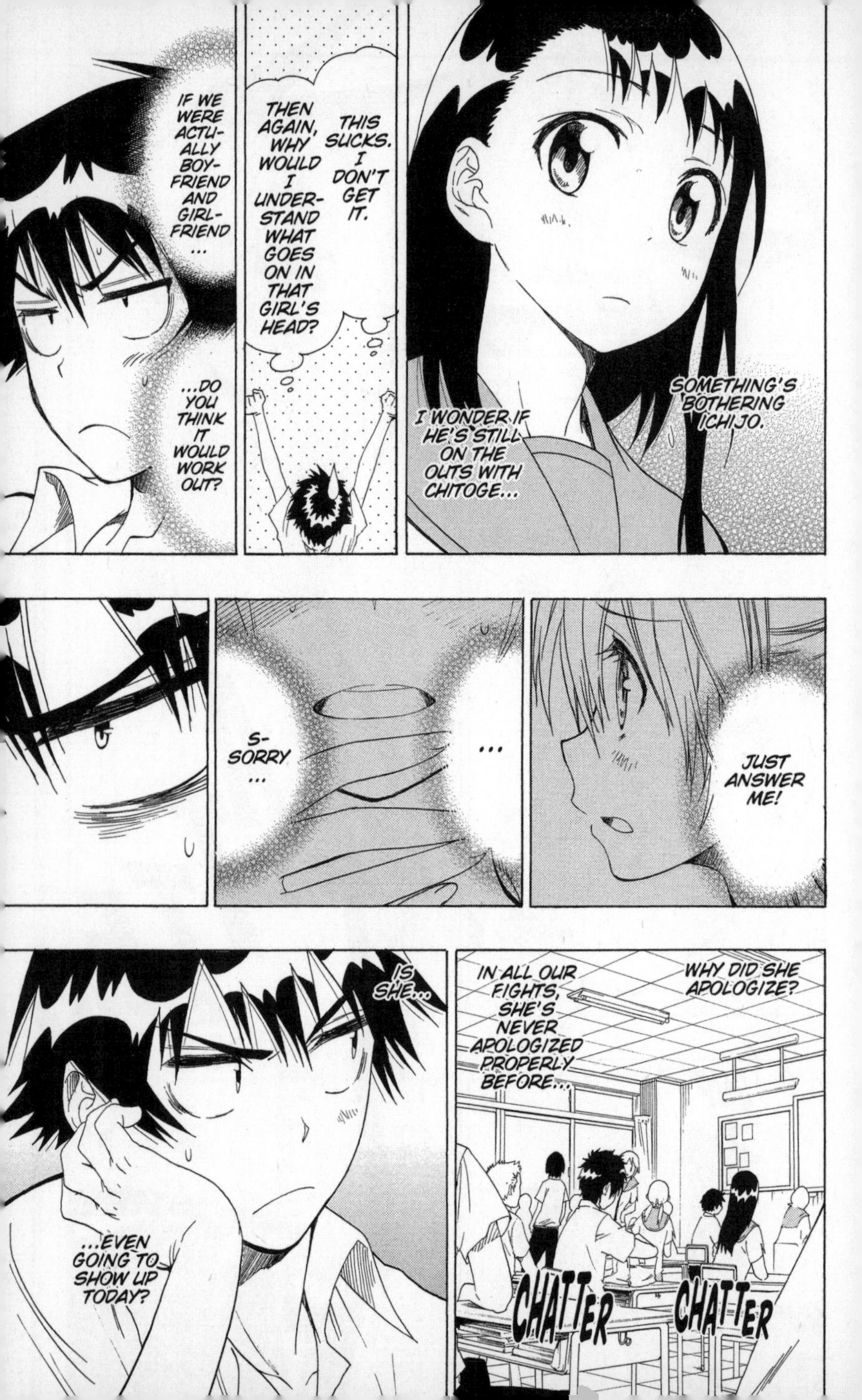
SOMETHING'S BOTHERING ICHIJO.
I WONDER IF HE'S STILL ON THE OUTS WITH CHITOGE...
THIS SUCKS. I DON'T GET IT.
THEN AGAIN, WHY WOULD I UNDERSTAND WHAT GOES ON IN THAT GIRL'S HEAD?
IF WE WERE ACTUALLY BOYFRIEND AND GIRLFRIEND...
...DO YOU THINK IT WOULD WORK OUT?
JUST ANSWER ME!
...
S-SORRY...
WHY DID SHE APOLOGIZE?
IN ALL OUR FIGHTS, SHE'S NEVER APOLOGIZED PROPERLY BEFORE...
CHATTER
CHATTER
IS SHE...
...EVEN GOING TO SHOW UP TODAY?

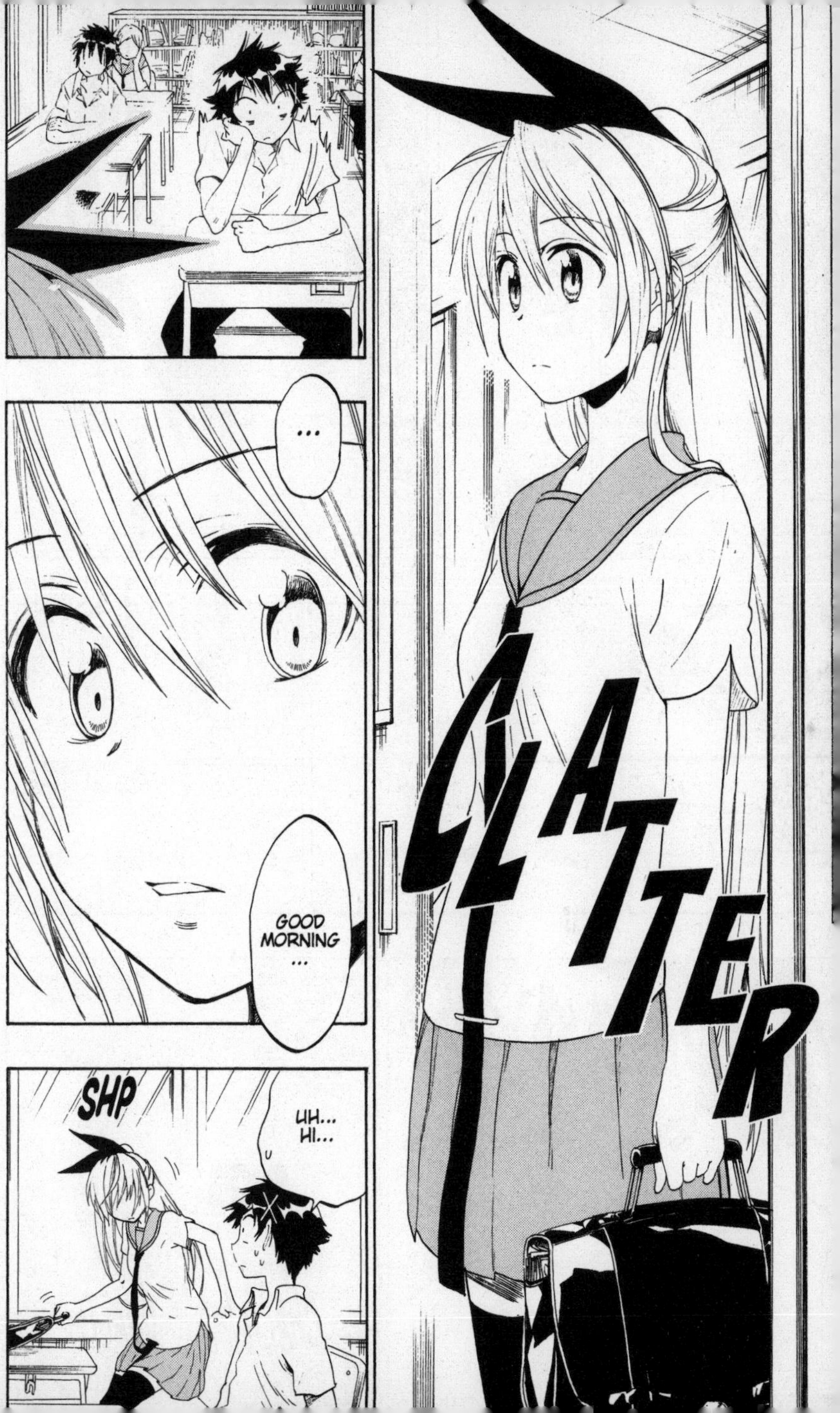
CLATTER
...
GOOD MORNING ...
SHP
UH... HI...

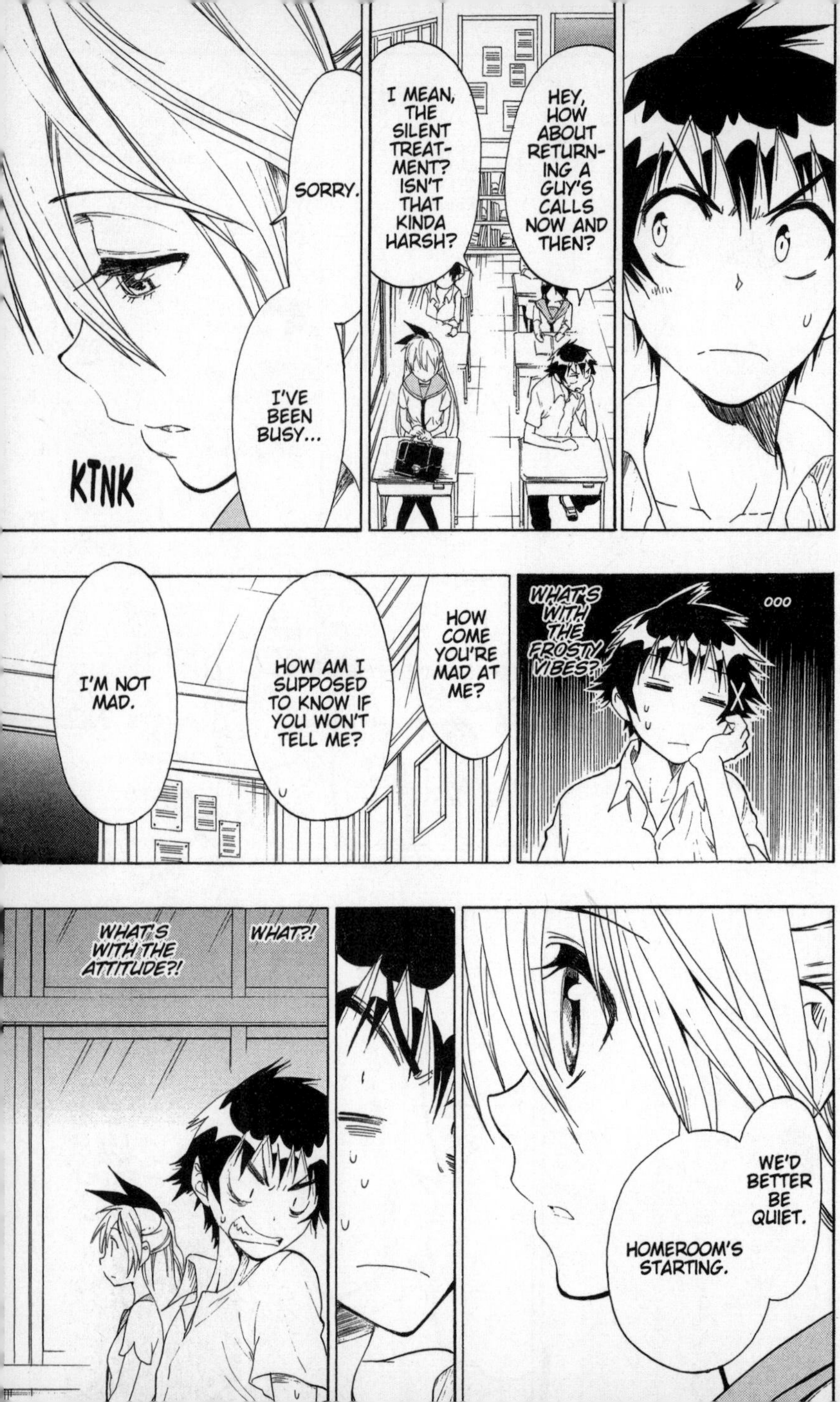
HEY, HOW ABOUT RETURNING A GUY'S CALLS NOW AND THEN?
I MEAN, THE SILENT TREATMENT? ISN'T THAT KINDA HARSH?
SORRY.
I'VE BEEN BUSY...
KTNK
WHAT'S WITH THE FROSTY VIBES?
HOW COME YOU'RE MAD AT ME?
HOW AM I SUPPOSED TO KNOW IF YOU WON'T TELL ME?
I'M NOT MAD.
WE'D BETTER BE QUIET.
HOMEROOM'S STARTING.
WHAT?!
WHAT'S WITH THE ATTITUDE?!

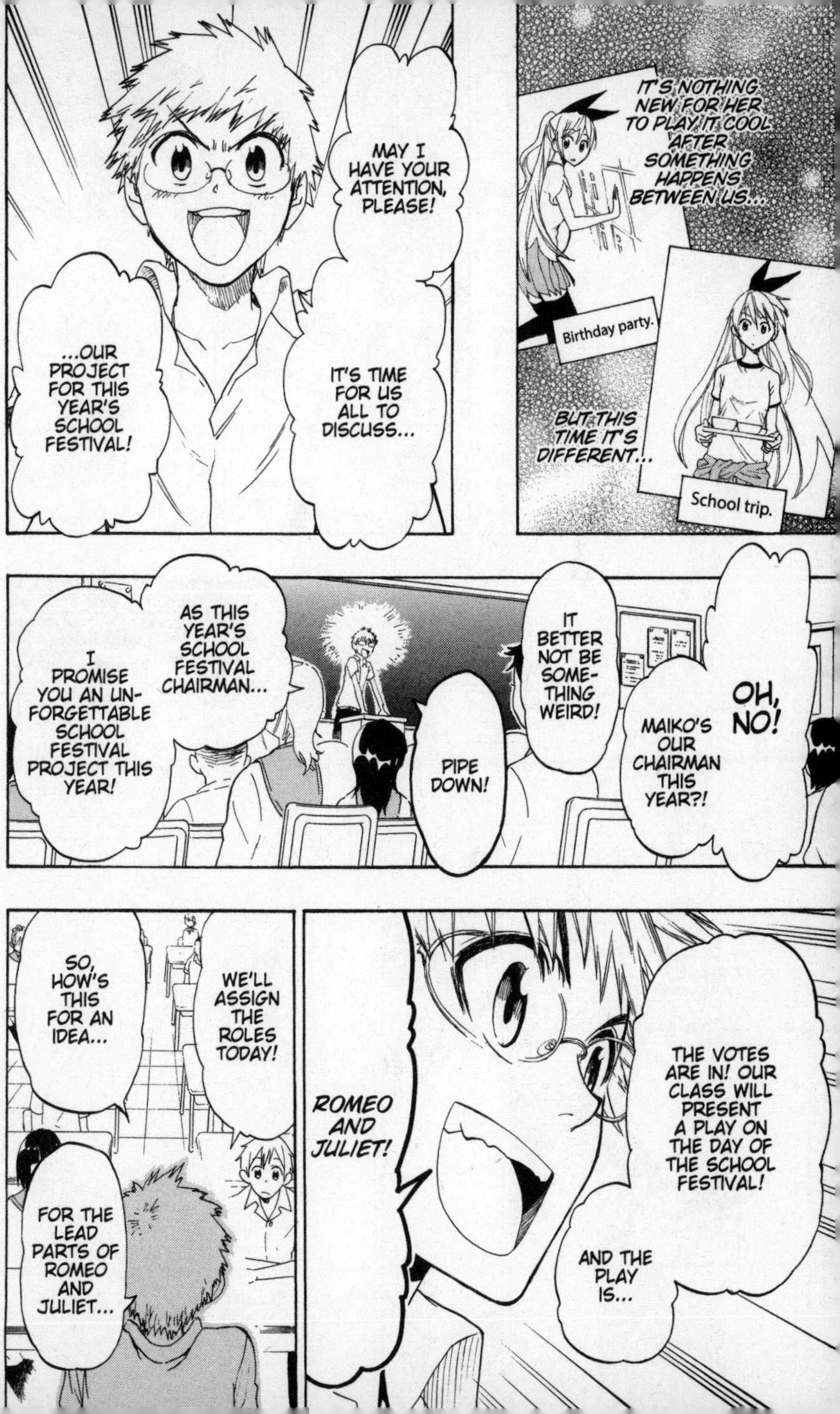
IT'S NOTHING NEW FOR HER TO PLAY IT COOL AFTER SOMETHING HAPPENS BETWEEN US...
Birthday party.
School trip.
BUT THIS TIME IT'S DIFFERENT...
MAY I HAVE YOUR ATTENTION, PLEASE!
IT'S TIME FOR US ALL TO DISCUSS...
...OUR PROJECT FOR THIS YEAR'S SCHOOL FESTIVAL!
OH, NO!
MAIKO'S OUR CHAIRMAN THIS YEAR?!
IT BETTER NOT BE SOMETHING WEIRD!
PIPE DOWN!
AS THIS YEAR'S SCHOOL FESTIVAL CHAIRMAN...
I PROMISE YOU AN UNFORGETTABLE SCHOOL FESTIVAL PROJECT THIS YEAR!
THE VOTES ARE IN! OUR CLASS WILL PRESENT A PLAY ON THE DAY OF THE SCHOOL FESTIVAL!
AND THE PLAY IS...
ROMEO AND JULIET!
WE'LL ASSIGN THE ROLES TODAY!
SO, HOW'S THIS FOR AN IDEA...
FOR THE LEAD PARTS OF ROMEO AND JULIET...

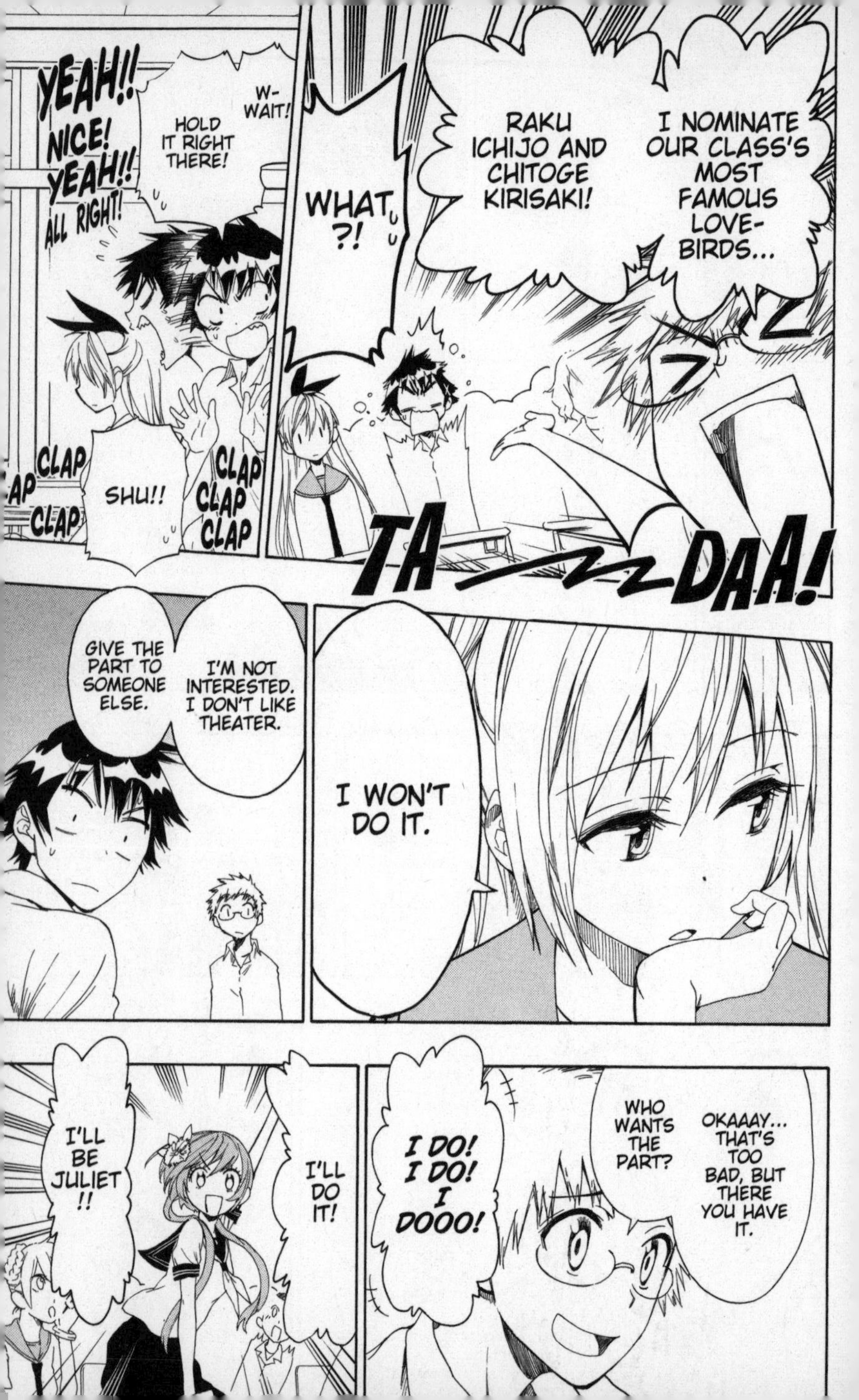
I NOMINATE OUR CLASS'S MOST FAMOUS LOVE-BIRDS...
RAKU ICHIJO AND CHITOGE KIRISAKI!
WHAT?!
TA-DAA!
W-WAIT!
HOLD IT RIGHT THERE!
YEAH!! NICE! YEAH!! ALL RIGHT!
CLAP CLAP CLAP
SHU!!
CLAP AP CLAP
I WON'T DO IT.
I'M NOT INTERESTED. I DON'T LIKE THEATER.
GIVE THE PART TO SOMEONE ELSE.
OKAAAY... THAT'S TOO BAD, BUT THERE YOU HAVE IT.
WHO WANTS THE PART?
I DO! I DO! I DOOO!
I'LL DO IT!
I'LL BE JULIET!!

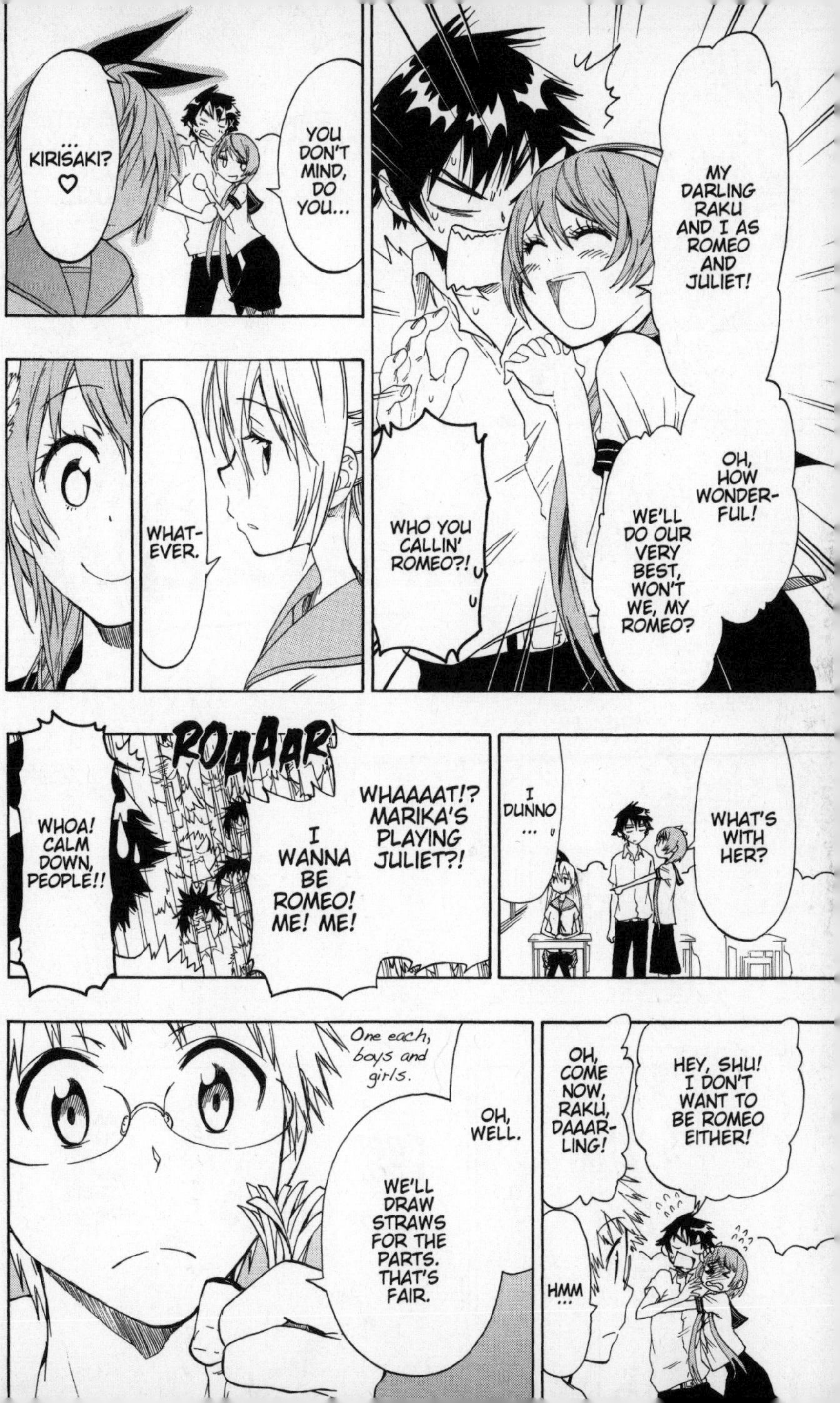
MY DARLING RAKU AND I AS ROMEO AND JULIET!
OH, HOW WONDERFUL!
WE'LL DO OUR VERY BEST, WON'T WE, MY ROMEO?
WHO YOU CALLIN' ROMEO?!
YOU DON'T MIND, DO YOU...
...KIRISAKI? ♡
WHAT-EVER.
WHAT'S WITH HER?
I DUNNO...
ROAAAR
WHAAAAT!? MARIKA'S PLAYING JULIET?!
I WANNA BE ROMEO! ME! ME!
WHOA! CALM DOWN, PEOPLE!!
HEY, SHU! I DON'T WANT TO BE ROMEO EITHER!
OH, COME NOW, RAKU, DAAAR-LING!
HMM...
OH, WELL.
One each, boys and girls.
WE'LL DRAW STRAWS FOR THE PARTS. THAT'S FAIR.

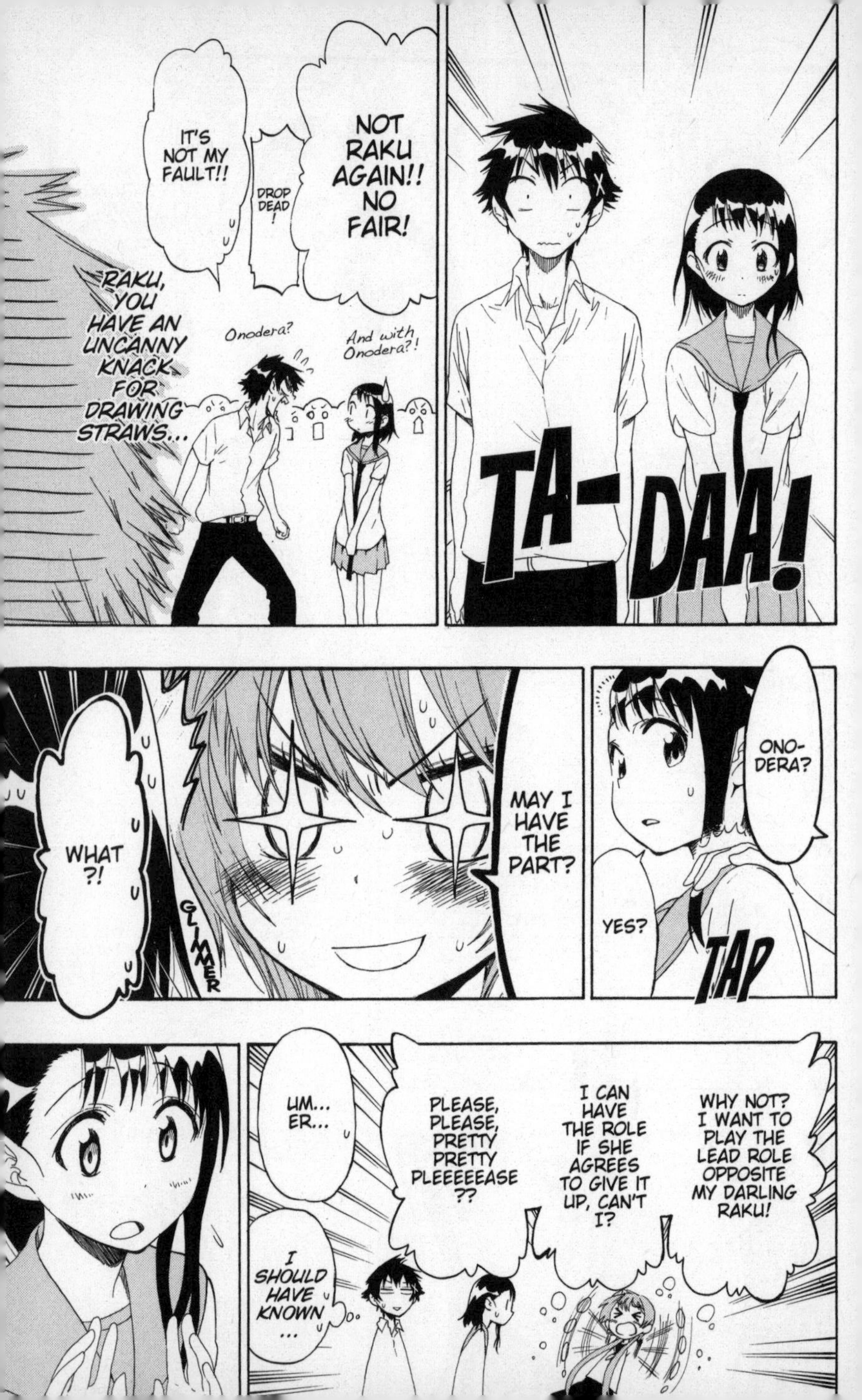
TA-DAA!
NOT RAKU AGAIN!! NO FAIR!
DROP DEAD!
IT'S NOT MY FAULT!!
And with Onodera?!
Onodera?
RAKU, YOU HAVE AN UNCANNY KNACK FOR DRAWING STRAWS...
ONO-DERA?
YES?
TAP
MAY I HAVE THE PART?
GLIMMER
WHAT?!
WHY NOT? I WANT TO PLAY THE LEAD ROLE OPPOSITE MY DARLING RAKU!
I CAN HAVE THE ROLE IF SHE AGREES TO GIVE IT UP, CAN'T I?
PLEASE, PLEASE, PRETTY PRETTY PLEEEEEASE??
UM... ER...
I SHOULD HAVE KNOWN...

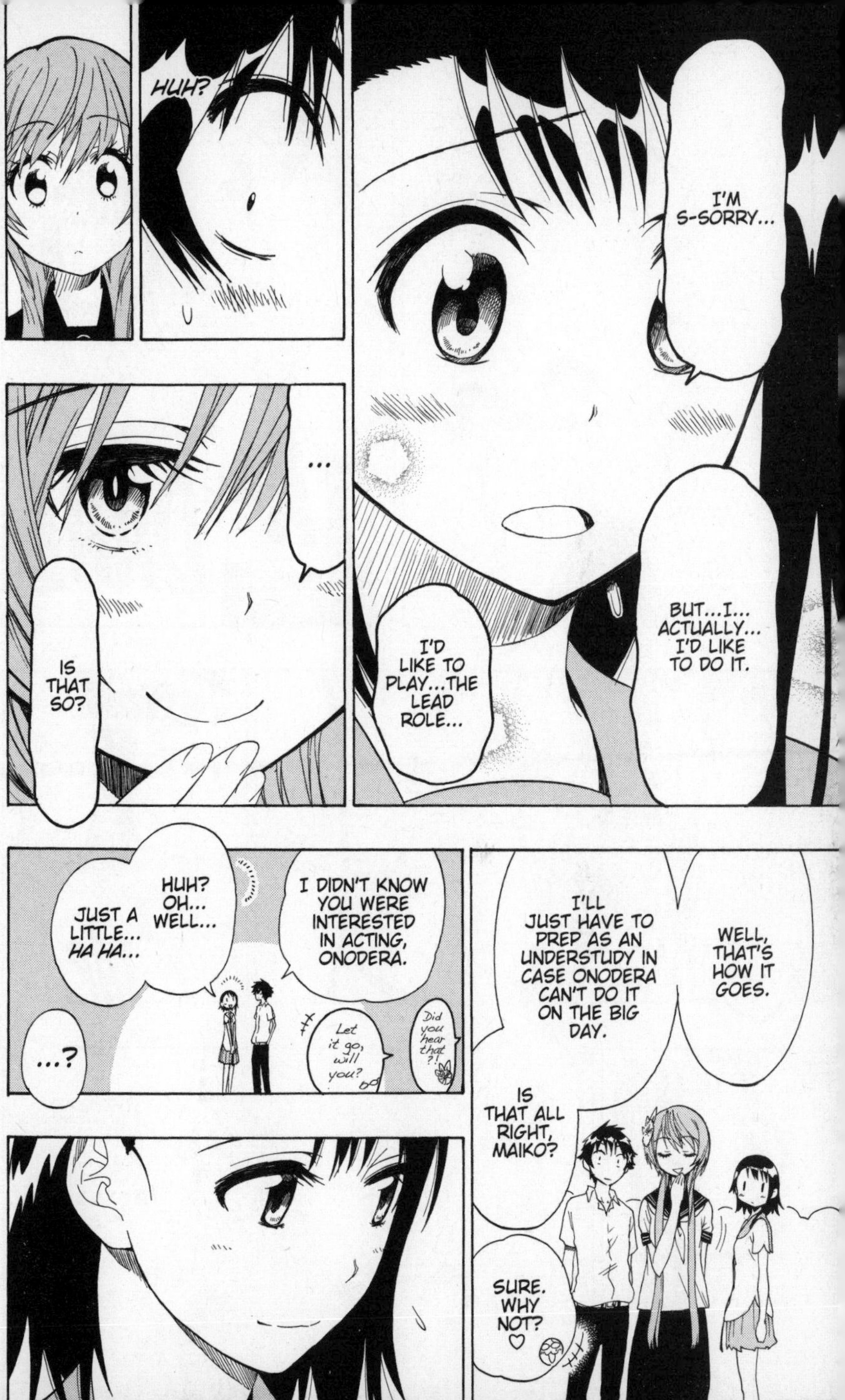
I'M S-SORRY...
BUT...I... ACTUALLY... I'D LIKE TO DO IT.
I'D LIKE TO PLAY...THE LEAD ROLE...
HUH?
...
IS THAT SO?
WELL, THAT'S HOW IT GOES.
I'LL JUST HAVE TO PREP AS AN UNDERSTUDY IN CASE ONODERA CAN'T DO IT ON THE BIG DAY.
IS THAT ALL RIGHT, MAIKO?
SURE. WHY NOT? ♡
I DIDN'T KNOW YOU WERE INTERESTED IN ACTING, ONODERA.
HUH? OH... WELL...
JUST A LITTLE... HA HA...
Did you hear that?!
Let it go, will you?
...?

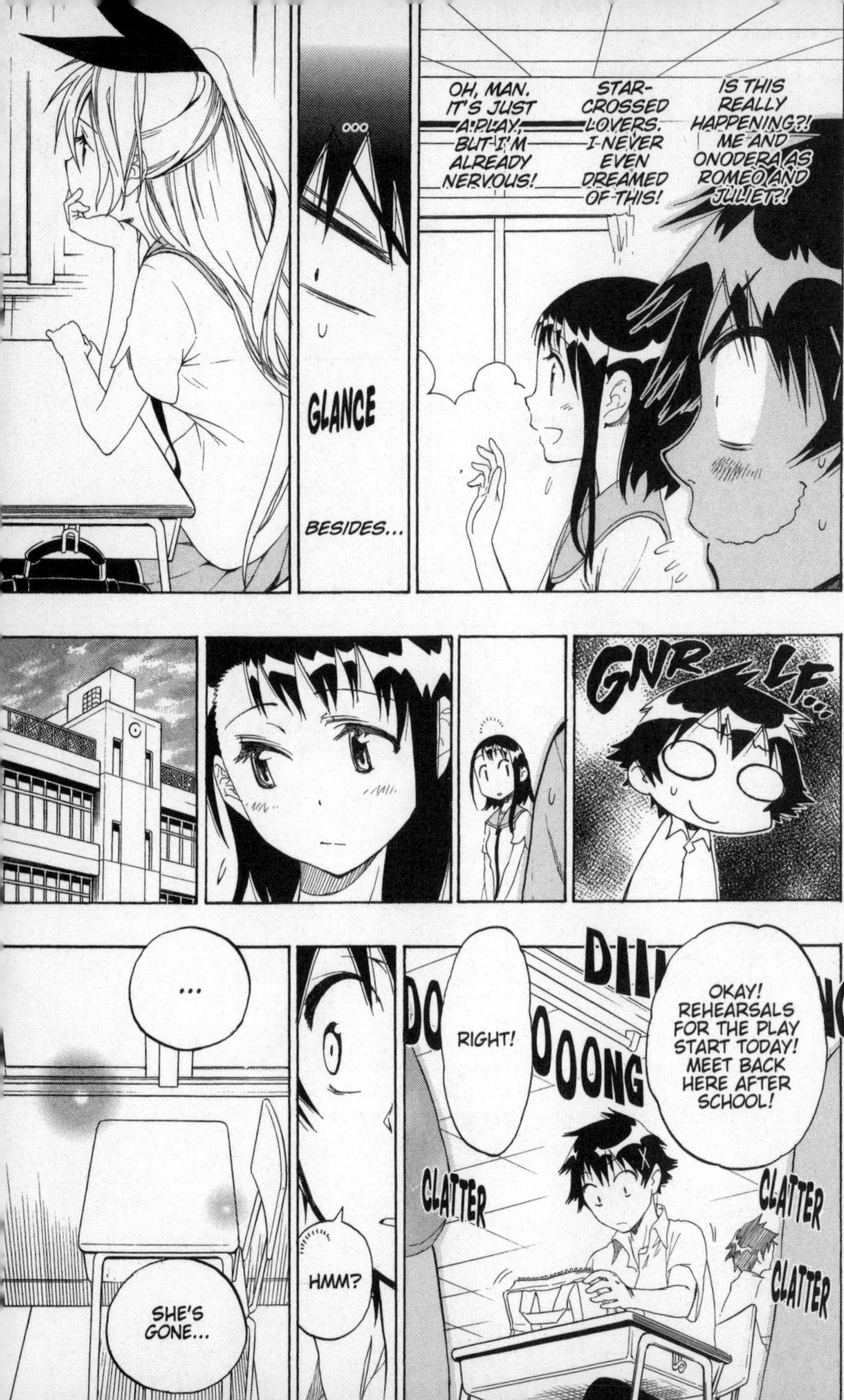
IS THIS REALLY HAPPENING?! ME AND ONODERA AS ROMEO AND JULIET?!
STAR-CROSSED LOVERS. I NEVER EVEN DREAMED OF THIS!
OH, MAN. IT'S JUST A PLAY, BUT I'M ALREADY NERVOUS!
GLANCE
BESIDES...
GNR
LF...
DIN
NG
DO
OOONG
OKAY! REHEARSALS FOR THE PLAY START TODAY! MEET BACK HERE AFTER SCHOOL!
RIGHT!
CLATTER
CLATTER
CLATTER
HMM?
...
SHE'S GONE...

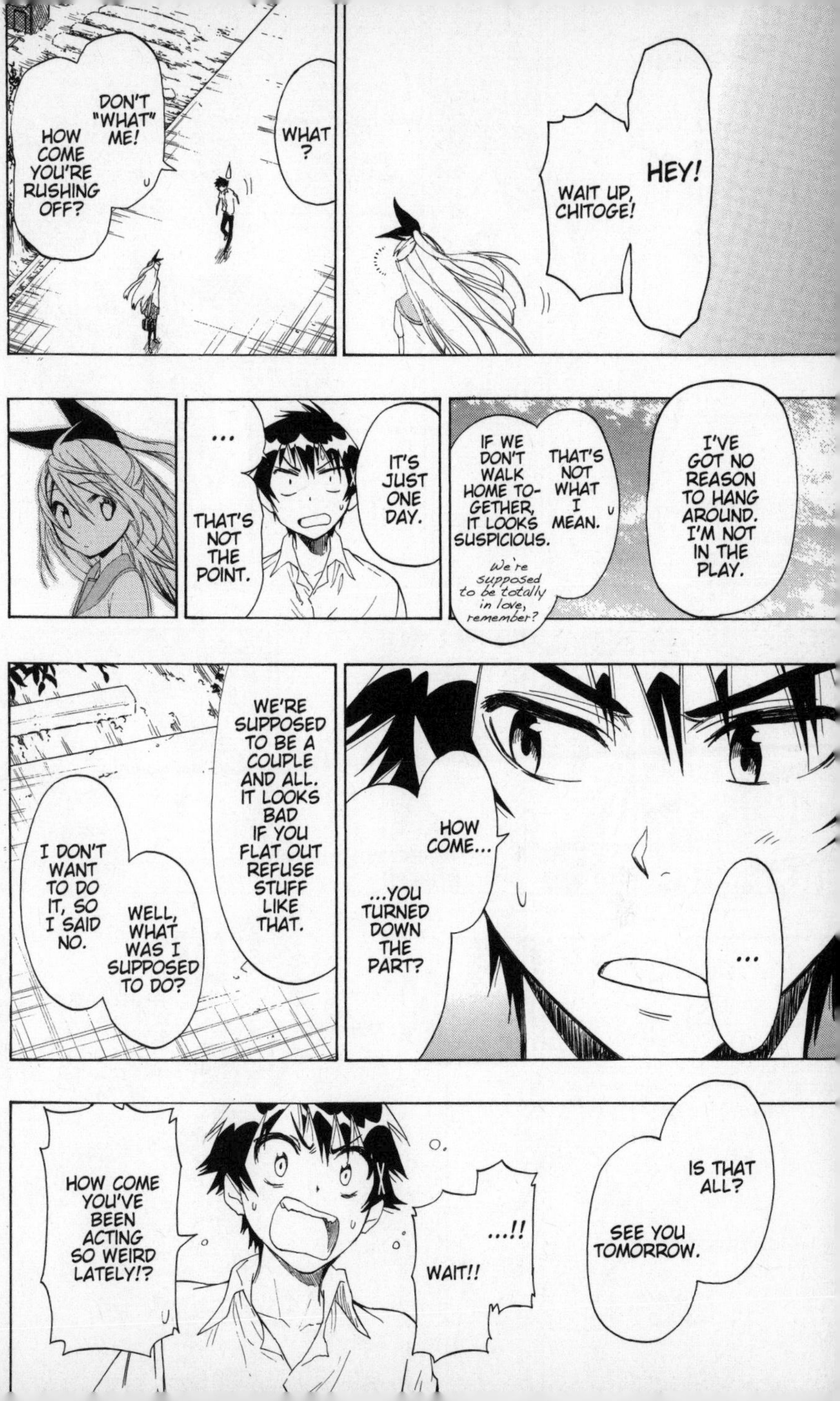
HEY!
WAIT UP, CHITOGE!
WHAT?
DON'T "WHAT" ME!
HOW COME YOU'RE RUSHING OFF?
I'VE GOT NO REASON TO HANG AROUND. I'M NOT IN THE PLAY.
THAT'S NOT WHAT I MEAN.
IF WE DON'T WALK HOME TO-GETHER, IT LOOKS SUSPICIOUS.
We're supposed to be totally in love, remember?
IT'S JUST ONE DAY.
...
THAT'S NOT THE POINT.
...
HOW COME...
...YOU TURNED DOWN THE PART?
WE'RE SUPPOSED TO BE A COUPLE AND ALL. IT LOOKS BAD IF YOU FLAT OUT REFUSE STUFF LIKE THAT.
WELL, WHAT WAS I SUPPOSED TO DO?
I DON'T WANT TO DO IT, SO I SAID NO.
IS THAT ALL?
SEE YOU TOMORROW.
...!!
WAIT!!
HOW COME YOU'VE BEEN ACTING SO WEIRD LATELY!?

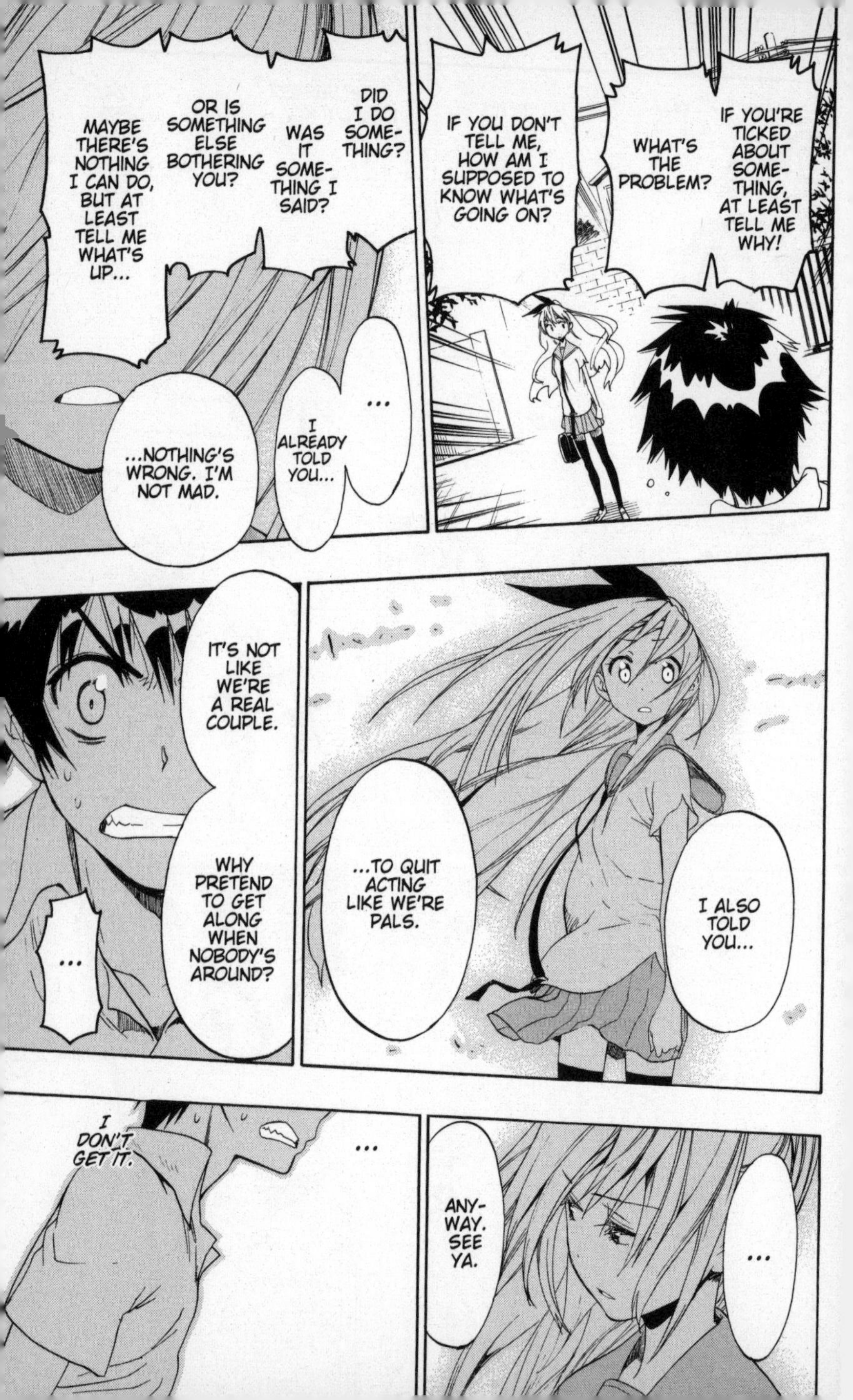
IF YOU'RE TICKED ABOUT SOMETHING, AT LEAST TELL ME WHY!
WHAT'S THE PROBLEM?
IF YOU DON'T TELL ME, HOW AM I SUPPOSED TO KNOW WHAT'S GOING ON?
DID I DO SOMETHING?
WAS IT SOMETHING I SAID?
OR IS SOMETHING ELSE BOTHERING YOU?
MAYBE THERE'S NOTHING I CAN DO, BUT AT LEAST TELL ME WHAT'S UP...
...
I ALREADY TOLD YOU...
...NOTHING'S WRONG. I'M NOT MAD.
I ALSO TOLD YOU...
...TO QUIT ACTING LIKE WE'RE PALS.
IT'S NOT LIKE WE'RE A REAL COUPLE.
WHY PRETEND TO GET ALONG WHEN NOBODY'S AROUND?
...
...
ANYWAY. SEE YA.
...
I DON'T GET IT.

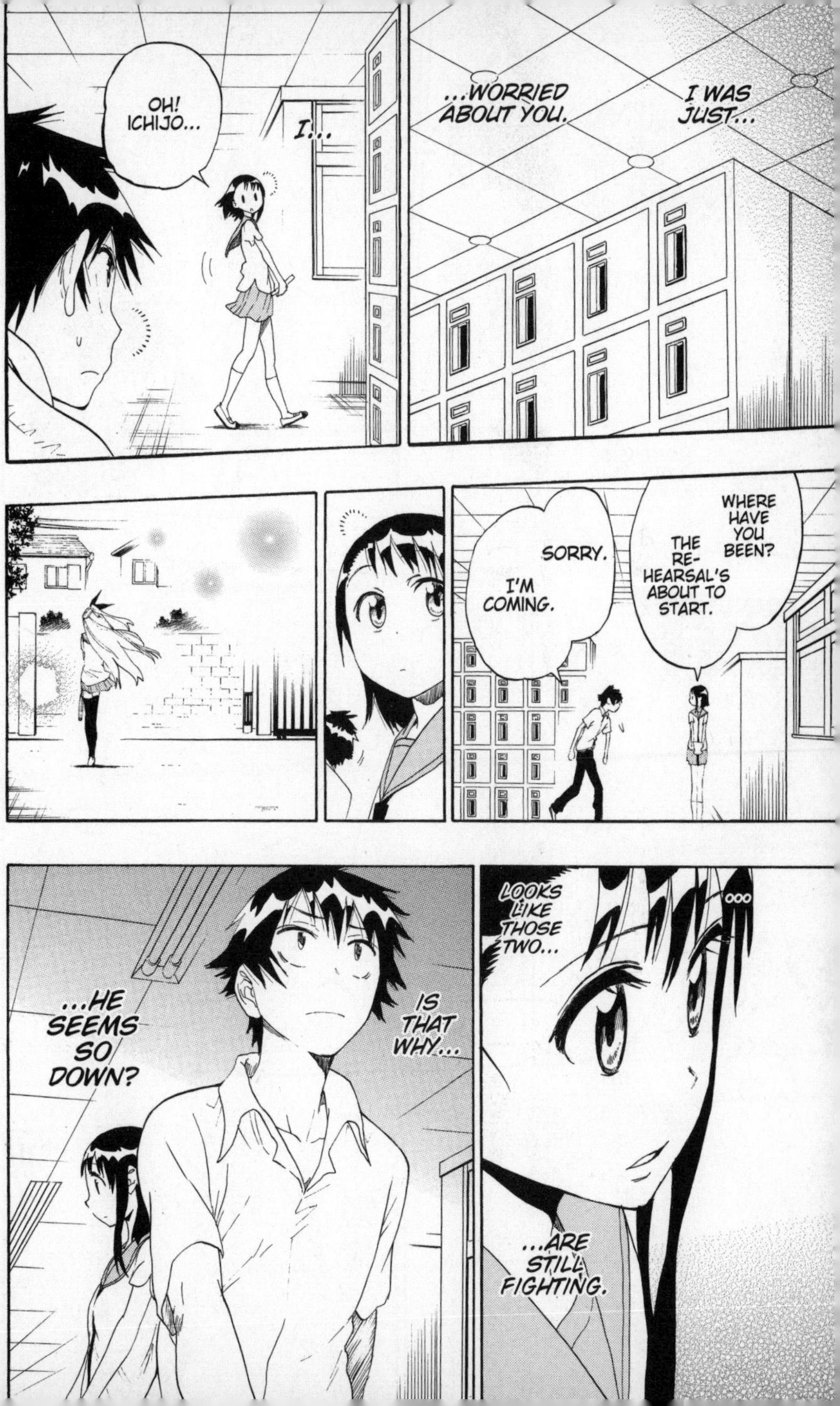
I WAS JUST...
...WORRIED ABOUT YOU.
I...
OH! ICHIJO...
WHERE HAVE YOU BEEN?
THE RE-HEARSAL'S ABOUT TO START.
SORRY.
I'M COMING.
LOOKS LIKE THOSE TWO...
...ARE STILL FIGHTING.
IS THAT WHY...
...HE SEEMS SO DOWN?

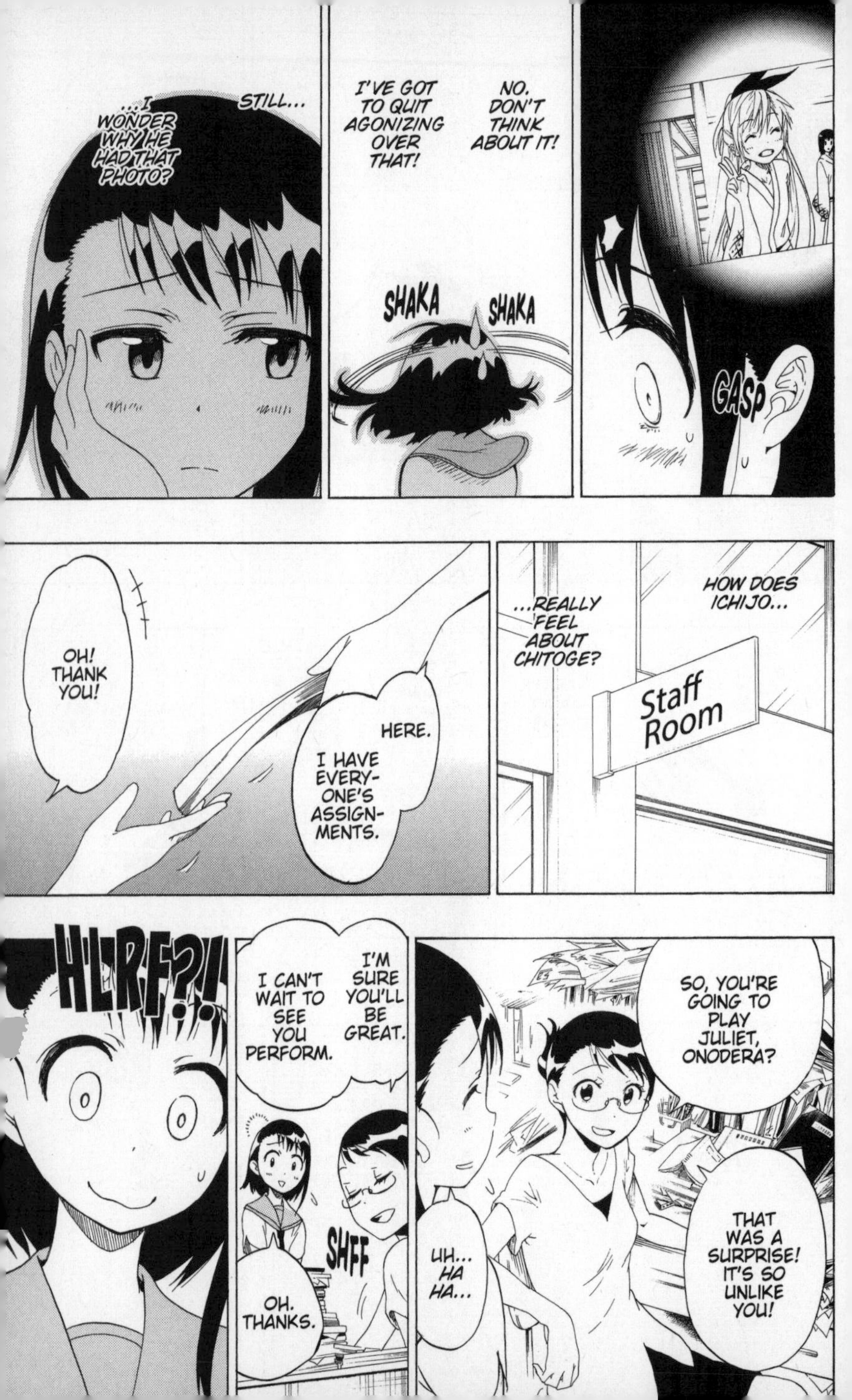
GASP
NO. DON'T THINK ABOUT IT!
I'VE GOT TO QUIT AGONIZING OVER THAT!
SHAKA
SHAKA
STILL...
...I WONDER WHY HE HAD THAT PHOTO?
HOW DOES ICHIJO...
...REALLY FEEL ABOUT CHITOGE?
Staff Room
HERE. I HAVE EVERYONE'S ASSIGNMENTS.
OH! THANK YOU!
SO, YOU'RE GOING TO PLAY JULIET, ONODERA?
THAT WAS A SURPRISE! IT'S SO UNLIKE YOU!
UH... HA HA...
I'M SURE YOU'LL BE GREAT.
I CAN'T WAIT TO SEE YOU PERFORM.
SHFF
OH. THANKS.
HLRF?!!

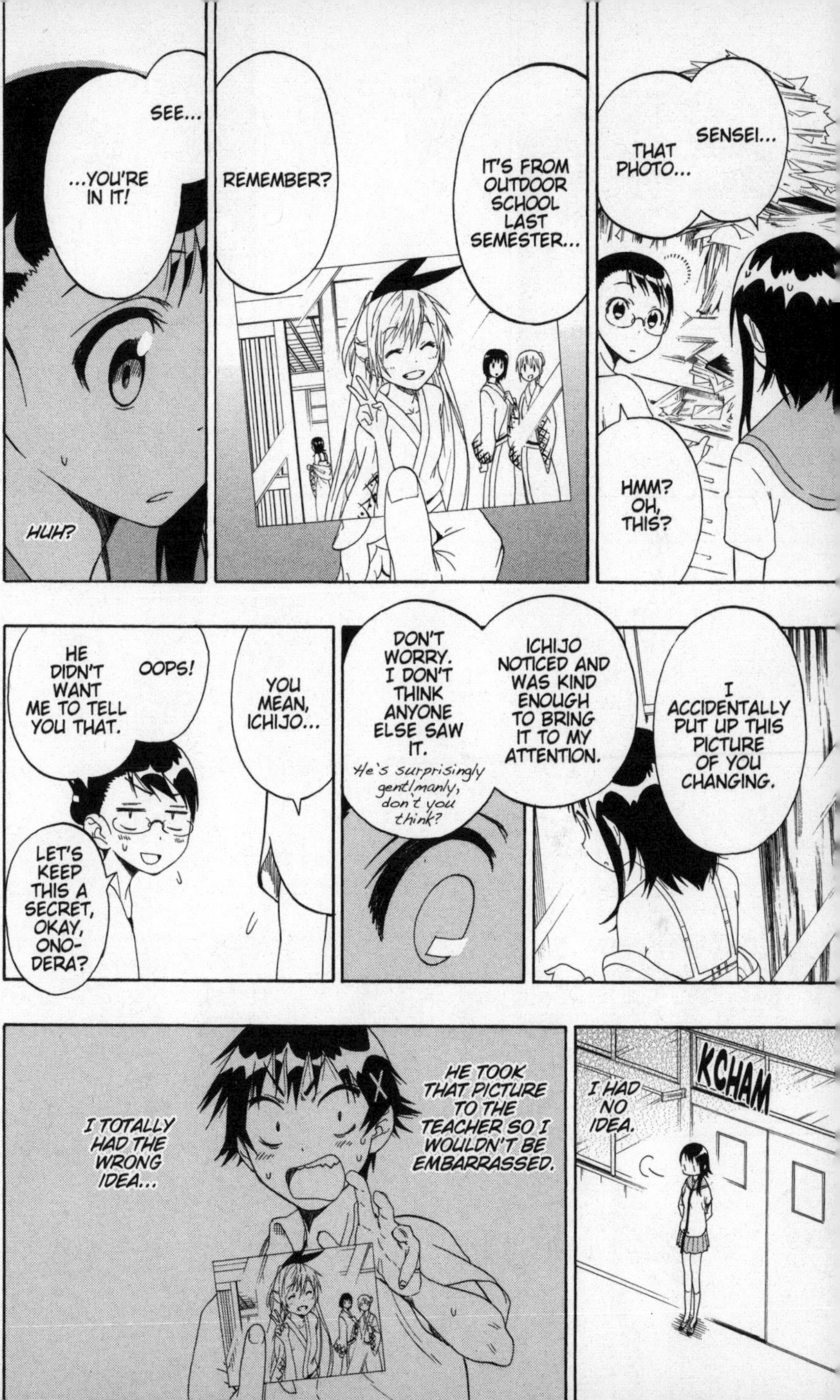
SENSEI...
THAT PHOTO...
HMM? OH, THIS?
IT'S FROM OUTDOOR SCHOOL LAST SEMESTER...
REMEMBER?
SEE...
...YOU'RE IN IT!
HUH?
I ACCIDENTALLY PUT UP THIS PICTURE OF YOU CHANGING.
ICHIJO NOTICED AND WAS KIND ENOUGH TO BRING IT TO MY ATTENTION.
DON'T WORRY. I DON'T THINK ANYONE ELSE SAW IT.
He's surprisingly gentlmanly, don't you think?
YOU MEAN, ICHIJO...
OOPS!
HE DIDN'T WANT ME TO TELL YOU THAT.
LET'S KEEP THIS A SECRET, OKAY, ONO-DERA?
KCHAM
I HAD NO IDEA.
HE TOOK THAT PICTURE TO THE TEACHER SO I WOULDN'T BE EMBARRASSED.
I TOTALLY HAD THE WRONG IDEA...

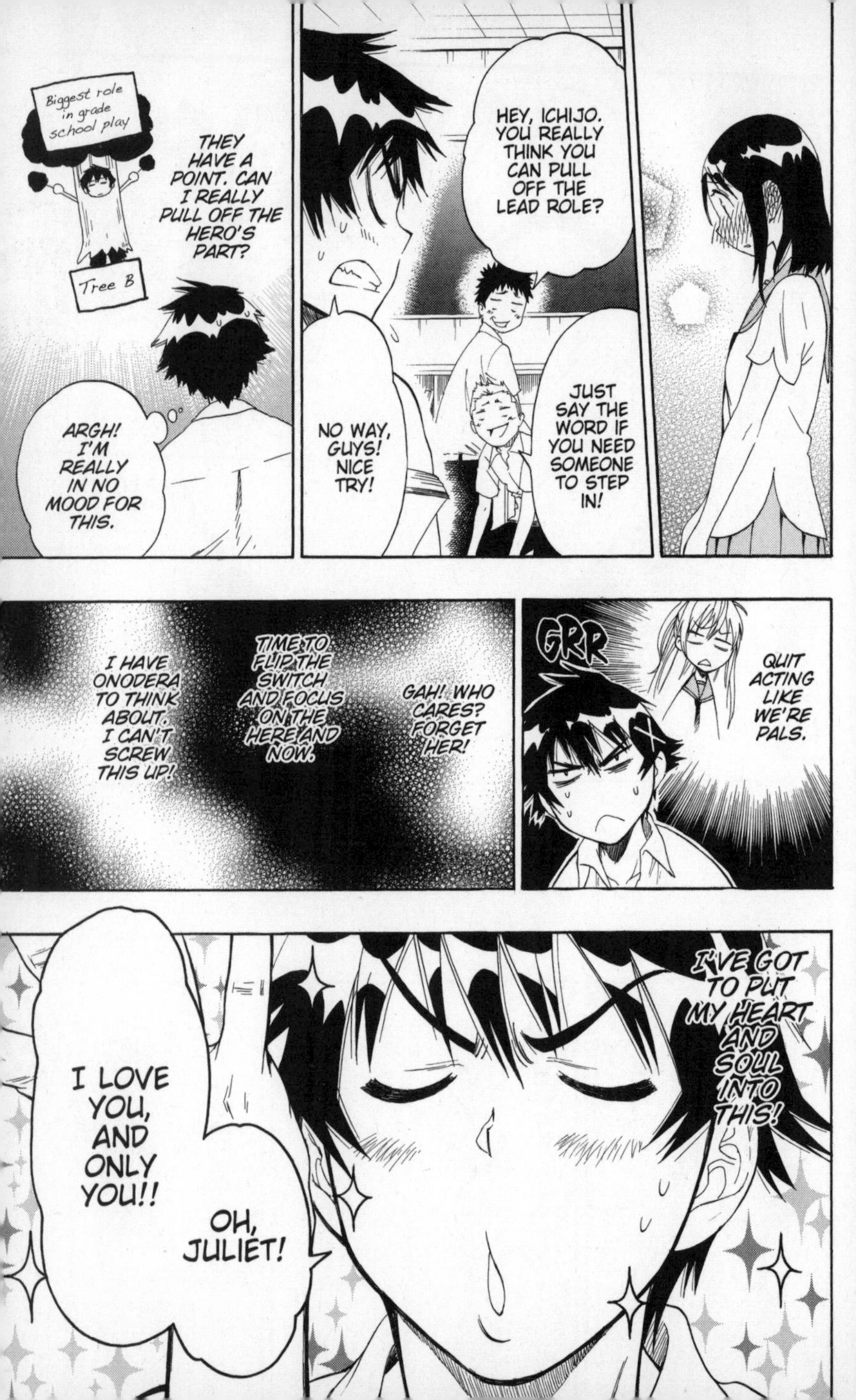

HEY, ICHIJO. YOU REALLY THINK YOU CAN PULL OFF THE LEAD ROLE?
JUST SAY THE WORD IF YOU NEED SOMEONE TO STEP IN!
NO WAY, GUYS! NICE TRY!
THEY HAVE A POINT. CAN I REALLY PULL OFF THE HERO'S PART?
Biggest role in grade school play
Tree B
ARGH! I'M REALLY IN NO MOOD FOR THIS.
GRR
QUIT ACTING LIKE WE'RE PALS.
GAH! WHO CARES? FORGET HER!
TIME TO FLIP THE SWITCH AND FOCUS ON THE HERE AND NOW.
I HAVE ONODERA TO THINK ABOUT. I CAN'T SCREW THIS UP!
I'VE GOT TO PUT MY HEART AND SOUL INTO THIS!
OH, JULIET!
I LOVE YOU, AND ONLY YOU!!

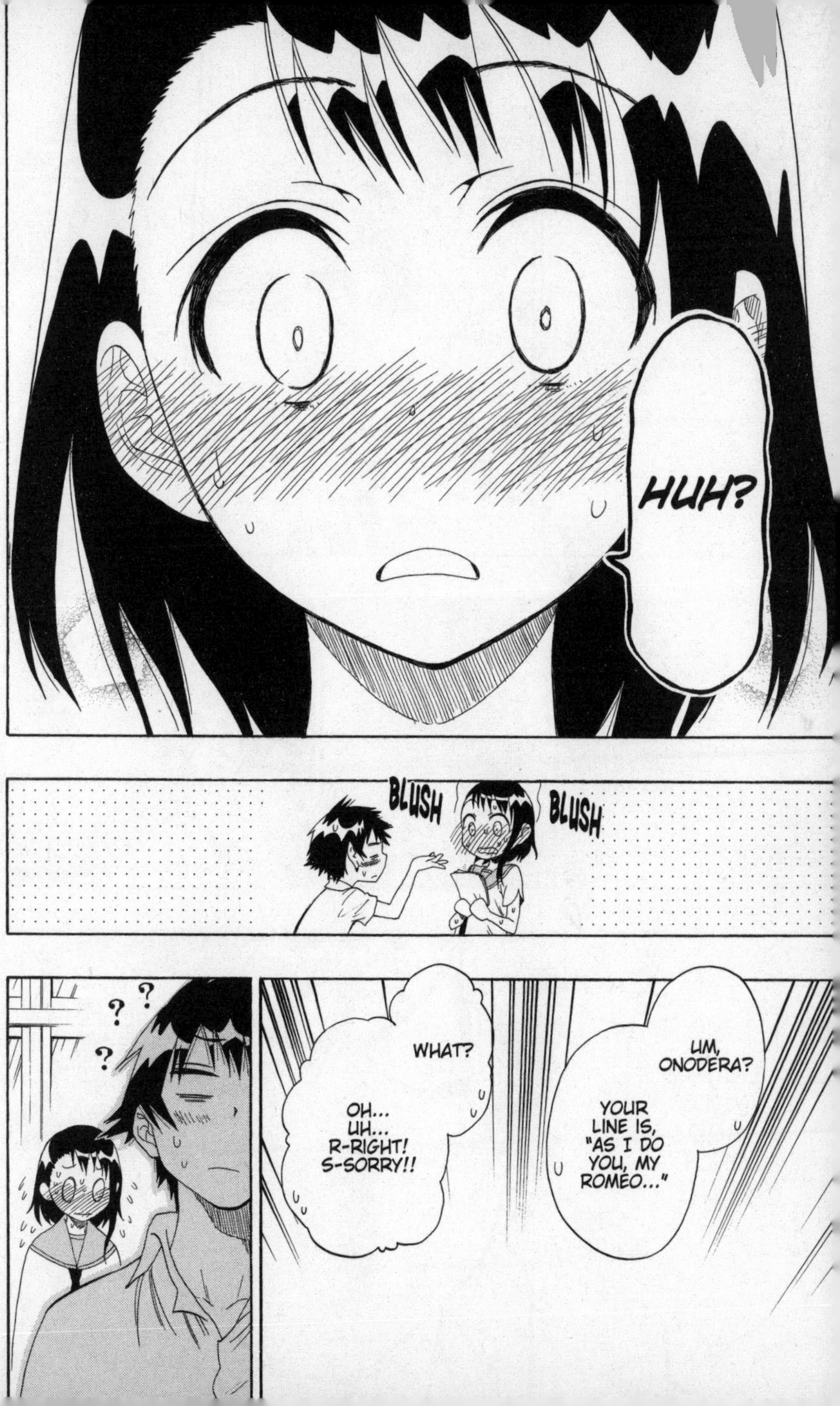
HUH?
BLUSH
BLUSH
UM, ONODERA?
YOUR LINE IS, "AS I DO YOU, MY ROMEO..."
WHAT?
OH... UH... R-RIGHT! S-SORRY!!

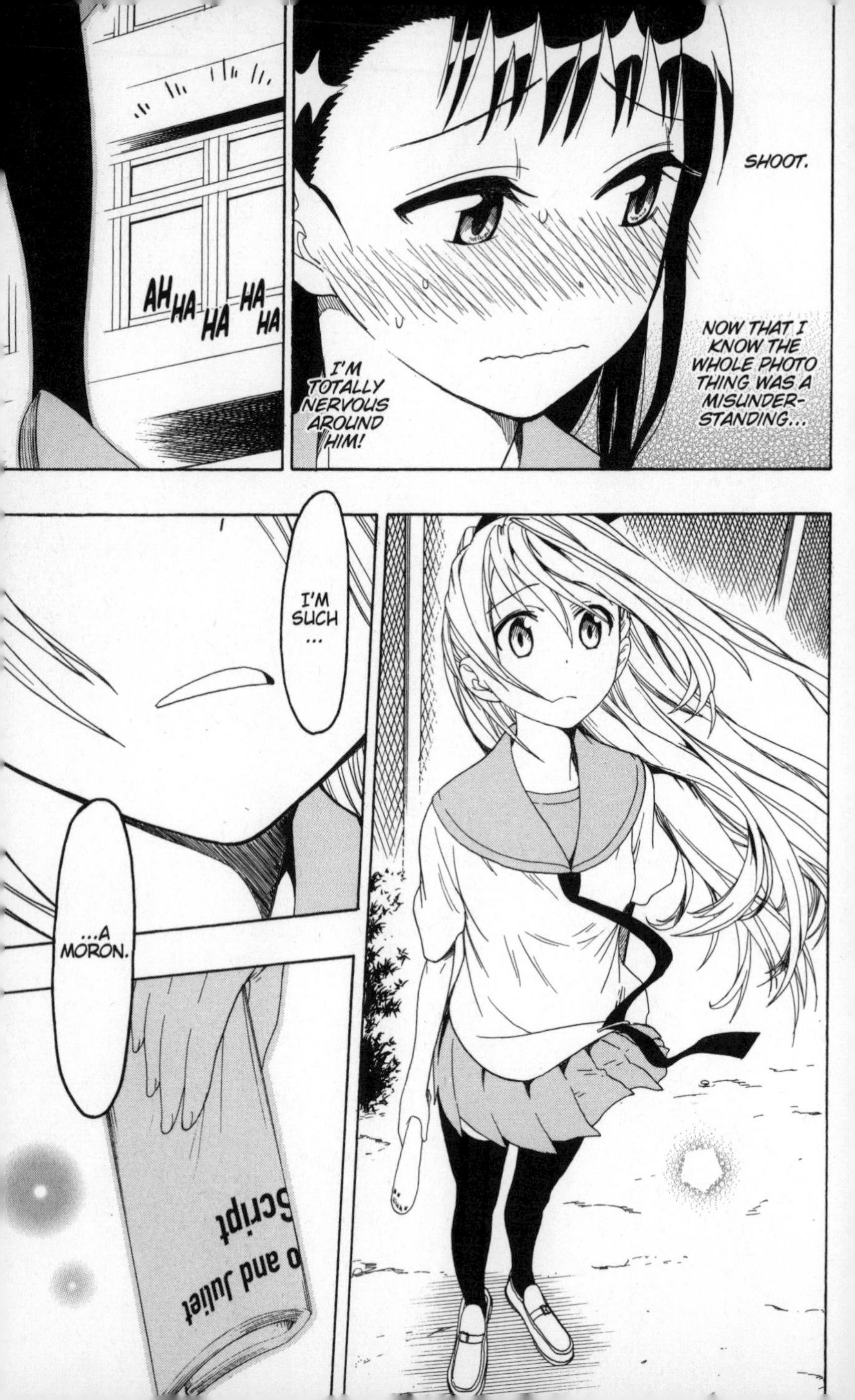
SHOOT.
NOW THAT I KNOW THE WHOLE PHOTO THING WAS A MISUNDER-STANDING...
I'M TOTALLY NERVOUS AROUND HIM!
AH HA HA HA HA
I'M SUCH...
...A MORON.

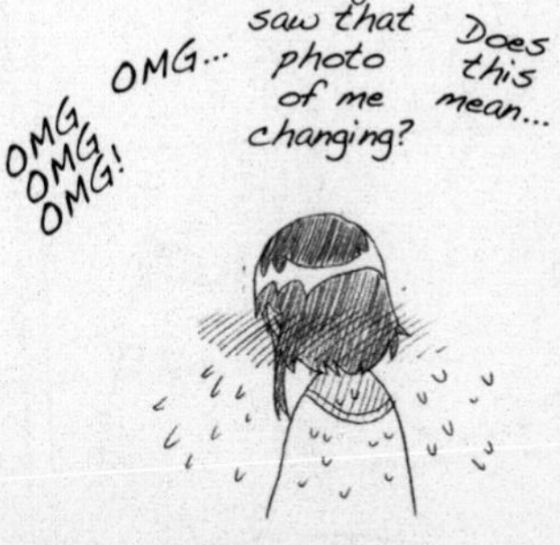
Does this mean...
...Ichijo saw that photo of me changing?
OMG...
OMG OMG OMG!

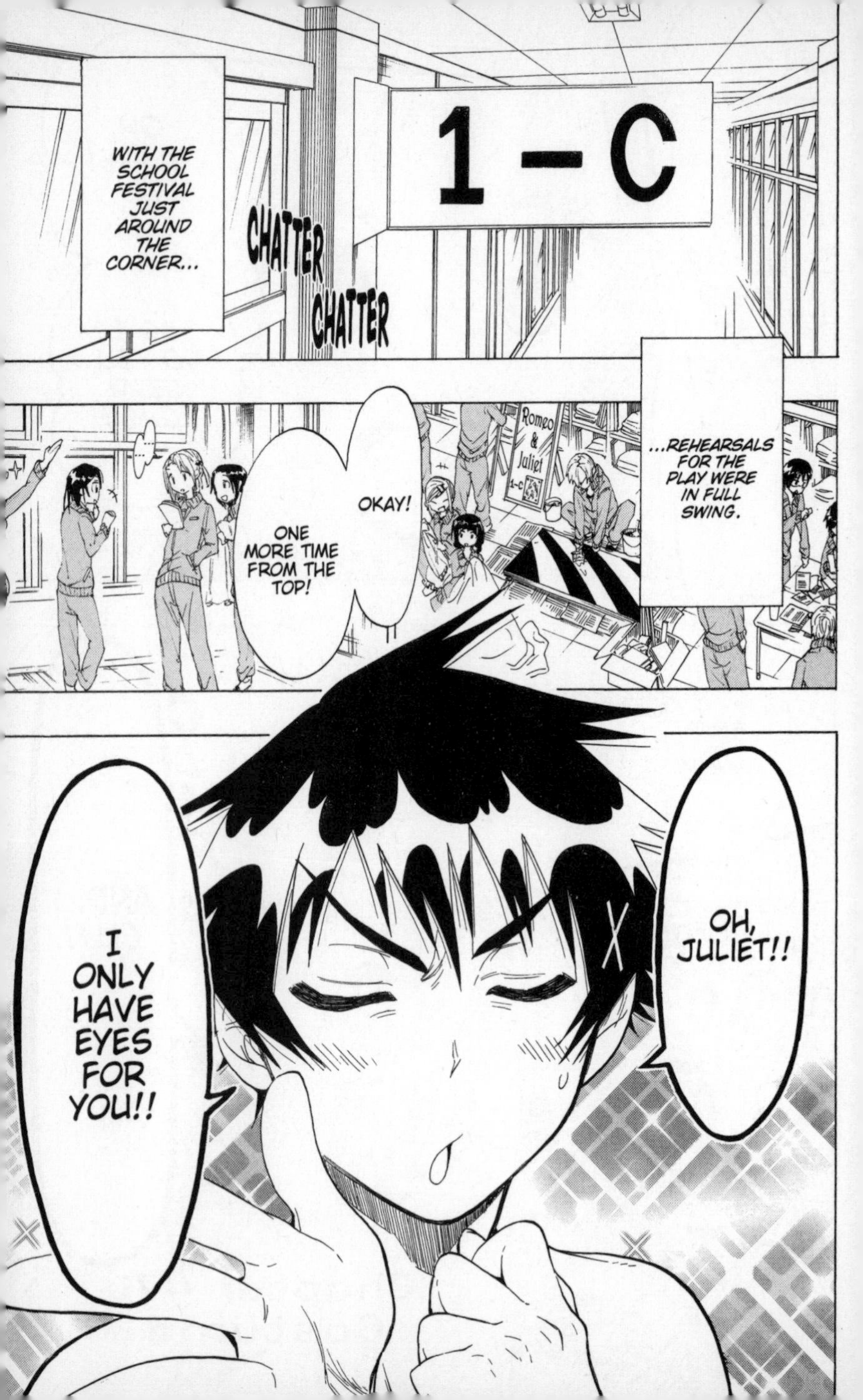
1 – C
WITH THE SCHOOL FESTIVAL JUST AROUND THE CORNER...
CHATTER
CHATTER
...REHEARSALS FOR THE PLAY WERE IN FULL SWING.
Romeo & Juliet 1-C
OKAY!
ONE MORE TIME FROM THE TOP!
...
OH, JULIET!!
I ONLY HAVE EYES FOR YOU!!

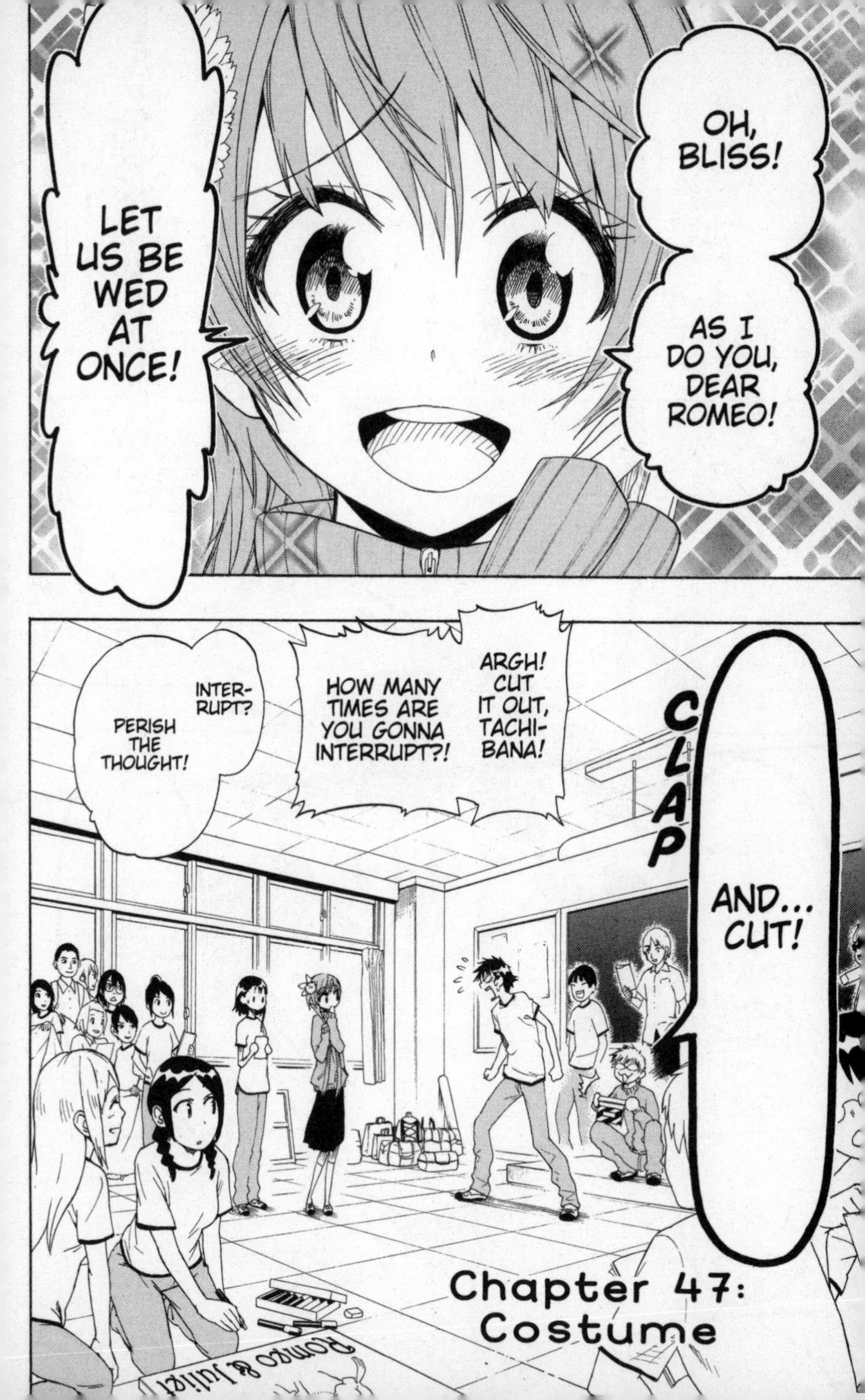
OH, BLISS!
AS I DO YOU, DEAR ROMEO!
LET US BE WED AT ONCE!
CLAP
AND... CUT!
ARGH! CUT IT OUT, TACHIBANA!
HOW MANY TIMES ARE YOU GONNA INTERRUPT?!
INTERRUPT?
PERISH THE THOUGHT!
Chapter 47: Costume
Romeo & Juliet

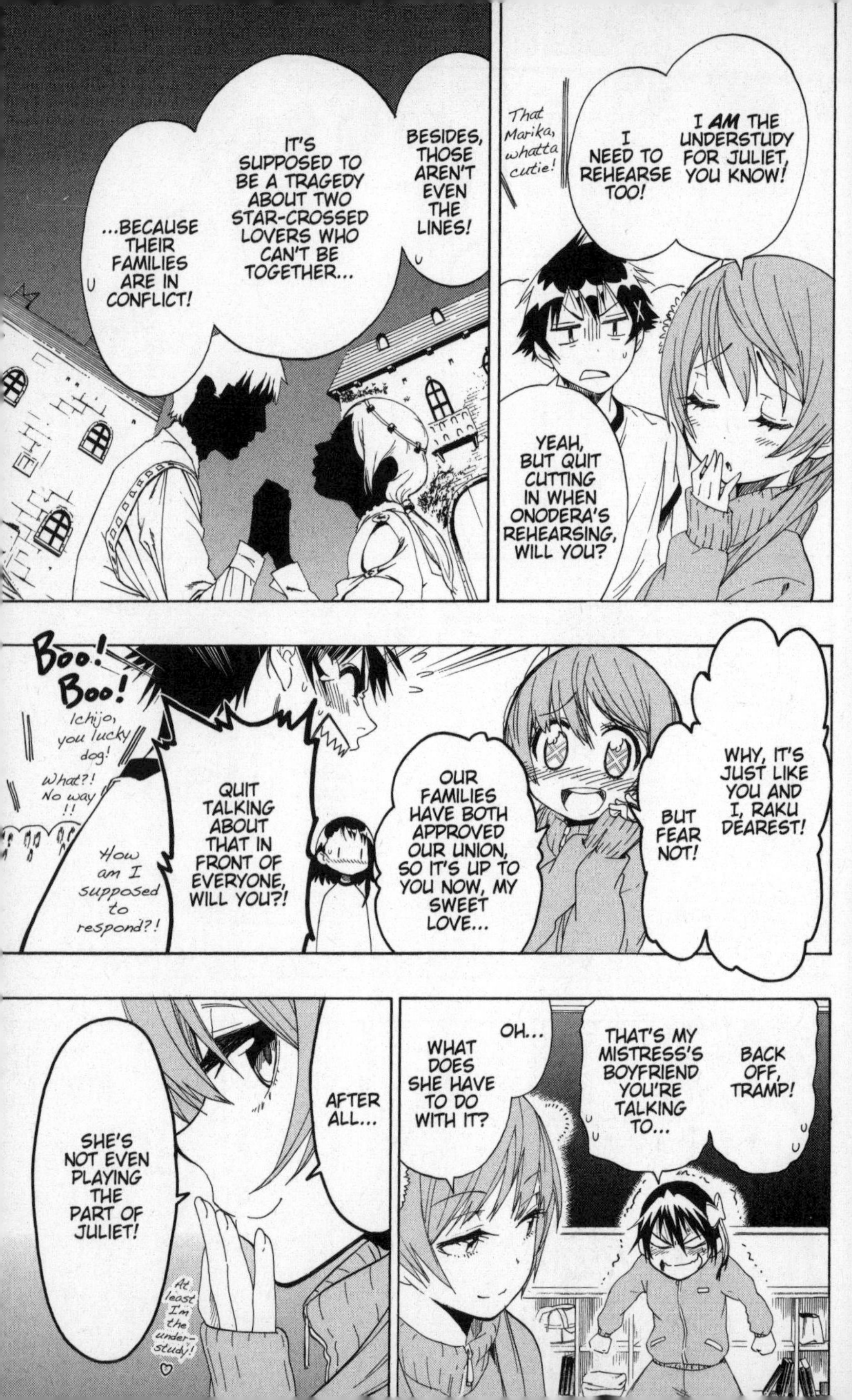
I AM THE UNDERSTUDY FOR JULIET, YOU KNOW!
I NEED TO REHEARSE TOO!
That Marika, whatta cutie!
YEAH, BUT QUIT CUTTING IN WHEN ONODERA'S REHEARSING, WILL YOU?
BESIDES, THOSE AREN'T EVEN THE LINES!
IT'S SUPPOSED TO BE A TRAGEDY ABOUT TWO STAR-CROSSED LOVERS WHO CAN'T BE TOGETHER...
...BECAUSE THEIR FAMILIES ARE IN CONFLICT!
WHY, IT'S JUST LIKE YOU AND I, RAKU DEAREST!
BUT FEAR NOT!
OUR FAMILIES HAVE BOTH APPROVED OUR UNION, SO IT'S UP TO YOU NOW, MY SWEET LOVE...
QUIT TALKING ABOUT THAT IN FRONT OF EVERYONE, WILL YOU?!
Boo! Boo!
Ichijo, you lucky dog!
What?! No way!!
How am I supposed to respond?!
BACK OFF, TRAMP!
THAT'S MY MISTRESS'S BOYFRIEND YOU'RE TALKING TO...
OH...
WHAT DOES SHE HAVE TO DO WITH IT?
AFTER ALL...
SHE'S NOT EVEN PLAYING THE PART OF JULIET!
At least I'm the under-study! ♡

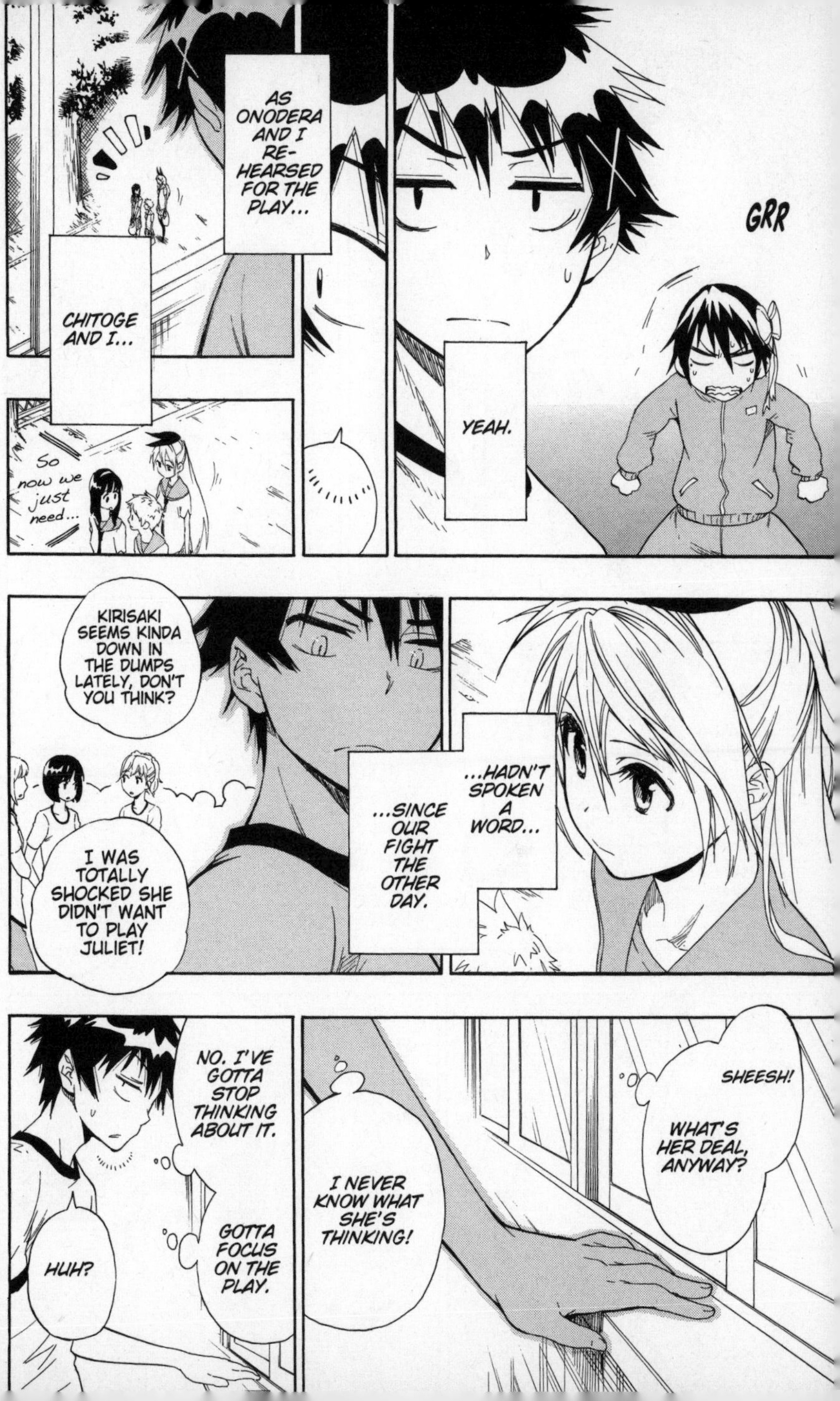
GRR
YEAH.
AS ONODERA AND I RE-HEARSED FOR THE PLAY...
CHITOGE AND I...
So now we just need...
...HADN'T SPOKEN A WORD...
...SINCE OUR FIGHT THE OTHER DAY.
KIRISAKI SEEMS KINDA DOWN IN THE DUMPS LATELY, DON'T YOU THINK?
I WAS TOTALLY SHOCKED SHE DIDN'T WANT TO PLAY JULIET!
SHEESH!
WHAT'S HER DEAL, ANYWAY?
I NEVER KNOW WHAT SHE'S THINKING!
NO. I'VE GOTTA STOP THINKING ABOUT IT.
GOTTA FOCUS ON THE PLAY.
HUH?

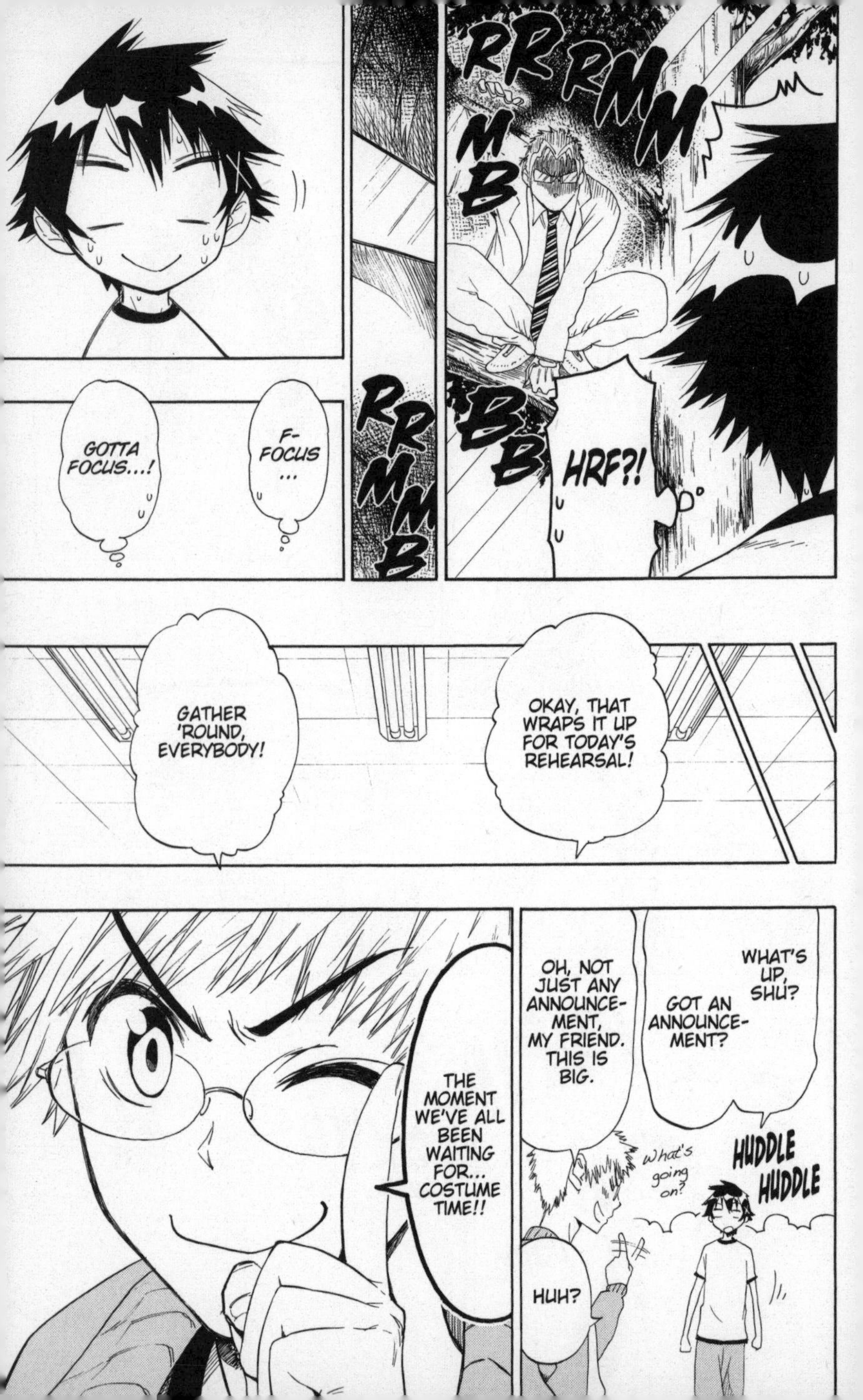
RRRMMMMB
BBB
HRF?!
RRMMMB
F-FOCUS...
GOTTA FOCUS...!
OKAY, THAT WRAPS IT UP FOR TODAY'S REHEARSAL!
GATHER 'ROUND, EVERYBODY!
WHAT'S UP, SHU?
GOT AN ANNOUNCEMENT?
OH, NOT JUST ANY ANNOUNCEMENT, MY FRIEND. THIS IS BIG.
HUDDLE HUDDLE
What's going on?
HUH?
THE MOMENT WE'VE ALL BEEN WAITING FOR... COSTUME TIME!!

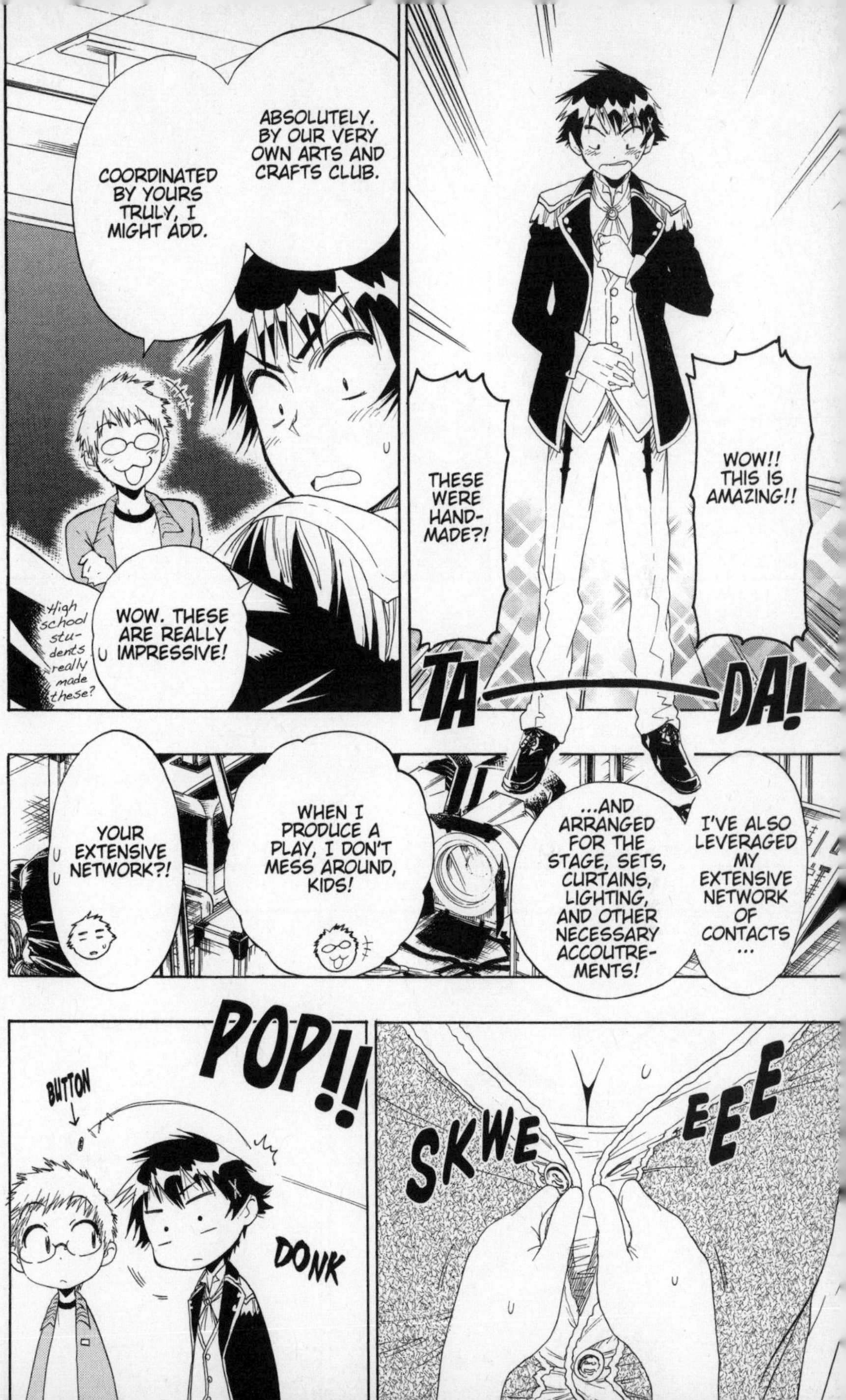

WOW!! THIS IS AMAZING!!
THESE WERE HAND-MADE?!
TA—DA!
ABSOLUTELY. BY OUR VERY OWN ARTS AND CRAFTS CLUB.
COORDINATED BY YOURS TRULY, I MIGHT ADD.
WOW. THESE ARE REALLY IMPRESSIVE!
High school students really made these?
I'VE ALSO LEVERAGED MY EXTENSIVE NETWORK OF CONTACTS...
...AND ARRANGED FOR THE STAGE, SETS, CURTAINS, LIGHTING, AND OTHER NECESSARY ACCOUTREMENTS!
WHEN I PRODUCE A PLAY, I DON'T MESS AROUND, KIDS!
YOUR EXTENSIVE NETWORK?!
SKWEEEE
POP!!
BUTTON
DONK

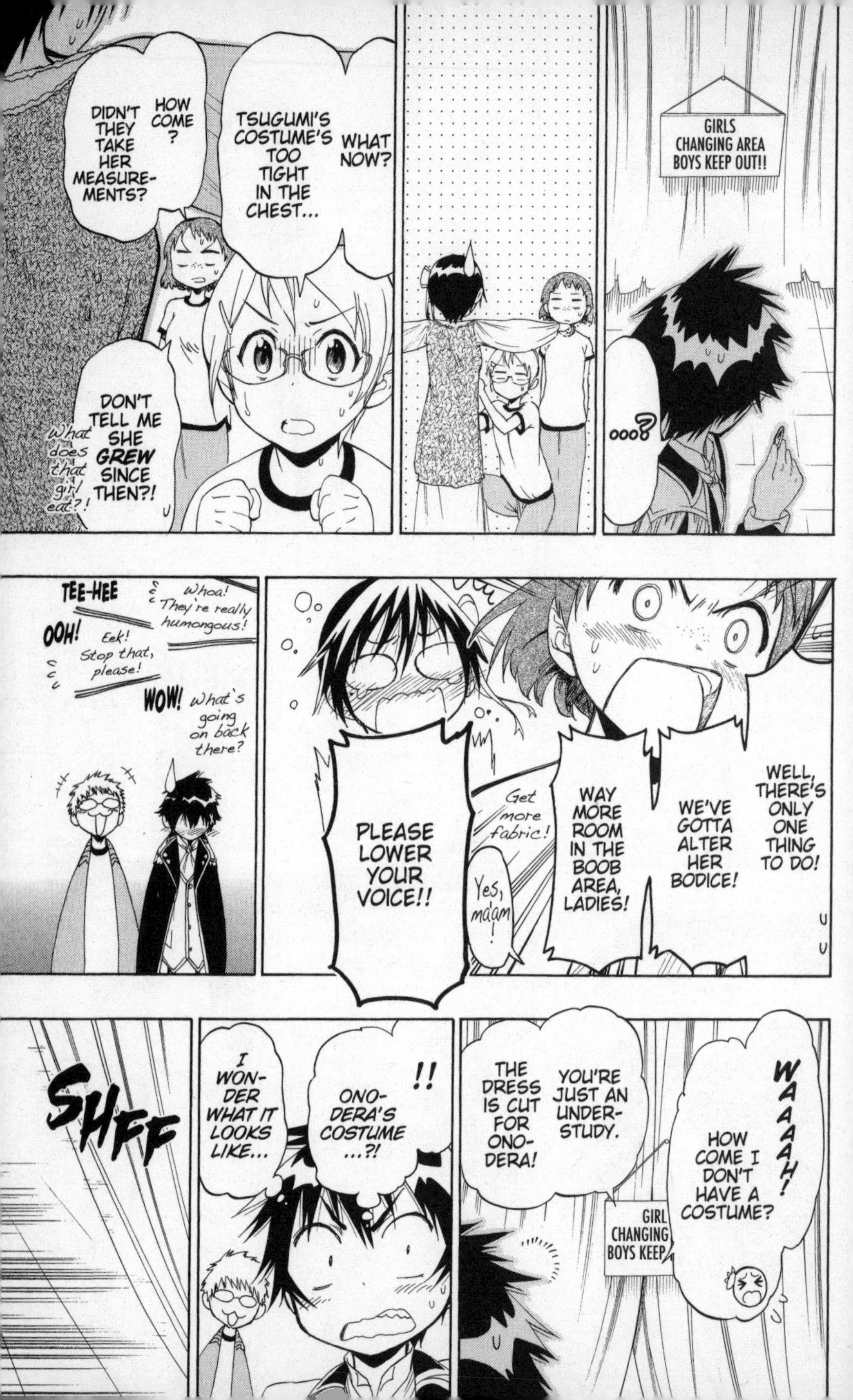
GIRLS CHANGING AREA BOYS KEEP OUT!!
ooo?
WHAT NOW?
TSUGUMI'S COSTUME'S TOO TIGHT IN THE CHEST...
HOW COME?
DIDN'T THEY TAKE HER MEASUREMENTS?
DON'T TELL ME SHE GREW SINCE THEN?!
What does that girl eat?!
WELL, THERE'S ONLY ONE THING TO DO!
WE'VE GOTTA ALTER HER BODICE!
WAY MORE ROOM IN THE BOOB AREA, LADIES!
Get more fabric!
Yes, ma'am!
PLEASE LOWER YOUR VOICE!!
Whoa! They're really humongous!
TEE-HEE
Eek! Stop that, please!
OOH!
What's going on back there?
WOW!
WAAAAH!
HOW COME I DON'T HAVE A COSTUME?
YOU'RE JUST AN UNDER-STUDY.
THE DRESS IS CUT FOR ONO-DERA!
GIRL CHANGING BOYS KEEP
!!
ONO-DERA'S COSTUME ...?!
I WON-DER WHAT IT LOOKS LIKE...
SHFF

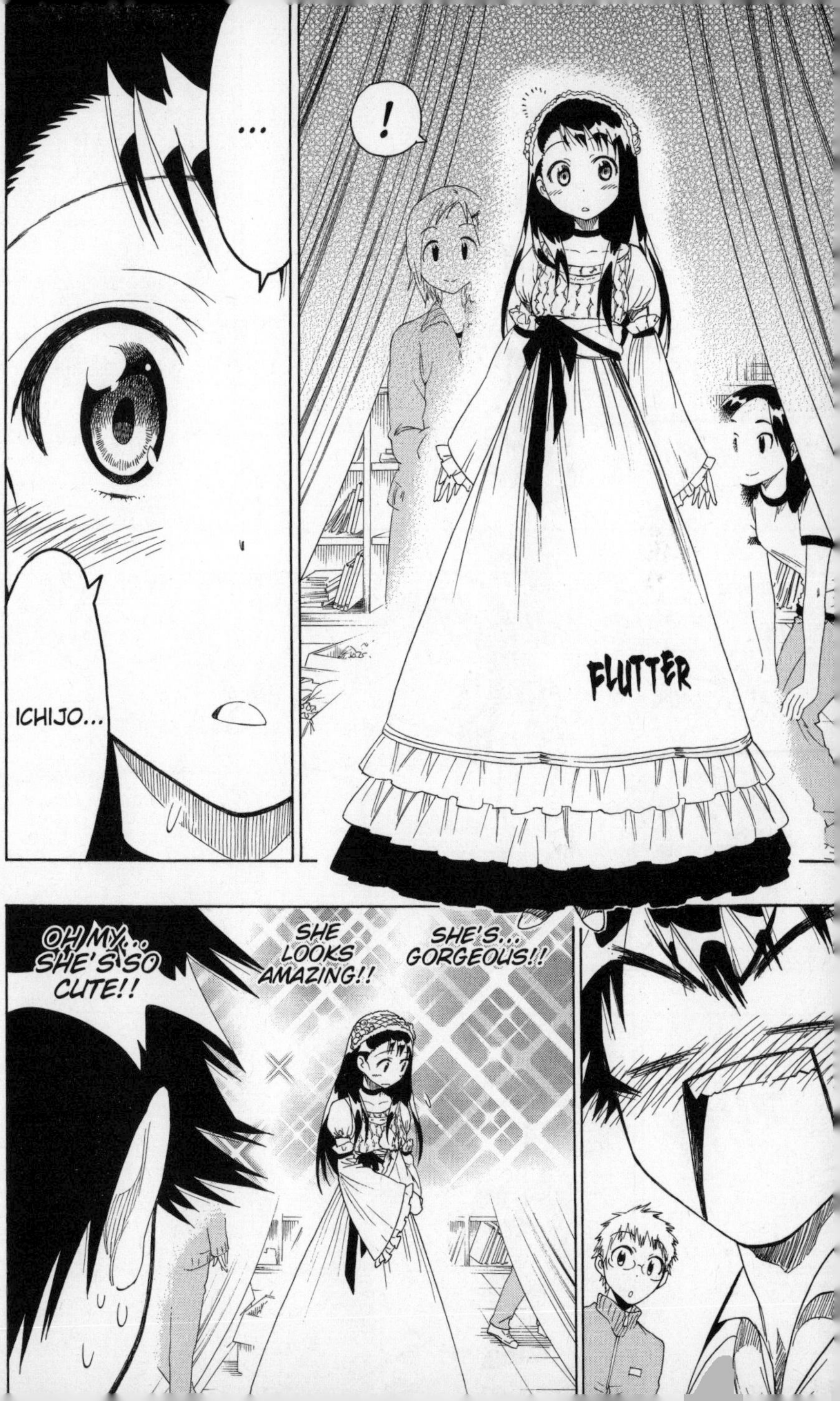
!
FLUTTER
...
ICHIJO...
SHE'S... GORGEOUS!!
SHE LOOKS AMAZING!!
OH MY... SHE'S SO CUTE!!

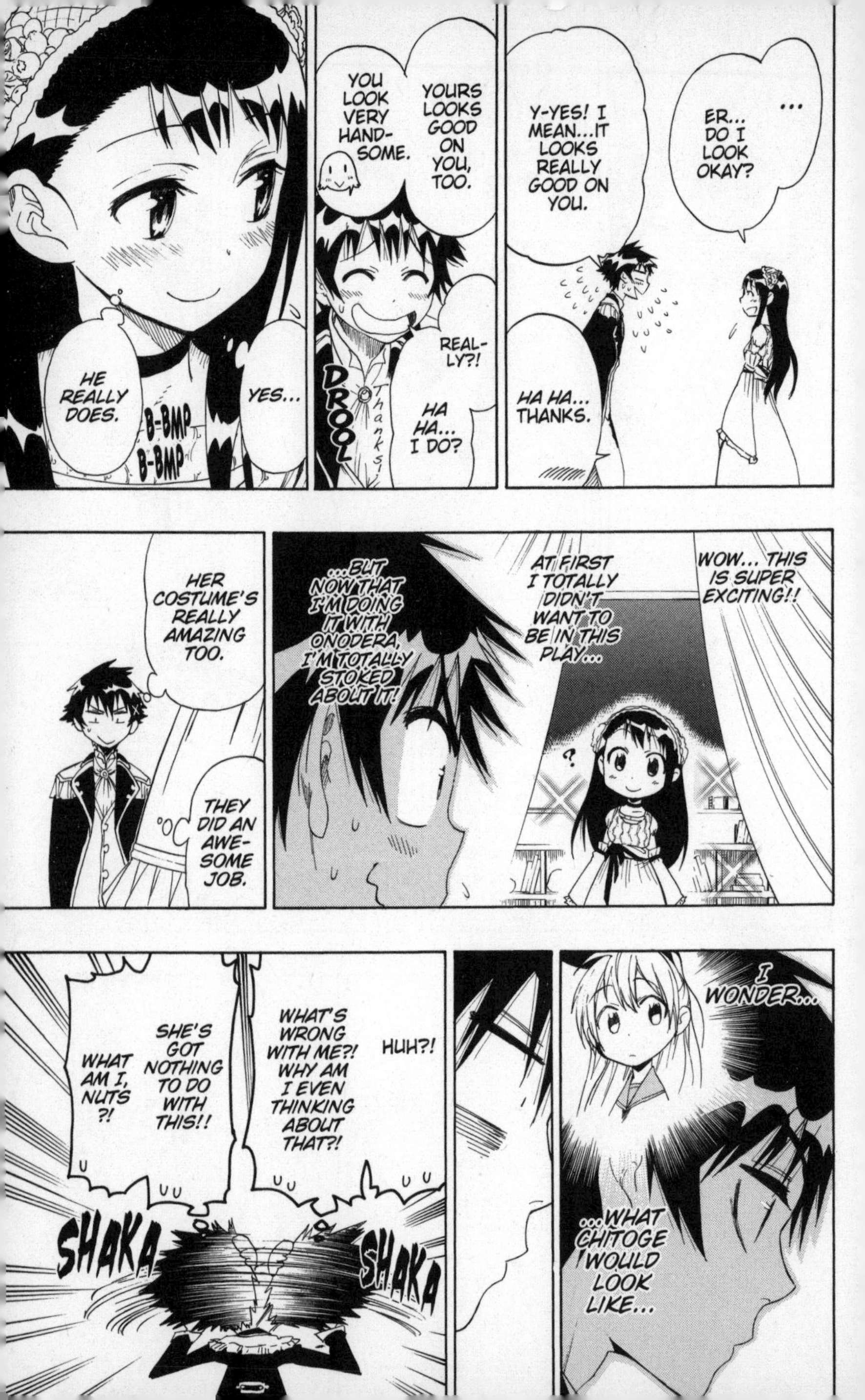
...
ER... DO I LOOK OKAY?
Y-YES! I MEAN...IT LOOKS REALLY GOOD ON YOU.
HA HA... THANKS.
YOURS LOOKS GOOD ON YOU, TOO.
YOU LOOK VERY HAND-SOME.
REAL-LY?!
HA HA... I DO?
Thanks!
DROOL
YES...
HE REALLY DOES.
B-BMP
B-BMP
WOW... THIS IS SUPER EXCITING!!
AT FIRST I TOTALLY DIDN'T WANT TO BE IN THIS PLAY...
?
...BUT NOW THAT I'M DOING IT WITH ONODERA, I'M TOTALLY STOKED ABOUT IT!
HER COSTUME'S REALLY AMAZING TOO.
THEY DID AN AWE-SOME JOB.
I WONDER...
...WHAT CHITOGE WOULD LOOK LIKE...
HUH?!
WHAT'S WRONG WITH ME?! WHY AM I EVEN THINKING ABOUT THAT?!
SHE'S GOT NOTHING TO DO WITH THIS!!
WHAT AM I, NUTS?!
SHAKA
SHAKA

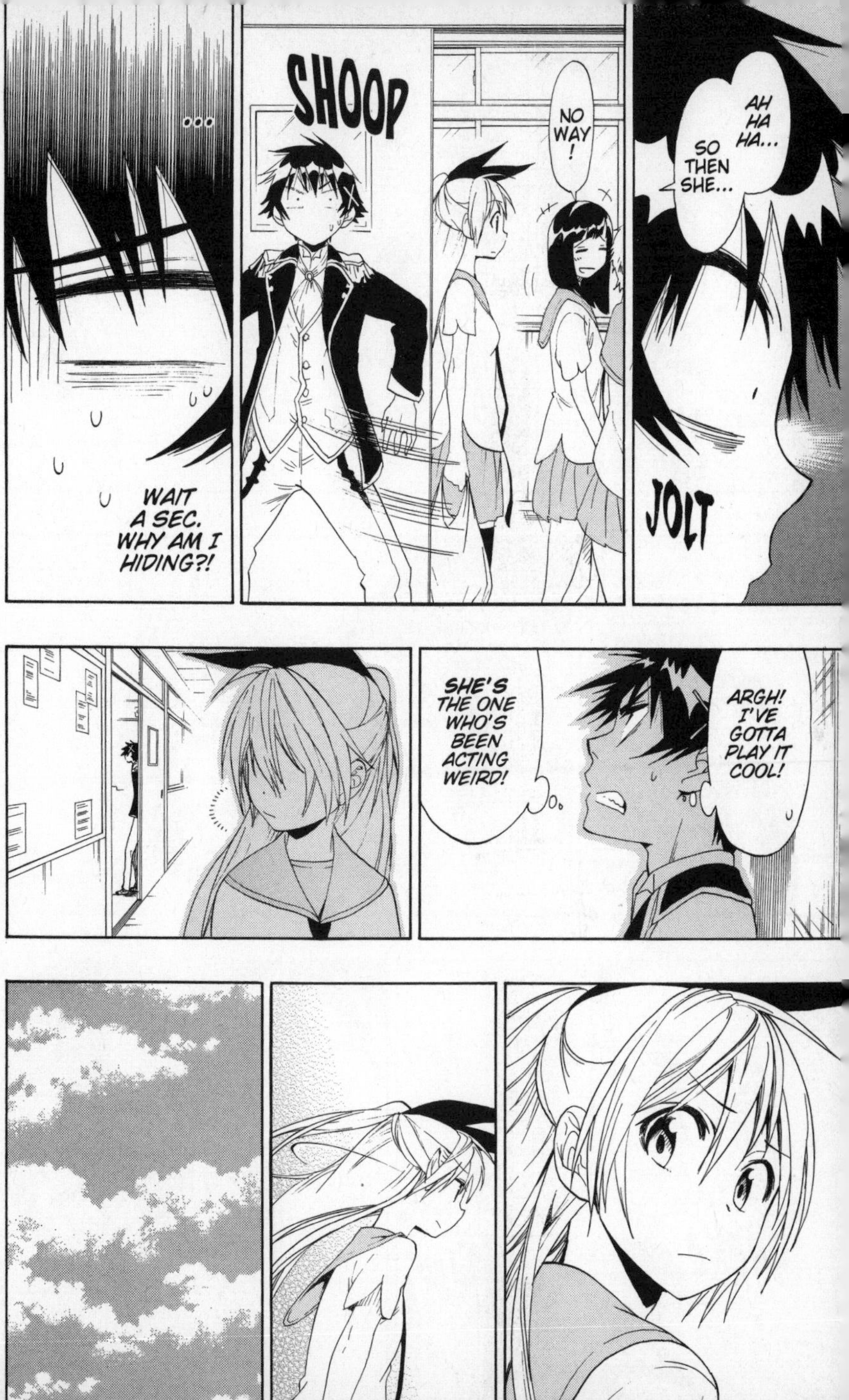
AH HA HA... SO THEN SHE...
JOLT
NO WAY!
SHOOP
...
WAIT A SEC. WHY AM I HIDING?!
ARGH! I'VE GOTTA PLAY IT COOL!
SHE'S THE ONE WHO'S BEEN ACTING WEIRD!

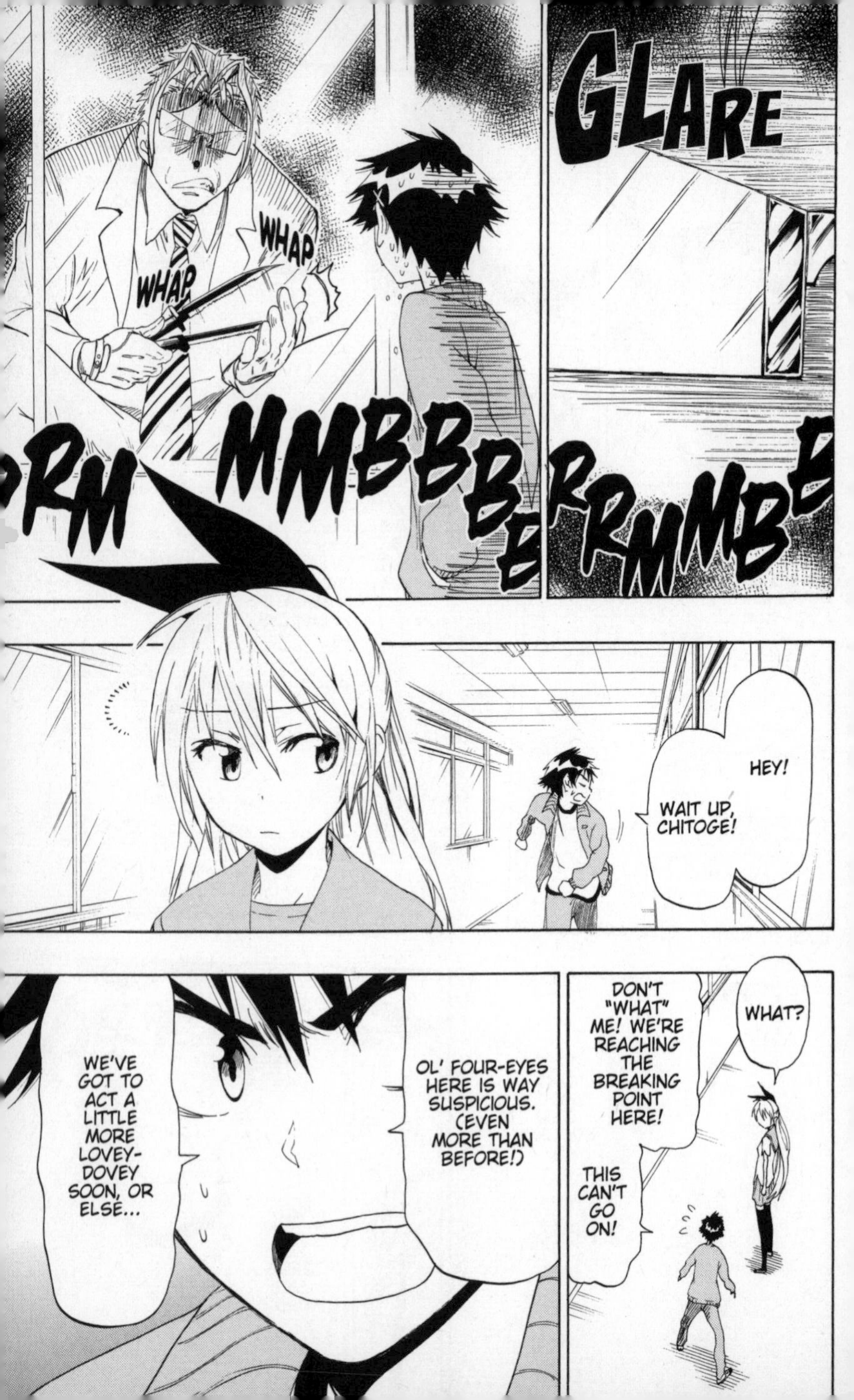
GLARE
RRMMBE
WHAP
WHAP
RM MMBBBBB
HEY!
WAIT UP, CHITOGE!
WHAT?
DON'T "WHAT" ME! WE'RE REACHING THE BREAKING POINT HERE!
THIS CAN'T GO ON!
OL' FOUR-EYES HERE IS WAY SUSPICIOUS. (EVEN MORE THAN BEFORE!)
WE'VE GOT TO ACT A LITTLE MORE LOVEY-DOVEY SOON, OR ELSE...

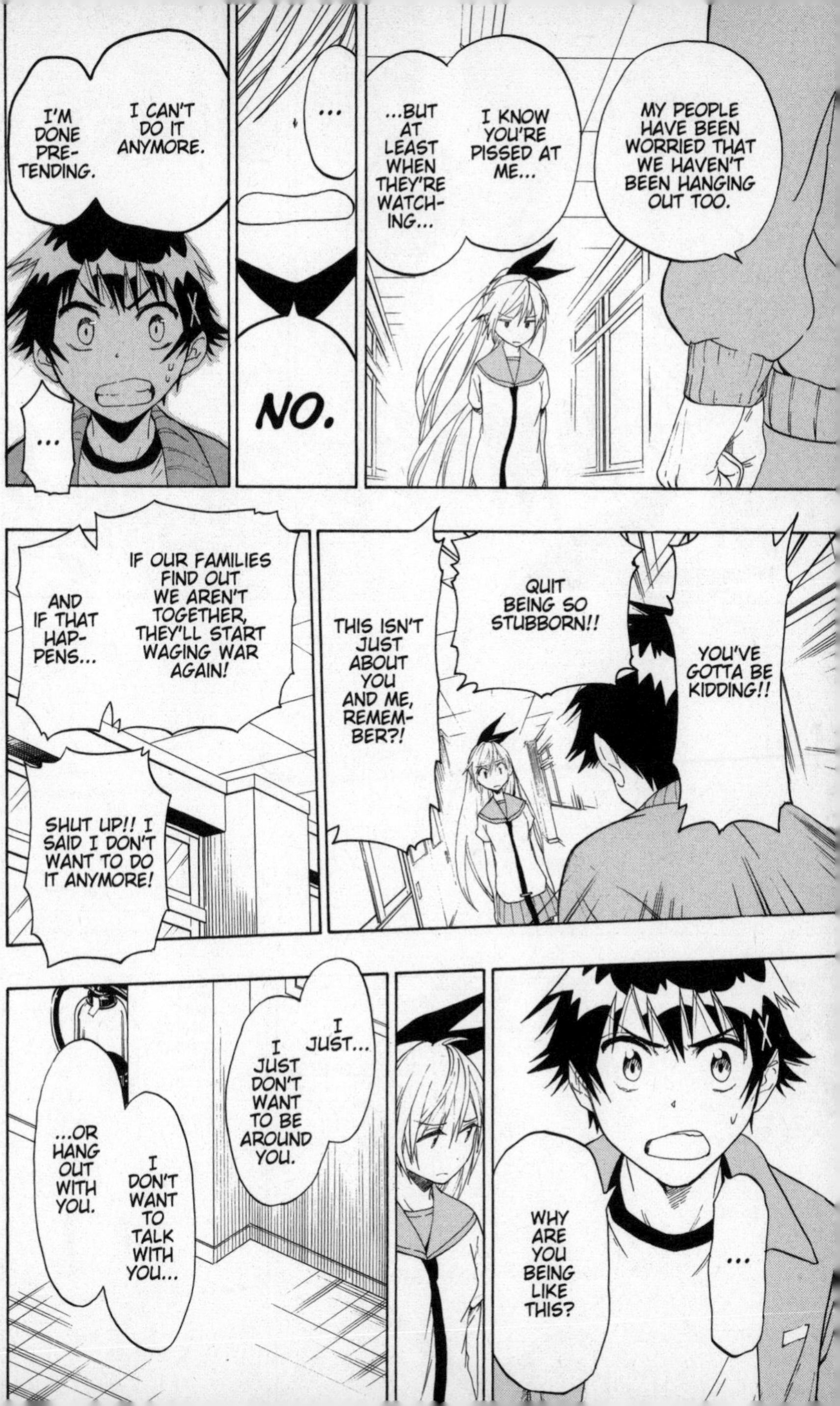
MY PEOPLE HAVE BEEN WORRIED THAT WE HAVEN'T BEEN HANGING OUT TOO.
I KNOW YOU'RE PISSED AT ME...
...BUT AT LEAST WHEN THEY'RE WATCH-ING...
...
NO.
I CAN'T DO IT ANYMORE.
I'M DONE PRE-TENDING.
...
YOU'VE GOTTA BE KIDDING!!
QUIT BEING SO STUBBORN!!
THIS ISN'T JUST ABOUT YOU AND ME, REMEM-BER?!
IF OUR FAMILIES FIND OUT WE AREN'T TOGETHER, THEY'LL START WAGING WAR AGAIN!
AND IF THAT HAP-PENS...
SHUT UP!! I SAID I DON'T WANT TO DO IT ANYMORE!
WHY ARE YOU BEING LIKE THIS?
...
I JUST...
I JUST DON'T WANT TO BE AROUND YOU.
I DON'T WANT TO TALK WITH YOU...
...OR HANG OUT WITH YOU.

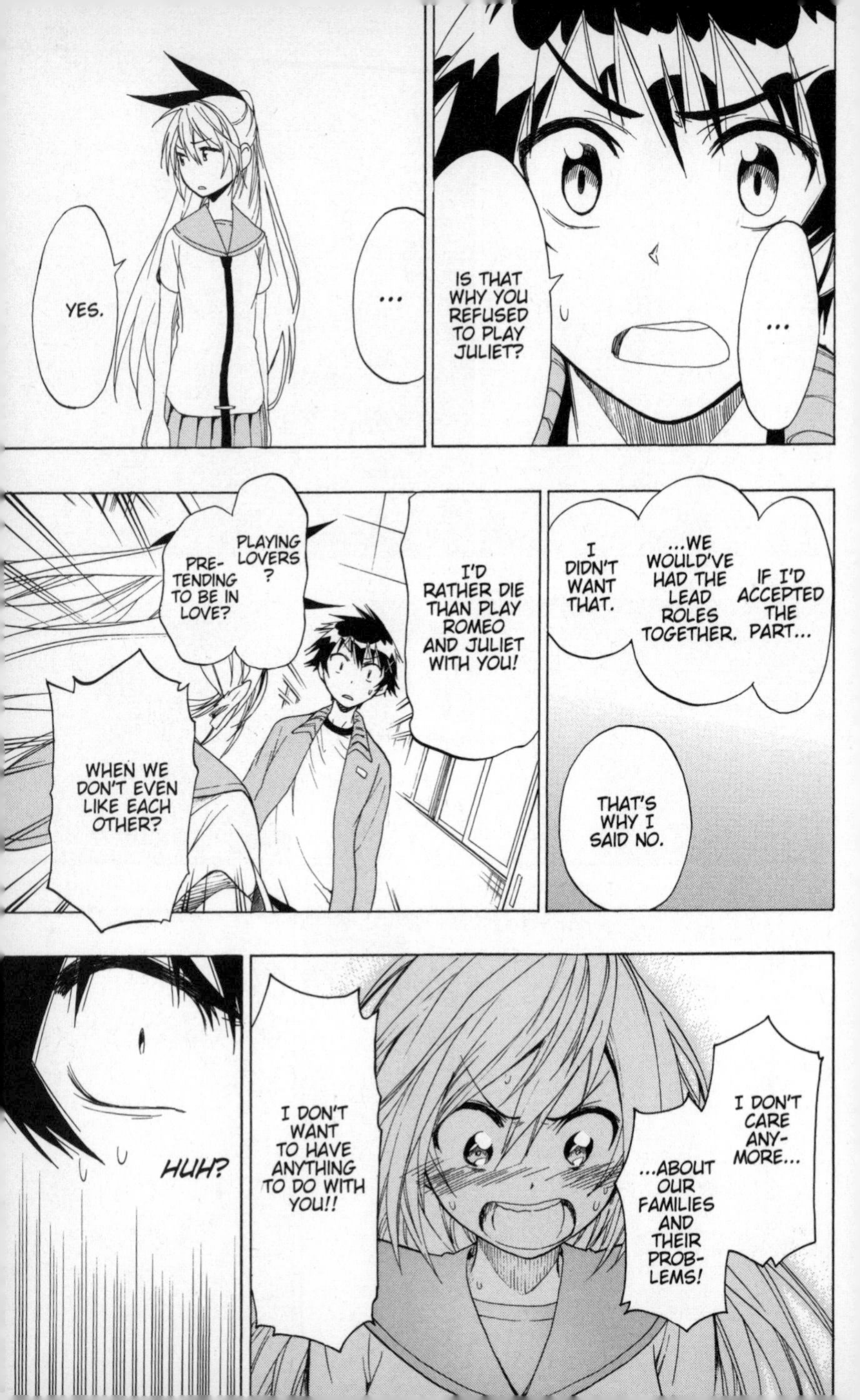
...
IS THAT WHY YOU REFUSED TO PLAY JULIET?
...
YES.
IF I'D ACCEPTED THE PART...
...WE WOULD'VE HAD THE LEAD ROLES TOGETHER.
I DIDN'T WANT THAT.
THAT'S WHY I SAID NO.
I'D RATHER DIE THAN PLAY ROMEO AND JULIET WITH YOU!
PLAYING LOVERS?
PRE-TENDING TO BE IN LOVE?
WHEN WE DON'T EVEN LIKE EACH OTHER?
I DON'T CARE ANY-MORE...
...ABOUT OUR FAMILIES AND THEIR PROB-LEMS!
I DON'T WANT TO HAVE ANYTHING TO DO WITH YOU!!
HUH?

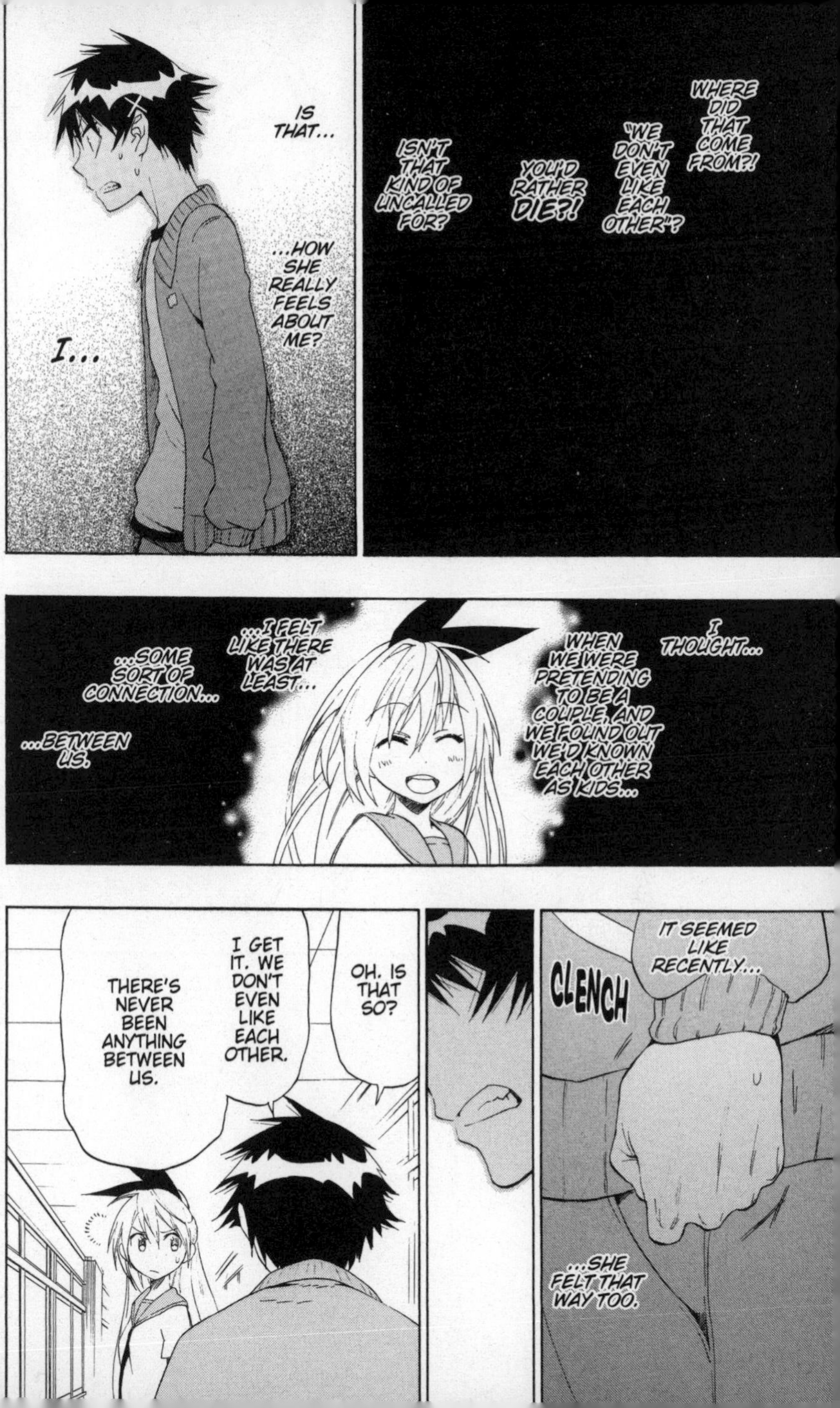
WHERE DID THAT COME FROM?!
"WE DON'T EVEN LIKE EACH OTHER"?
YOU'D RATHER DIE?!
ISN'T THAT KIND OF UNCALLED FOR?
IS THAT...
...HOW SHE REALLY FEELS ABOUT ME?
I...
I THOUGHT...
WHEN WE WERE PRETENDING TO BE A COUPLE, AND WE FOUND OUT WE'D KNOWN EACH OTHER AS KIDS...
...I FELT LIKE THERE WAS AT LEAST...
...SOME SORT OF CONNECTION...
...BETWEEN US.
IT SEEMED LIKE RECENTLY...
CLENCH
...SHE FELT THAT WAY TOO.
OH. IS THAT SO?
I GET IT. WE DON'T EVEN LIKE EACH OTHER.
THERE'S NEVER BEEN ANYTHING BETWEEN US.

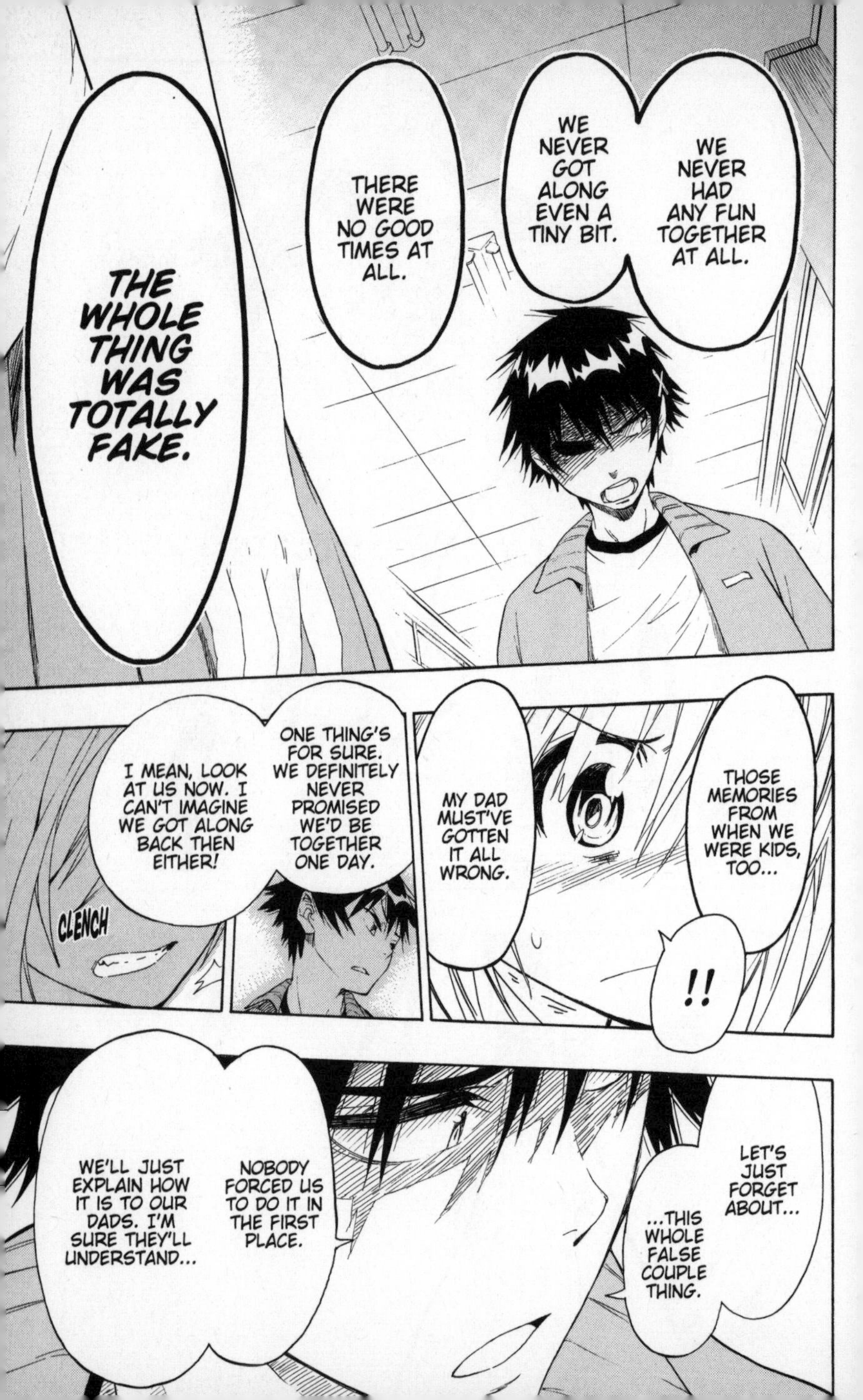
WE NEVER HAD ANY FUN TOGETHER AT ALL.
WE NEVER GOT ALONG EVEN A TINY BIT.
THERE WERE NO GOOD TIMES AT ALL.
THE WHOLE THING WAS TOTALLY FAKE.
THOSE MEMORIES FROM WHEN WE WERE KIDS, TOO...
!!
MY DAD MUST'VE GOTTEN IT ALL WRONG.
ONE THING'S FOR SURE. WE DEFINITELY NEVER PROMISED WE'D BE TOGETHER ONE DAY.
I MEAN, LOOK AT US NOW. I CAN'T IMAGINE WE GOT ALONG BACK THEN EITHER!
CLENCH
LET'S JUST FORGET ABOUT...
...THIS WHOLE FALSE COUPLE THING.
NOBODY FORCED US TO DO IT IN THE FIRST PLACE.
WE'LL JUST EXPLAIN HOW IT IS TO OUR DADS. I'M SURE THEY'LL UNDERSTAND...

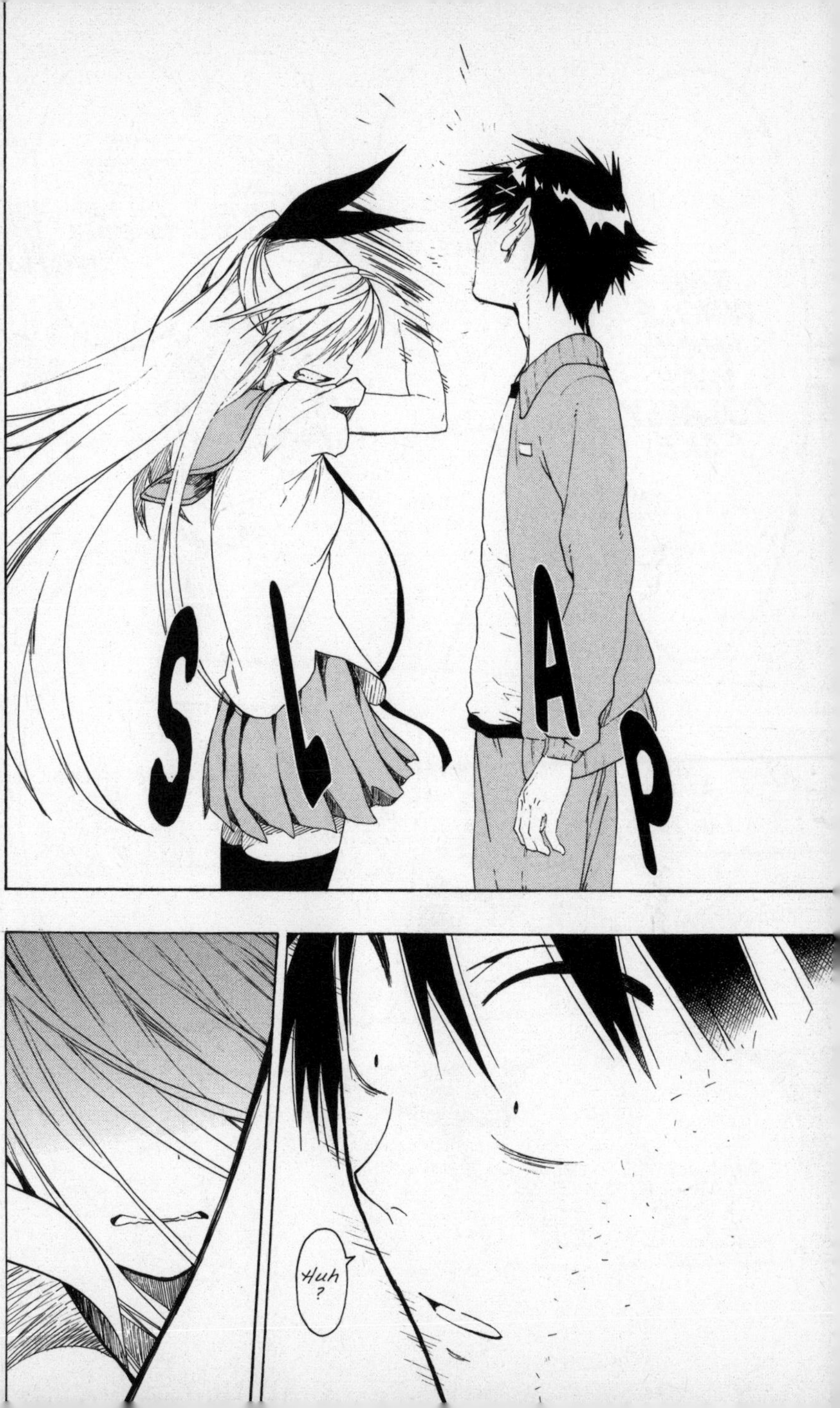
SLAP
Huh?

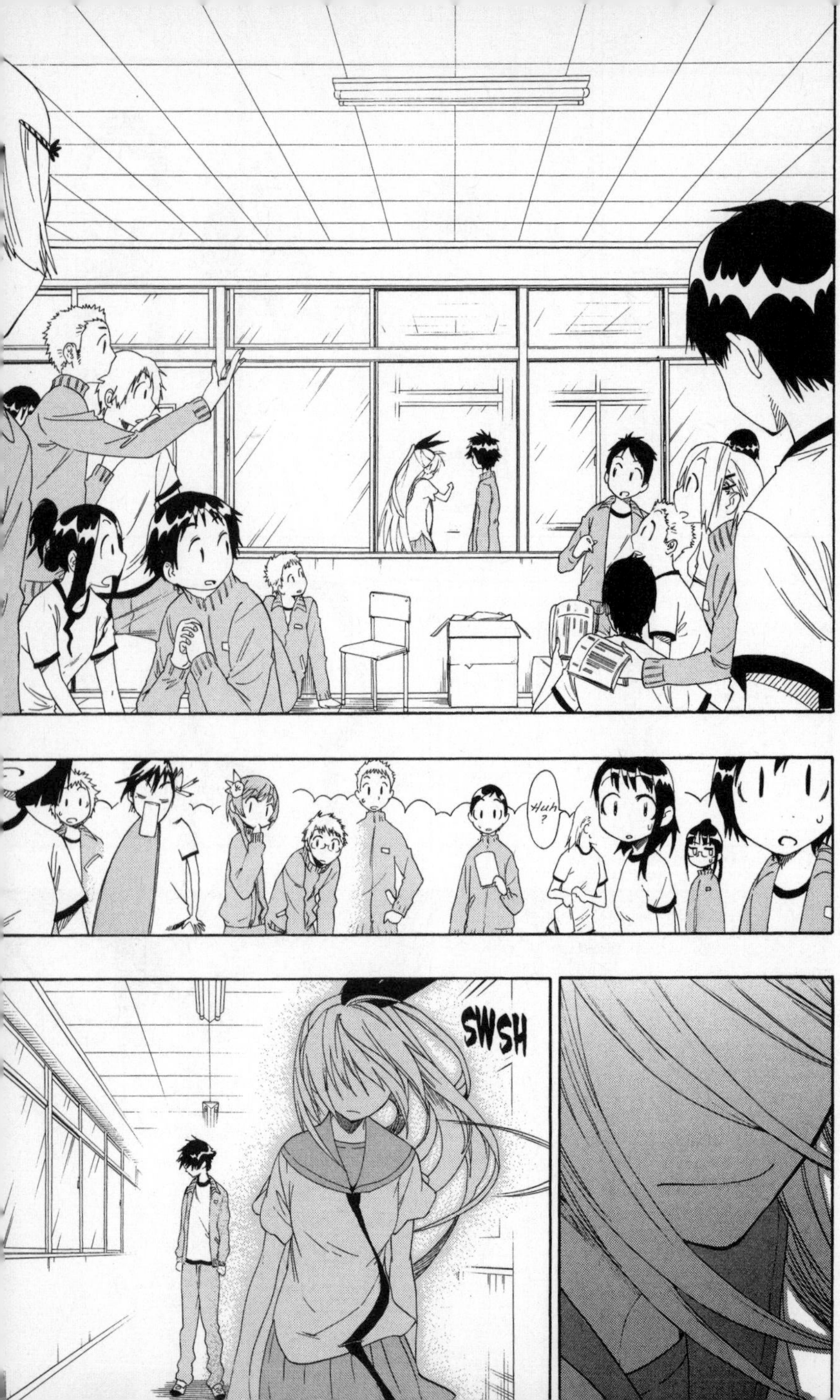
Huh?
SWSH

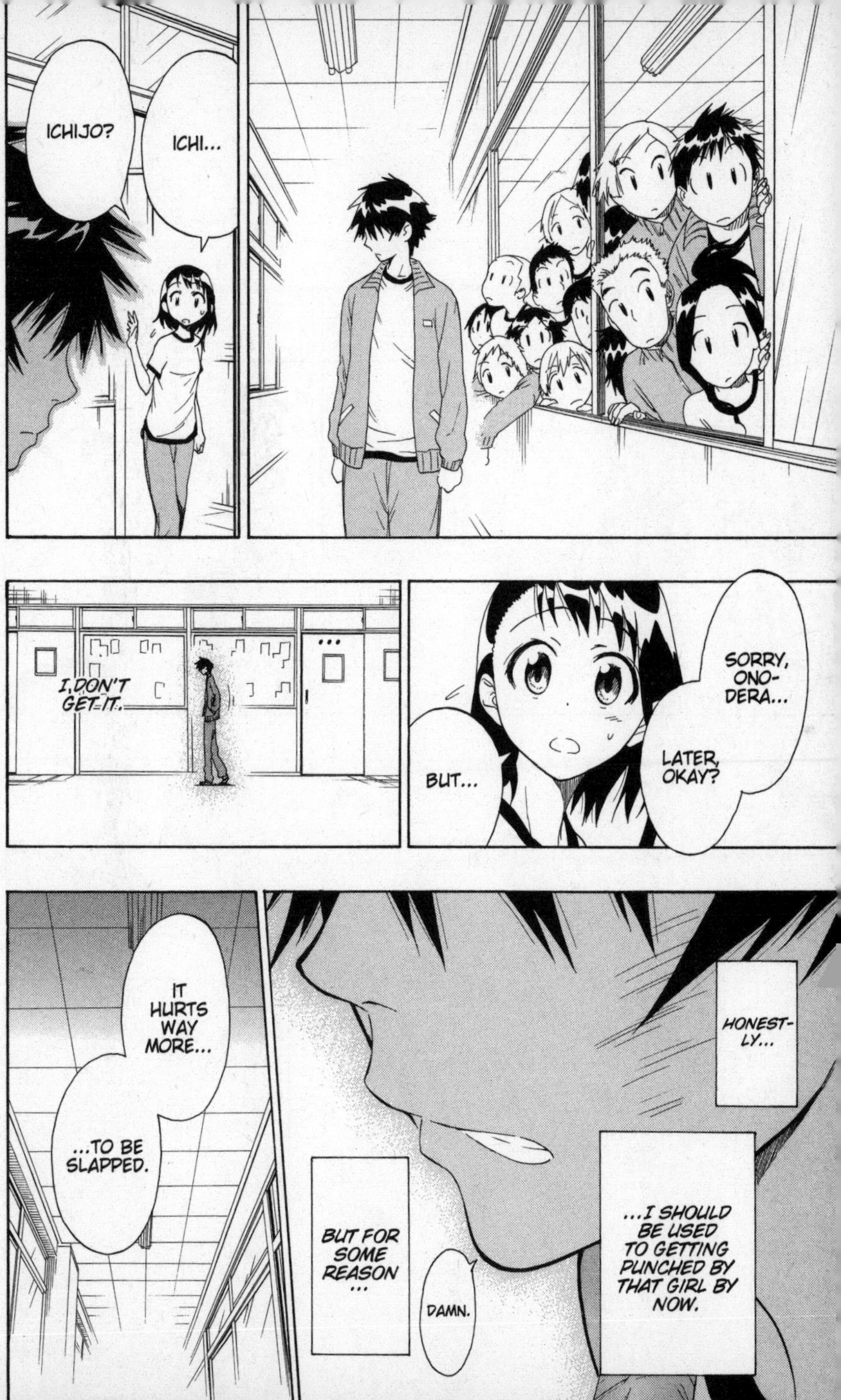
ICHI...
ICHIJO?
SORRY, ONO-DERA...
LATER, OKAY?
BUT...
I DON'T GET IT.
HONEST-LY...
...I SHOULD BE USED TO GETTING PUNCHED BY THAT GIRL BY NOW.
BUT FOR SOME REASON...
DAMN.
IT HURTS WAY MORE...
...TO BE SLAPPED.

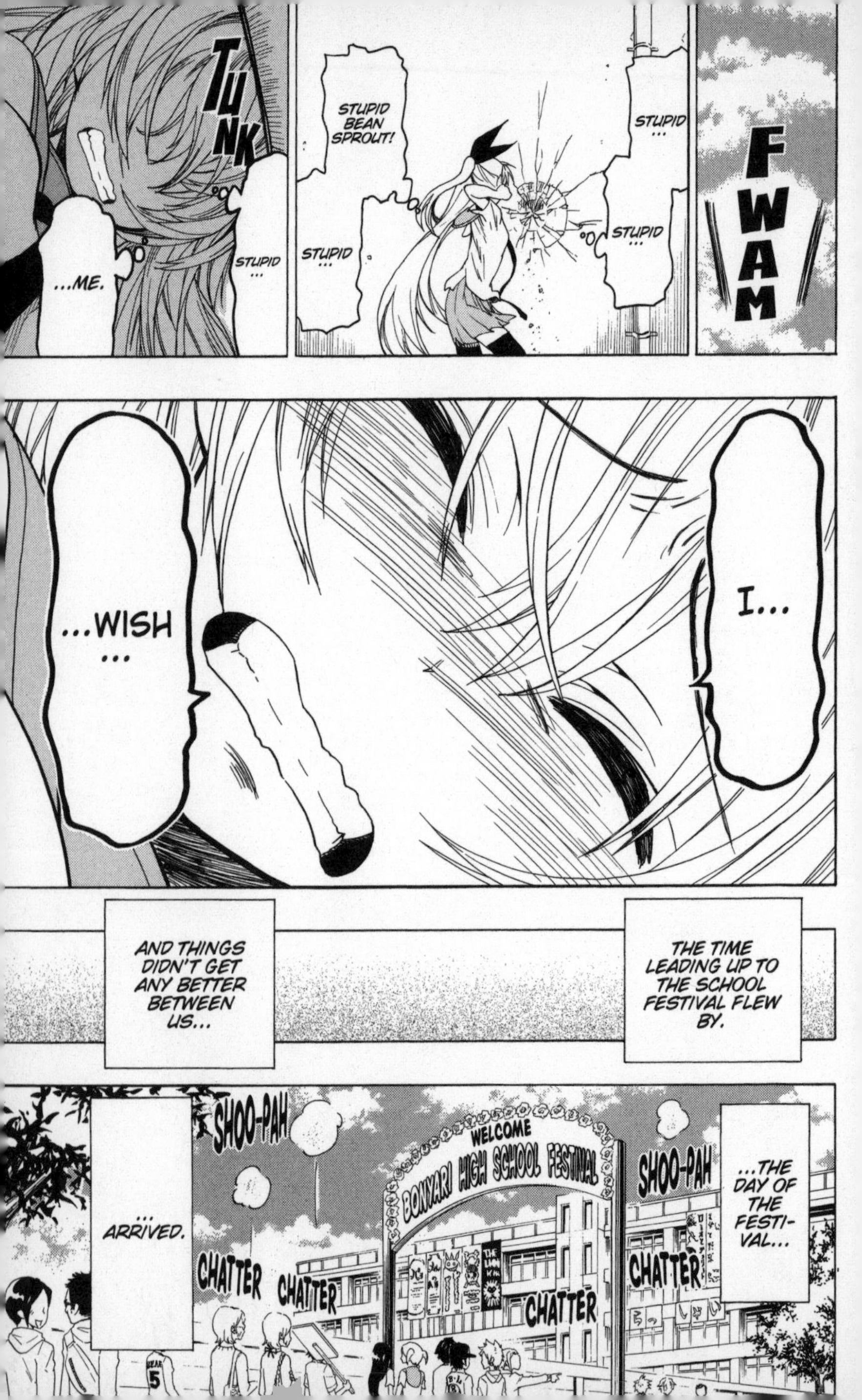
FWAM
STUPID ...
STUPID ...
STUPID BEAN SPROUT!
STUPID ...
TUNK
STUPID ...
...ME.
I...
...WISH ...
THE TIME LEADING UP TO THE SCHOOL FESTIVAL FLEW BY.
AND THINGS DIDN'T GET ANY BETTER BETWEEN US...
...THE DAY OF THE FESTI-VAL...
SHOO-PAH
CHATTER
WELCOME
BONYARI HIGH SCHOOL FESTIVAL
CHATTER
CHATTER
CHATTER
SHOO-PAH
... ARRIVED.

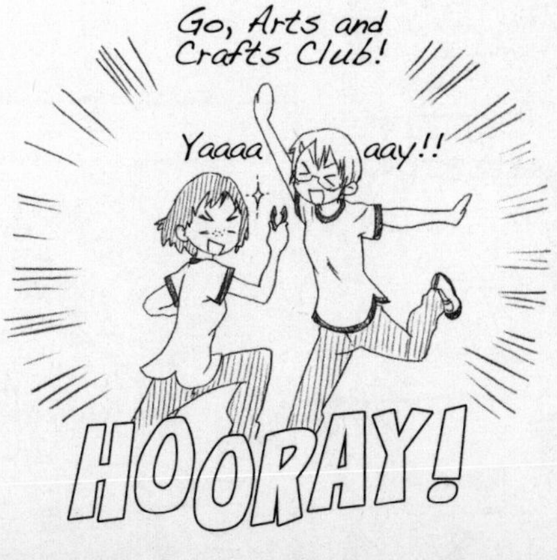
Go, Arts and Crafts Club!
Yaaaa aay!!
HOORAY!

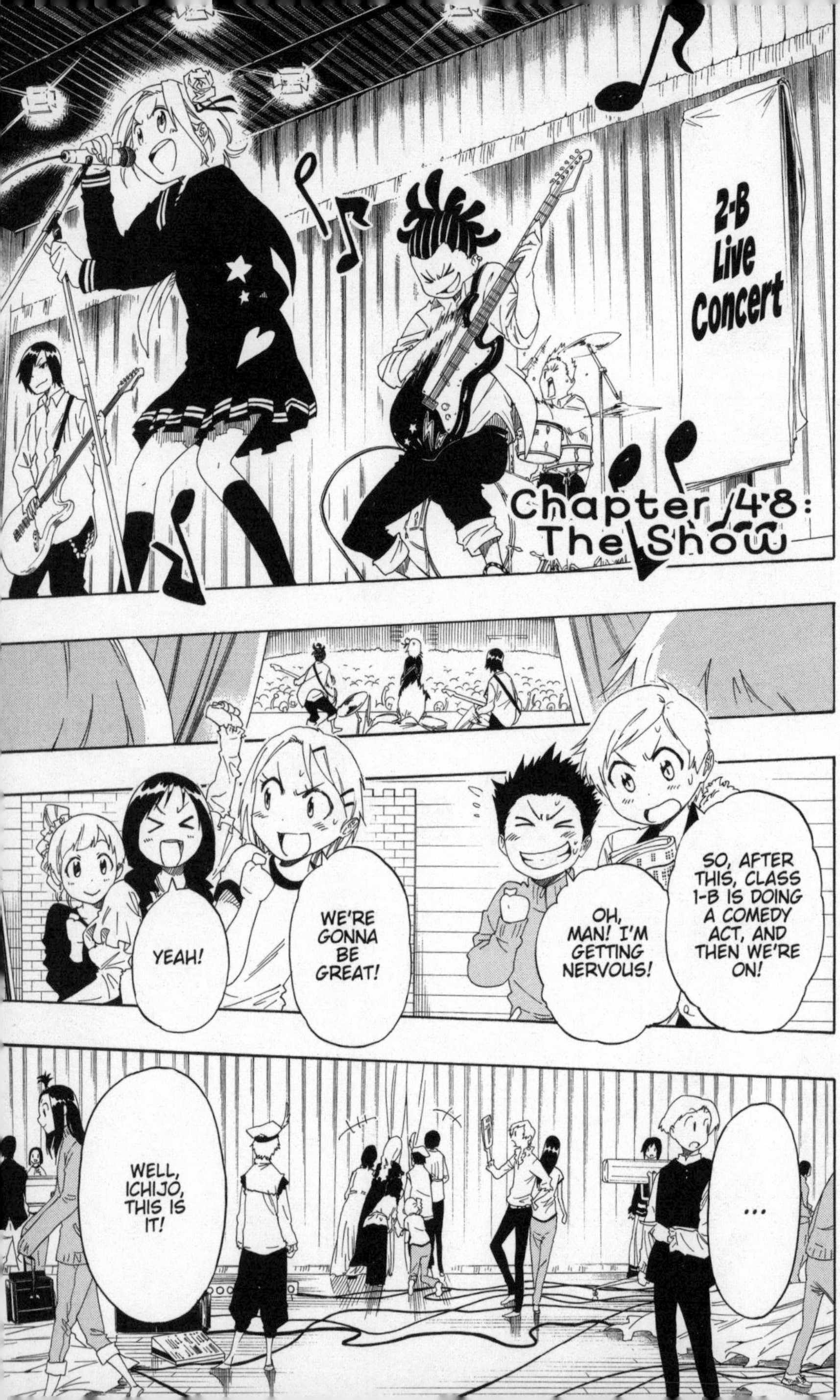
2-B Live Concert
Chapter 48: The Show
SO, AFTER THIS, CLASS 1-B IS DOING A COMEDY ACT, AND THEN WE'RE ON!
OH, MAN! I'M GETTING NERVOUS!
WE'RE GONNA BE GREAT!
YEAH!
...
WELL, ICHIJO, THIS IS IT!

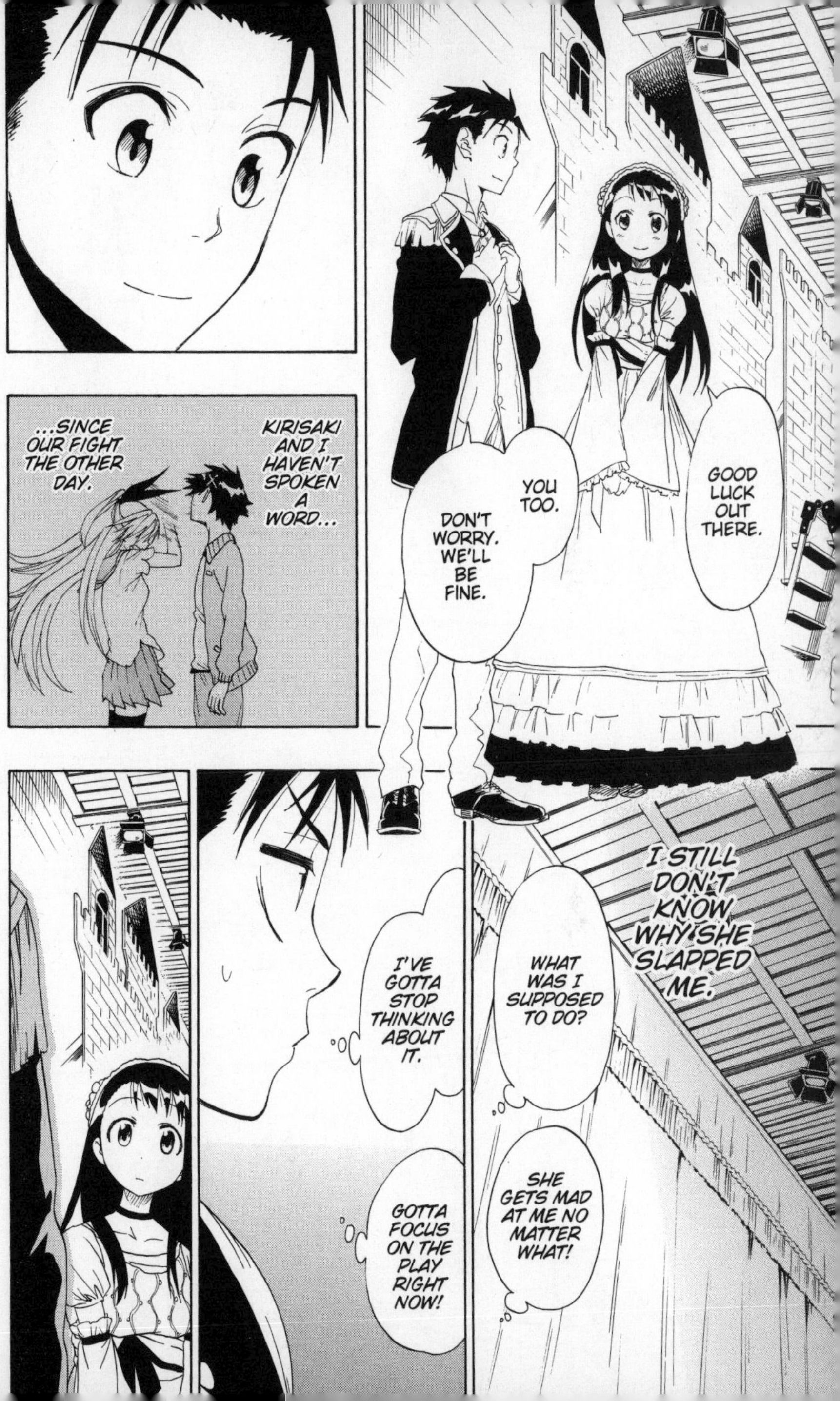
GOOD LUCK OUT THERE.
YOU TOO.
DON'T WORRY. WE'LL BE FINE.
KIRISAKI AND I HAVEN'T SPOKEN A WORD...
...SINCE OUR FIGHT THE OTHER DAY.
I STILL DON'T KNOW WHY SHE SLAPPED ME.
WHAT WAS I SUPPOSED TO DO?
SHE GETS MAD AT ME NO MATTER WHAT!
I'VE GOTTA STOP THINKING ABOUT IT.
GOTTA FOCUS ON THE PLAY RIGHT NOW!

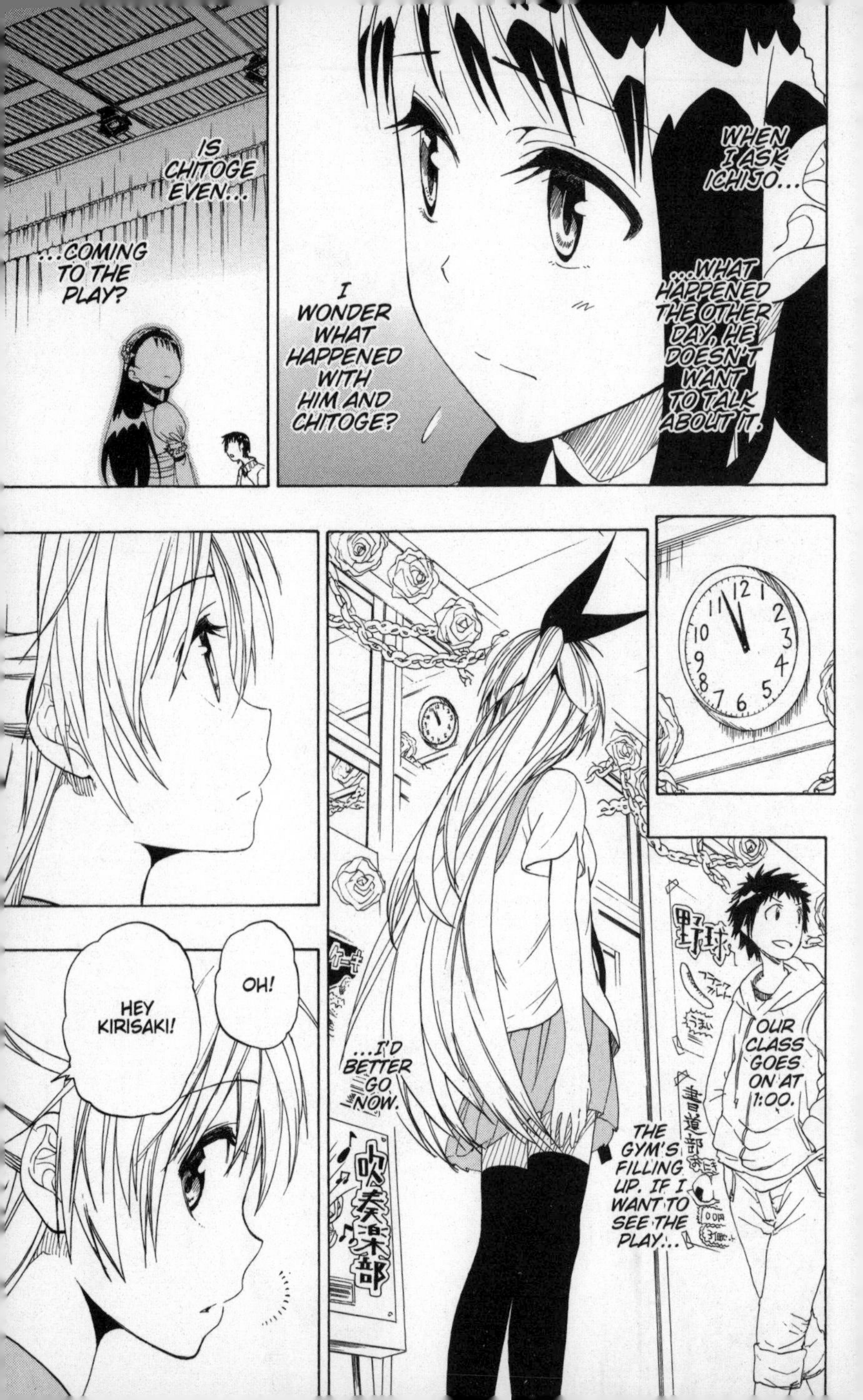

WHEN I ASK ICHIJO...
...WHAT HAPPENED THE OTHER DAY, HE DOESN'T WANT TO TALK ABOUT IT.
I WONDER WHAT HAPPENED WITH HIM AND CHITOGE?
IS CHITOGE EVEN...
...COMING TO THE PLAY?
OUR CLASS GOES ON AT 1:00.
野球
書道部
THE GYM'S FILLING UP. IF I WANT TO SEE THE PLAY...
...I'D BETTER GO NOW.
吹奏楽部
OH!
HEY KIRISAKI!

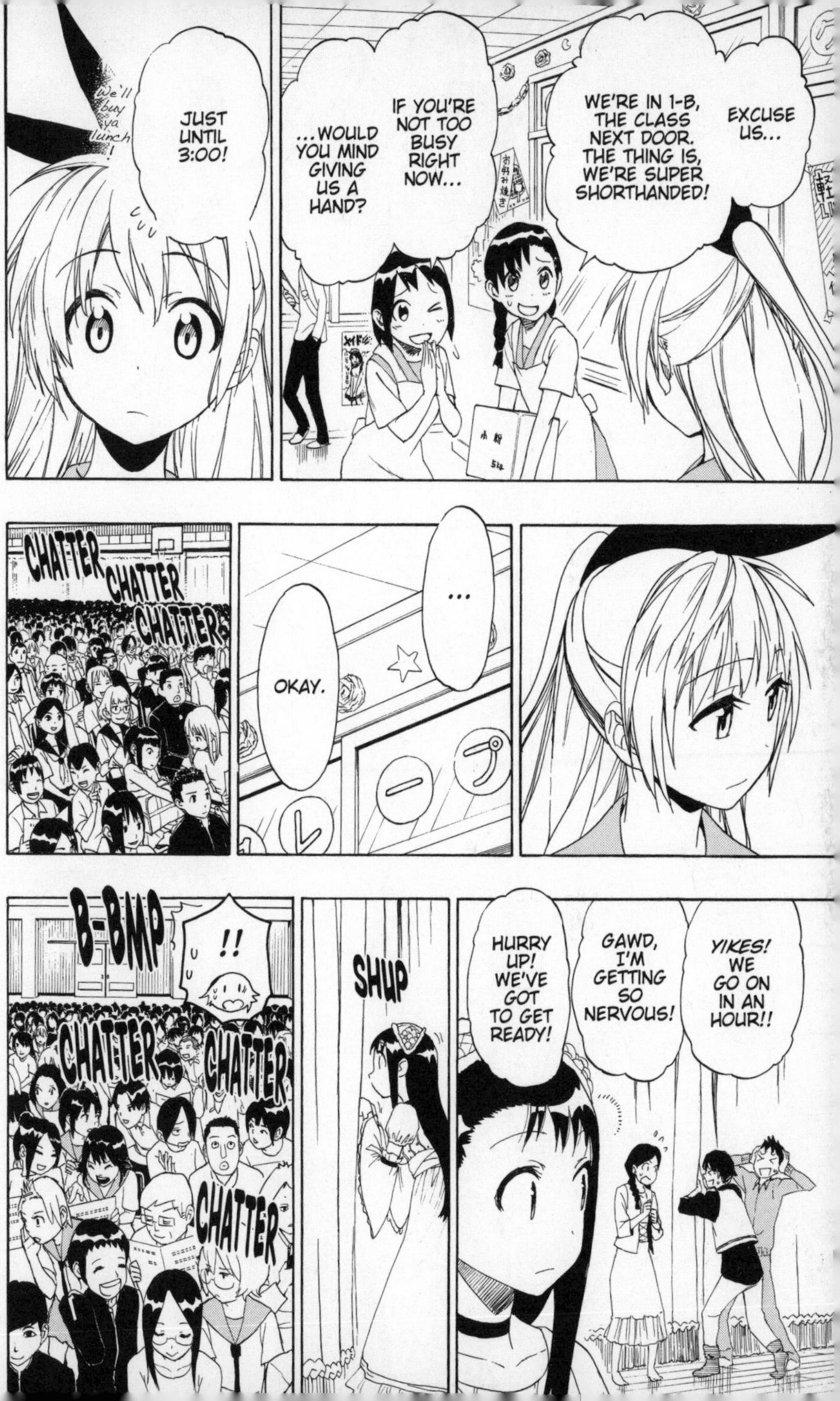
EXCUSE US...
WE'RE IN 1-B, THE CLASS NEXT DOOR. THE THING IS, WE'RE SUPER SHORTHANDED!
IF YOU'RE NOT TOO BUSY RIGHT NOW...
...WOULD YOU MIND GIVING US A HAND?
JUST UNTIL 3:00!
We'll buy ya lunch!
...
OKAY.
CHATTER
CHATTER
CHATTER
YIKES! WE GO ON IN AN HOUR!!
GAWD, I'M GETTING SO NERVOUS!
HURRY UP! WE'VE GOT TO GET READY!
SHUP
B-BMP
!!
CHATTER
CHATTER
CHATTER

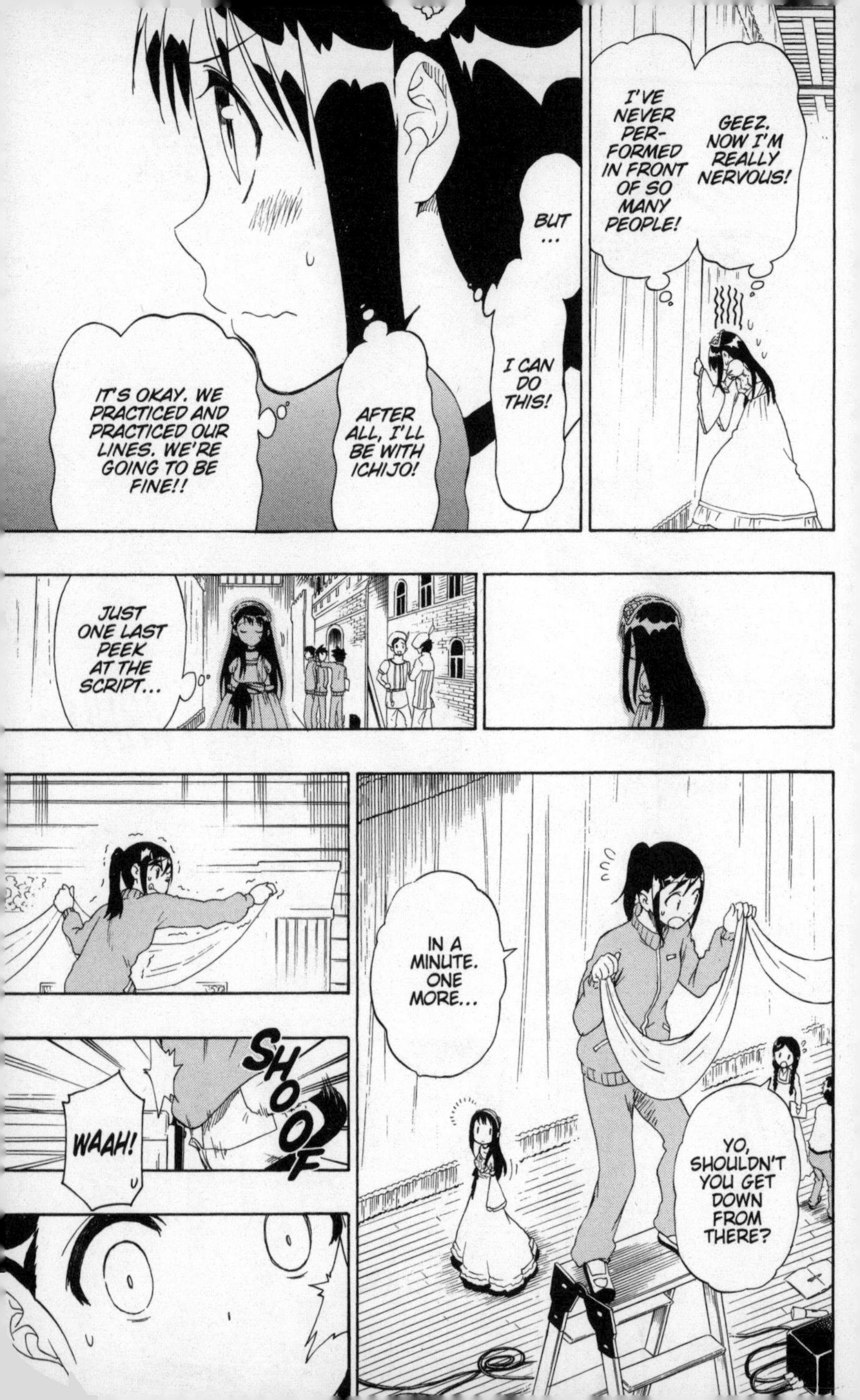
GEEZ. NOW I'M REALLY NERVOUS!
I'VE NEVER PER-FORMED IN FRONT OF SO MANY PEOPLE!
BUT ... I CAN DO THIS!
AFTER ALL, I'LL BE WITH ICHIJO!
IT'S OKAY. WE PRACTICED AND PRACTICED OUR LINES. WE'RE GOING TO BE FINE!!
JUST ONE LAST PEEK AT THE SCRIPT...
YO, SHOULDN'T YOU GET DOWN FROM THERE?
IN A MINUTE. ONE MORE...
SHOOF
WAAH!

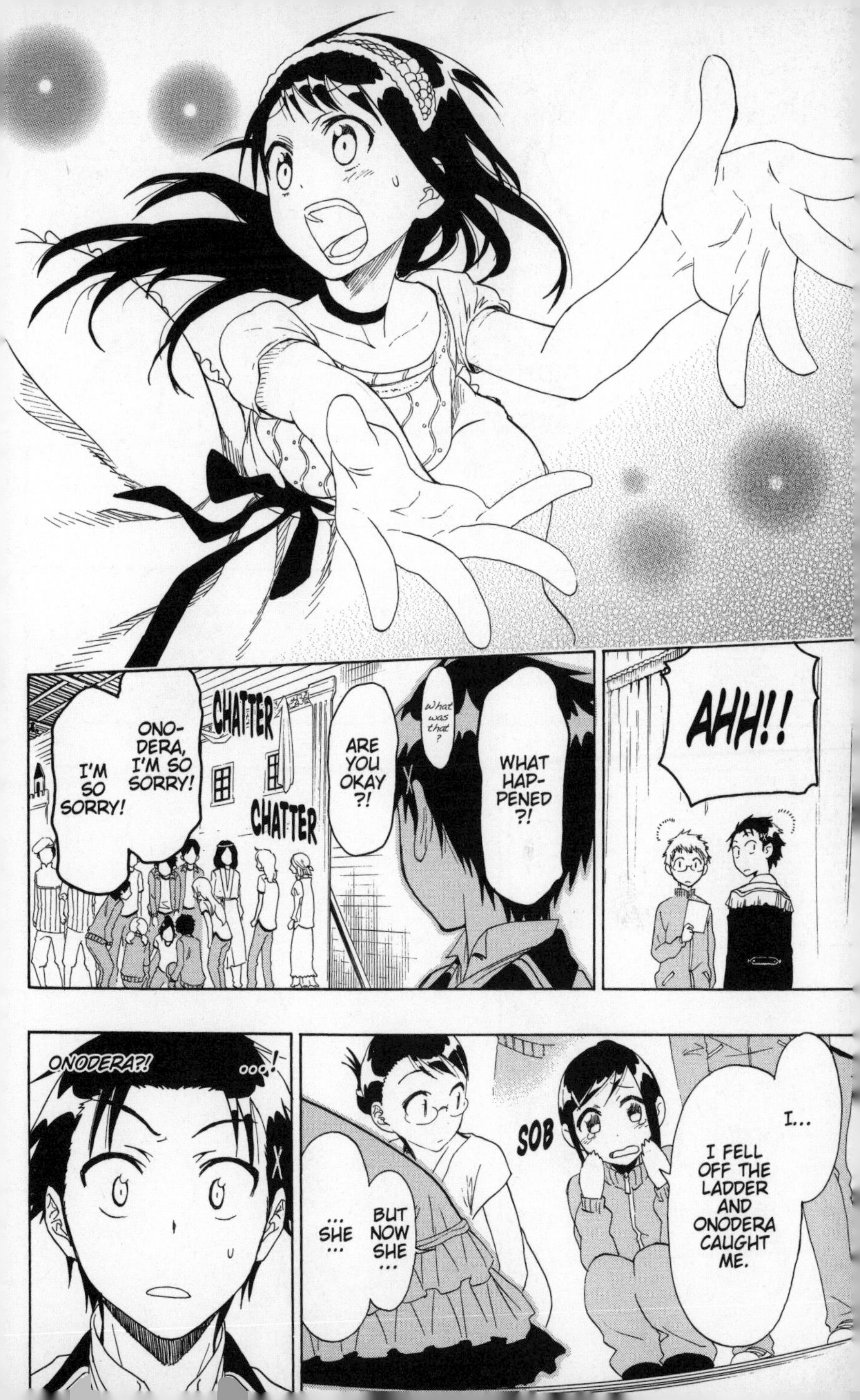

AHH!!
WHAT HAP-PENED?!
What was that?
ARE YOU OKAY?!
CHATTER
CHATTER
ONO-DERA, I'M SO SORRY!
I'M SO SORRY!
I...
I FELL OFF THE LADDER AND ONODERA CAUGHT ME.
SOB
BUT NOW SHE...
...SHE...
...!
ONODERA?!

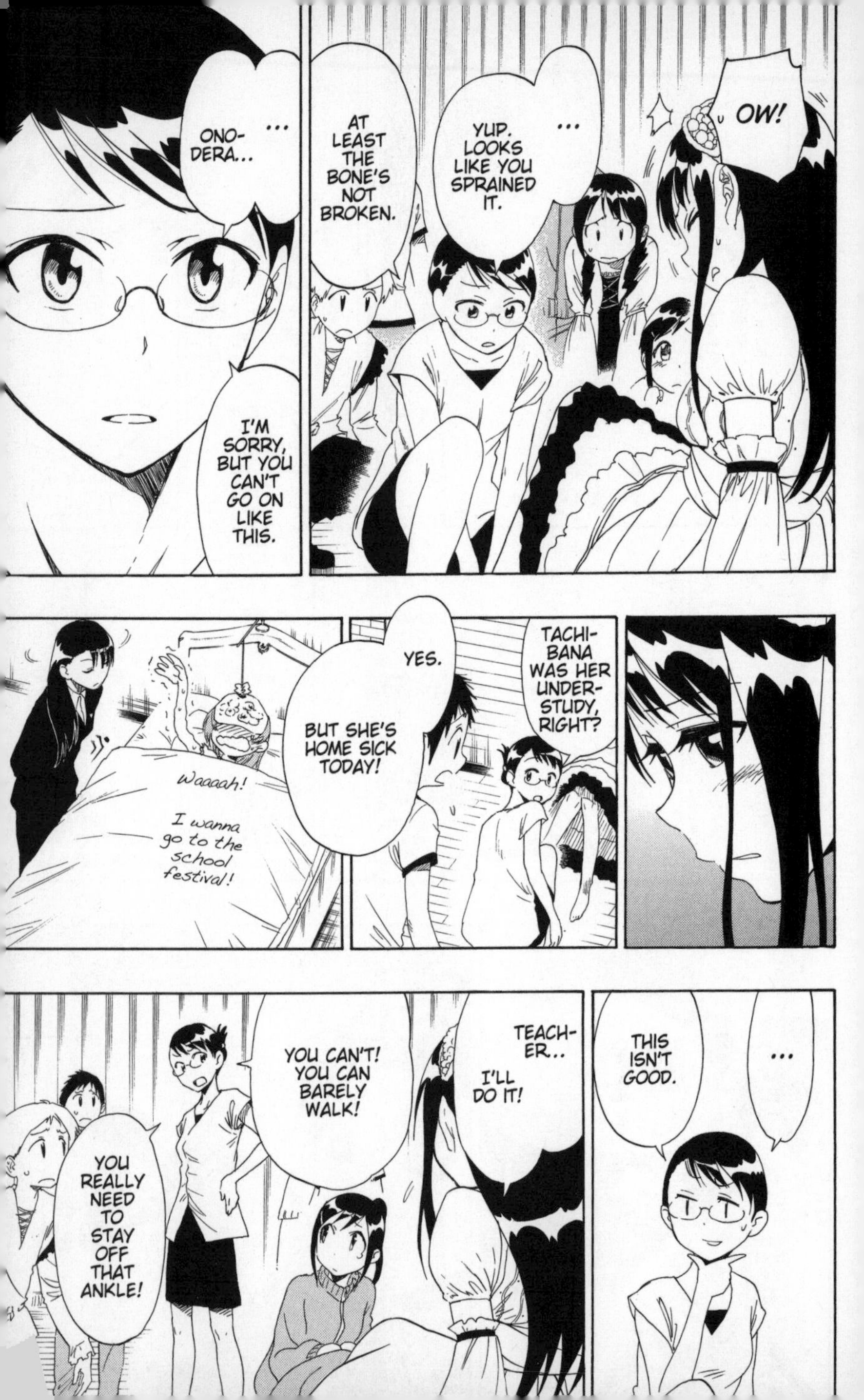
OW!
...
YUP. LOOKS LIKE YOU SPRAINED IT.
AT LEAST THE BONE'S NOT BROKEN.
...
ONO-DERA...
I'M SORRY, BUT YOU CAN'T GO ON LIKE THIS.
TACHI-BANA WAS HER UNDER-STUDY, RIGHT?
YES.
BUT SHE'S HOME SICK TODAY!
Waaaah!
I wanna go to the school festival!
...
THIS ISN'T GOOD.
TEACH-ER...
I'LL DO IT!
YOU CAN'T! YOU CAN BARELY WALK!
YOU REALLY NEED TO STAY OFF THAT ANKLE!

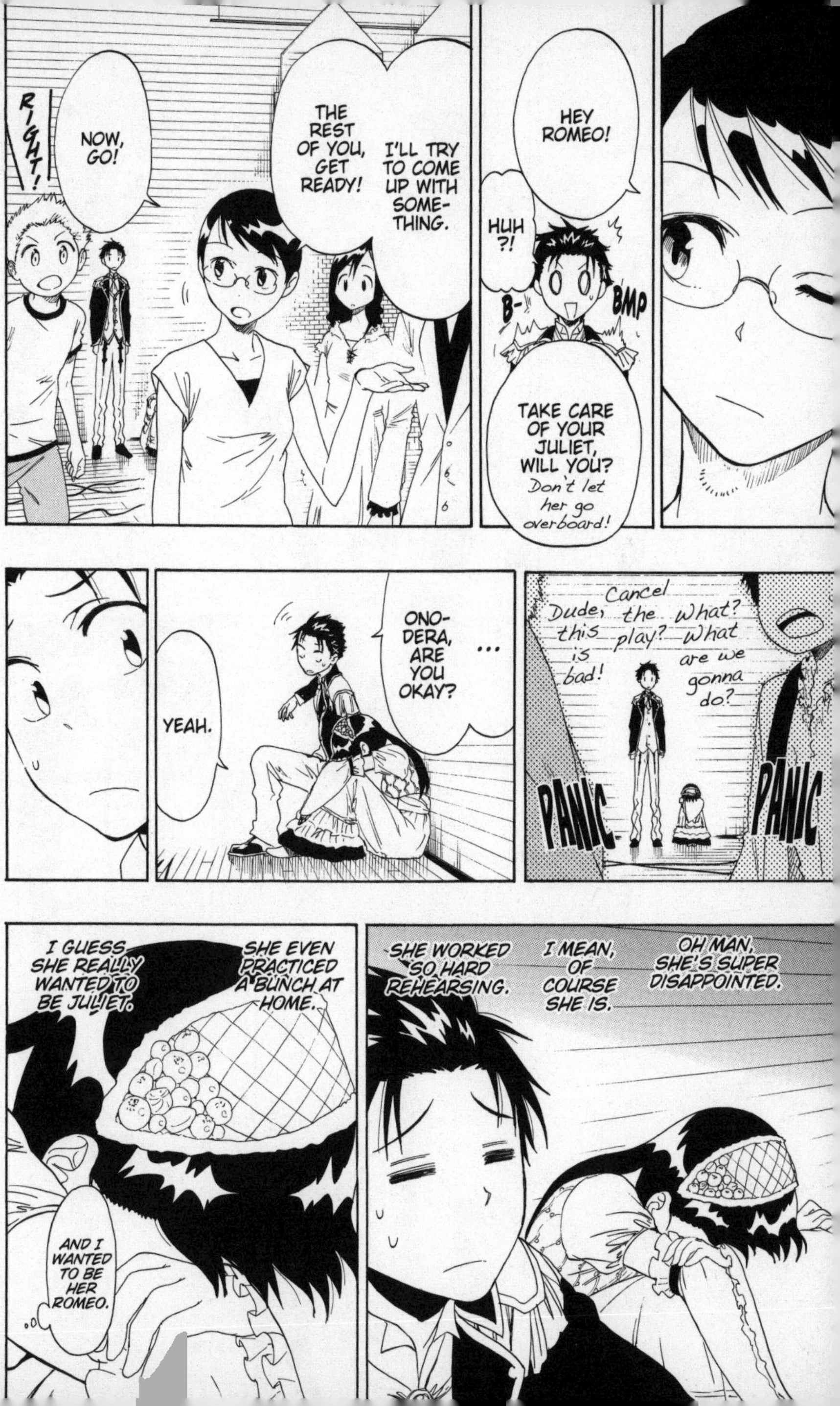
HEY ROMEO!
HUH ?!
B-BMP
TAKE CARE OF YOUR JULIET, WILL YOU? Don't let her go overboard!
THE REST OF YOU, GET READY! I'LL TRY TO COME UP WITH SOME-THING.
NOW, GO!
RIGHT!
Cancel the play?
What? What are we gonna do?
Dude, this is bad!
PANIC
PANIC
ONO-DERA, ARE YOU OKAY?
...
YEAH.
OH MAN, SHE'S SUPER DISAPPOINTED.
I MEAN, OF COURSE SHE IS.
SHE WORKED SO HARD REHEARSING.
SHE EVEN PRACTICED A BUNCH AT HOME.
I GUESS SHE REALLY WANTED TO BE JULIET.
AND I WANTED TO BE HER ROMEO.

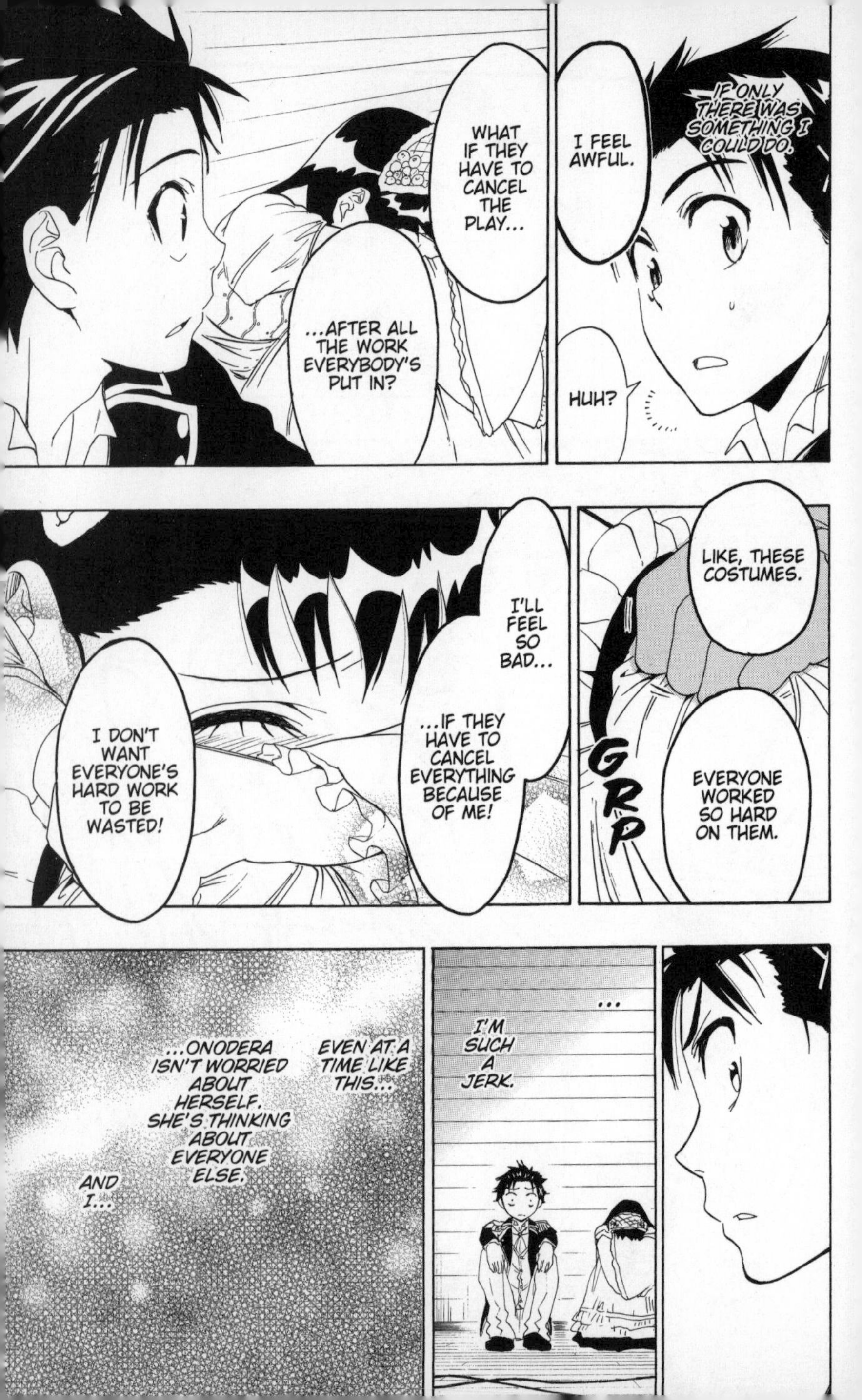
IF ONLY THERE WAS SOMETHING I COULD DO.
I FEEL AWFUL.
HUH?
WHAT IF THEY HAVE TO CANCEL THE PLAY...
...AFTER ALL THE WORK EVERYBODY'S PUT IN?
LIKE, THESE COSTUMES.
GRP
EVERYONE WORKED SO HARD ON THEM.
I'LL FEEL SO BAD...
...IF THEY HAVE TO CANCEL EVERYTHING BECAUSE OF ME!
I DON'T WANT EVERYONE'S HARD WORK TO BE WASTED!
...
I'M SUCH A JERK.
EVEN AT A TIME LIKE THIS...
...ONODERA ISN'T WORRIED ABOUT HERSELF. SHE'S THINKING ABOUT EVERYONE ELSE.
AND I...

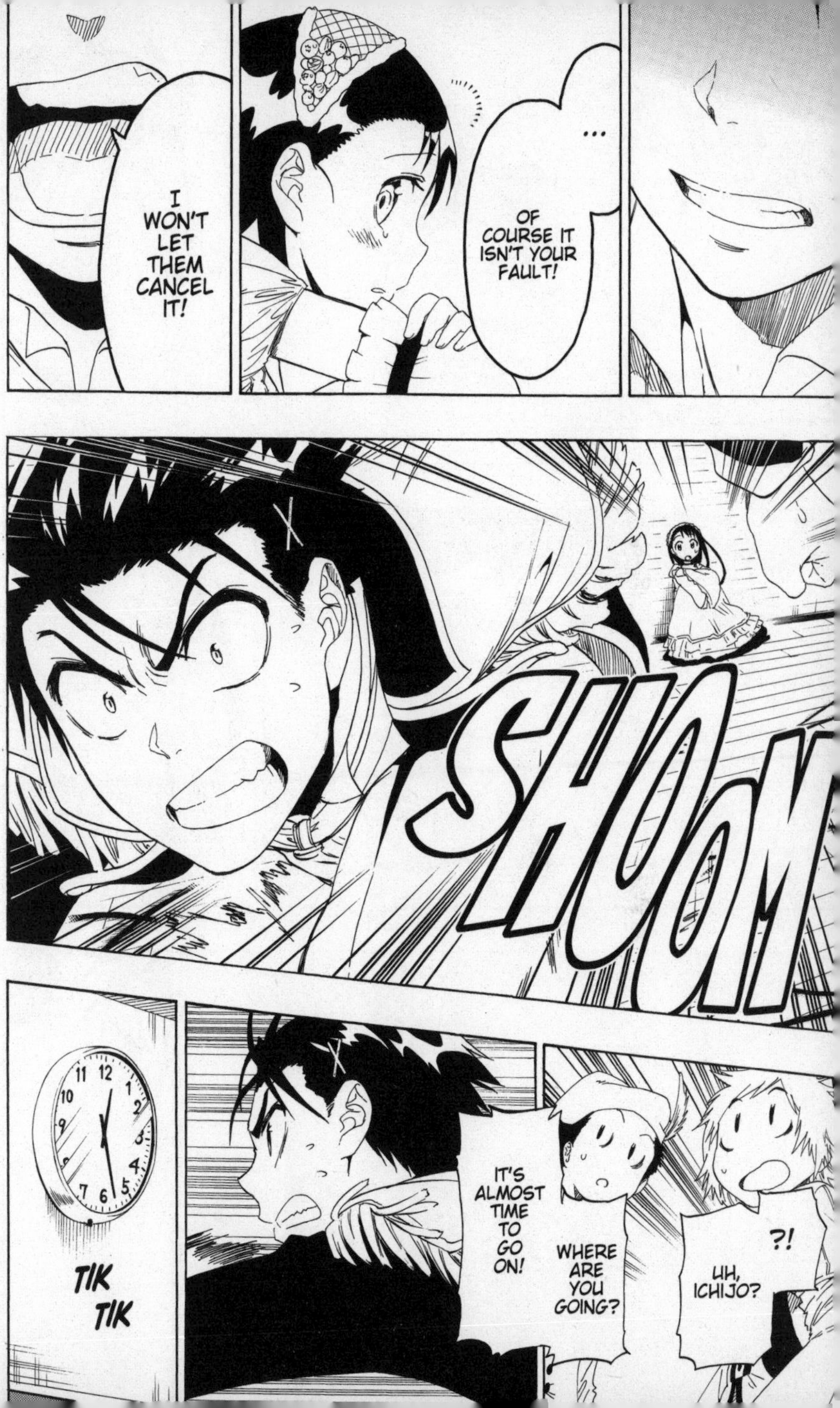
...
OF COURSE IT ISN'T YOUR FAULT!
I WON'T LET THEM CANCEL IT!
SHOOM
?!
UH, ICHIJO?
WHERE ARE YOU GOING?
IT'S ALMOST TIME TO GO ON!
TIK TIK

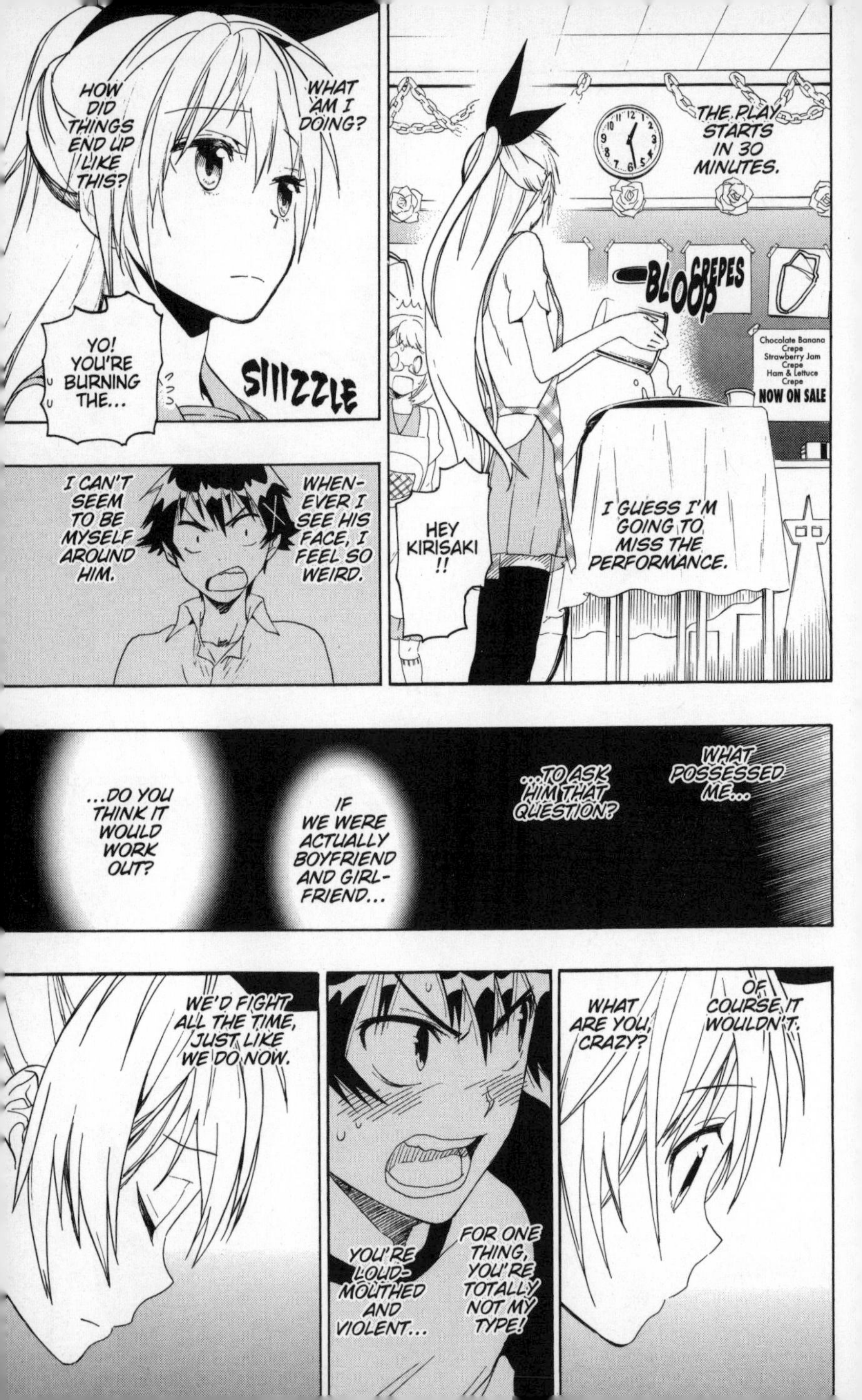
THE PLAY STARTS IN 30 MINUTES.
BLOOP
CREPES
Chocolate Banana Crepe
Strawberry Jam Crepe
Ham & Lettuce Crepe
NOW ON SALE
I GUESS I'M GOING TO MISS THE PERFORMANCE.
HEY KIRISAKI !!
WHAT AM I DOING?
HOW DID THINGS END UP LIKE THIS?
YO! YOU'RE BURNING THE...
SIIIZZLE
WHEN-EVER I SEE HIS FACE, I FEEL SO WEIRD.
I CAN'T SEEM TO BE MYSELF AROUND HIM.
WHAT POSSESSED ME...
...TO ASK HIM THAT QUESTION?
IF WE WERE ACTUALLY BOYFRIEND AND GIRL-FRIEND...
...DO YOU THINK IT WOULD WORK OUT?
OF COURSE IT WOULDN'T.
WHAT ARE YOU, CRAZY?
FOR ONE THING, YOU'RE TOTALLY NOT MY TYPE!
YOU'RE LOUD-MOUTHED AND VIOLENT...
WE'D FIGHT ALL THE TIME, JUST LIKE WE DO NOW.

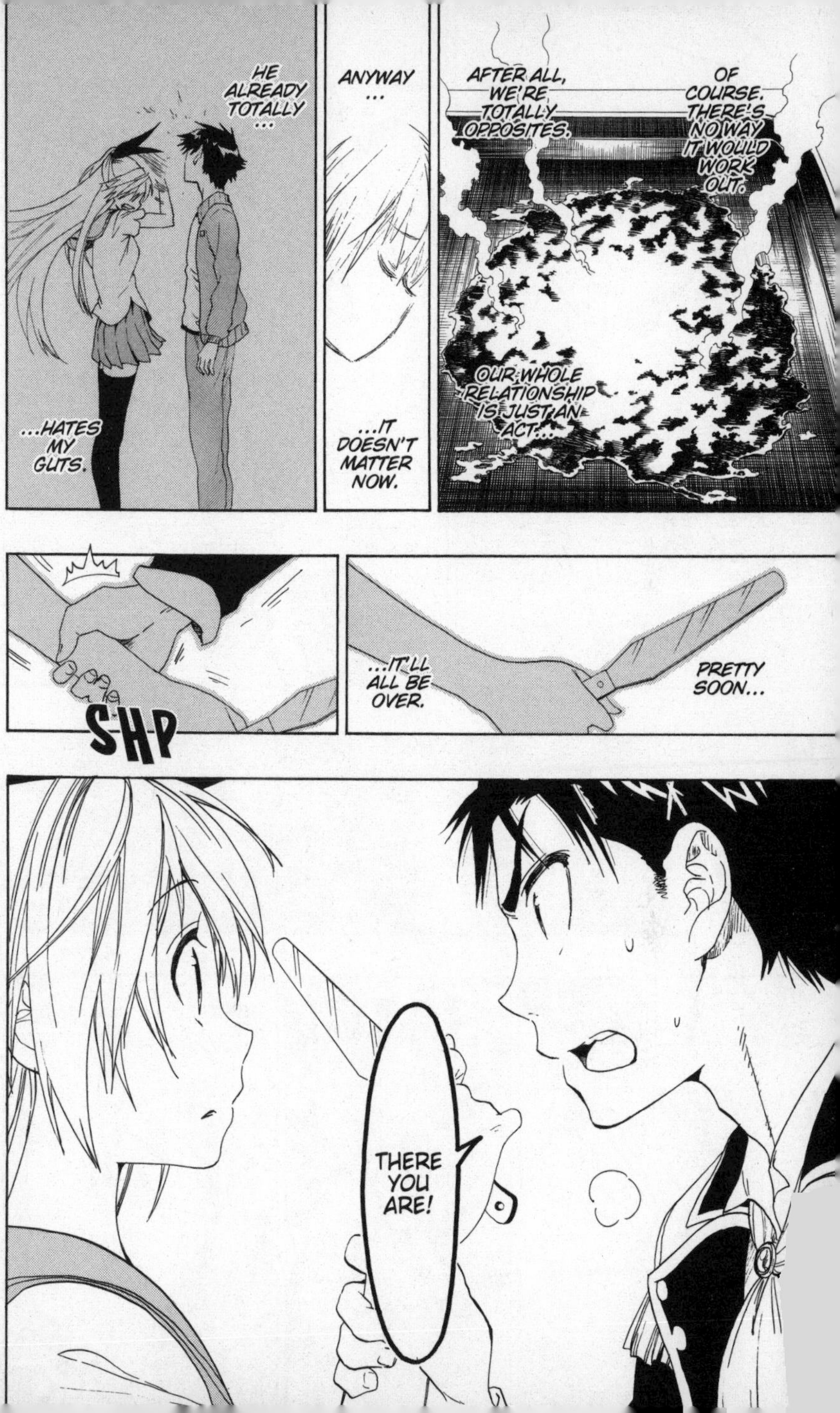
OF COURSE. THERE'S NO WAY IT WOULD WORK OUT.
AFTER ALL, WE'RE TOTALLY OPPOSITES.
OUR WHOLE RELATIONSHIP IS JUST AN ACT...
ANYWAY...
...IT DOESN'T MATTER NOW.
HE ALREADY TOTALLY...
...HATES MY GUTS.
PRETTY SOON...
...IT'LL ALL BE OVER.
SHP
THERE YOU ARE!

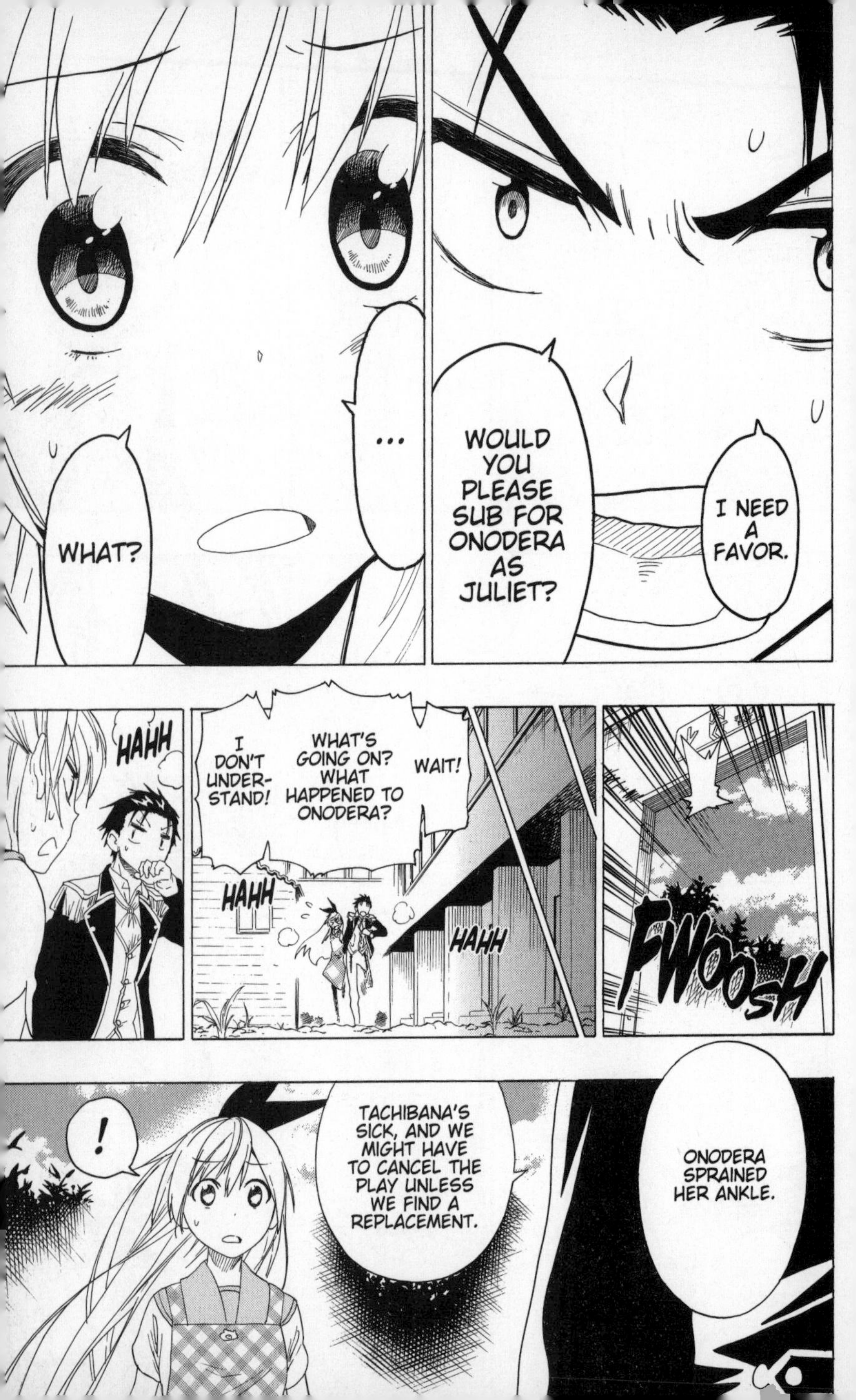
I NEED A FAVOR.
WOULD YOU PLEASE SUB FOR ONODERA AS JULIET?
...
WHAT?
FWOOSH
HAHH
WAIT!
WHAT'S GOING ON? WHAT HAPPENED TO ONODERA?
I DON'T UNDER-STAND!
HAHH
HAHH
ONODERA SPRAINED HER ANKLE.
TACHIBANA'S SICK, AND WE MIGHT HAVE TO CANCEL THE PLAY UNLESS WE FIND A REPLACEMENT.
!

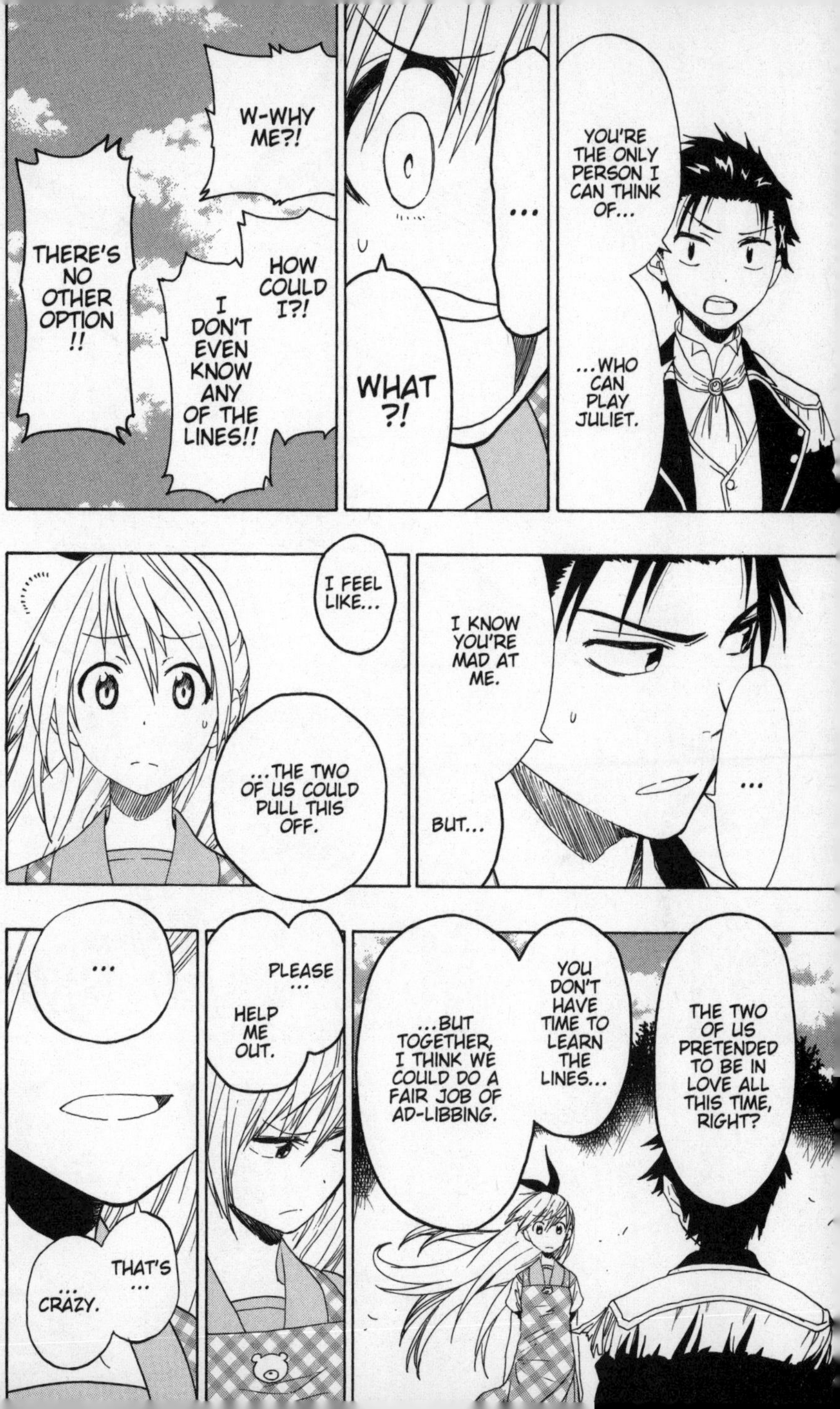
YOU'RE THE ONLY PERSON I CAN THINK OF...
...WHO CAN PLAY JULIET.
...
WHAT ?!
W-WHY ME?!
HOW COULD I?!
I DON'T EVEN KNOW ANY OF THE LINES!!
THERE'S NO OTHER OPTION !!
...
I KNOW YOU'RE MAD AT ME.
BUT...
I FEEL LIKE...
...THE TWO OF US COULD PULL THIS OFF.
THE TWO OF US PRETENDED TO BE IN LOVE ALL THIS TIME, RIGHT?
YOU DON'T HAVE TIME TO LEARN THE LINES...
...BUT TOGETHER, I THINK WE COULD DO A FAIR JOB OF AD-LIBBING.
PLEASE...
HELP ME OUT.
...
THAT'S... CRAZY.

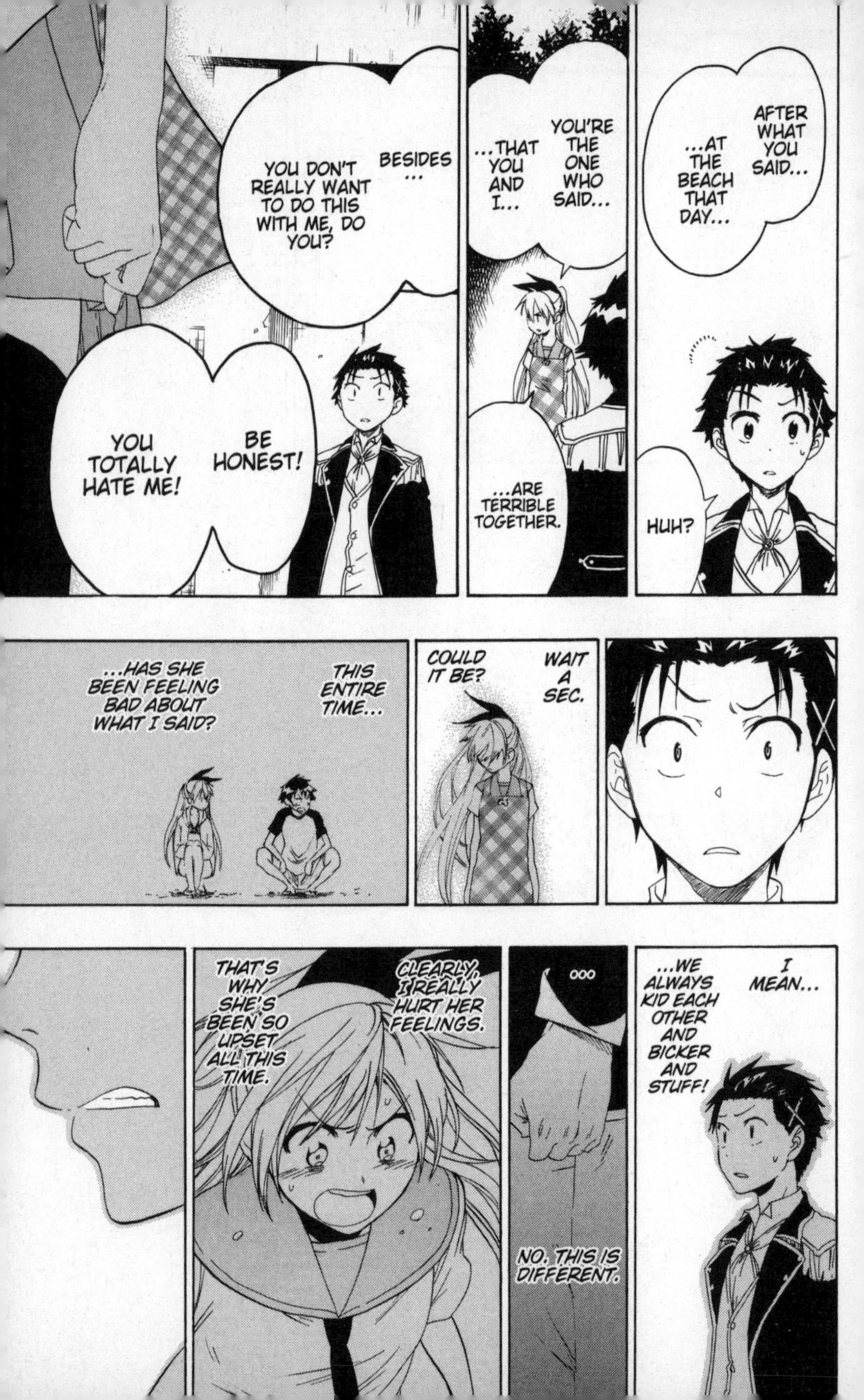
AFTER WHAT YOU SAID...
...AT THE BEACH THAT DAY...
HUH?
YOU'RE THE ONE WHO SAID...
...THAT YOU AND I...
...ARE TERRIBLE TOGETHER.
BESIDES...
YOU DON'T REALLY WANT TO DO THIS WITH ME, DO YOU?
BE HONEST!
YOU TOTALLY HATE ME!
WAIT A SEC.
COULD IT BE?
THIS ENTIRE TIME...
...HAS SHE BEEN FEELING BAD ABOUT WHAT I SAID?
I MEAN...
...WE ALWAYS KID EACH OTHER AND BICKER AND STUFF!
ooo
NO. THIS IS DIFFERENT.
CLEARLY, I REALLY HURT HER FEELINGS.
THAT'S WHY SHE'S BEEN SO UPSET ALL THIS TIME.

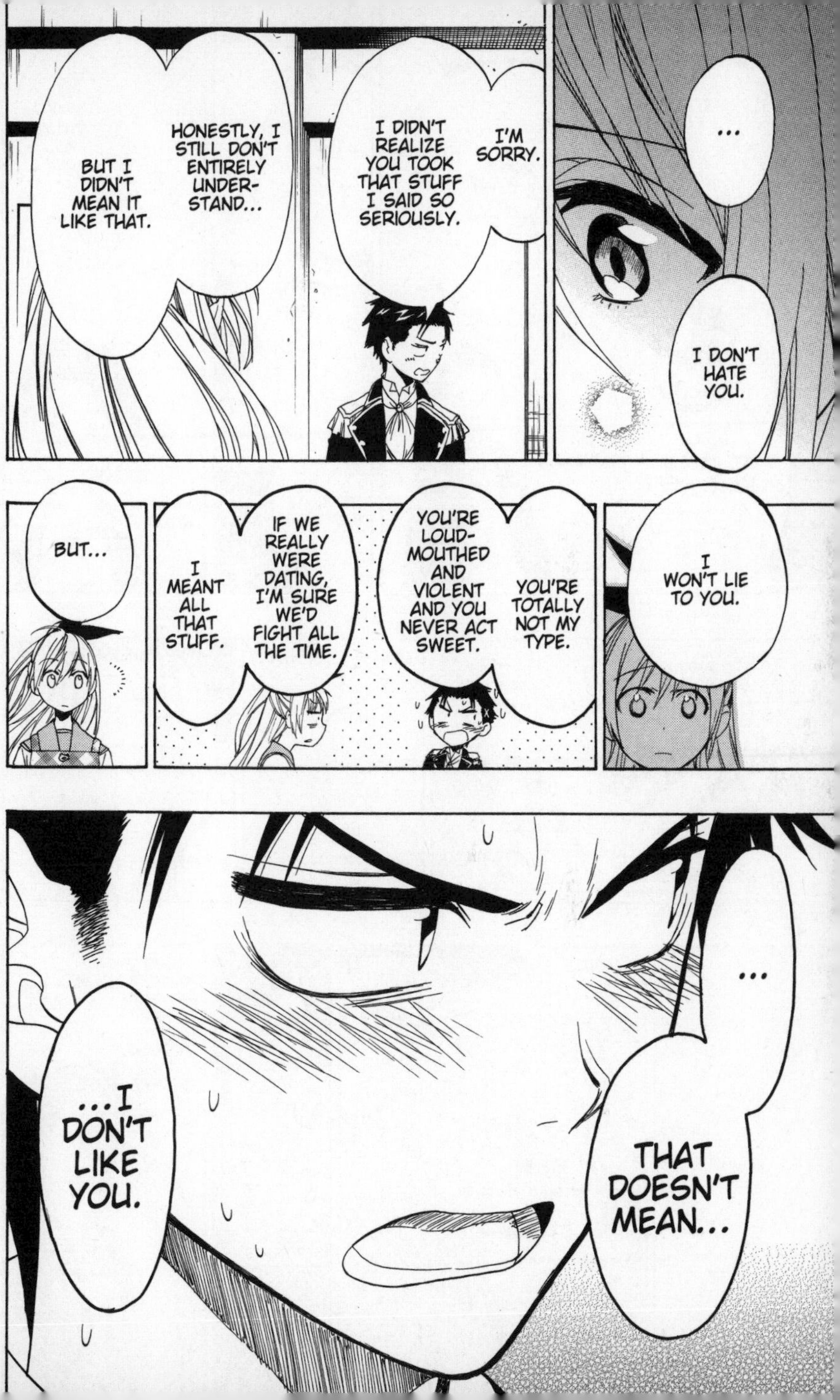
...
I DON'T HATE YOU.
I'M SORRY.
I DIDN'T REALIZE YOU TOOK THAT STUFF I SAID SO SERIOUSLY.
HONESTLY, I STILL DON'T ENTIRELY UNDER-STAND...
BUT I DIDN'T MEAN IT LIKE THAT.
I WON'T LIE TO YOU.
YOU'RE TOTALLY NOT MY TYPE.
YOU'RE LOUD-MOUTHED AND VIOLENT AND YOU NEVER ACT SWEET.
IF WE REALLY WERE DATING, I'M SURE WE'D FIGHT ALL THE TIME.
I MEANT ALL THAT STUFF.
BUT...
...
THAT DOESN'T MEAN...
...I DON'T LIKE YOU.

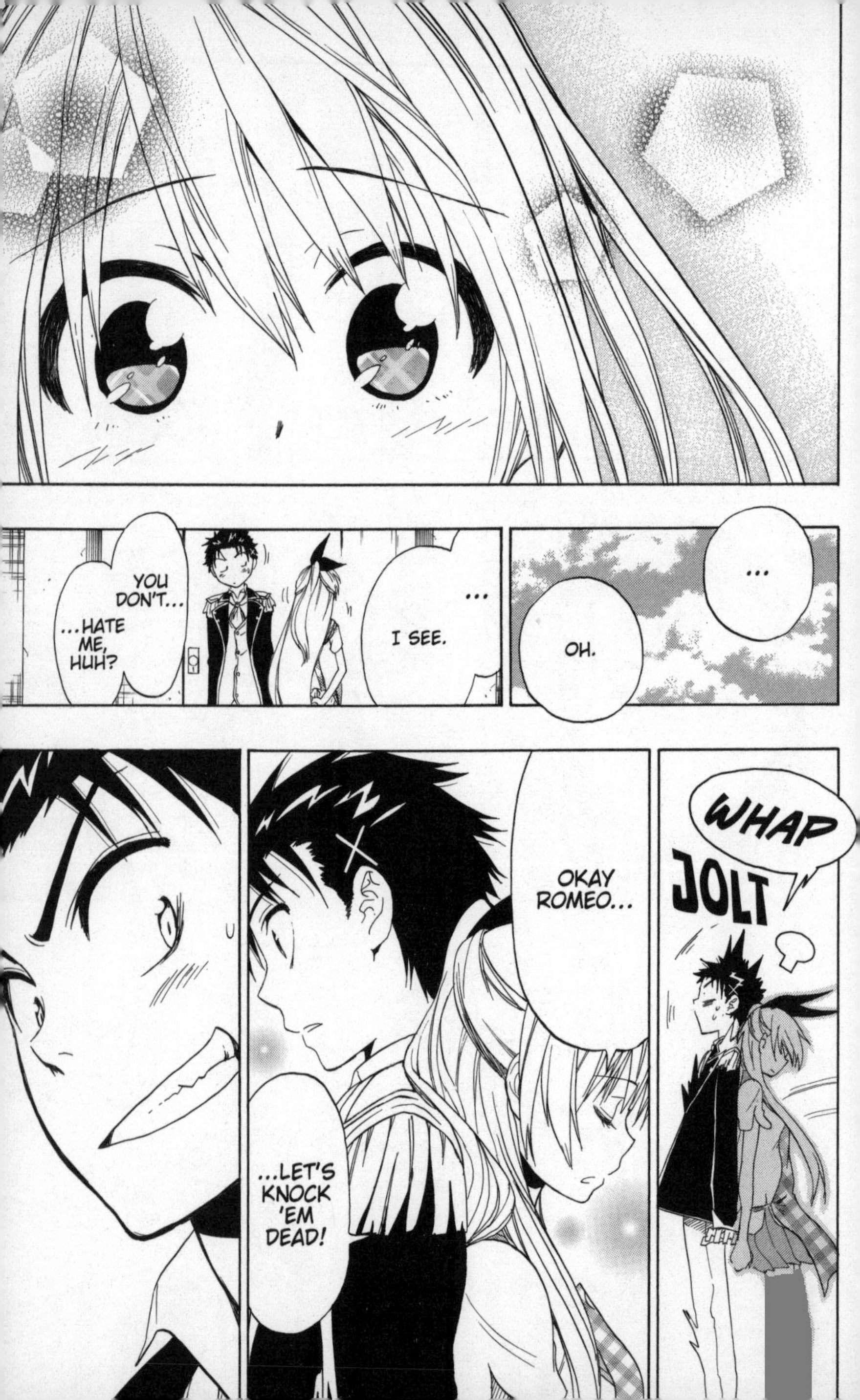
...
OH.
...
I SEE.
YOU DON'T...
...HATE ME, HUH?
WHAP
JOLT
OKAY ROMEO...
...LET'S KNOCK 'EM DEAD!

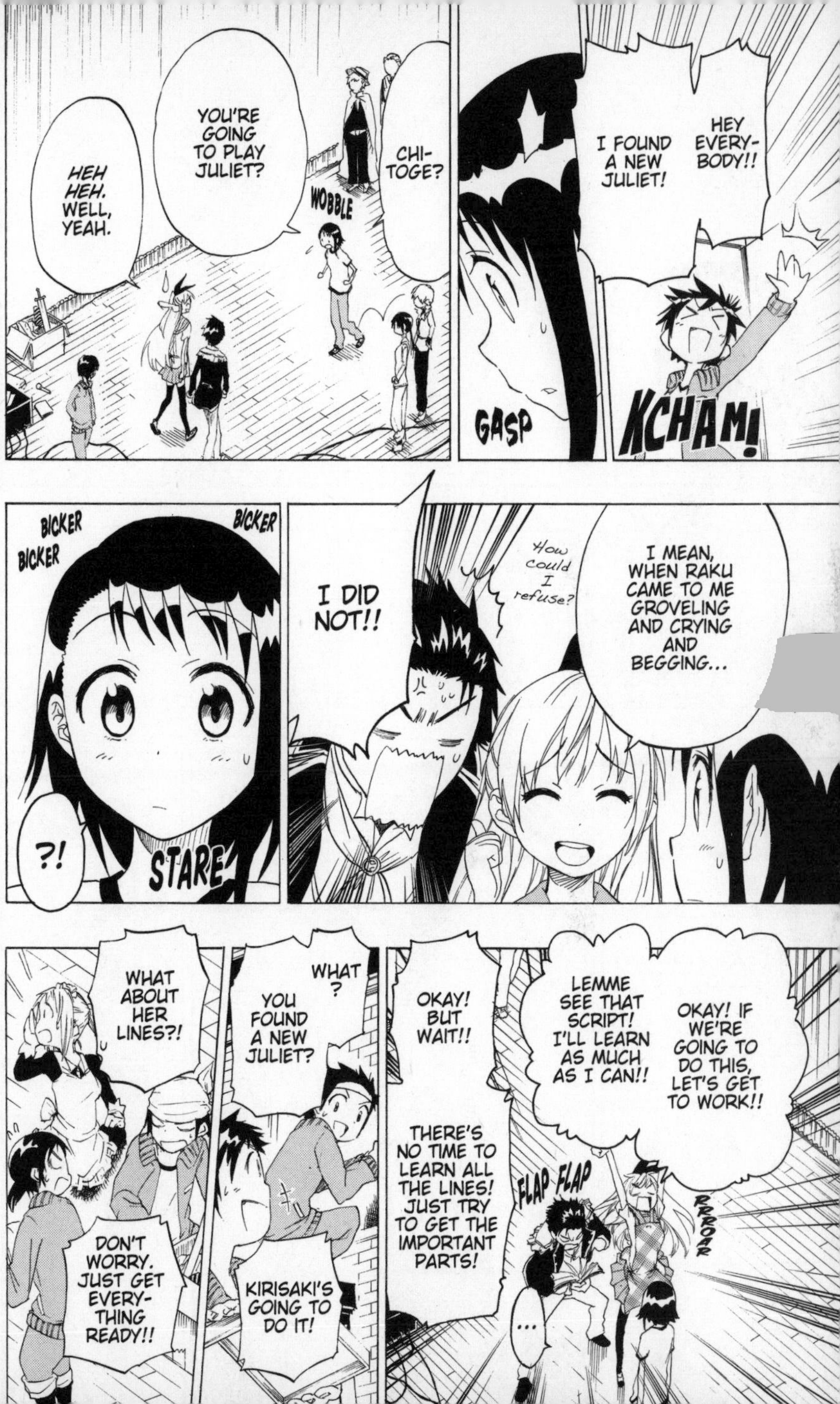
HEY EVERY-BODY!!
I FOUND A NEW JULIET!
KCHAM!
GASP
CHI-TOGE?
WOBBLE
YOU'RE GOING TO PLAY JULIET?
HEH HEH. WELL, YEAH.
I MEAN, WHEN RAKU CAME TO ME GROVELING AND CRYING AND BEGGING...
How could I refuse?
I DID NOT!!
BICKER
BICKER
BICKER
?!
STARE
OKAY! IF WE'RE GOING TO DO THIS, LET'S GET TO WORK!!
LEMME SEE THAT SCRIPT! I'LL LEARN AS MUCH AS I CAN!!
RRROAR
FLAP FLAP
...
OKAY! BUT WAIT!!
THERE'S NO TIME TO LEARN ALL THE LINES! JUST TRY TO GET THE IMPORTANT PARTS!
WHAT?
YOU FOUND A NEW JULIET?
KIRISAKI'S GOING TO DO IT!
WHAT ABOUT HER LINES?!
DON'T WORRY. JUST GET EVERY-THING READY!!

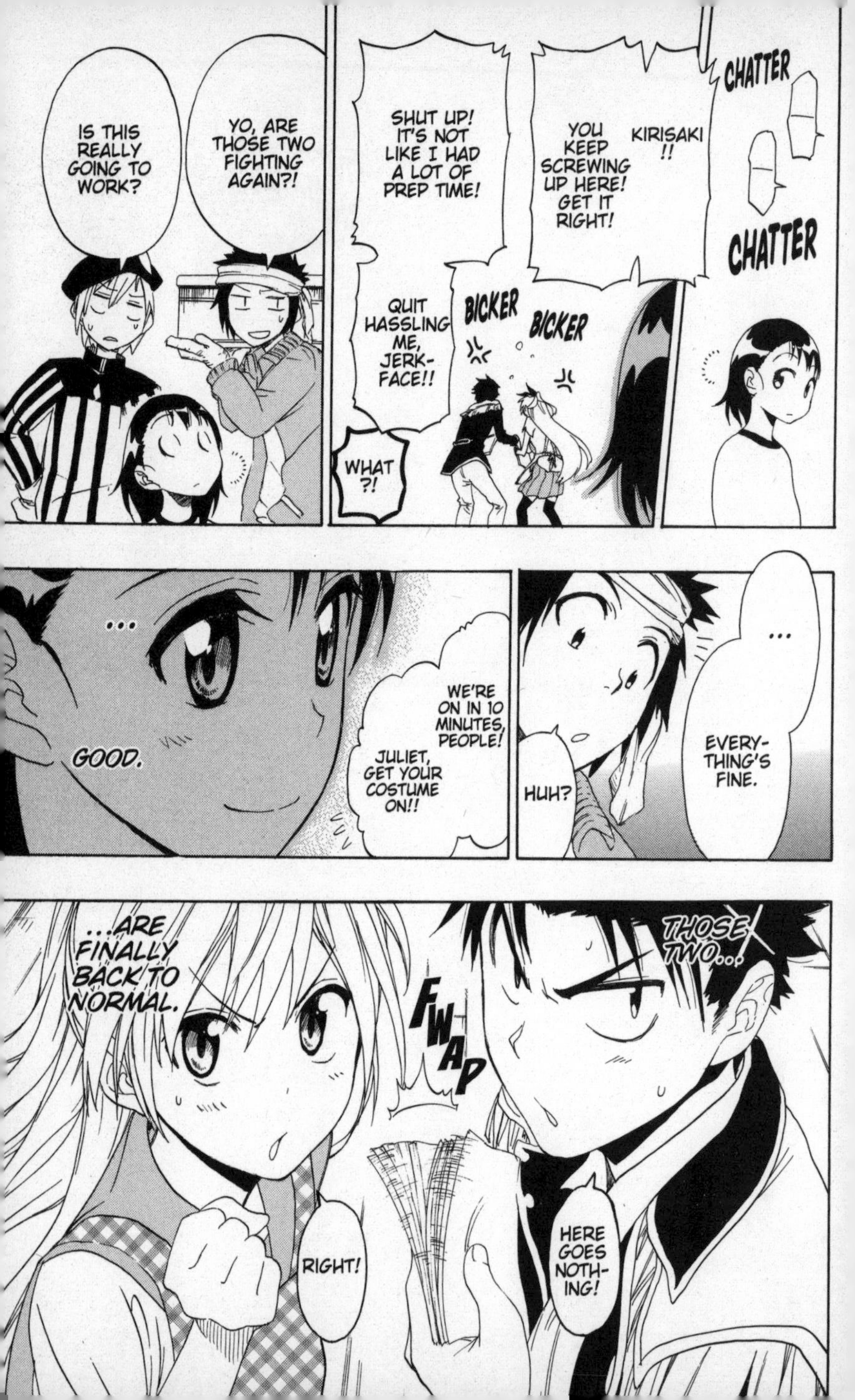
CHATTER
CHATTER
KIRISAKI!!
YOU KEEP SCREWING UP HERE! GET IT RIGHT!
SHUT UP! IT'S NOT LIKE I HAD A LOT OF PREP TIME!
BICKER
BICKER
QUIT HASSLING ME, JERK-FACE!!
WHAT?!
YO, ARE THOSE TWO FIGHTING AGAIN?!
IS THIS REALLY GOING TO WORK?
...
EVERY-THING'S FINE.
HUH?
WE'RE ON IN 10 MINUTES, PEOPLE!
JULIET, GET YOUR COSTUME ON!!
...
GOOD.
THOSE TWO...
...ARE FINALLY BACK TO NORMAL.
FWAP
HERE GOES NOTHING!
RIGHT!

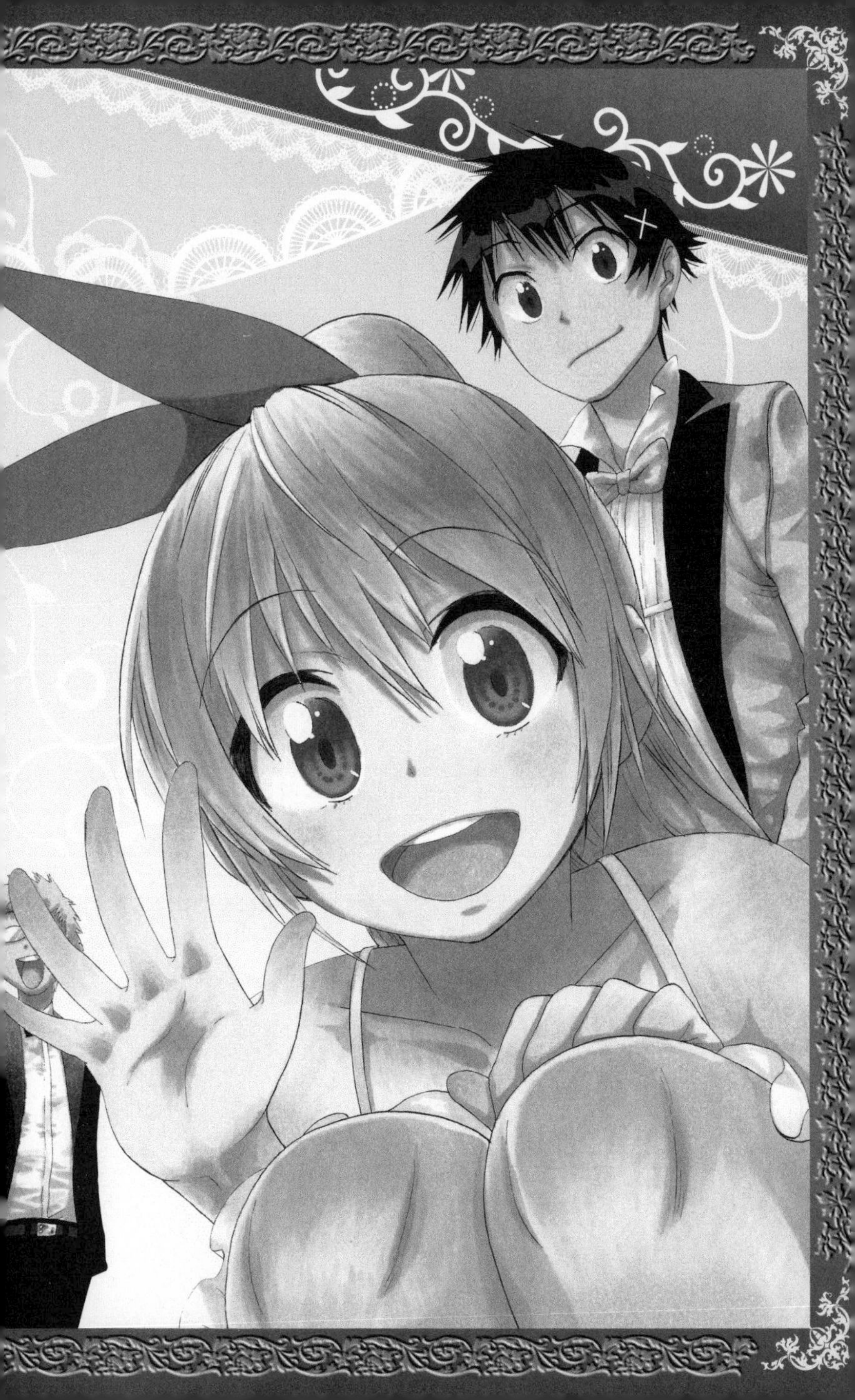

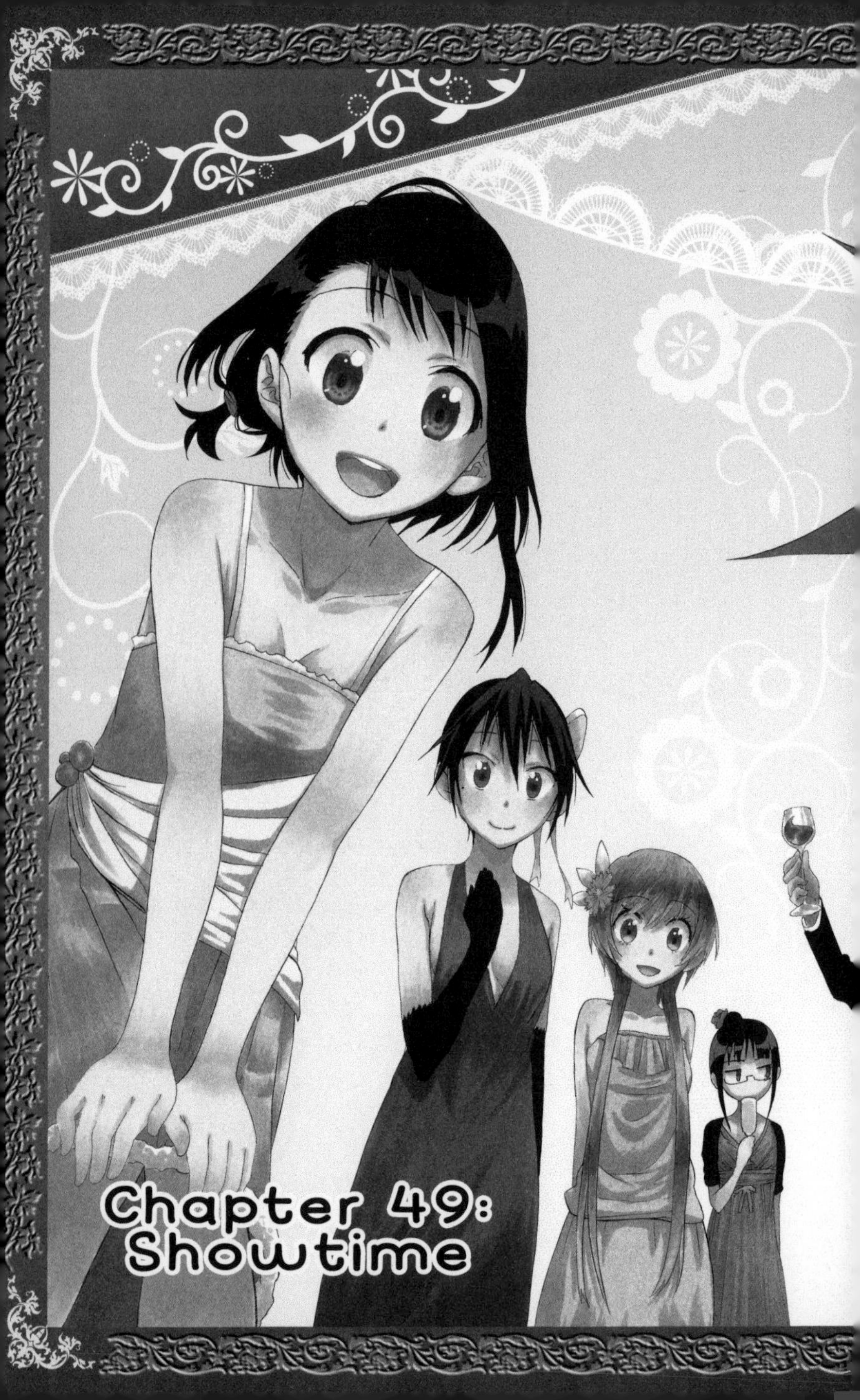
Chapter 49:
Showtime

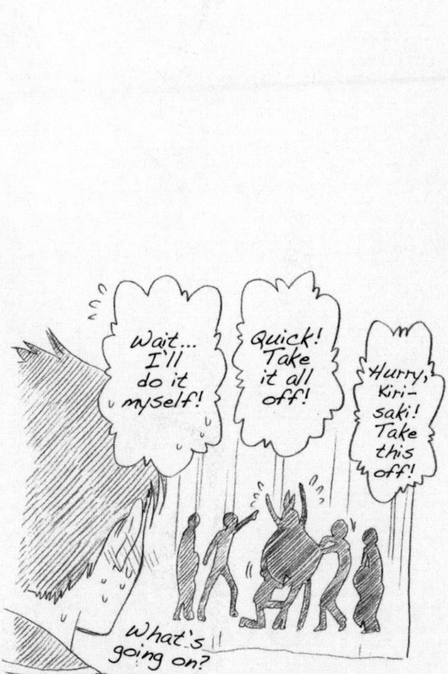
Hurry, Kiri-saki! Take this off!
Quick! Take it all off!
Wait... I'll do it myself!
What's going on?

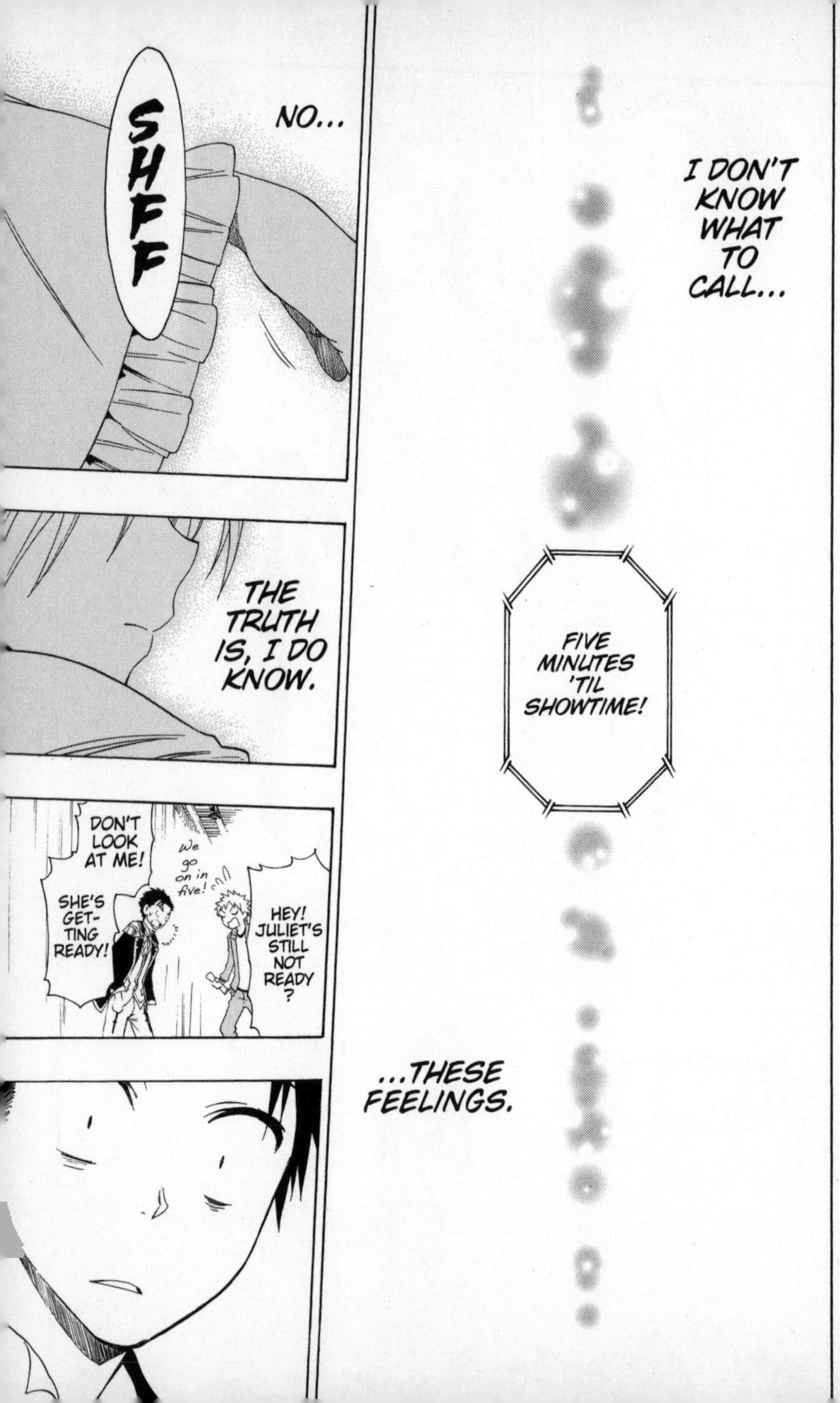
I DON'T KNOW WHAT TO CALL...
FIVE MINUTES 'TIL SHOWTIME!
...THESE FEELINGS.
NO...
SHFF
THE TRUTH IS, I DO KNOW.
HEY! JULIET'S STILL NOT READY?
We go on in five!
DON'T LOOK AT ME!
SHE'S GET-TING READY!

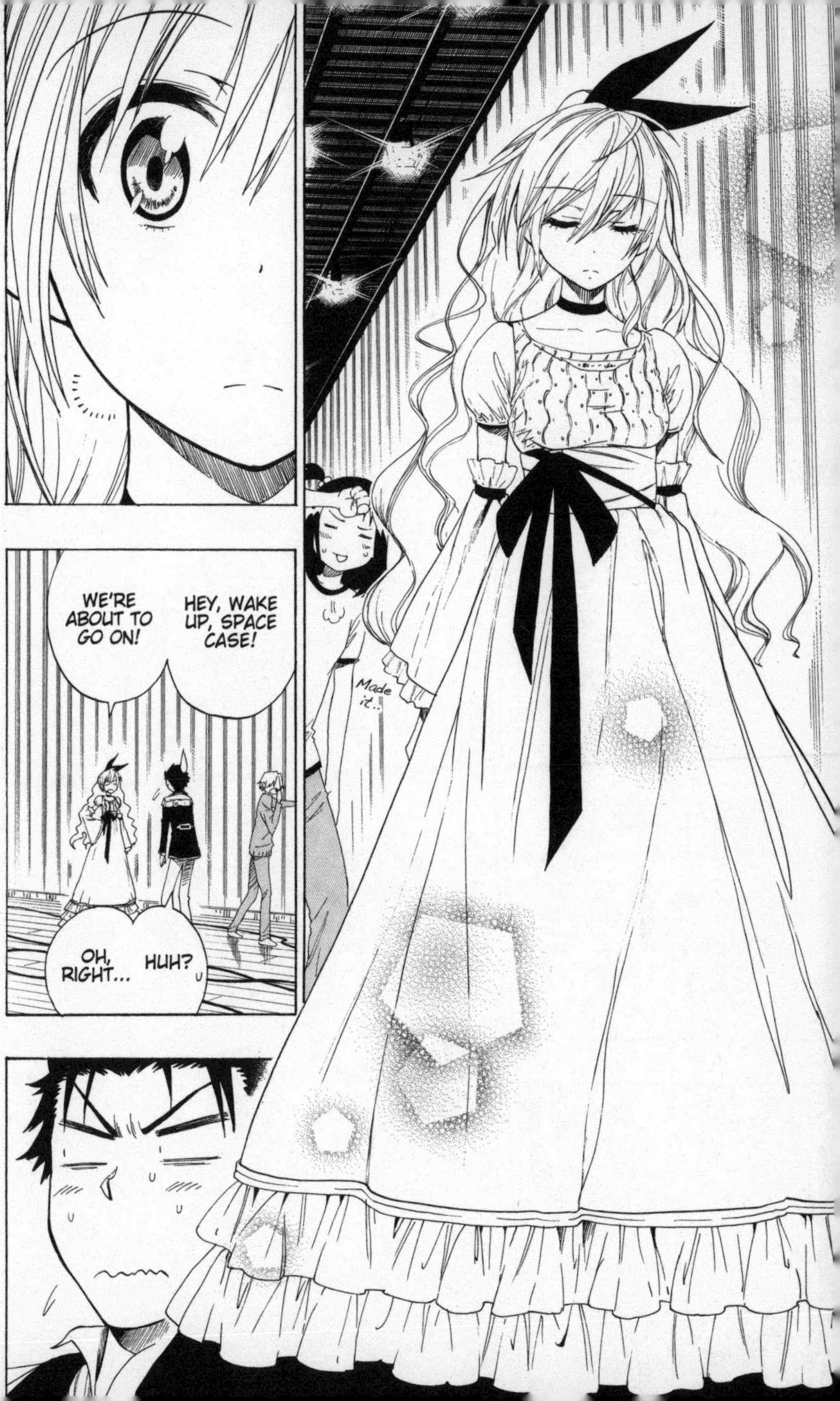
Made it..
HEY, WAKE UP, SPACE CASE!
WE'RE ABOUT TO GO ON!
HUH?
OH, RIGHT...

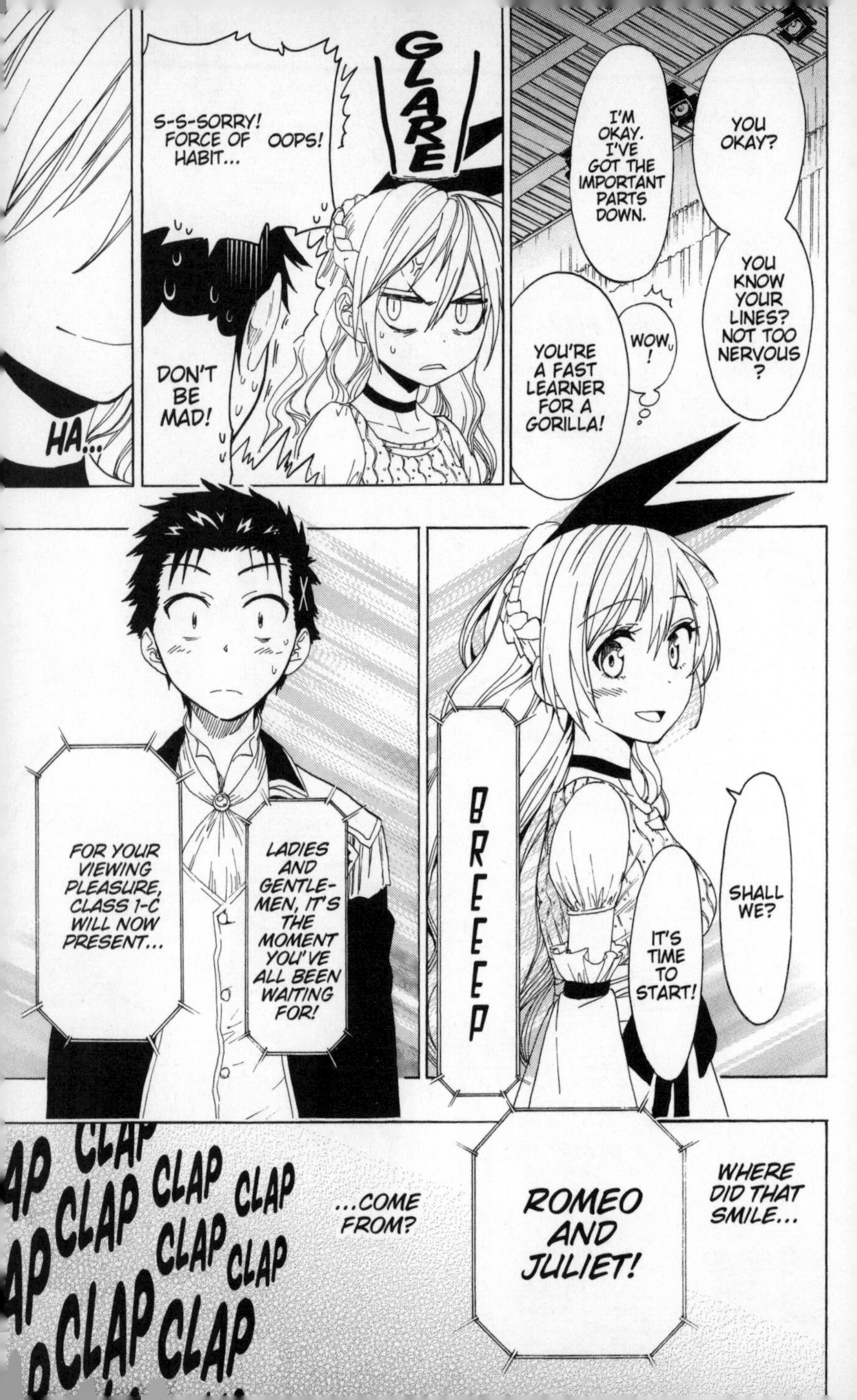
YOU OKAY?
I'M OKAY. I'VE GOT THE IMPORTANT PARTS DOWN.
YOU KNOW YOUR LINES? NOT TOO NERVOUS?
WOW!
YOU'RE A FAST LEARNER FOR A GORILLA!
GLARE
OOPS!
S-S-SORRY! FORCE OF HABIT...
DON'T BE MAD!
HA...
SHALL WE?
IT'S TIME TO START!
BREEEP
LADIES AND GENTLEMEN, IT'S THE MOMENT YOU'VE ALL BEEN WAITING FOR!
FOR YOUR VIEWING PLEASURE, CLASS 1-C WILL NOW PRESENT...
WHERE DID THAT SMILE...
ROMEO AND JULIET!
...COME FROM?
CLAP CLAP CLAP CLAP CLAP CLAP CLAP CLAP CLAP

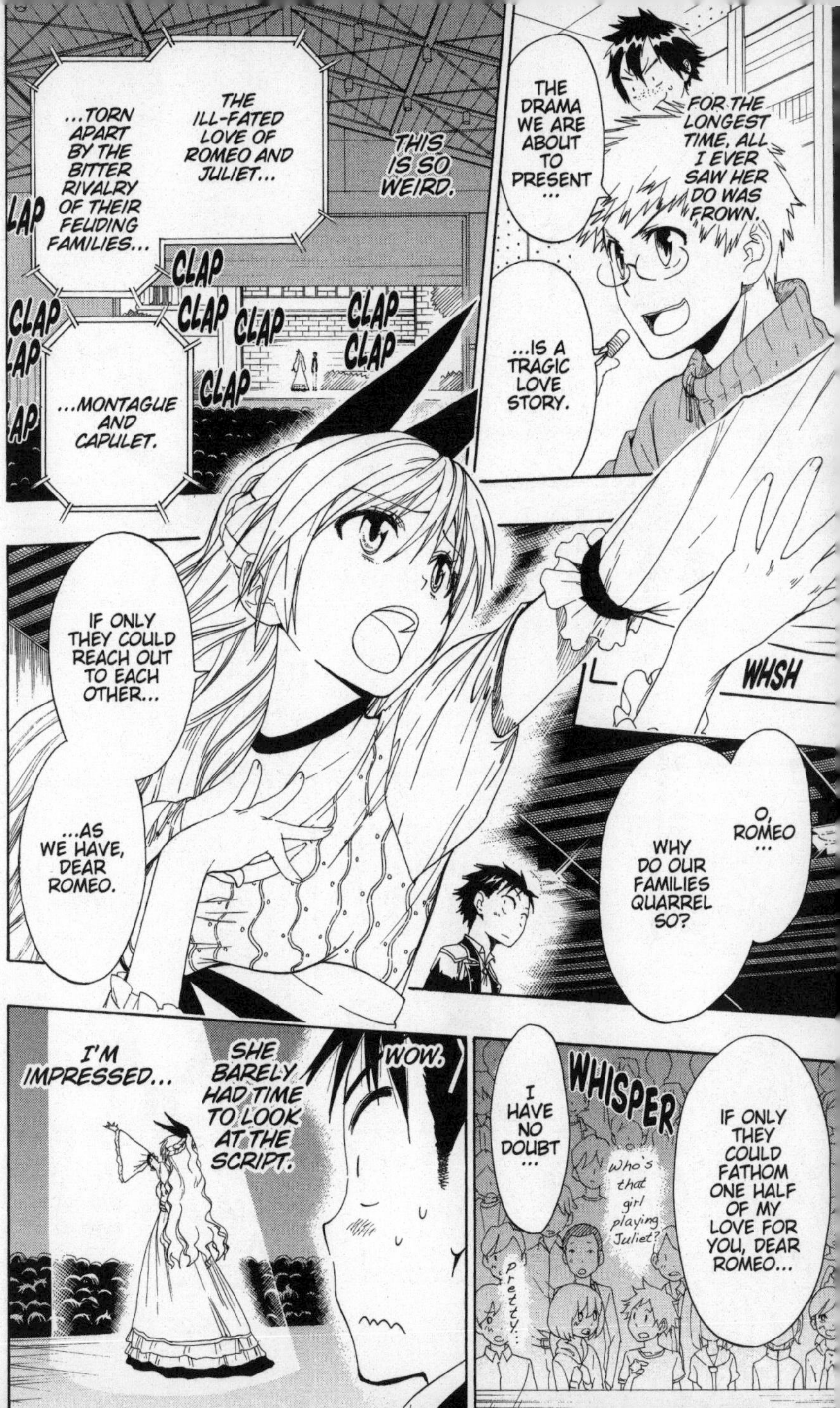
FOR THE LONGEST TIME, ALL I EVER SAW HER DO WAS FROWN.
THE DRAMA WE ARE ABOUT TO PRESENT...
...IS A TRAGIC LOVE STORY.
THIS IS SO WEIRD.
THE ILL-FATED LOVE OF ROMEO AND JULIET...
...TORN APART BY THE BITTER RIVALRY OF THEIR FEUDING FAMILIES...
CLAP CLAP
CLAP CLAP
CLAP
CLAP
CLAP
LAP
CLAP
LAP
AP
...MONTAGUE AND CAPULET.
WHSH
O, ROMEO...
WHY DO OUR FAMILIES QUARREL SO?
IF ONLY THEY COULD REACH OUT TO EACH OTHER...
...AS WE HAVE, DEAR ROMEO.
IF ONLY THEY COULD FATHOM ONE HALF OF MY LOVE FOR YOU, DEAR ROMEO...
WHISPER
I HAVE NO DOUBT...
Who's that girl playing Juliet?
Pretty...
WOW.
SHE BARELY HAD TIME TO LOOK AT THE SCRIPT.
I'M IMPRESSED...

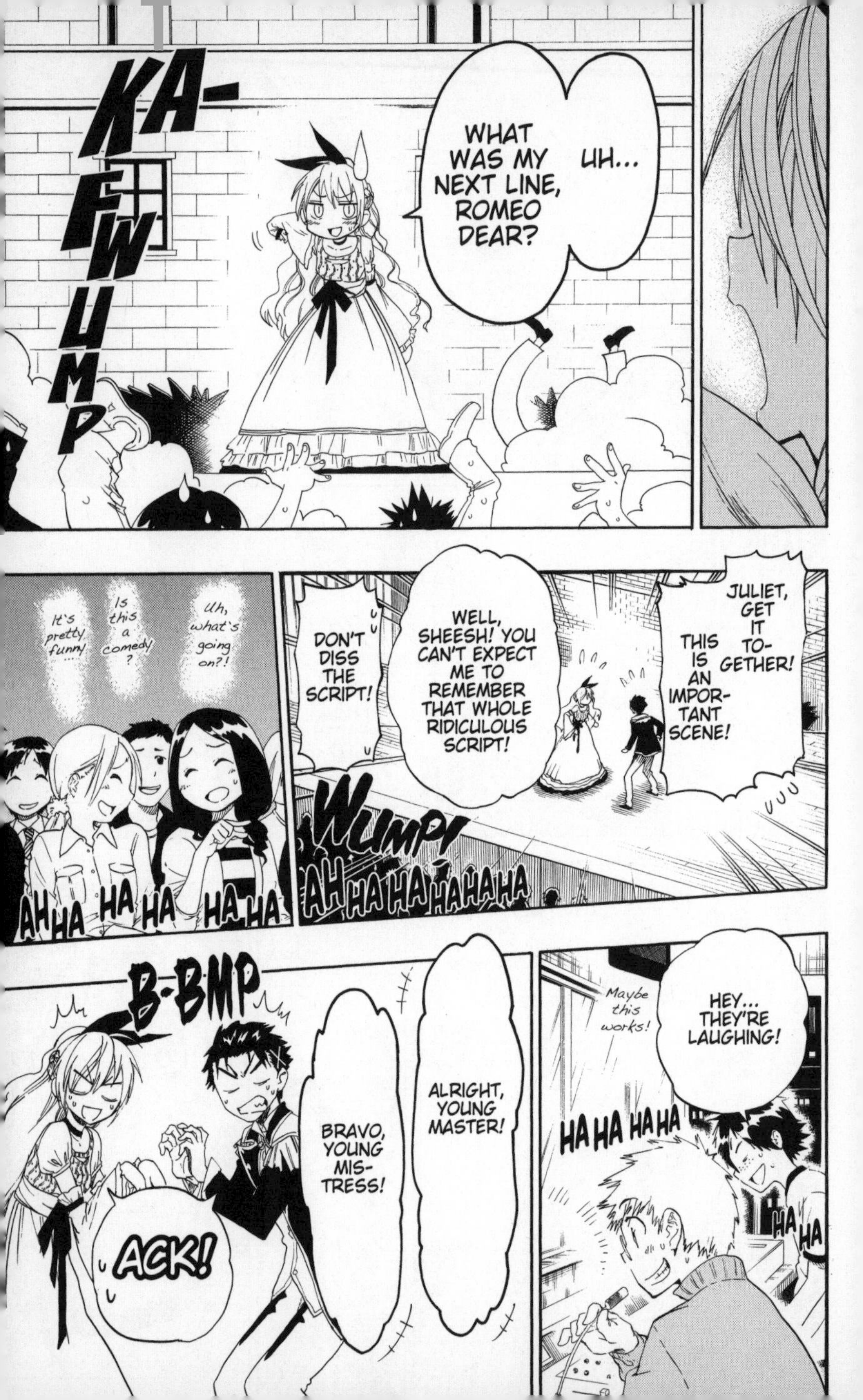
KA-FWUMP
UH...
WHAT WAS MY NEXT LINE, ROMEO DEAR?
JULIET, GET IT TO-GETHER!
THIS IS AN IMPOR-TANT SCENE!
WELL, SHEESH! YOU CAN'T EXPECT ME TO REMEMBER THAT WHOLE RIDICULOUS SCRIPT!
DON'T DISS THE SCRIPT!
WUMP!
AH HA HA HAHAHA
Uh, what's going on?!
Is this a comedy?
It's pretty funny...
AH HA HA HA HA HA
HEY... THEY'RE LAUGHING!
Maybe this works!
HA HA HA HA
HA HA
B-BMP
ALRIGHT, YOUNG MASTER!
BRAVO, YOUNG MIS-TRESS!
ACK!

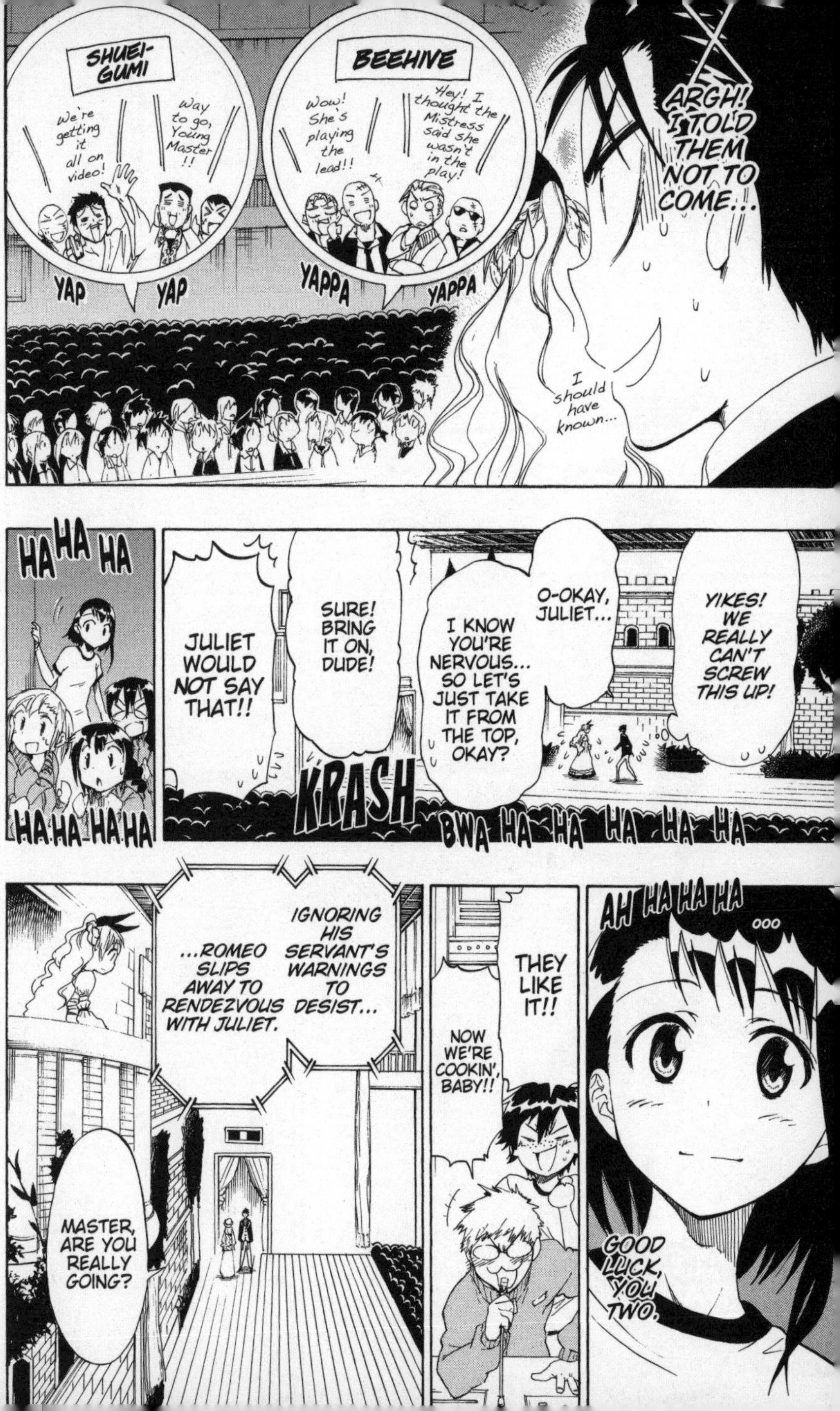
ARGH! I TOLD THEM NOT TO COME...
BEEHIVE
Hey! I thought the Mistress said she wasn't in the play!
Wow! She's playing the lead!!
YAPPA YAPPA
SHUEI-GUMI
Way to go, Young Master!!
We're getting it all on video!
YAP YAP
I should have known...
YIKES! WE REALLY CAN'T SCREW THIS UP!
O-OKAY, JULIET...
I KNOW YOU'RE NERVOUS... SO LET'S JUST TAKE IT FROM THE TOP, OKAY?
SURE! BRING IT ON, DUDE!
JULIET WOULD NOT SAY THAT!!
KRASH
BWA HA HA HA HA HA
HA HA HA
HA HA HA HA
AH HA HA HA HA
GOOD LUCK, YOU TWO.
THEY LIKE IT!!
NOW WE'RE COOKIN', BABY!!
IGNORING HIS SERVANT'S WARNINGS TO DESIST...
...ROMEO SLIPS AWAY TO RENDEZVOUS WITH JULIET.
MASTER, ARE YOU REALLY GOING?

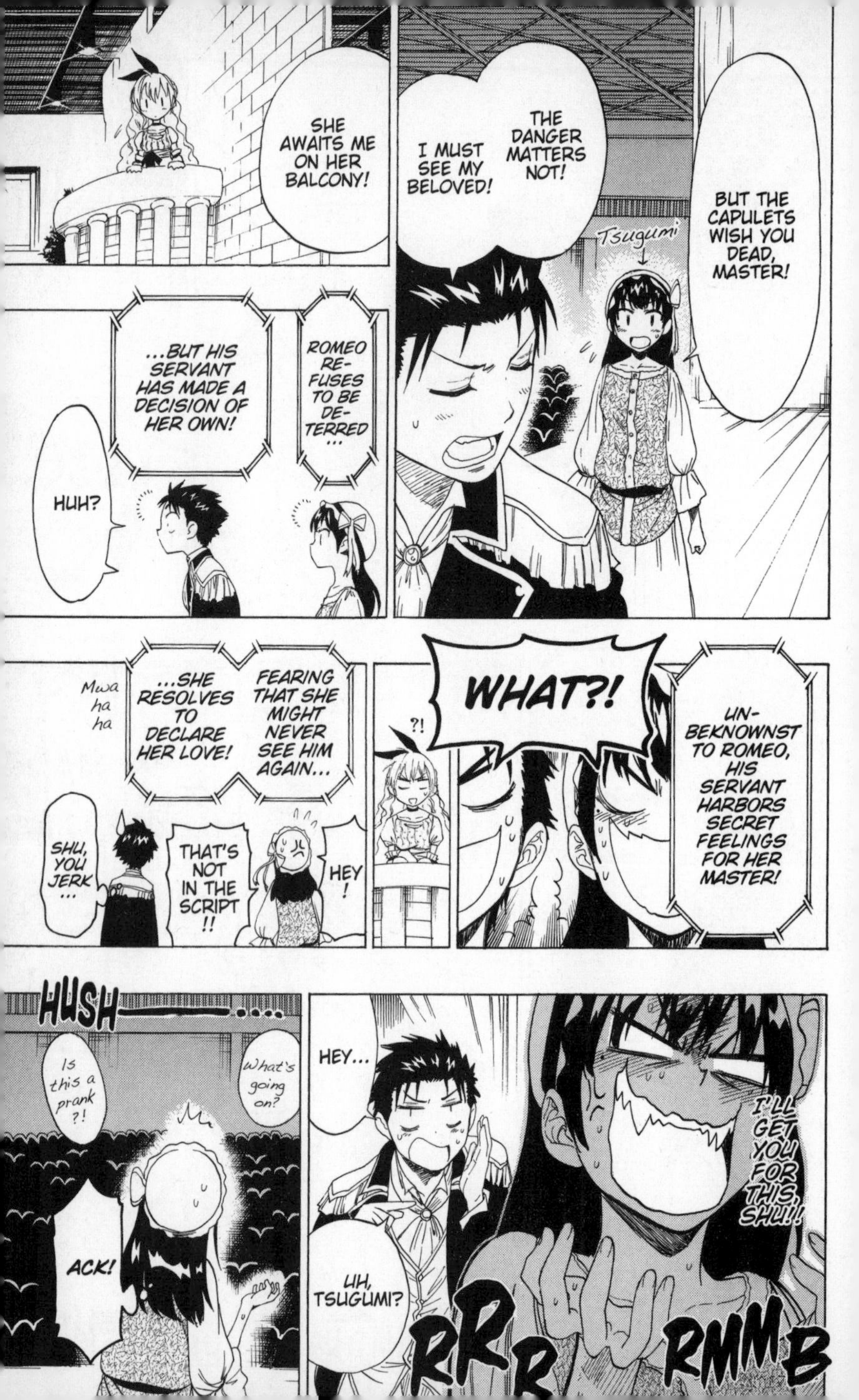
BUT THE CAPULETS WISH YOU DEAD, MASTER!
Tsugumi
THE DANGER MATTERS NOT!
I MUST SEE MY BELOVED!
SHE AWAITS ME ON HER BALCONY!
ROMEO RE-FUSES TO BE DE-TERRED...
...BUT HIS SERVANT HAS MADE A DECISION OF HER OWN!
HUH?
UN-BEKNOWNST TO ROMEO, HIS SERVANT HARBORS SECRET FEELINGS FOR HER MASTER!
WHAT?!
?!
FEARING THAT SHE MIGHT NEVER SEE HIM AGAIN...
...SHE RESOLVES TO DECLARE HER LOVE!
Mwa ha ha
HEY!
THAT'S NOT IN THE SCRIPT!!
SHU, YOU JERK...
I'LL GET YOU FOR THIS, SHU!!
HEY...
UH, TSUGUMI?
RRRR
RMMB
HUSH—....
What's going on?
Is this a prank?!
ACK!

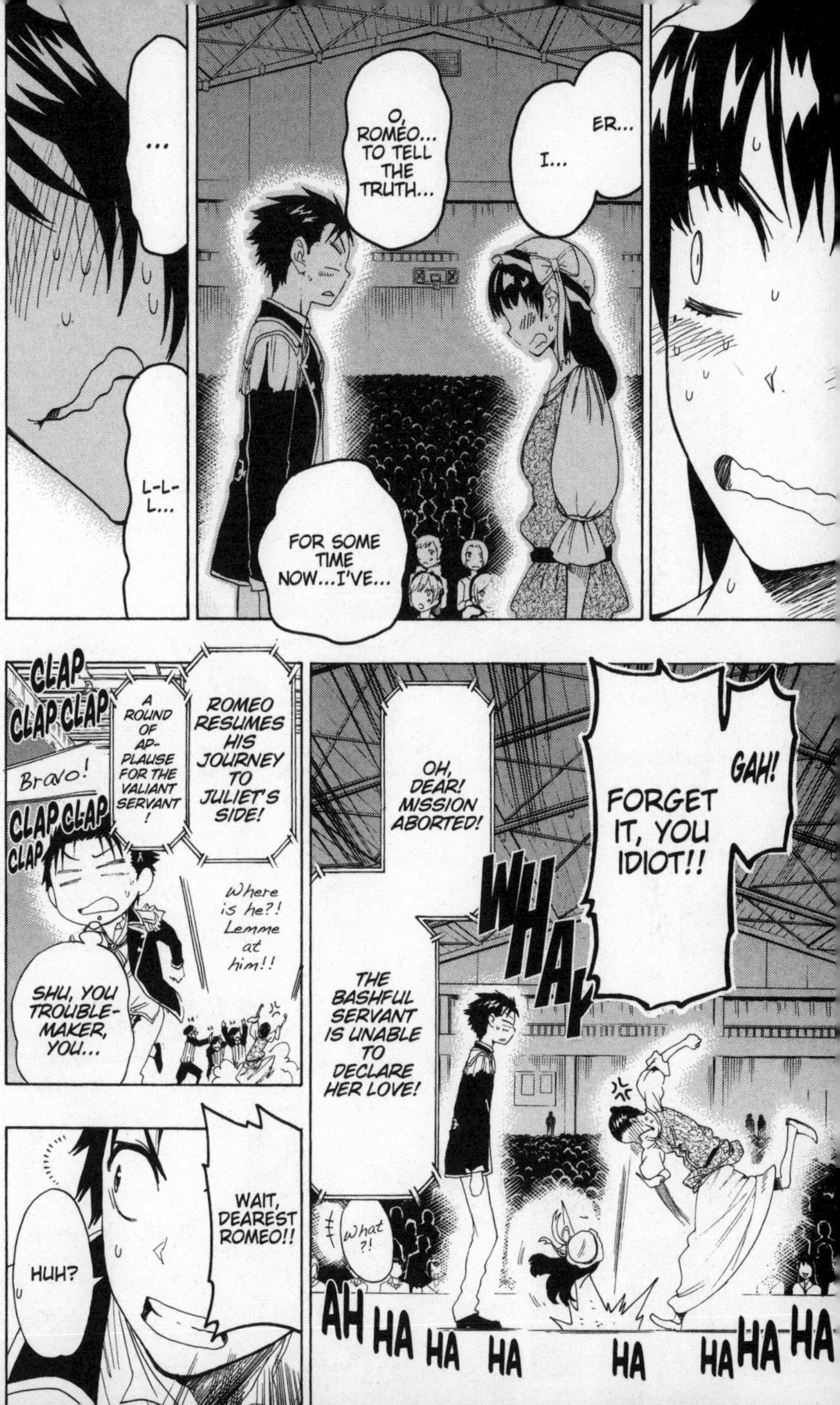

ER...
I...
O, ROMEO... TO TELL THE TRUTH...
...
FOR SOME TIME NOW...I'VE...
L-L-L...
GAH!
FORGET IT, YOU IDIOT!!
WHAM
OH, DEAR! MISSION ABORTED!
THE BASHFUL SERVANT IS UNABLE TO DECLARE HER LOVE!
What?!
AH HA HA HA HA HA HA HA
ROMEO RESUMES HIS JOURNEY TO JULIET'S SIDE!
A ROUND OF AP-PLAUSE FOR THE VALIANT SERVANT!
CLAP CLAP CLAP
Bravo!
CLAP CLAP CLAP
Where is he?! Lemme at him!!
SHU, YOU TROUBLE-MAKER, YOU...
WAIT, DEAREST ROMEO!!
HUH?

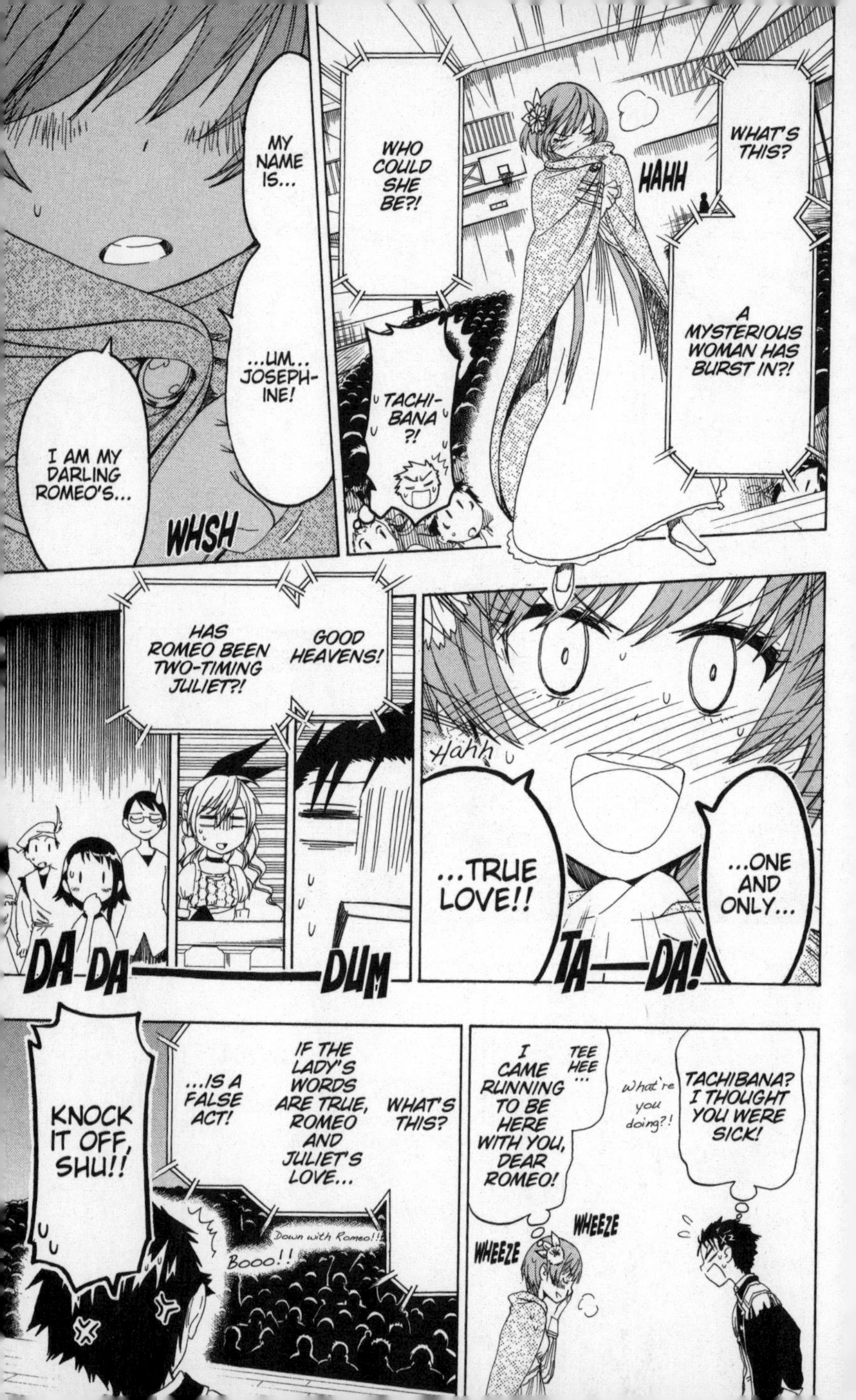
WHAT'S THIS?
A MYSTERIOUS WOMAN HAS BURST IN?!
HAHH
WHO COULD SHE BE?!
TACHIBANA?!
MY NAME IS...
...UM... JOSEPHINE!
I AM MY DARLING ROMEO'S...
WHSH
...ONE AND ONLY...
...TRUE LOVE!!
Hahh
TA—DA!
GOOD HEAVENS!
HAS ROMEO BEEN TWO-TIMING JULIET?!
DA DA—DUM
TACHIBANA? I THOUGHT YOU WERE SICK!
What're you doing?!
TEE HEE...
I CAME RUNNING TO BE HERE WITH YOU, DEAR ROMEO!
WHEEZE
WHEEZE
WHAT'S THIS?
IF THE LADY'S WORDS ARE TRUE, ROMEO AND JULIET'S LOVE...
...IS A FALSE ACT!
Down with Romeo!!
Booo!!
KNOCK IT OFF, SHU!!

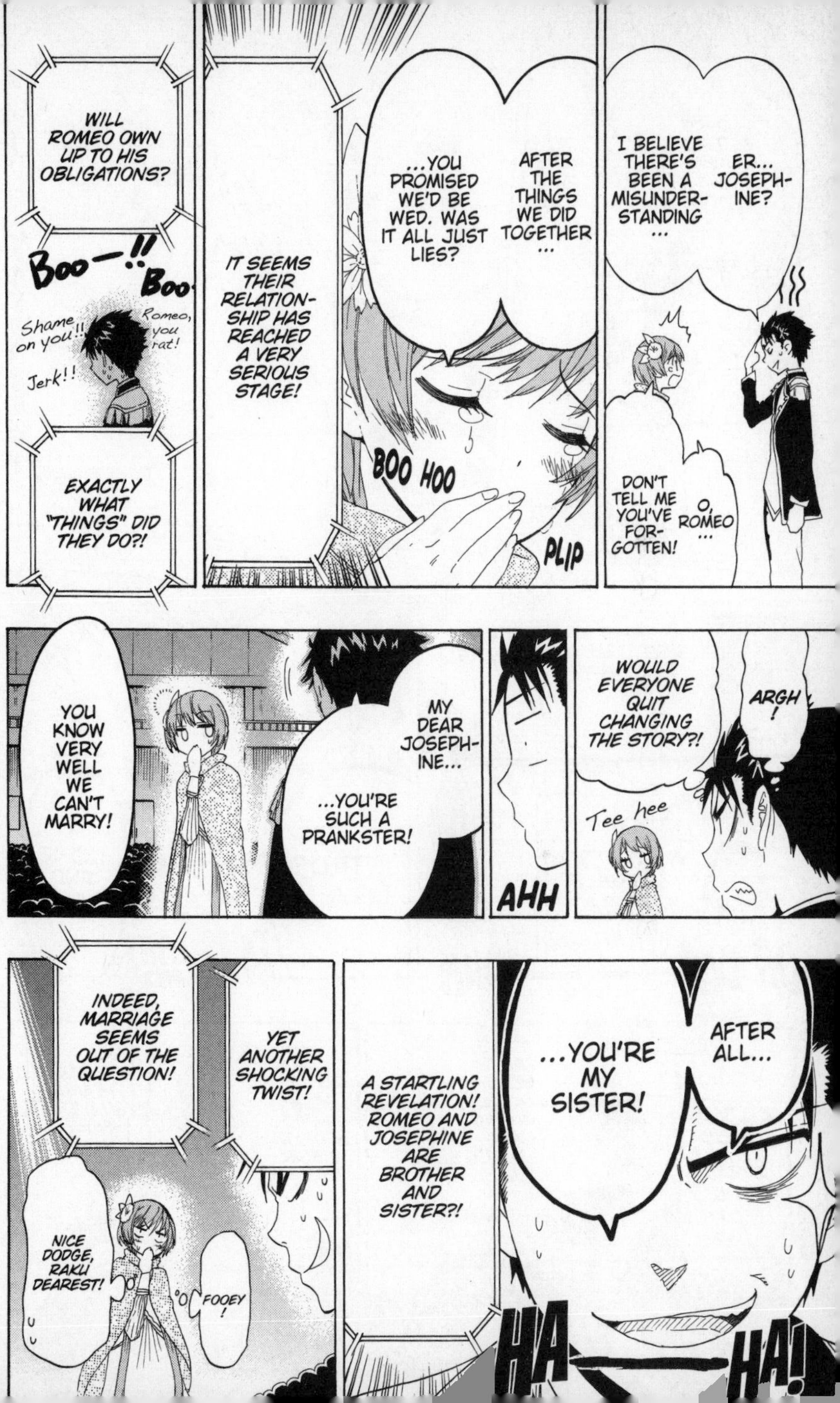
ER... JOSEPHINE?
I BELIEVE THERE'S BEEN A MISUNDERSTANDING...
O, ROMEO...
DON'T TELL ME YOU'VE FORGOTTEN!
AFTER THE THINGS WE DID TOGETHER...
...YOU PROMISED WE'D BE WED. WAS IT ALL JUST LIES?
BOO HOO
PLIP
IT SEEMS THEIR RELATIONSHIP HAS REACHED A VERY SERIOUS STAGE!
WILL ROMEO OWN UP TO HIS OBLIGATIONS?
Boo—!!
Boo
Romeo, you rat!
Shame on you!!
Jerk!!
EXACTLY WHAT "THINGS" DID THEY DO?!
ARGH!
WOULD EVERYONE QUIT CHANGING THE STORY?!
Tee hee
AHH
MY DEAR JOSEPHINE...
...YOU'RE SUCH A PRANKSTER!
YOU KNOW VERY WELL WE CAN'T MARRY!
AFTER ALL...
...YOU'RE MY SISTER!
HA——HA!
A STARTLING REVELATION! ROMEO AND JOSEPHINE ARE BROTHER AND SISTER?!
YET ANOTHER SHOCKING TWIST!
INDEED, MARRIAGE SEEMS OUT OF THE QUESTION!
FOOEY!
NICE DODGE, RAKU DEAREST!

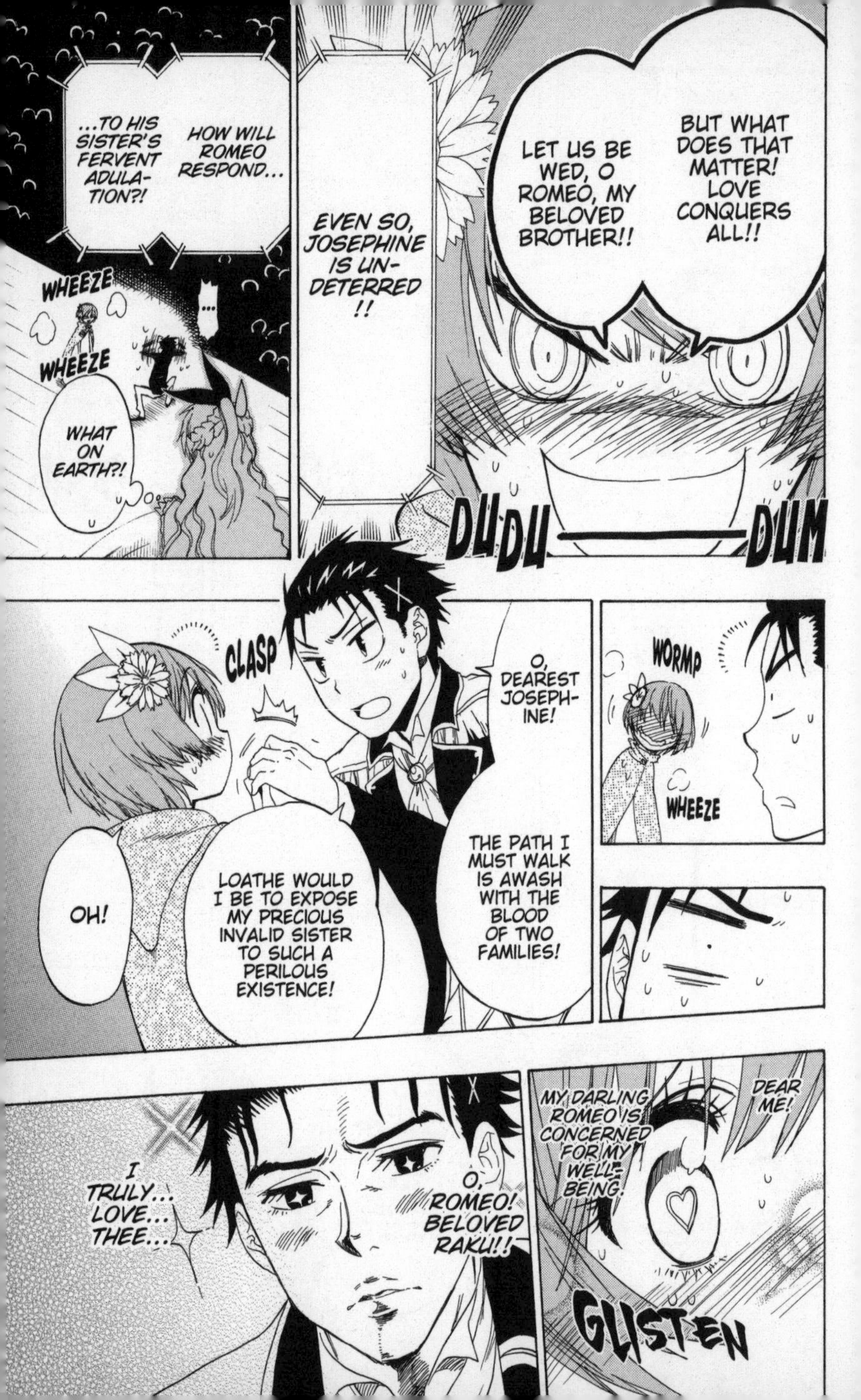
BUT WHAT DOES THAT MATTER! LOVE CONQUERS ALL!!
LET US BE WED, O ROMEO, MY BELOVED BROTHER!!
DUDU——DUM
EVEN SO, JOSEPHINE IS UN-DETERRED!!
HOW WILL ROMEO RESPOND...
...TO HIS SISTER'S FERVENT ADULA-TION?!
WHEEZE
WHEEZE
...
WHAT ON EARTH?!
WORMP
WHEEZE
O, DEAREST JOSEPH-INE!
THE PATH I MUST WALK IS AWASH WITH THE BLOOD OF TWO FAMILIES!
CLASP
LOATHE WOULD I BE TO EXPOSE MY PRECIOUS INVALID SISTER TO SUCH A PERILOUS EXISTENCE!
OH!
DEAR ME!
MY DARLING ROMEO IS CONCERNED FOR MY WELL-BEING.
O, ROMEO! BELOVED RAKU!!
GLISTEN
I TRULY... LOVE... THEE...

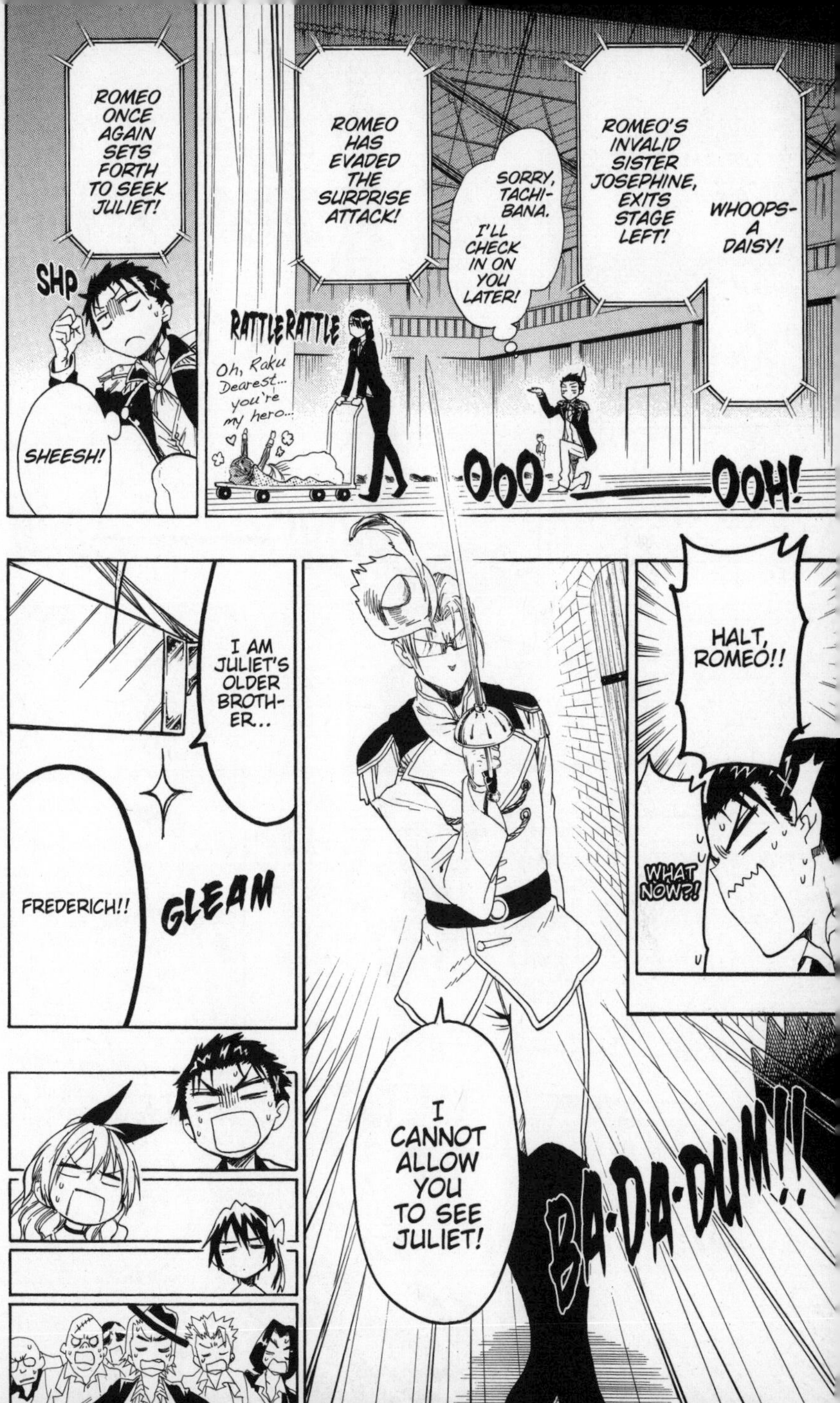
WHOOPS-A DAISY!
ROMEO'S INVALID SISTER JOSEPHINE, EXITS STAGE LEFT!
SORRY, TACHIBANA. I'LL CHECK IN ON YOU LATER!
ROMEO HAS EVADED THE SURPRISE ATTACK!
RATTLE RATTLE
Oh, Raku Dearest... you're my hero...
OOO——OOH!
ROMEO ONCE AGAIN SETS FORTH TO SEEK JULIET!
SHP
SHEESH!
HALT, ROMEO!!
WHAT NOW?!
I AM JULIET'S OLDER BROTHER...
FREDERICH!!
GLEAM
I CANNOT ALLOW YOU TO SEE JULIET!
BA-DA-DUM!!

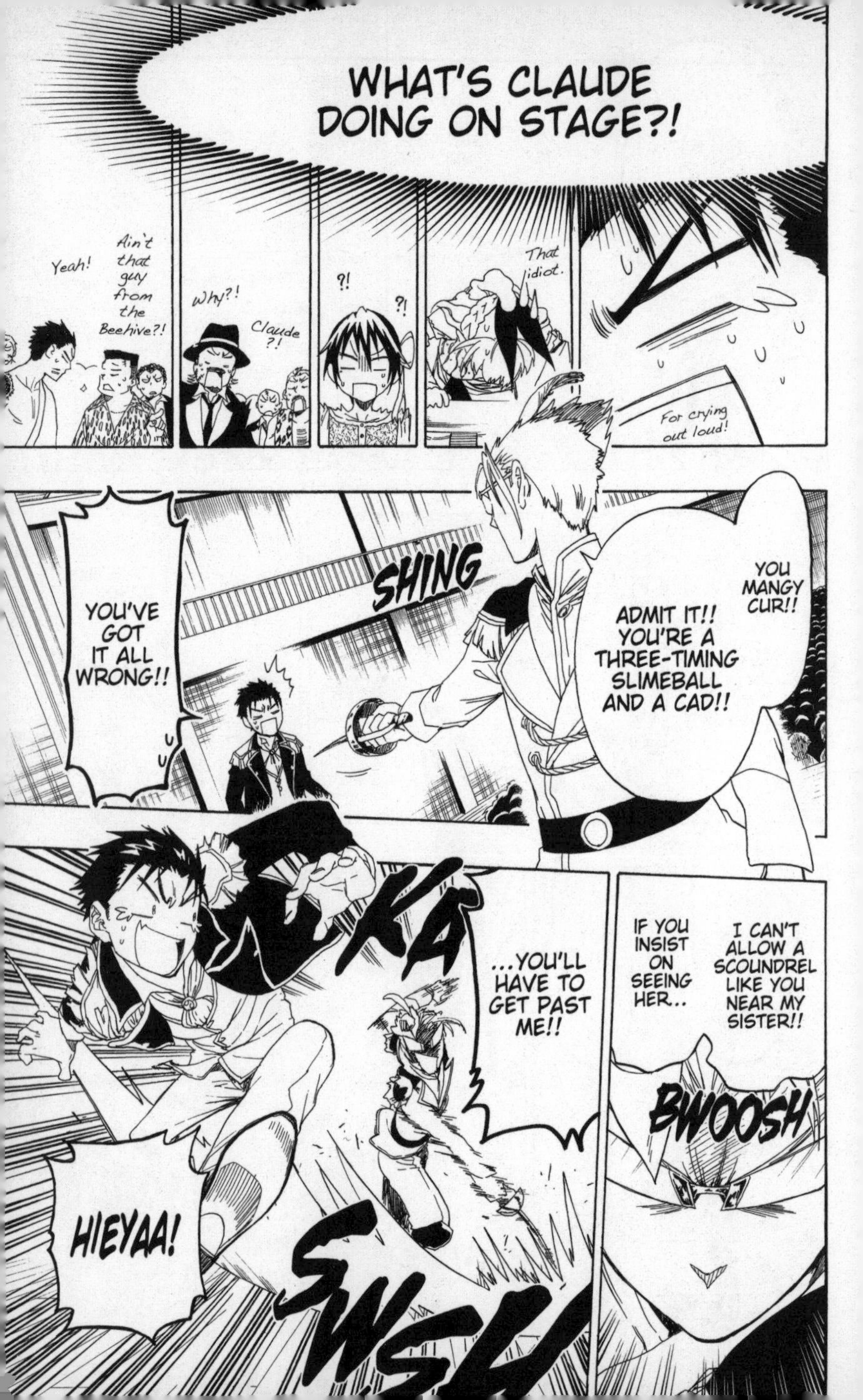
WHAT'S CLAUDE DOING ON STAGE?!
For crying out loud!
That idiot.
?!
?!
Why?!
Claude ?!
Ain't that guy from the Beehive?!
Yeah!
YOU MANGY CUR!!
ADMIT IT!! YOU'RE A THREE-TIMING SLIMEBALL AND A CAD!!
SHING
YOU'VE GOT IT ALL WRONG!!
I CAN'T ALLOW A SCOUNDREL LIKE YOU NEAR MY SISTER!!
IF YOU INSIST ON SEEING HER...
BWOOSH
...YOU'LL HAVE TO GET PAST ME!!
KA
HIEYAA!
SWSH

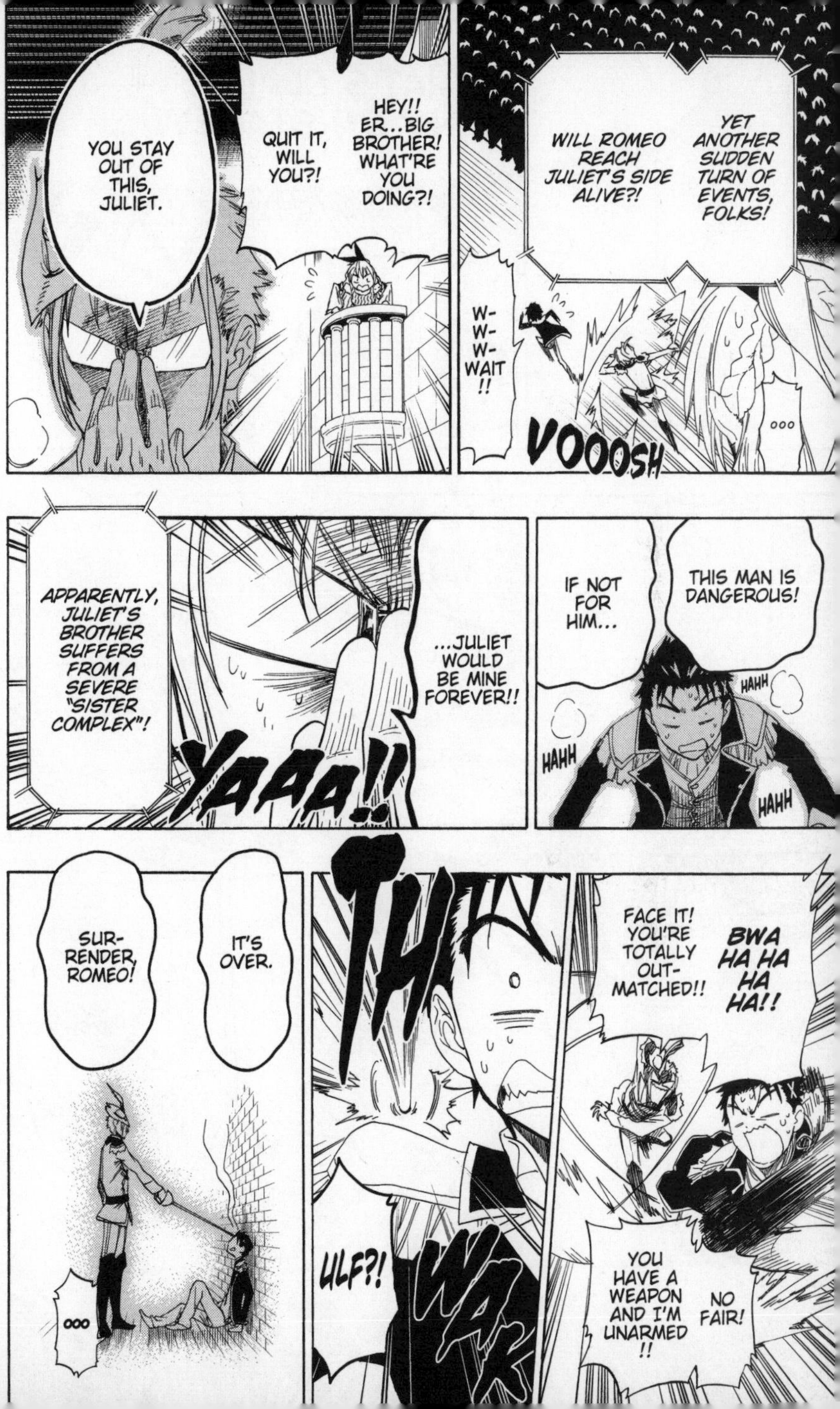
YET ANOTHER SUDDEN TURN OF EVENTS, FOLKS!
WILL ROMEO REACH JULIET'S SIDE ALIVE?!
W- W- W- WAIT !!
VOOOSH
...
HEY!! ER...BIG BROTHER! WHAT'RE YOU DOING?!
QUIT IT, WILL YOU?!
YOU STAY OUT OF THIS, JULIET.
THIS MAN IS DANGEROUS!
IF NOT FOR HIM...
HAHH
HAHH
HAHH
...JULIET WOULD BE MINE FOREVER!!
YAAAA!!
APPARENTLY, JULIET'S BROTHER SUFFERS FROM A SEVERE "SISTER COMPLEX"!
BWA HA HA HA HA!!
FACE IT! YOU'RE TOTALLY OUT-MATCHED!!
NO FAIR!
YOU HAVE A WEAPON AND I'M UNARMED !!
TH
WAK
ULF?!
IT'S OVER.
SUR-RENDER, ROMEO!
...

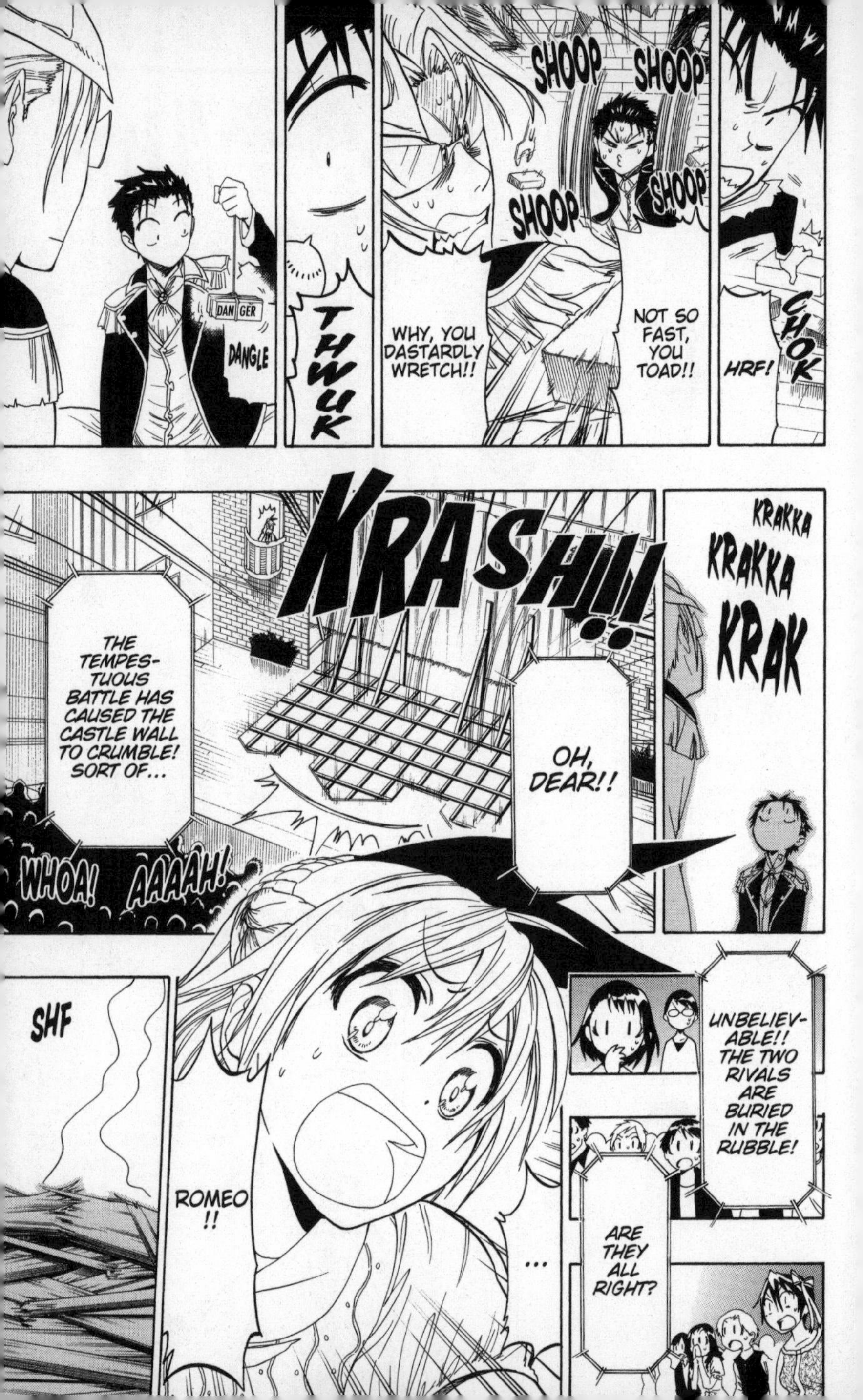
HRF!
CHOK
SHOOP SHOOP
SHOOP SHOOP
NOT SO FAST, YOU TOAD!!
WHY, YOU DASTARDLY WRETCH!!
THWUK
DANGER
DANGLE
KRAKKA
KRAKKA
KRAK
KRASH!!
THE TEMPESTUOUS BATTLE HAS CAUSED THE CASTLE WALL TO CRUMBLE! SORT OF...
OH, DEAR!!
WHOA!
AAAAH!
UNBELIEVABLE!! THE TWO RIVALS ARE BURIED IN THE RUBBLE!
ARE THEY ALL RIGHT?
...
ROMEO!!
SHF

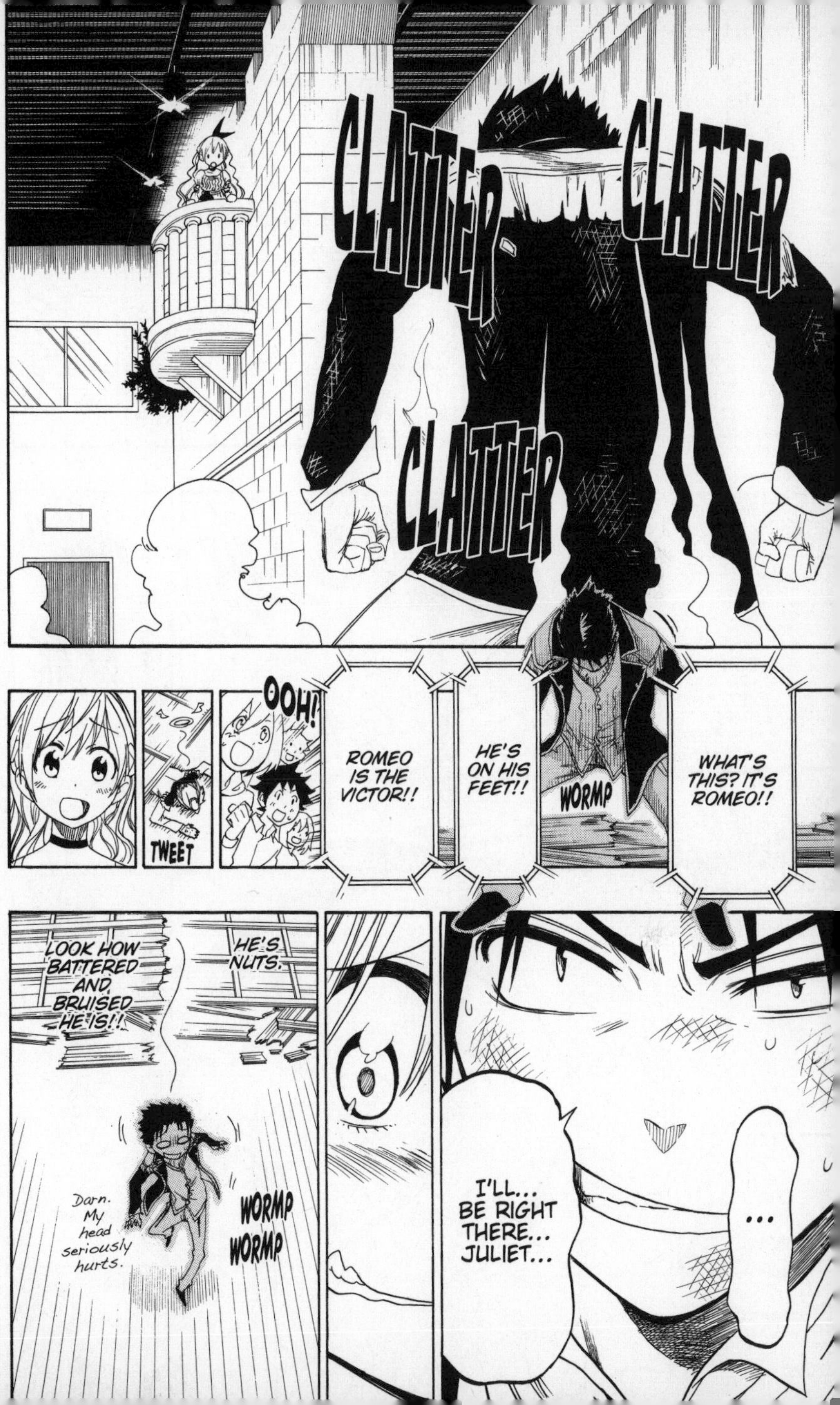
CLATTER-
CLATTER
CLATTER
WHAT'S THIS? IT'S ROMEO!!
WORMP
HE'S ON HIS FEET!!
ROMEO IS THE VICTOR!!
OOH!
TWEET
...
I'LL... BE RIGHT THERE... JULIET...
HE'S NUTS.
LOOK HOW BATTERED AND BRUISED HE IS!!
WORMP WORMP
Darn. My head seriously hurts.

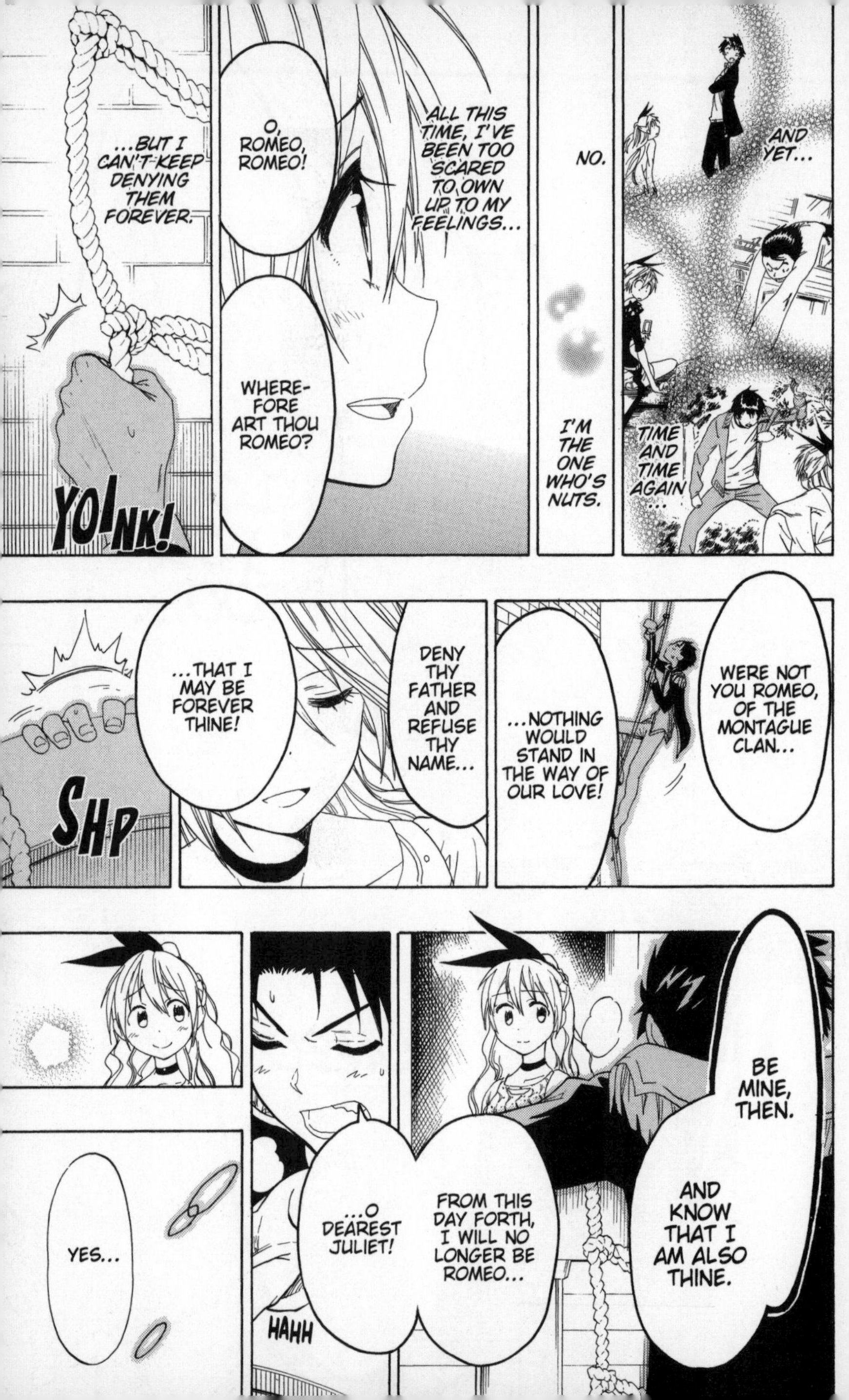
AND YET...
TIME AND TIME AGAIN...
NO.
I'M THE ONE WHO'S NUTS.
ALL THIS TIME, I'VE BEEN TOO SCARED TO OWN UP TO MY FEELINGS...
O, ROMEO, ROMEO!
WHEREFORE ART THOU ROMEO?
...BUT I CAN'T KEEP DENYING THEM FOREVER.
YOINK!
WERE NOT YOU ROMEO, OF THE MONTAGUE CLAN...
...NOTHING WOULD STAND IN THE WAY OF OUR LOVE!
DENY THY FATHER AND REFUSE THY NAME...
...THAT I MAY BE FOREVER THINE!
SHP
BE MINE, THEN.
AND KNOW THAT I AM ALSO THINE.
FROM THIS DAY FORTH, I WILL NO LONGER BE ROMEO...
...O DEAREST JULIET!
HAHH
YES...

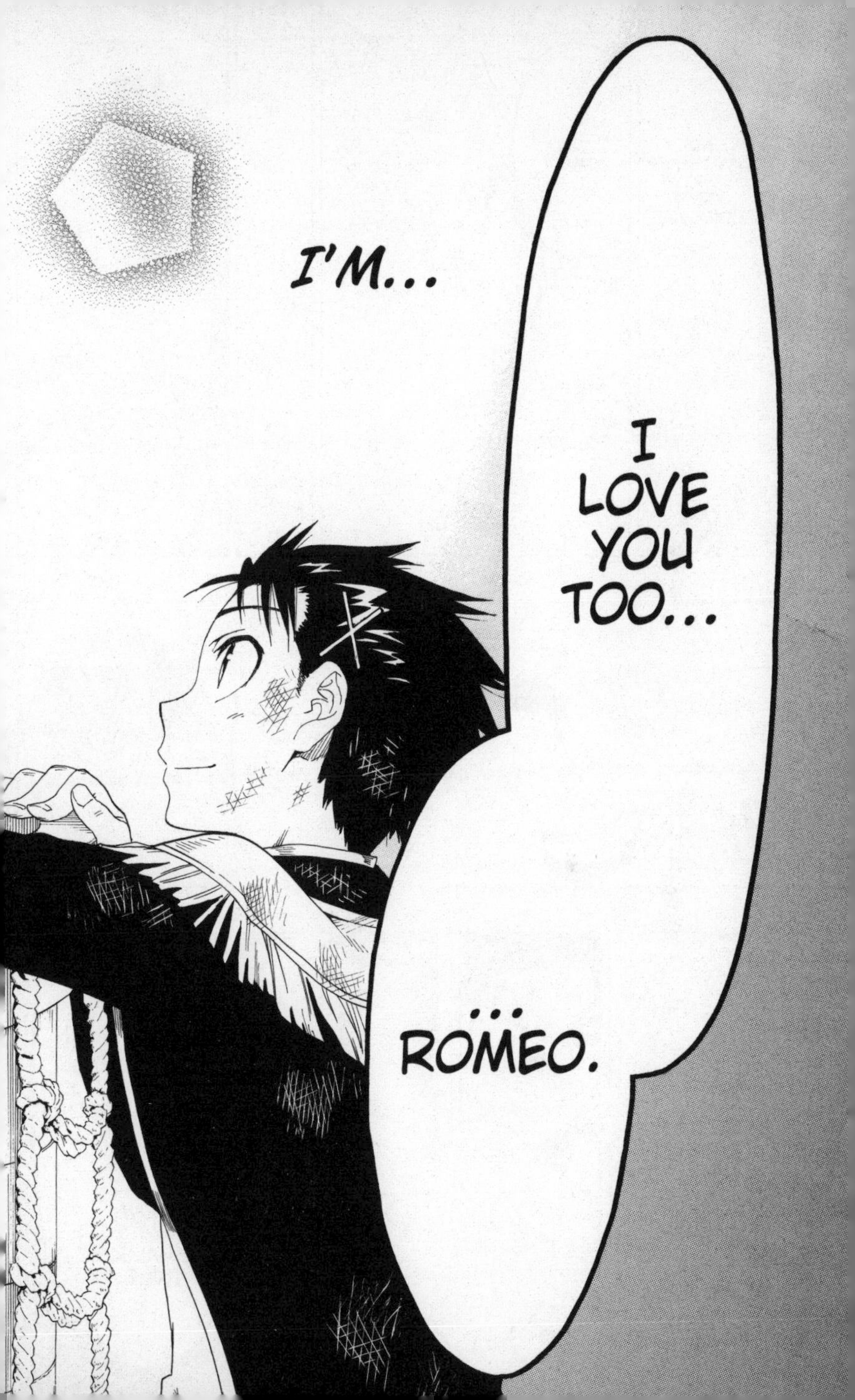
I'M...
I LOVE YOU TOO...
...ROMEO.

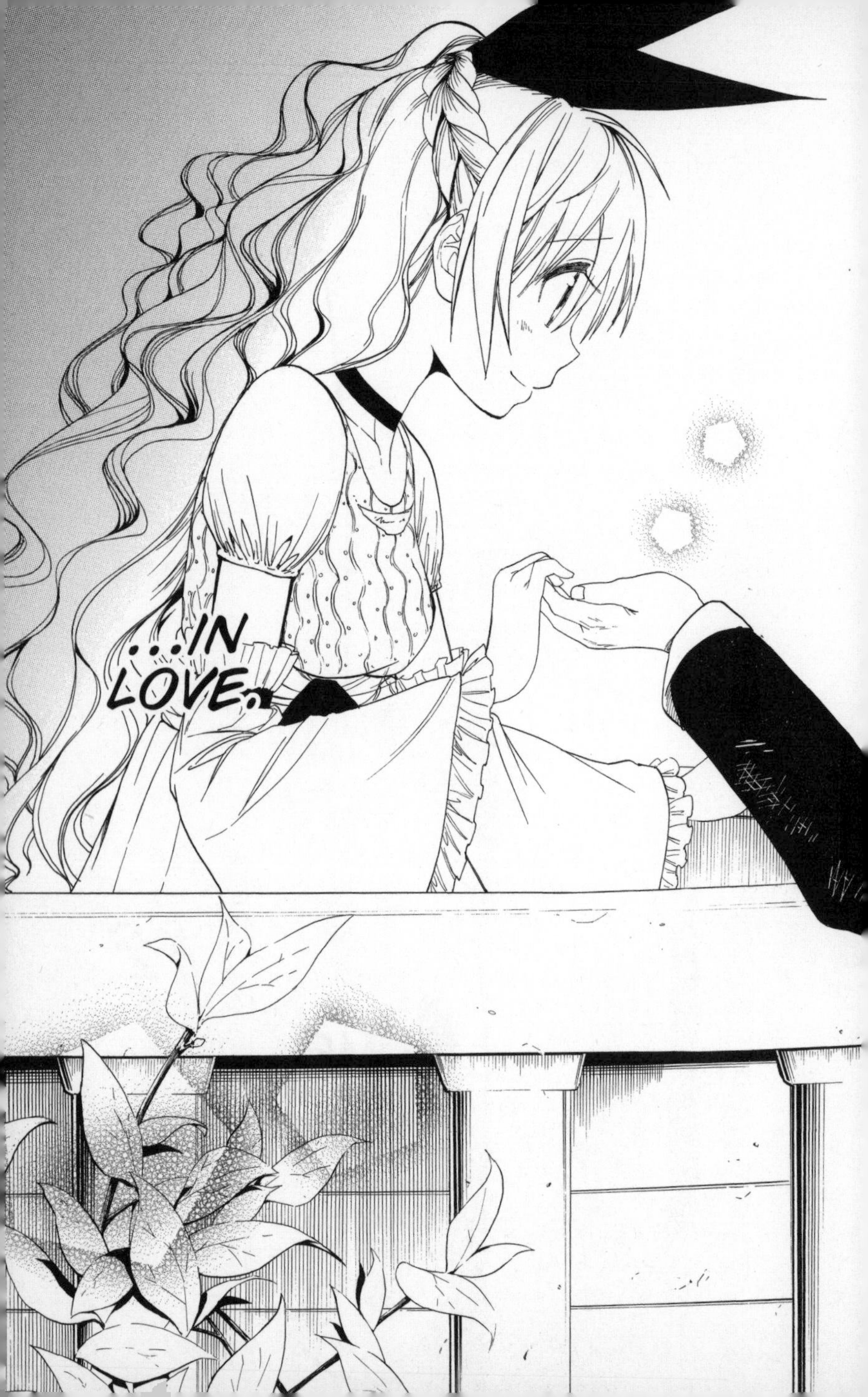
...IN LOVE.

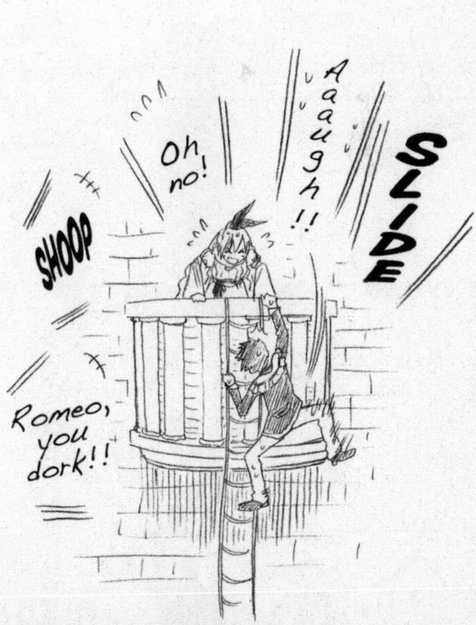
SLIDE
Aaaugh!!
Oh no!
SHOOP
Romeo, you dork!!

Chapter 50: The Stars

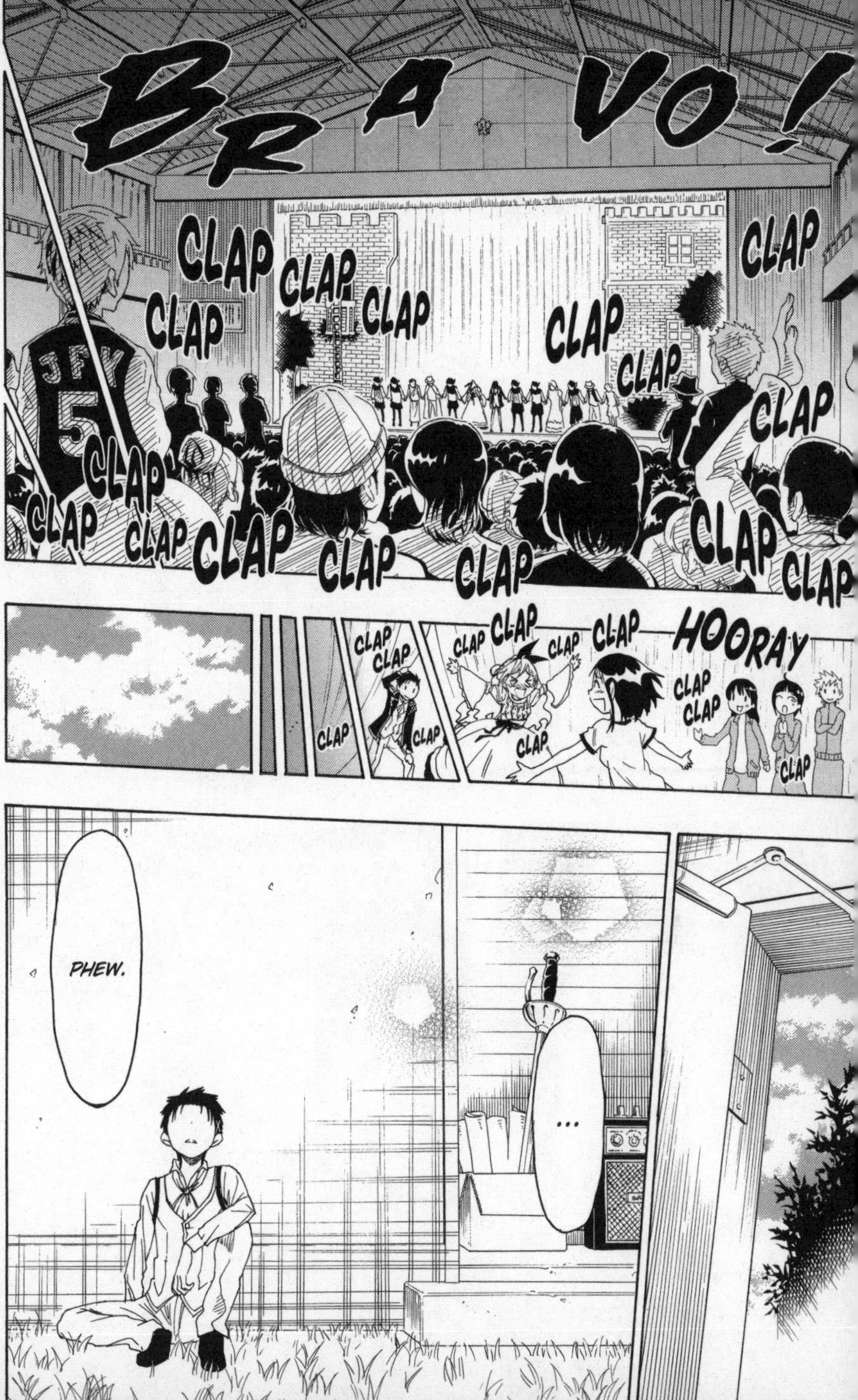
BRAVO!
CLAP
CLAP
CLAP
CLAP
CLAP
CLAP
CLAP
CLAP
CLAP
CLAP
CLAP
CLAP
CLAP
CLAP
CLAP
CLAP
HOORAY
CLAP
CLAP
CLAP
CLAP
CLAP
CLAP
CLAP
CLAP
CLAP
CLAP
CLAP
CLAP
...
PHEW.

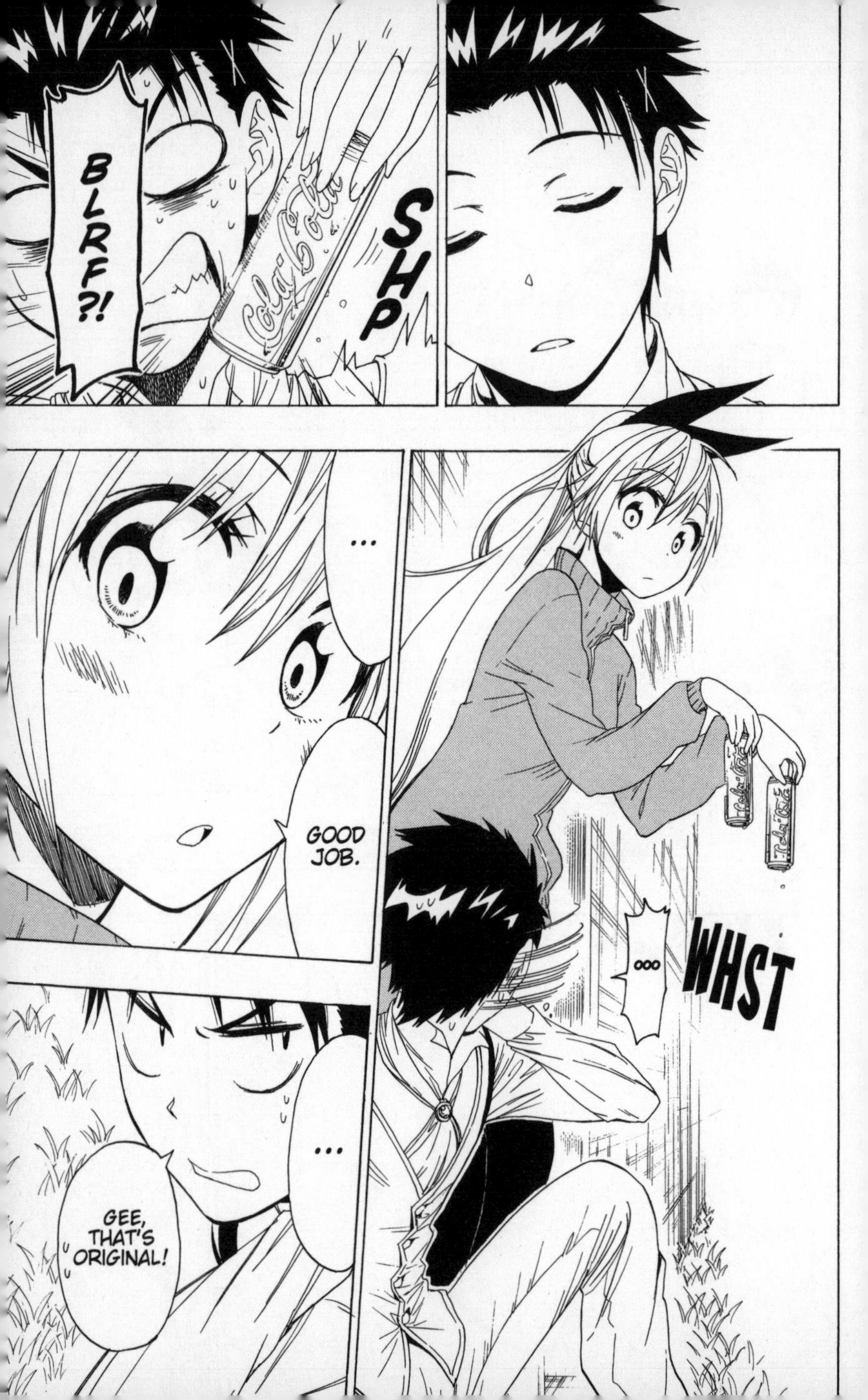
SHP
BLRF?!
WHST
...
...
GOOD JOB.
...
GEE, THAT'S ORIGINAL!

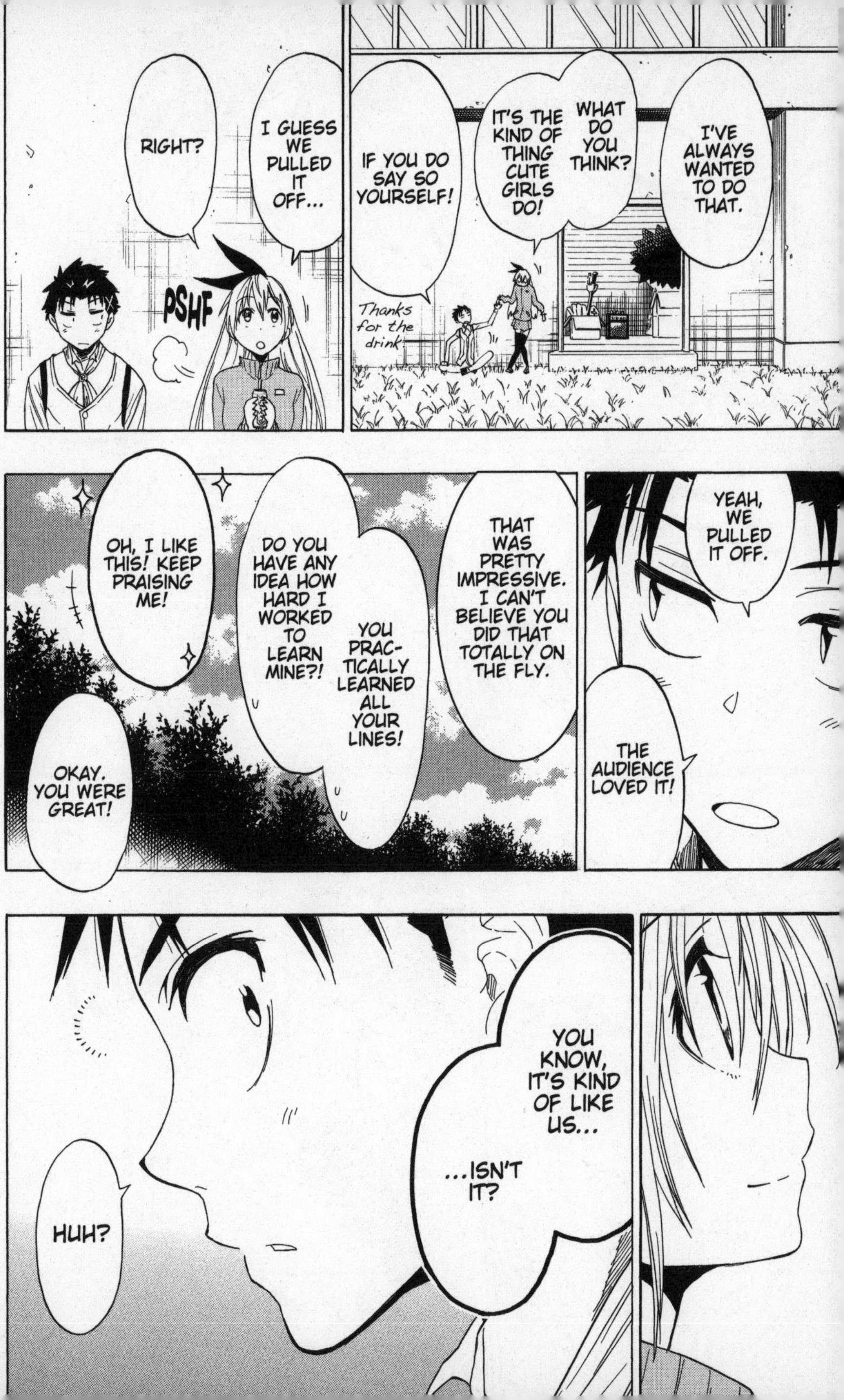
I'VE ALWAYS WANTED TO DO THAT.
WHAT DO YOU THINK?
IT'S THE KIND OF THING CUTE GIRLS DO!
IF YOU DO SAY SO YOURSELF!
Thanks for the drink.
I GUESS WE PULLED IT OFF...
PSHF
RIGHT?
YEAH, WE PULLED IT OFF.
THE AUDIENCE LOVED IT!
THAT WAS PRETTY IMPRESSIVE. I CAN'T BELIEVE YOU DID THAT TOTALLY ON THE FLY.
YOU PRAC-TICALLY LEARNED ALL YOUR LINES!
DO YOU HAVE ANY IDEA HOW HARD I WORKED TO LEARN MINE?!
OH, I LIKE THIS! KEEP PRAISING ME!
OKAY. YOU WERE GREAT!
YOU KNOW, IT'S KIND OF LIKE US...
...ISN'T IT?
HUH?

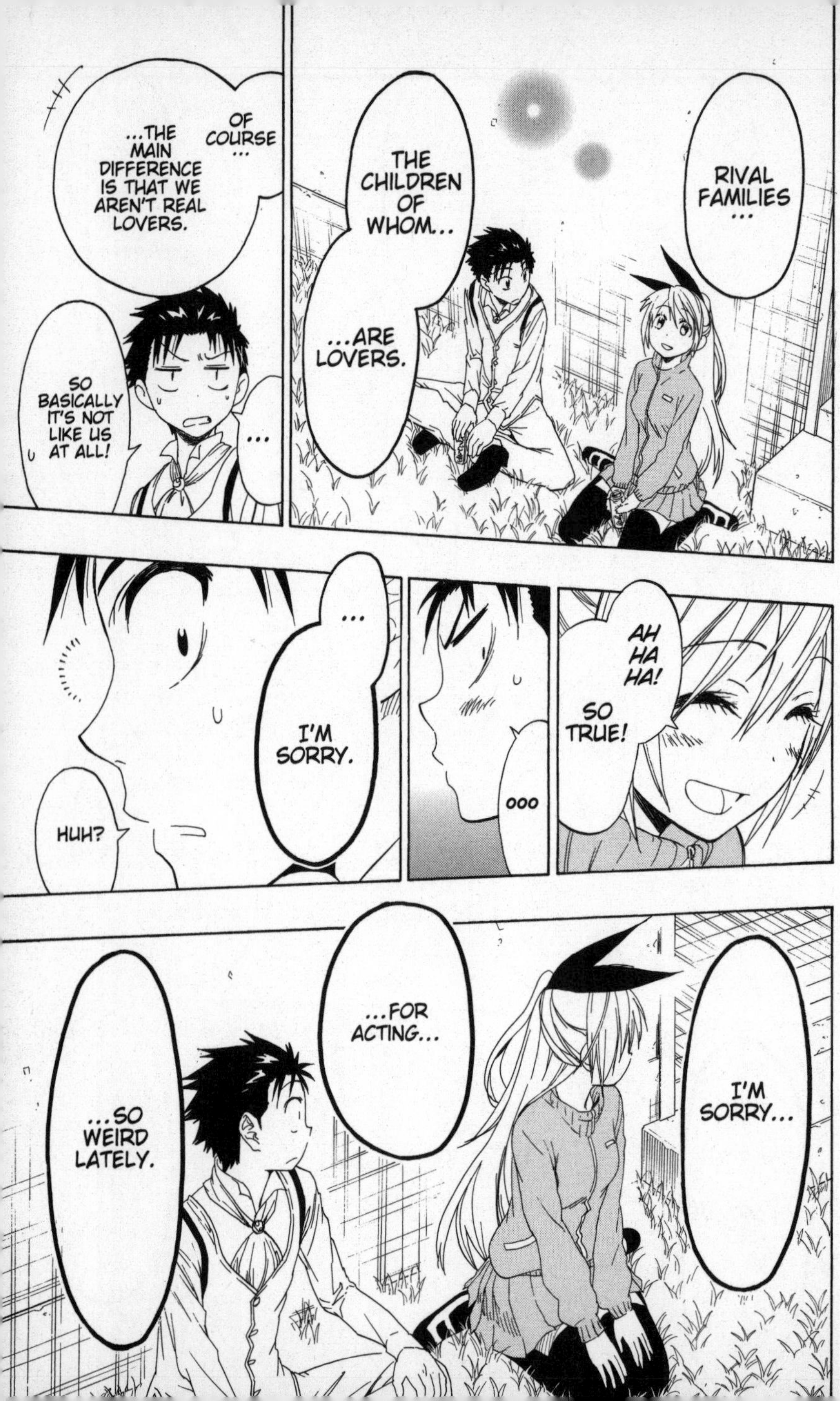
RIVAL FAMILIES...
THE CHILDREN OF WHOM...
...ARE LOVERS.
OF COURSE...
...THE MAIN DIFFERENCE IS THAT WE AREN'T REAL LOVERS.
...
SO BASICALLY IT'S NOT LIKE US AT ALL!
AH HA HA!
SO TRUE!
ooo
...
I'M SORRY.
HUH?
I'M SORRY...
...FOR ACTING...
...SO WEIRD LATELY.

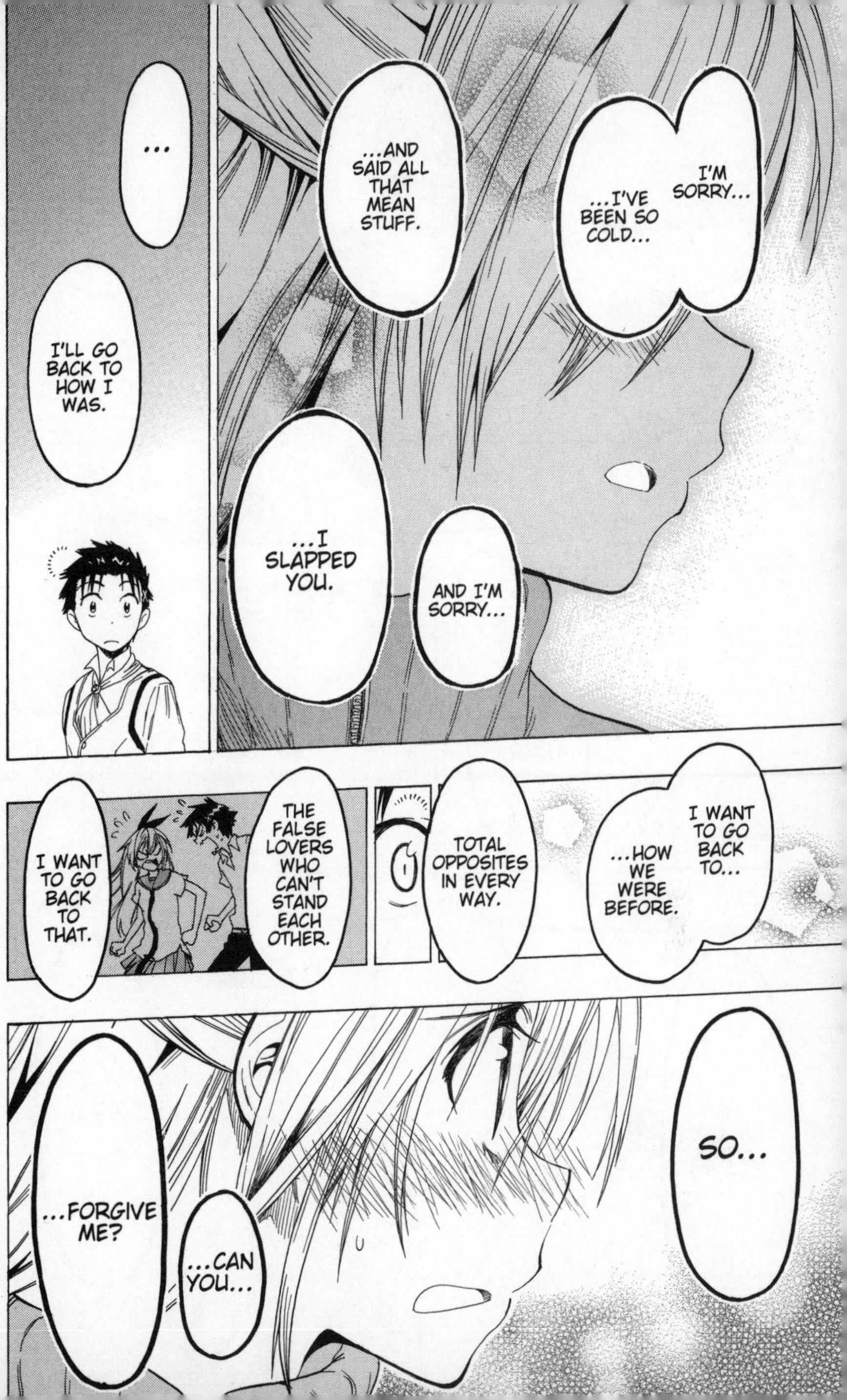
I'M SORRY...
...I'VE BEEN SO COLD...
...AND SAID ALL THAT MEAN STUFF.
AND I'M SORRY...
...I SLAPPED YOU.
...
I'LL GO BACK TO HOW I WAS.
I WANT TO GO BACK TO...
...HOW WE WERE BEFORE.
TOTAL OPPOSITES IN EVERY WAY.
THE FALSE LOVERS WHO CAN'T STAND EACH OTHER.
I WANT TO GO BACK TO THAT.
SO...
...CAN YOU...
...FORGIVE ME?

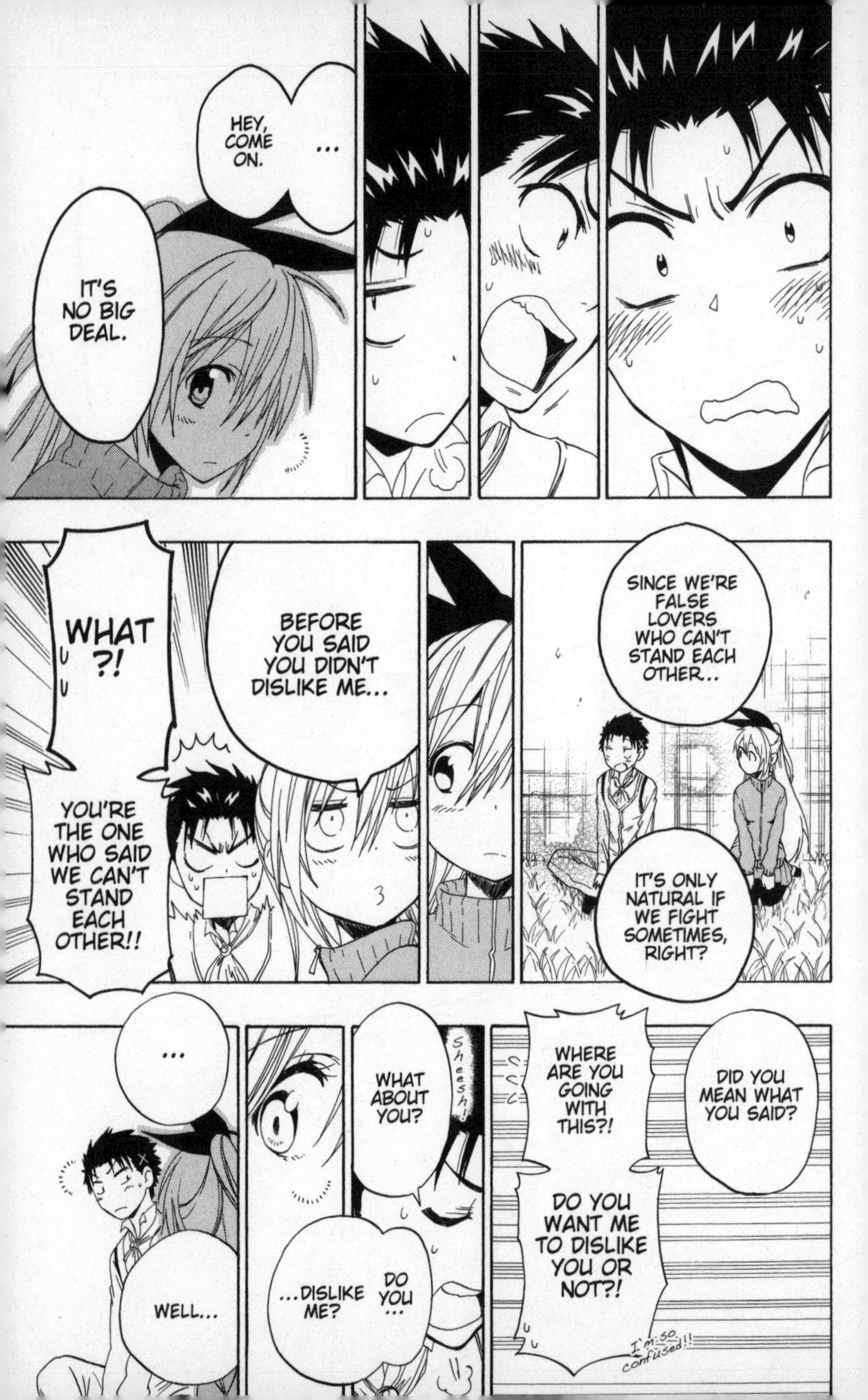
...
HEY, COME ON.
IT'S NO BIG DEAL.
SINCE WE'RE FALSE LOVERS WHO CAN'T STAND EACH OTHER...
IT'S ONLY NATURAL IF WE FIGHT SOMETIMES, RIGHT?
BEFORE YOU SAID YOU DIDN'T DISLIKE ME...
WHAT ?!
YOU'RE THE ONE WHO SAID WE CAN'T STAND EACH OTHER!!
DID YOU MEAN WHAT YOU SAID?
WHERE ARE YOU GOING WITH THIS?!
DO YOU WANT ME TO DISLIKE YOU OR NOT?!
I'm so confused!!
Sheesh!
WHAT ABOUT YOU?
DO YOU...
...DISLIKE ME?
...
WELL...

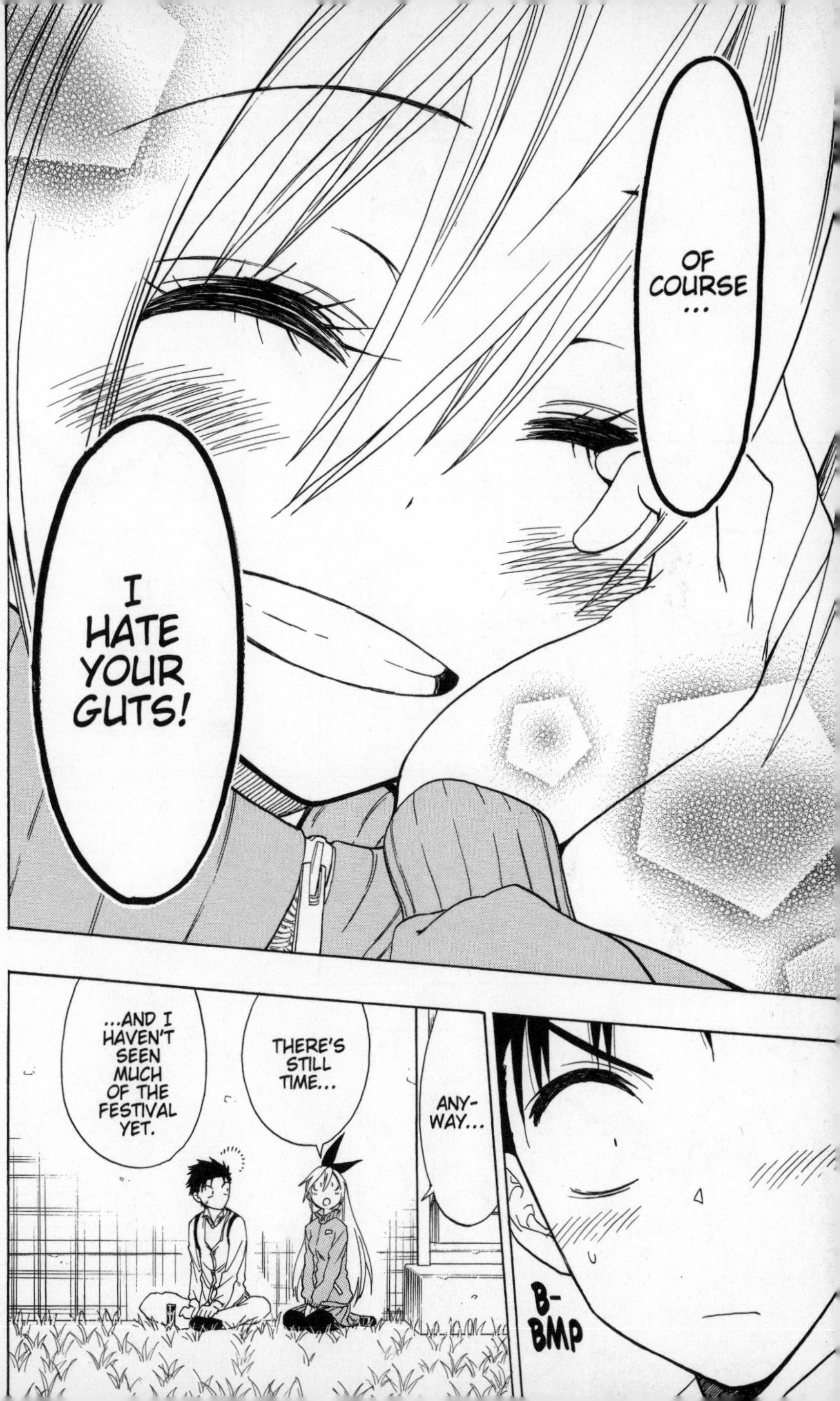
OF COURSE...
I HATE YOUR GUTS!
ANY-WAY...
B-BMP
THERE'S STILL TIME...
...AND I HAVEN'T SEEN MUCH OF THE FESTIVAL YET.

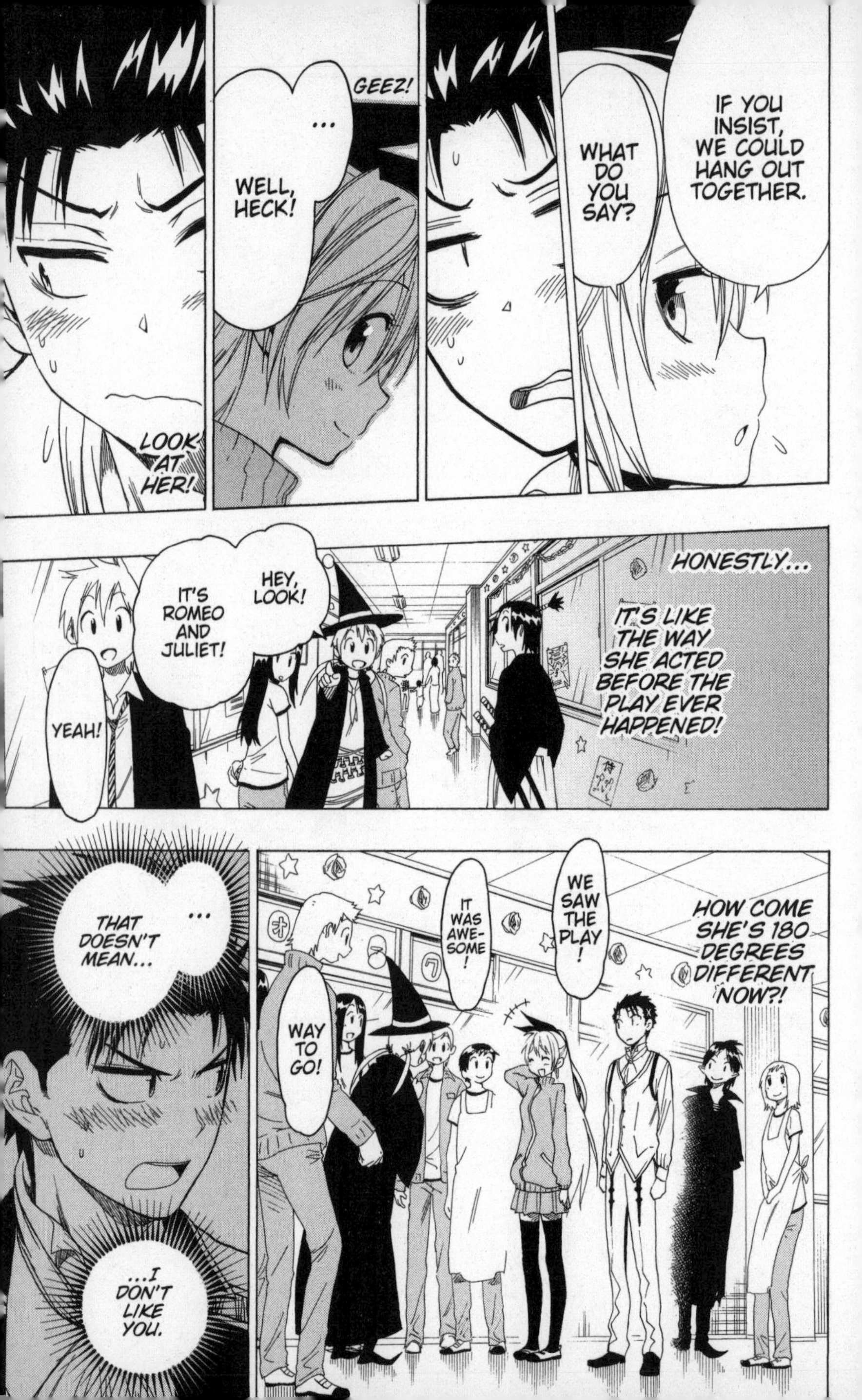
IF YOU INSIST, WE COULD HANG OUT TOGETHER.
WHAT DO YOU SAY?
GEEZ!
...
WELL, HECK!
LOOK AT HER!
HONESTLY...
IT'S LIKE THE WAY SHE ACTED BEFORE THE PLAY EVER HAPPENED!
HEY, LOOK!
IT'S ROMEO AND JULIET!
YEAH!
HOW COME SHE'S 180 DEGREES DIFFERENT NOW?!
WE SAW THE PLAY!
IT WAS AWE-SOME!
WAY TO GO!
...
THAT DOESN'T MEAN...
...I DON'T LIKE YOU.

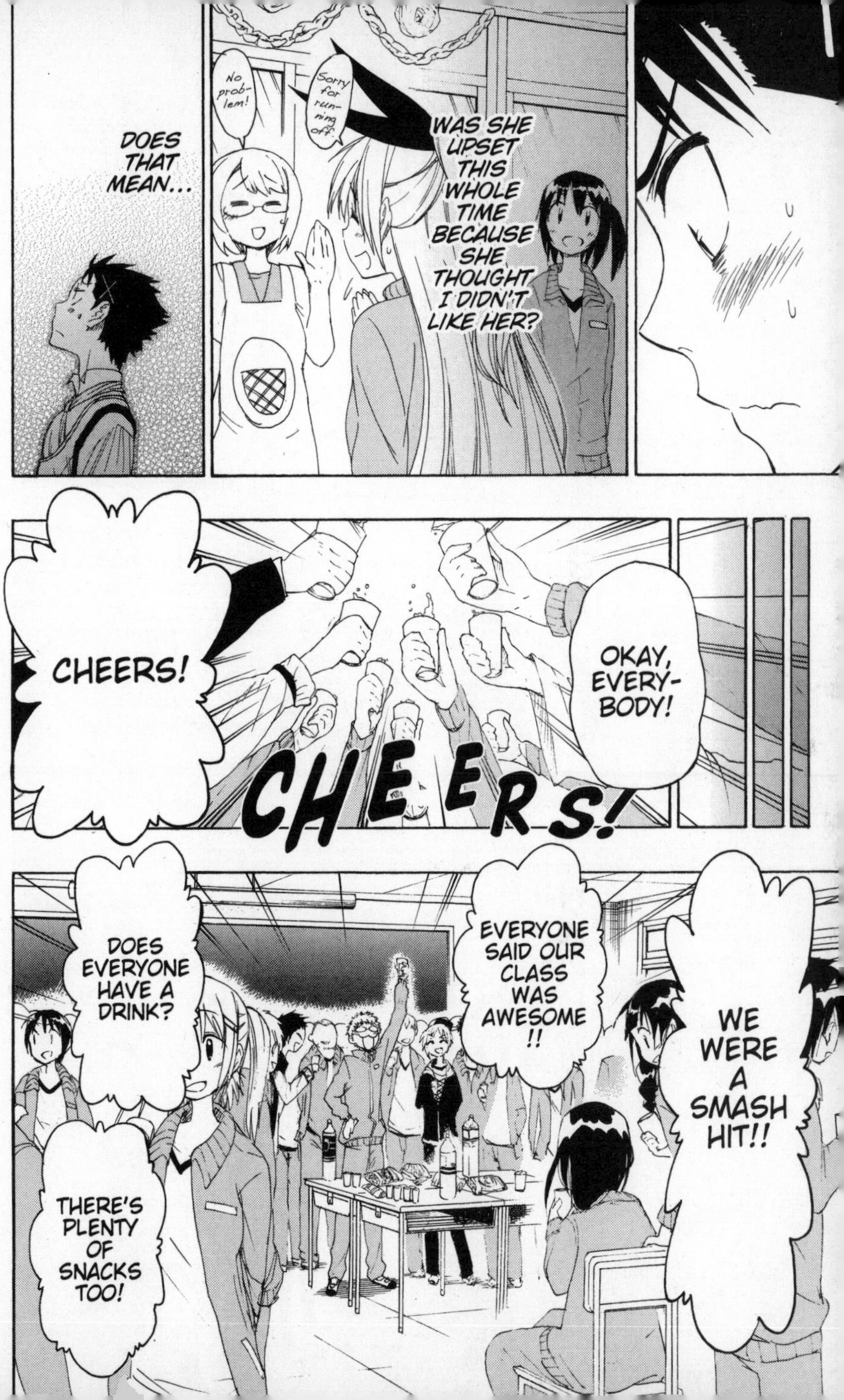
Sorry for running off.
No problem!
WAS SHE UPSET THIS WHOLE TIME BECAUSE SHE THOUGHT I DIDN'T LIKE HER?
DOES THAT MEAN...
OKAY, EVERYBODY!
CHEERS!
CHEERS!
WE WERE A SMASH HIT!!
EVERYONE SAID OUR CLASS WAS AWESOME!!
DOES EVERYONE HAVE A DRINK?
THERE'S PLENTY OF SNACKS TOO!

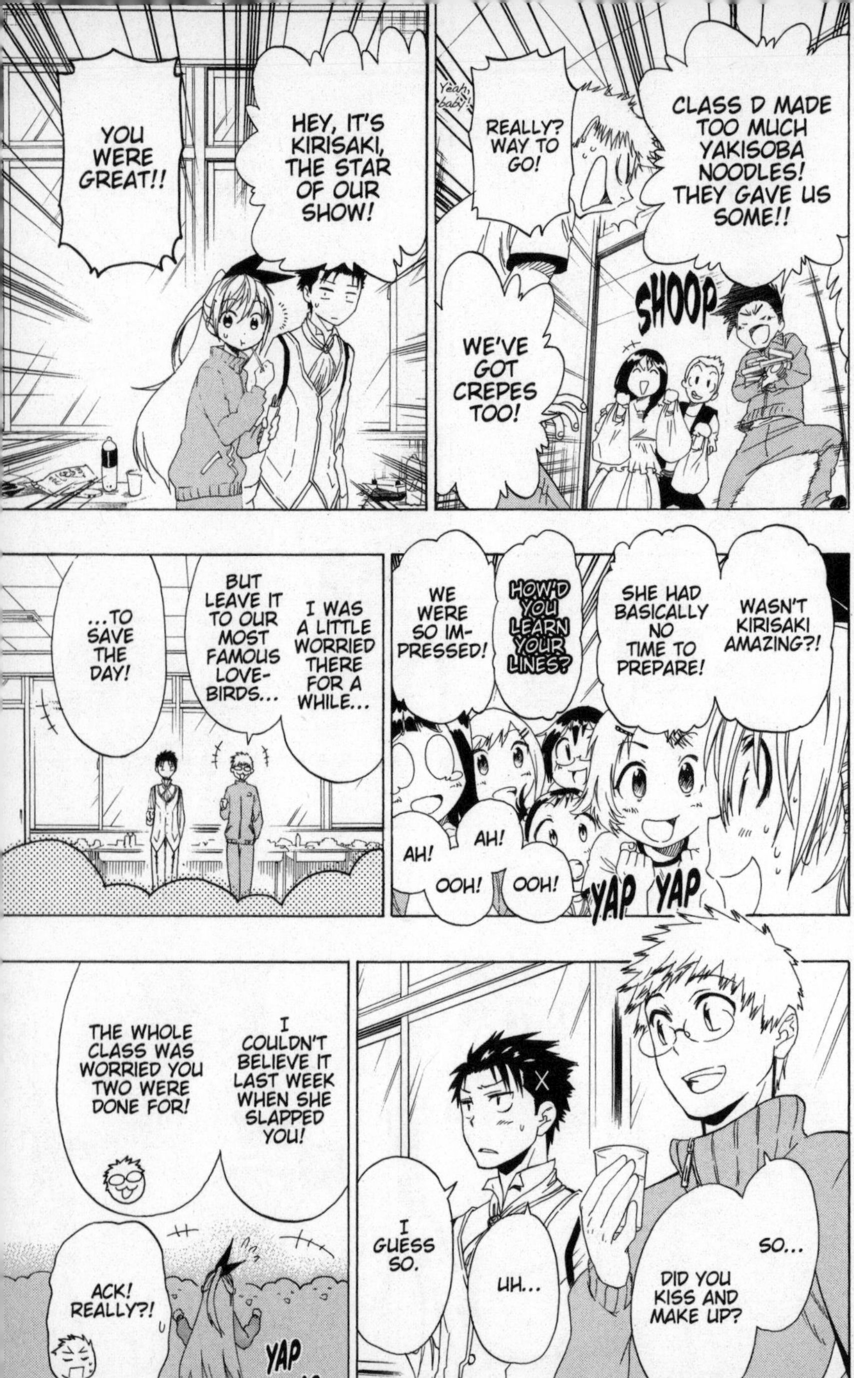
CLASS D MADE TOO MUCH YAKISOBA NOODLES! THEY GAVE US SOME!!
Yeah, baby!
REALLY? WAY TO GO!
SHOOP
WE'VE GOT CREPES TOO!
HEY, IT'S KIRISAKI, THE STAR OF OUR SHOW!
YOU WERE GREAT!!
WASN'T KIRISAKI AMAZING?!
SHE HAD BASICALLY NO TIME TO PREPARE!
HOW'D YOU LEARN YOUR LINES?
WE WERE SO IMPRESSED!
AH!
AH!
OOH!
OOH!
YAP YAP
I WAS A LITTLE WORRIED THERE FOR A WHILE...
BUT LEAVE IT TO OUR MOST FAMOUS LOVE-BIRDS...
...TO SAVE THE DAY!
SO...
DID YOU KISS AND MAKE UP?
UH...
I GUESS SO.
I COULDN'T BELIEVE IT LAST WEEK WHEN SHE SLAPPED YOU!
THE WHOLE CLASS WAS WORRIED YOU TWO WERE DONE FOR!
ACK! REALLY?!
YAP
YAP
YAP

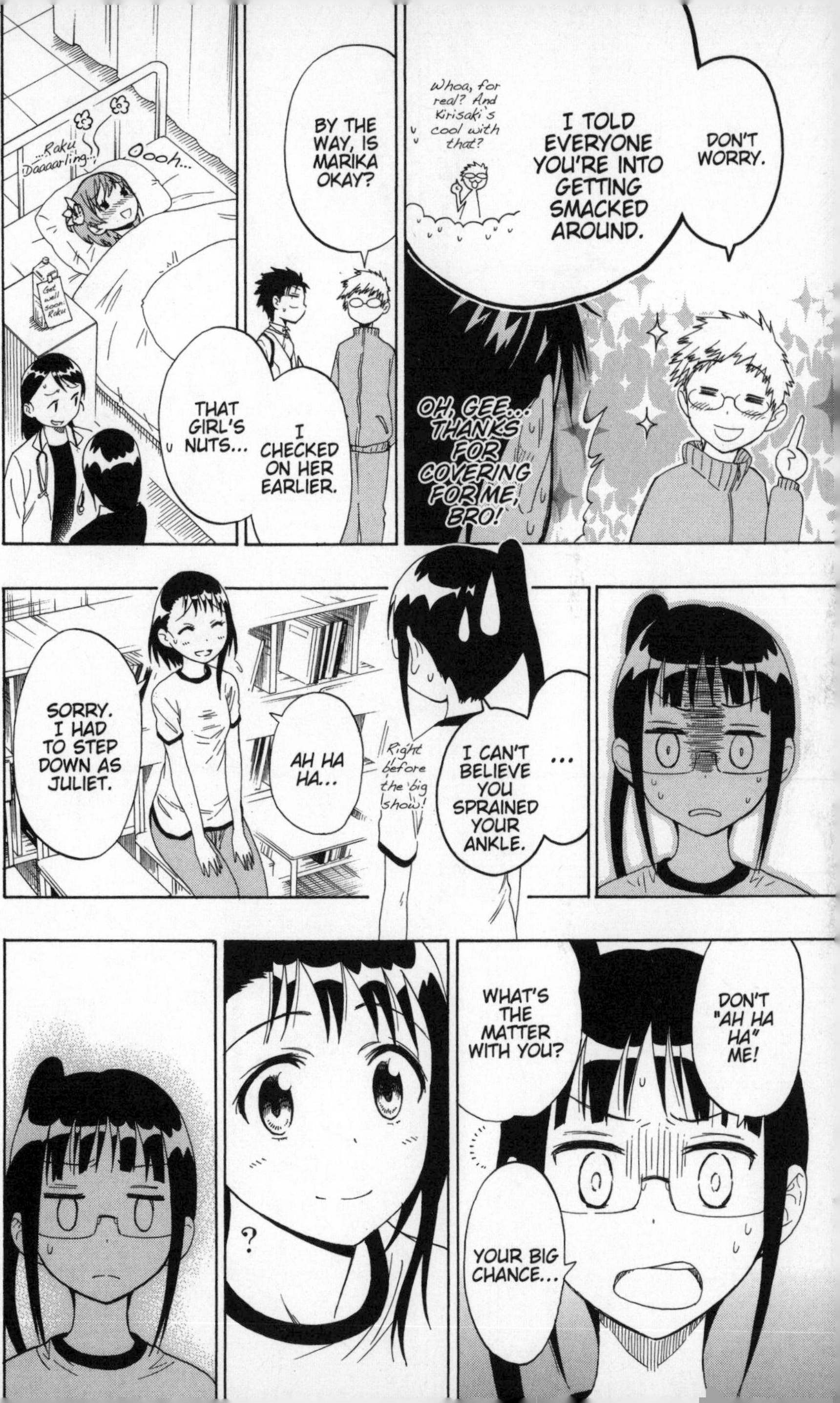
DON'T WORRY.
I TOLD EVERYONE YOU'RE INTO GETTING SMACKED AROUND.
Whoa, for real? And Kirisaki's cool with that?
OH, GEE... THANKS FOR COVERING FOR ME, BRO!
BY THE WAY, IS MARIKA OKAY?
I CHECKED ON HER EARLIER.
THAT GIRL'S NUTS...
...Raku Daaaarling...
Oooh...
Get well soon. Raku
...
I CAN'T BELIEVE YOU SPRAINED YOUR ANKLE.
Right before the big show!
AH HA HA...
SORRY. I HAD TO STEP DOWN AS JULIET.
DON'T "AH HA HA" ME!
WHAT'S THE MATTER WITH YOU?
YOUR BIG CHANCE...
?

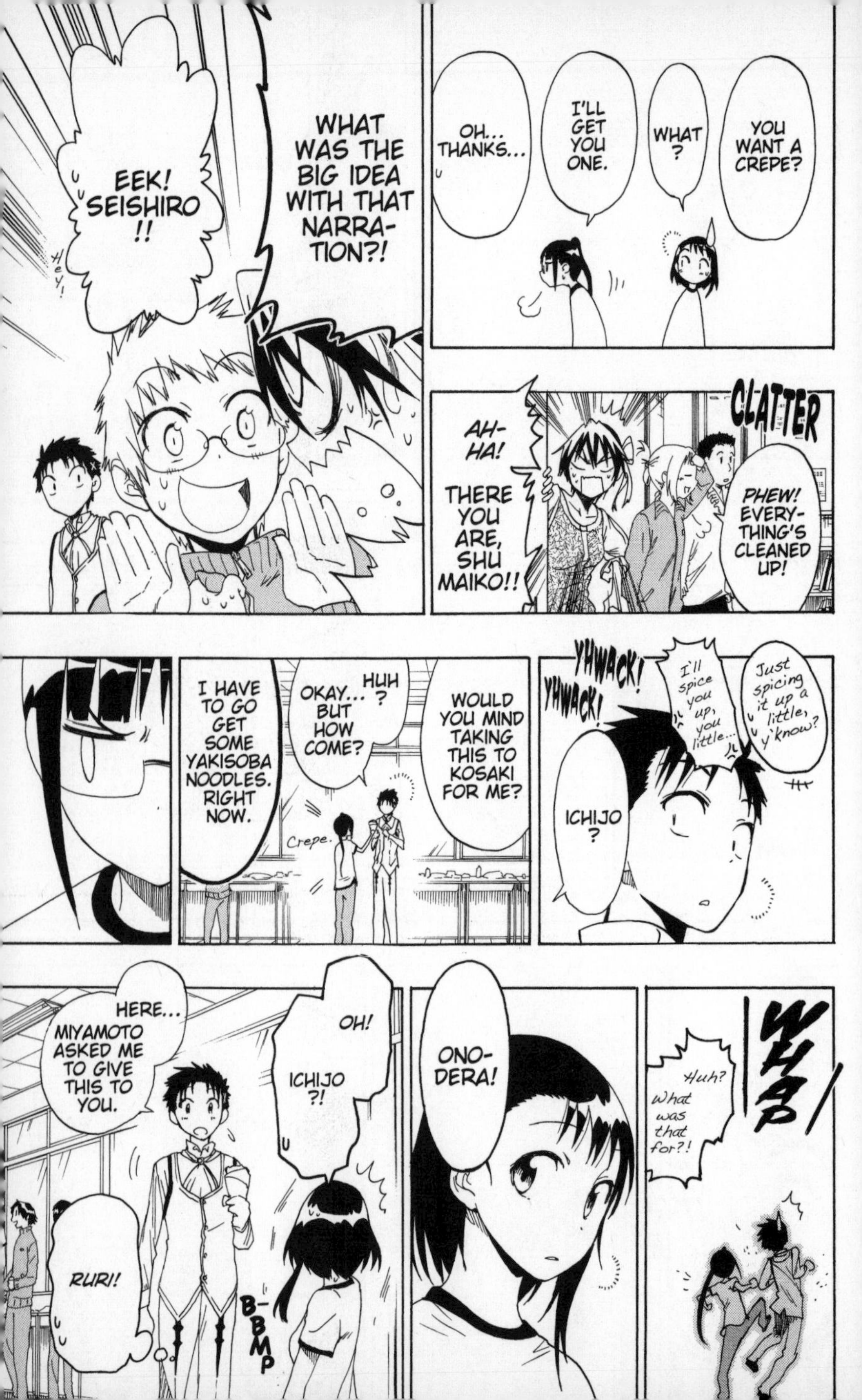
YOU WANT A CREPE?
WHAT?
I'LL GET YOU ONE.
OH... THANKS...
CLATTER
PHEW! EVERYTHING'S CLEANED UP!
AH-HA! THERE YOU ARE, SHU MAIKO!!
WHAT WAS THE BIG IDEA WITH THAT NARRATION?!
EEK! SEISHIRO!!
Hey!
Just spicing it up a little, y'know?
I'll spice you up, you little...
YHWACK!
YHWACK!
ICHIJO?
WOULD YOU MIND TAKING THIS TO KOSAKI FOR ME?
HUH?
OKAY... BUT HOW COME?
I HAVE TO GO GET SOME YAKISOBA NOODLES. RIGHT NOW.
Crepe.
WHAP
Huh? What was that for?!
ONO-DERA!
OH!
ICHIJO?!
B-BMP
HERE... MIYAMOTO ASKED ME TO GIVE THIS TO YOU.
RURI!

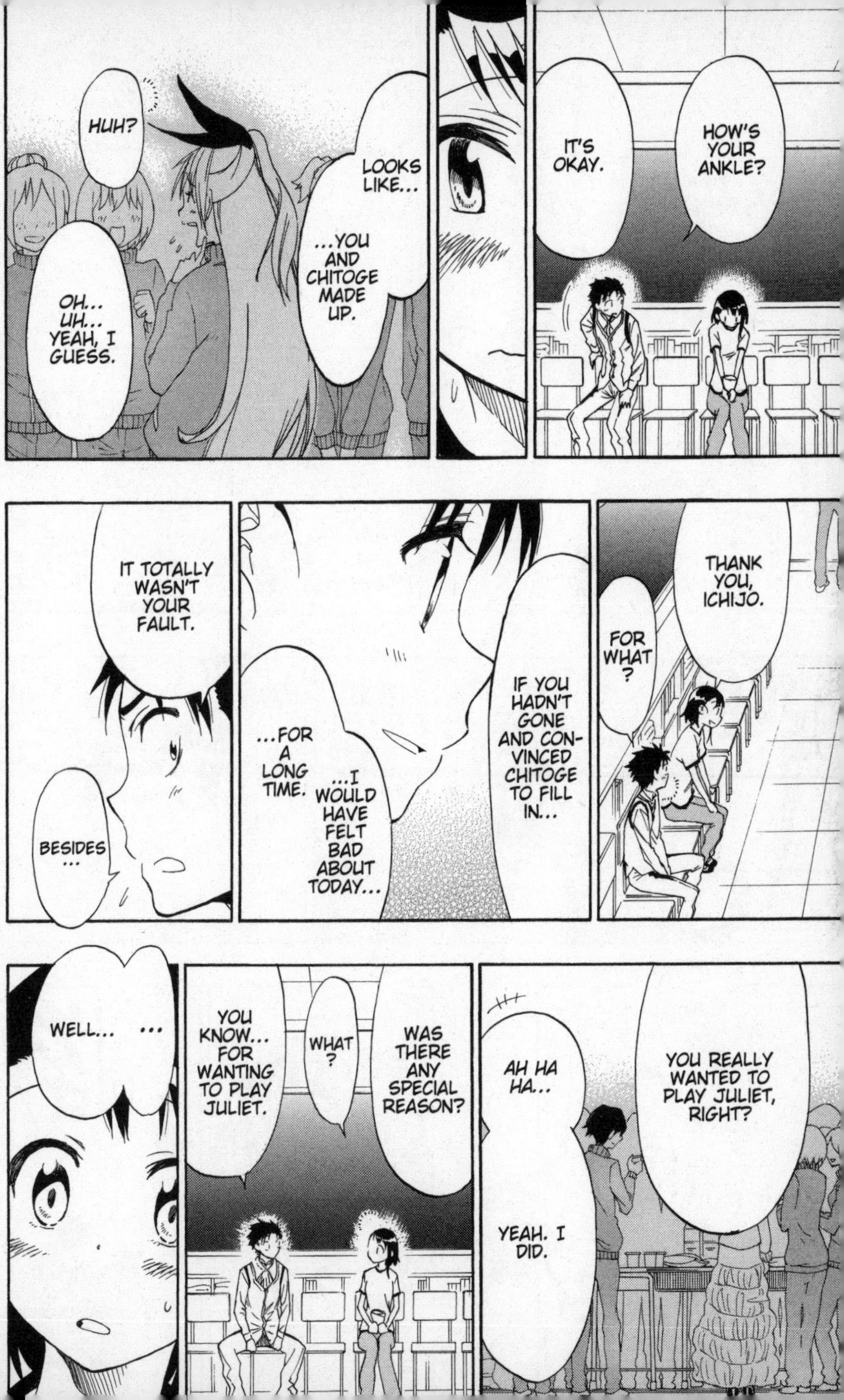
HOW'S YOUR ANKLE?
IT'S OKAY.
LOOKS LIKE...
...YOU AND CHITOGE MADE UP.
HUH?
OH... UH... YEAH, I GUESS.
THANK YOU, ICHIJO.
FOR WHAT?
IF YOU HADN'T GONE AND CONVINCED CHITOGE TO FILL IN...
...I WOULD HAVE FELT BAD ABOUT TODAY...
...FOR A LONG TIME.
IT TOTALLY WASN'T YOUR FAULT.
BESIDES...
YOU REALLY WANTED TO PLAY JULIET, RIGHT?
AH HA HA...
YEAH. I DID.
WAS THERE ANY SPECIAL REASON?
WHAT?
YOU KNOW... FOR WANTING TO PLAY JULIET.
...
WELL...

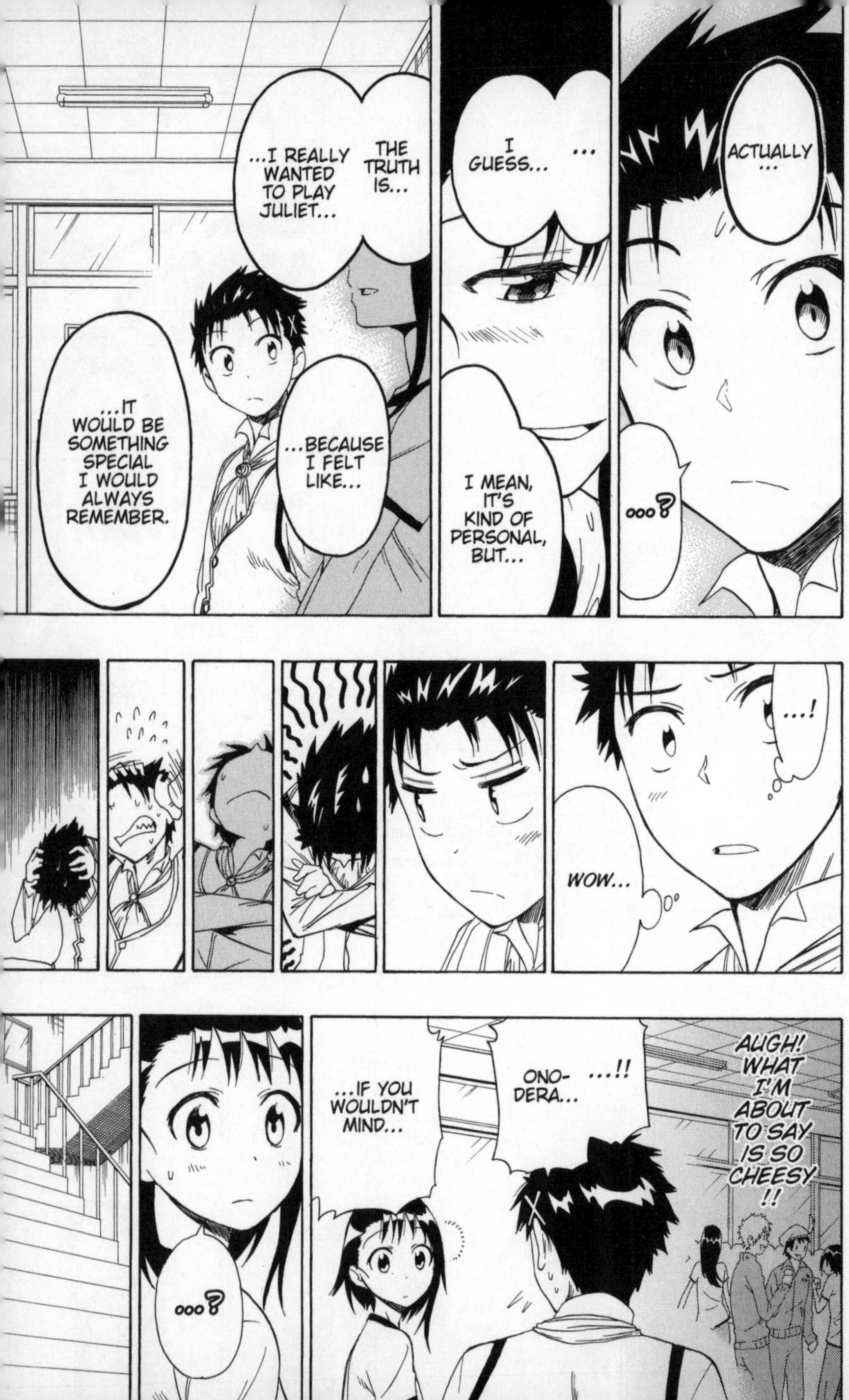
ACTUALLY ...
ooo?
...
I GUESS...
I MEAN, IT'S KIND OF PERSONAL, BUT...
THE TRUTH IS...
...I REALLY WANTED TO PLAY JULIET...
...BECAUSE I FELT LIKE...
...IT WOULD BE SOMETHING SPECIAL I WOULD ALWAYS REMEMBER.
...!
WOW...
AUGH! WHAT I'M ABOUT TO SAY IS SO CHEESY!!
...!!
ONO-DERA...
...IF YOU WOULDN'T MIND...
ooo?

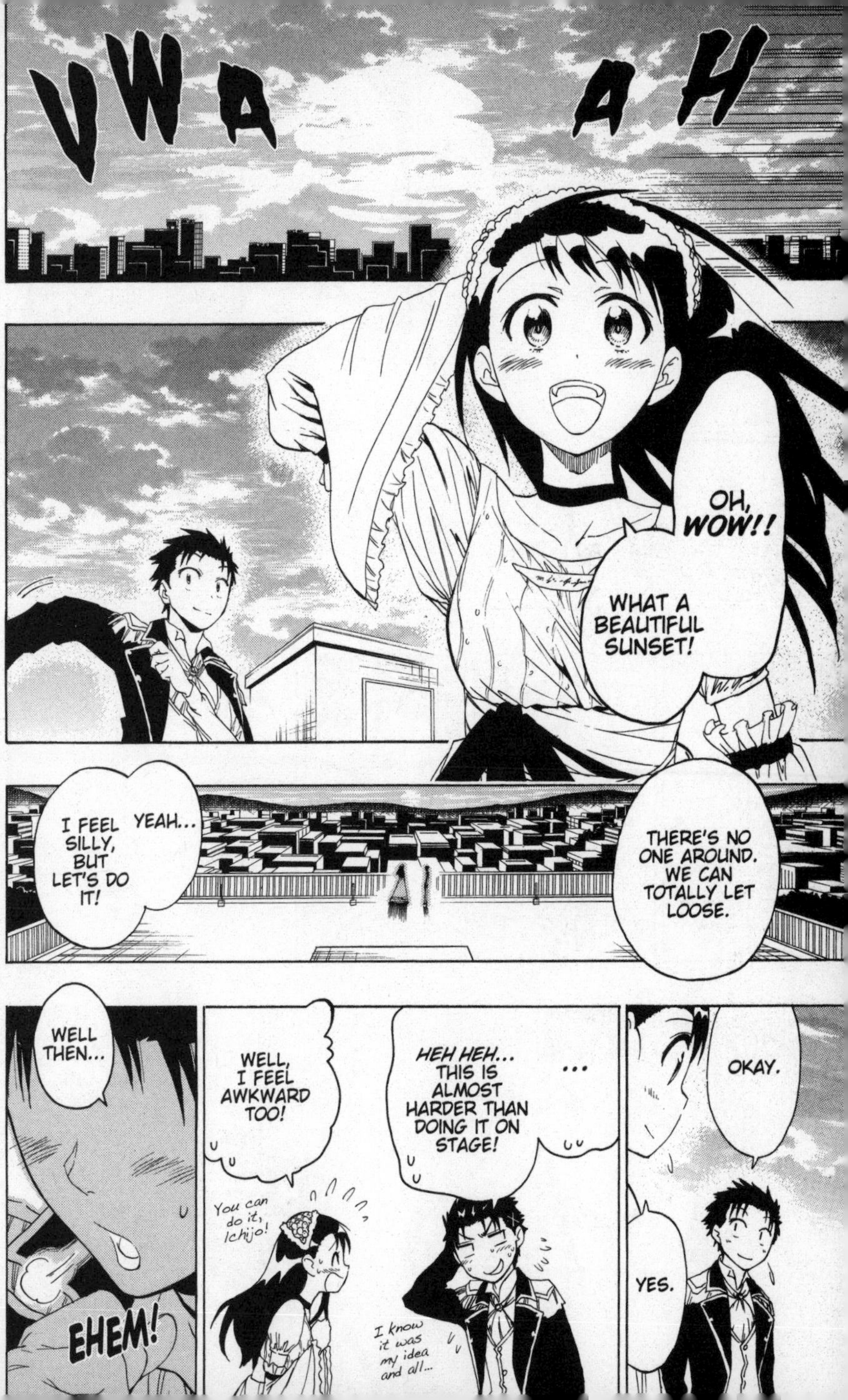
UWA AH
OH, WOW!!
WHAT A BEAUTIFUL SUNSET!
THERE'S NO ONE AROUND. WE CAN TOTALLY LET LOOSE.
YEAH... I FEEL SILLY, BUT LET'S DO IT!
OKAY.
YES.
...
HEH HEH... THIS IS ALMOST HARDER THAN DOING IT ON STAGE!
WELL, I FEEL AWKWARD TOO!
You can do it, Ichijo!
I know it was my idea and all...
WELL THEN...
EHEM!

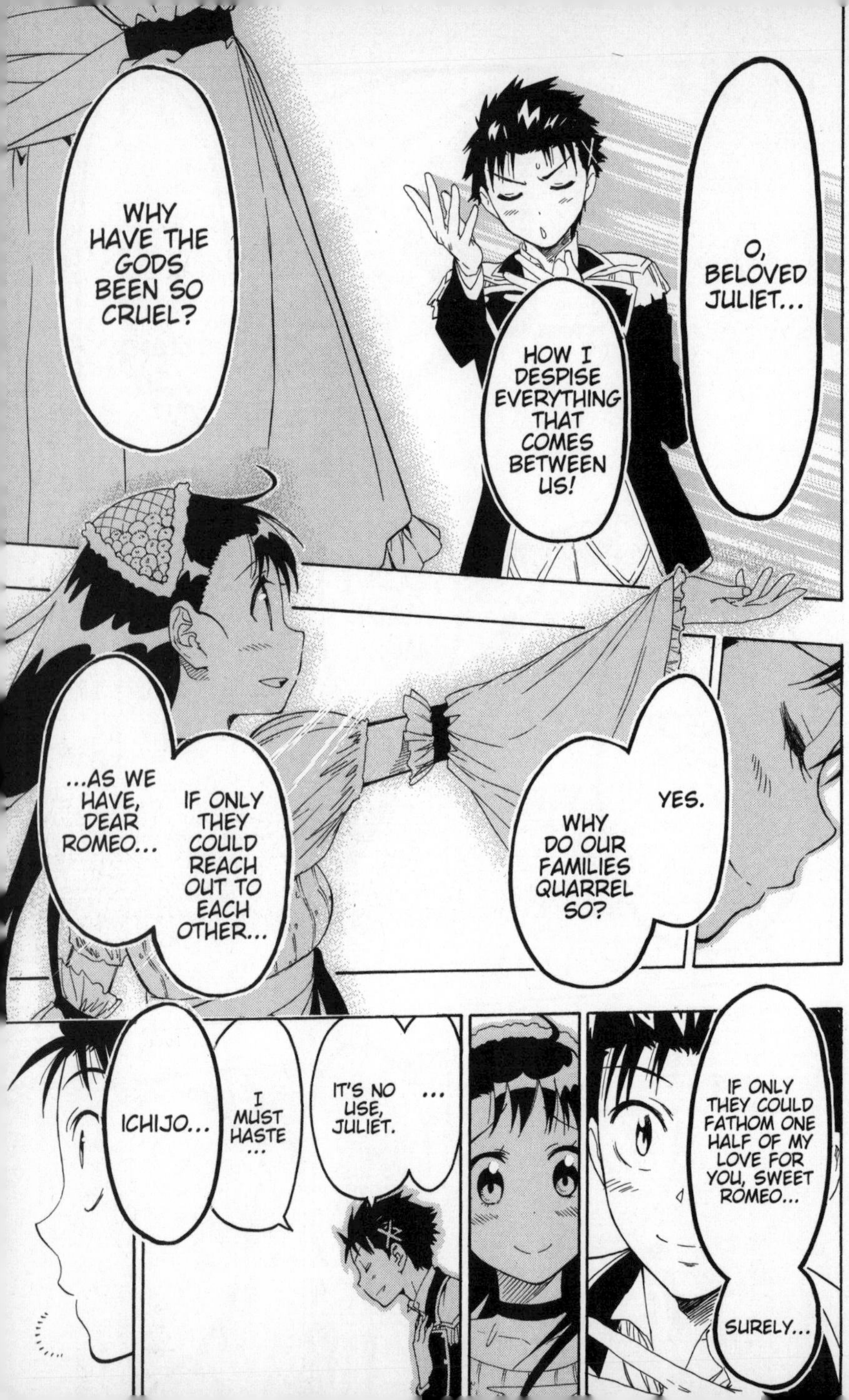
O, BELOVED JULIET...
HOW I DESPISE EVERYTHING THAT COMES BETWEEN US!
WHY HAVE THE GODS BEEN SO CRUEL?
YES.
WHY DO OUR FAMILIES QUARREL SO?
IF ONLY THEY COULD REACH OUT TO EACH OTHER...
...AS WE HAVE, DEAR ROMEO...
IF ONLY THEY COULD FATHOM ONE HALF OF MY LOVE FOR YOU, SWEET ROMEO...
SURELY...
...
IT'S NO USE, JULIET.
I MUST HASTE ...
ICHIJO...

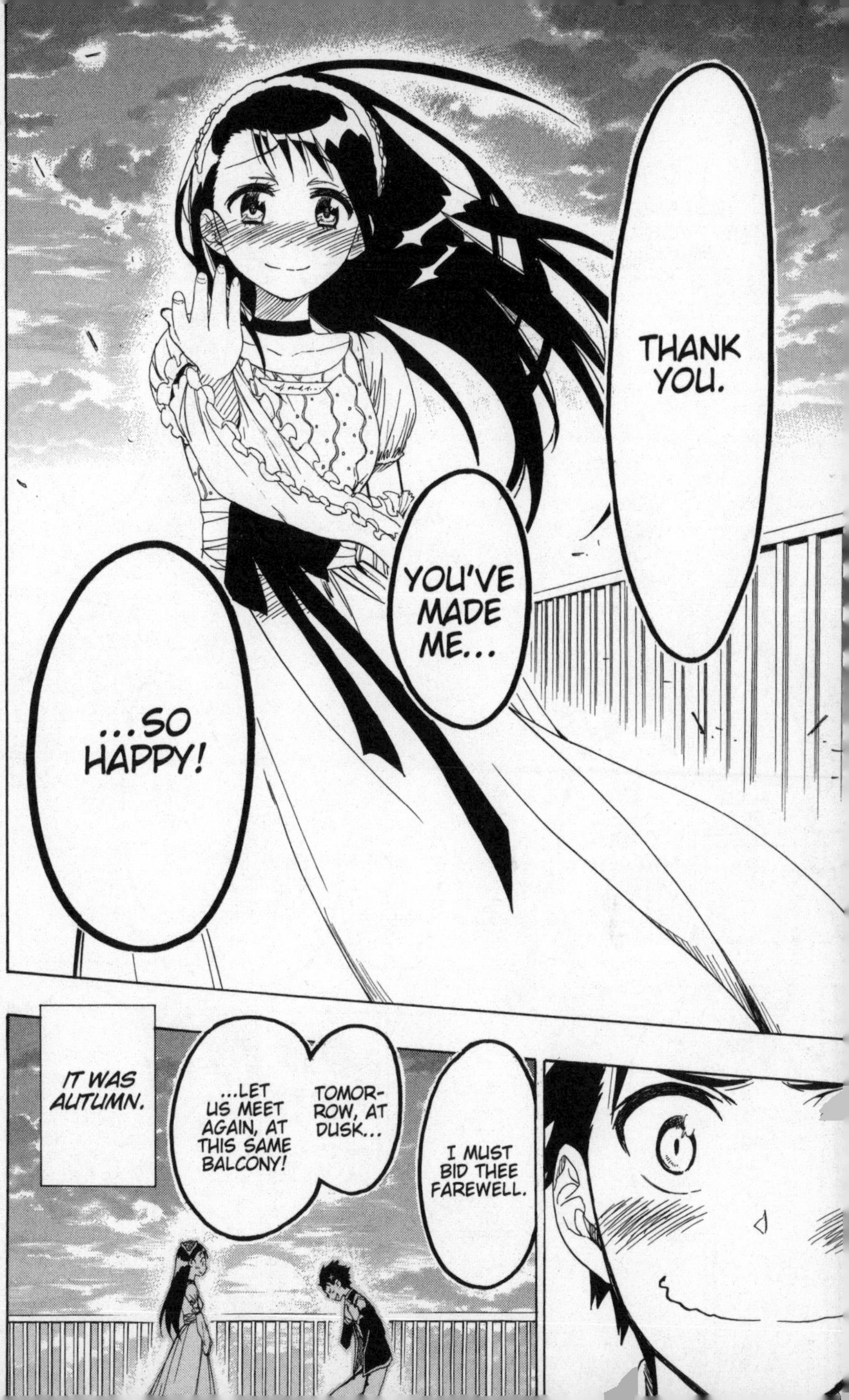
THANK YOU.
YOU'VE MADE ME...
...SO HAPPY!
I MUST BID THEE FAREWELL.
TOMORROW, AT DUSK...
...LET US MEET AGAIN, AT THIS SAME BALCONY!
IT WAS AUTUMN.

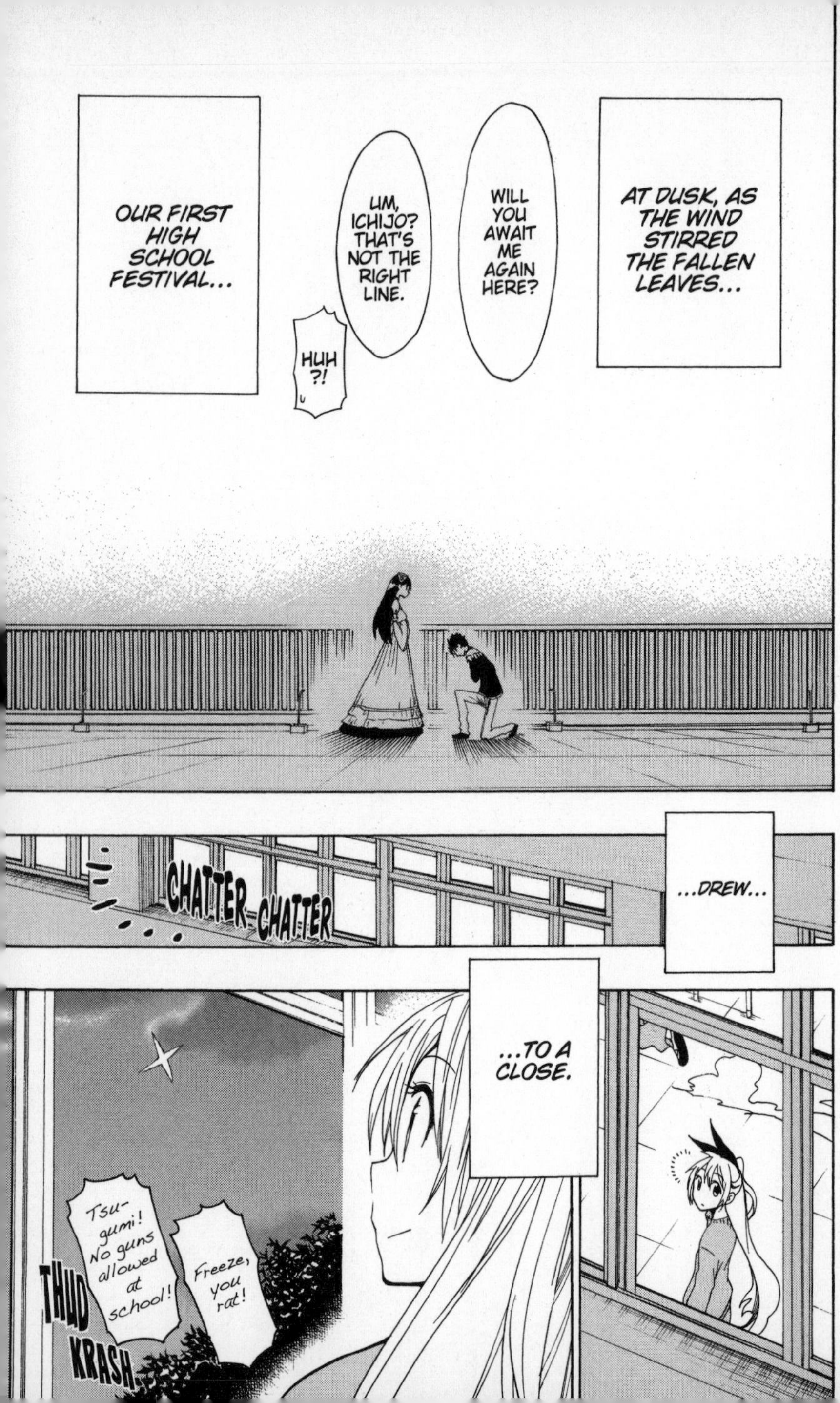
AT DUSK, AS THE WIND STIRRED THE FALLEN LEAVES…
WILL YOU AWAIT ME AGAIN HERE?
UM, ICHIJO? THAT'S NOT THE RIGHT LINE.
HUH ?!
OUR FIRST HIGH SCHOOL FESTIVAL…
…DREW…
CHATTER CHATTER
…TO A CLOSE.
Freeze, you rat!
Tsu-gumi! No guns allowed at school!
THUD
KRASH

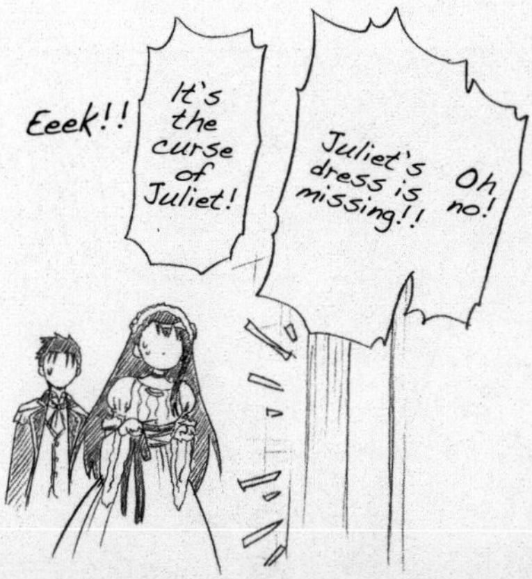
Oh no!
Juliet's dress is missing!!
It's the curse of Juliet!
Eeek!!

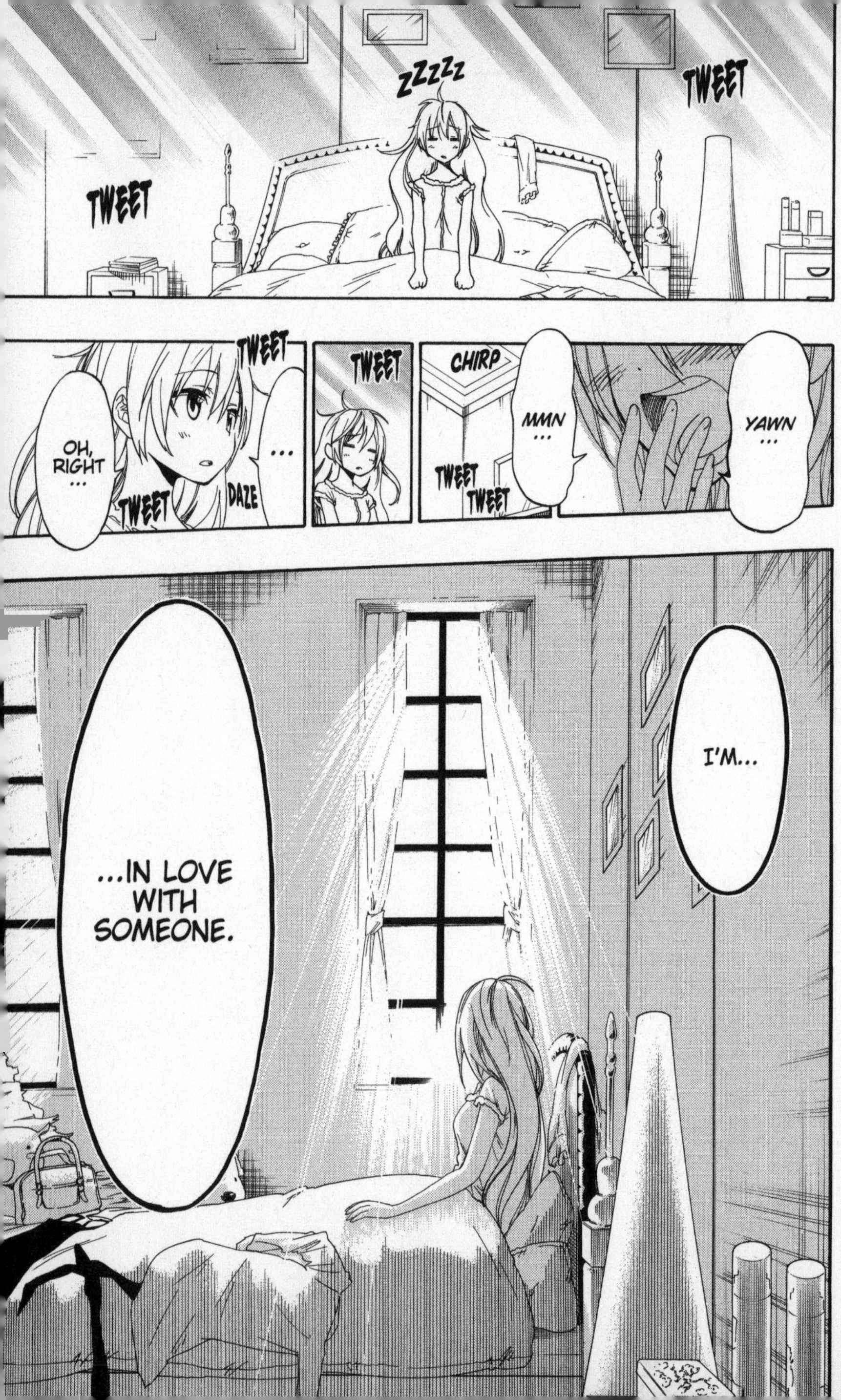
TWEET
ZZZZZ
TWEET
YAWN...
MMN...
CHIRP
TWEET
TWEET
TWEET
TWEET
...
DAZE
OH, RIGHT...
TWEET
I'M...
...IN LOVE WITH SOMEONE.

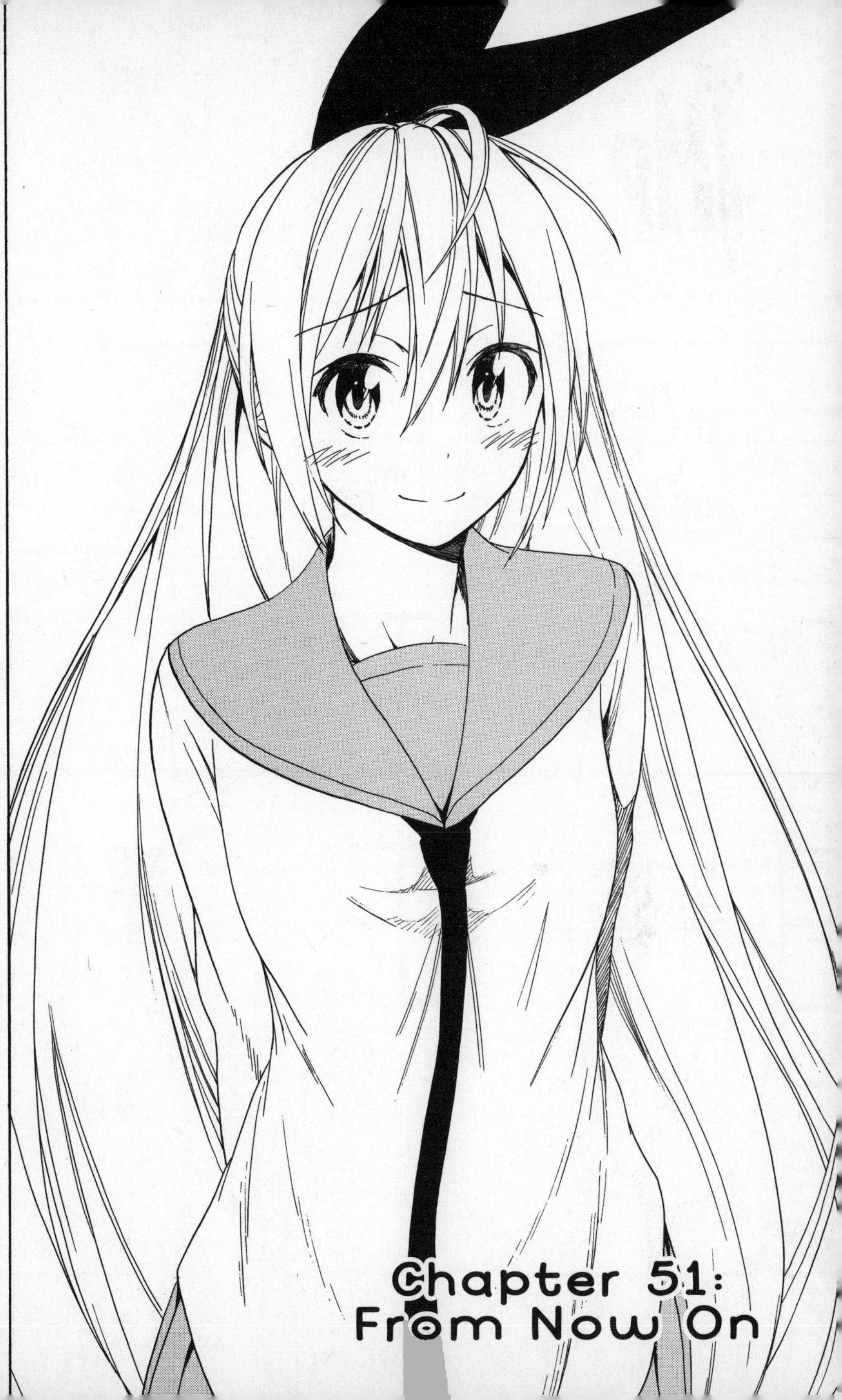
Chapter 51:
From Now On

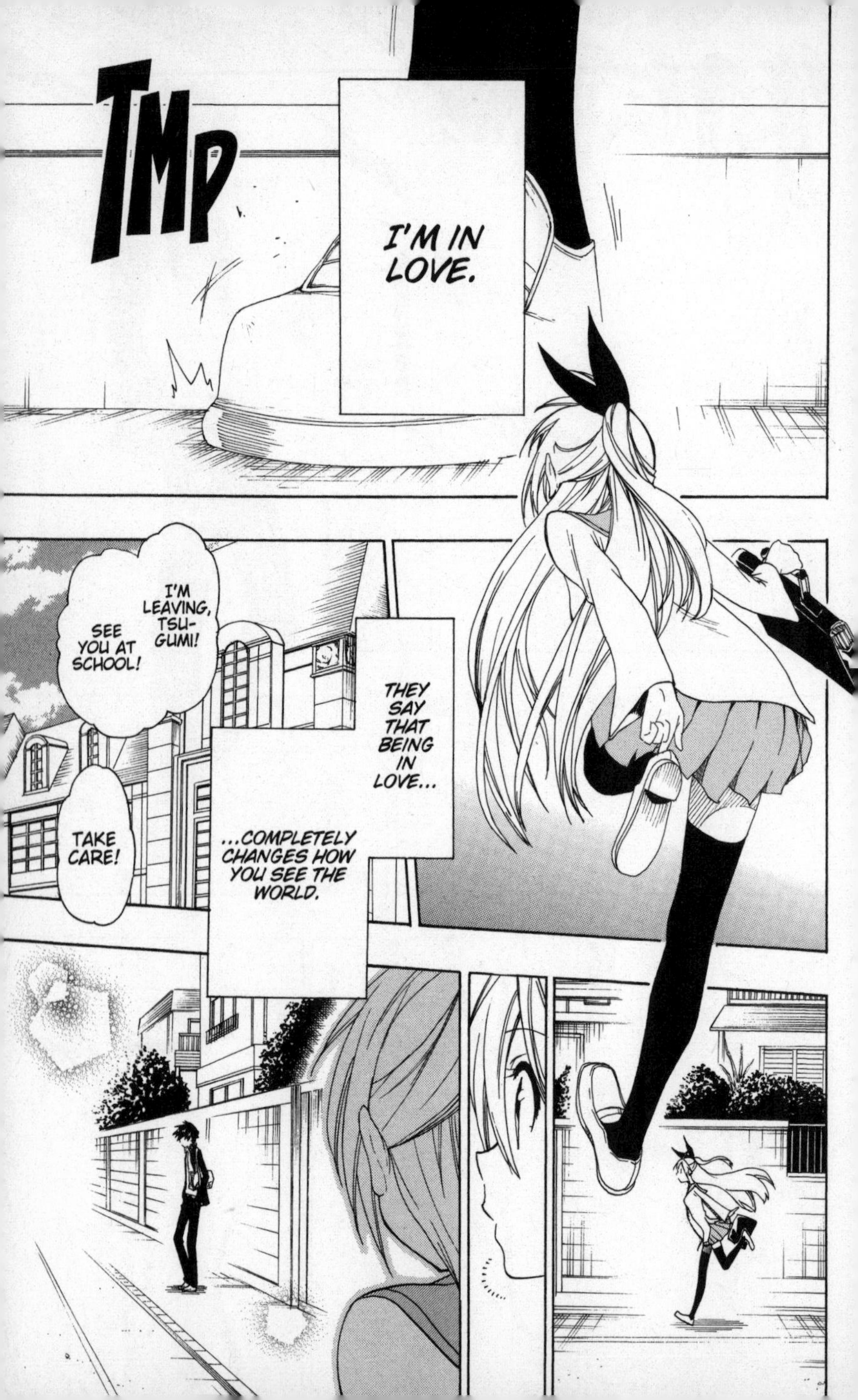
I'M IN LOVE.
TMP
THEY SAY THAT BEING IN LOVE...
...COMPLETELY CHANGES HOW YOU SEE THE WORLD.
I'M LEAVING, TSU-GUMI! SEE YOU AT SCHOOL!
TAKE CARE!

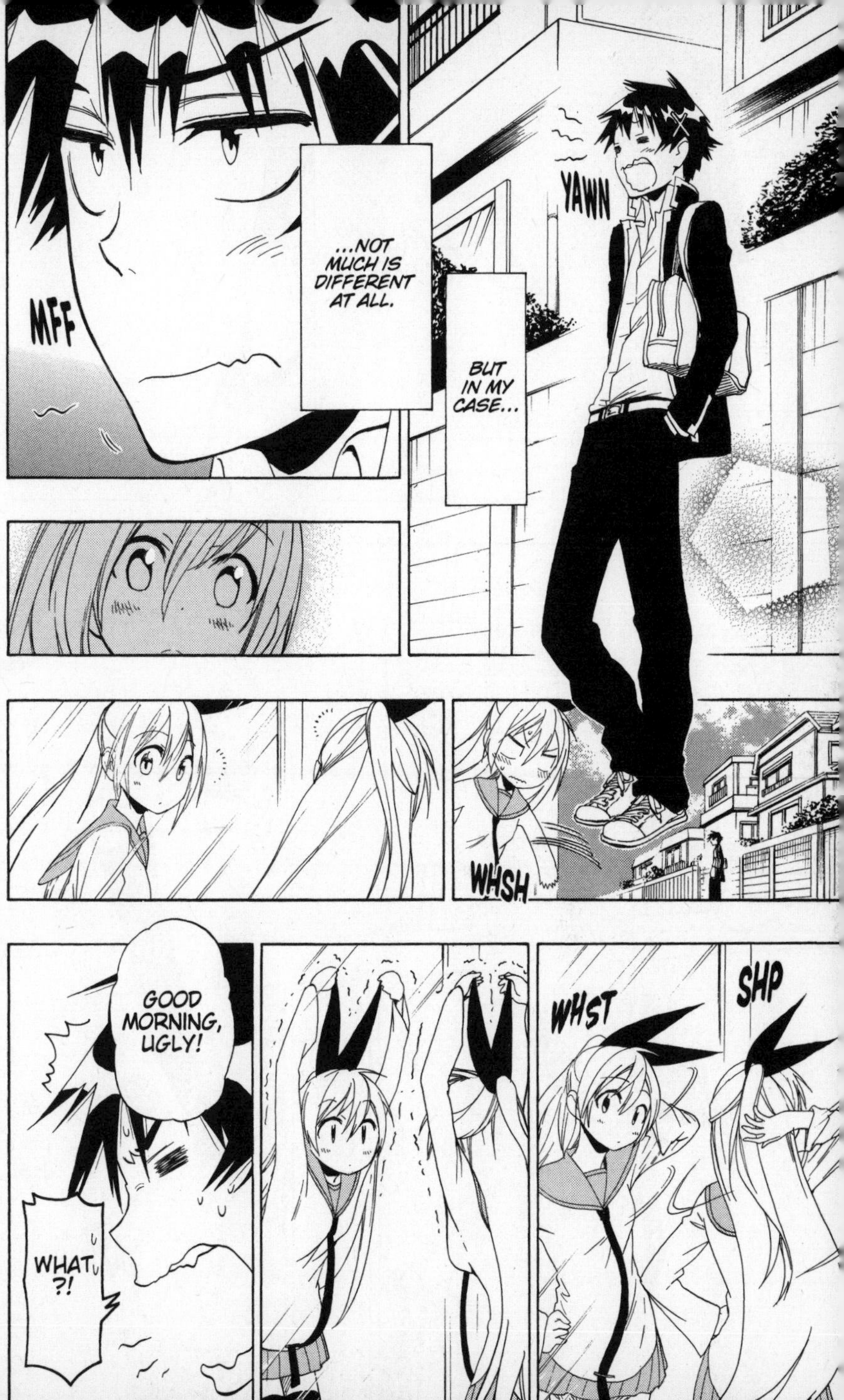
...NOT MUCH IS DIFFERENT AT ALL.
BUT IN MY CASE...
YAWN
MFF
WHSH
SHP
WHST
GOOD MORNING, UGLY!
WHAT?!

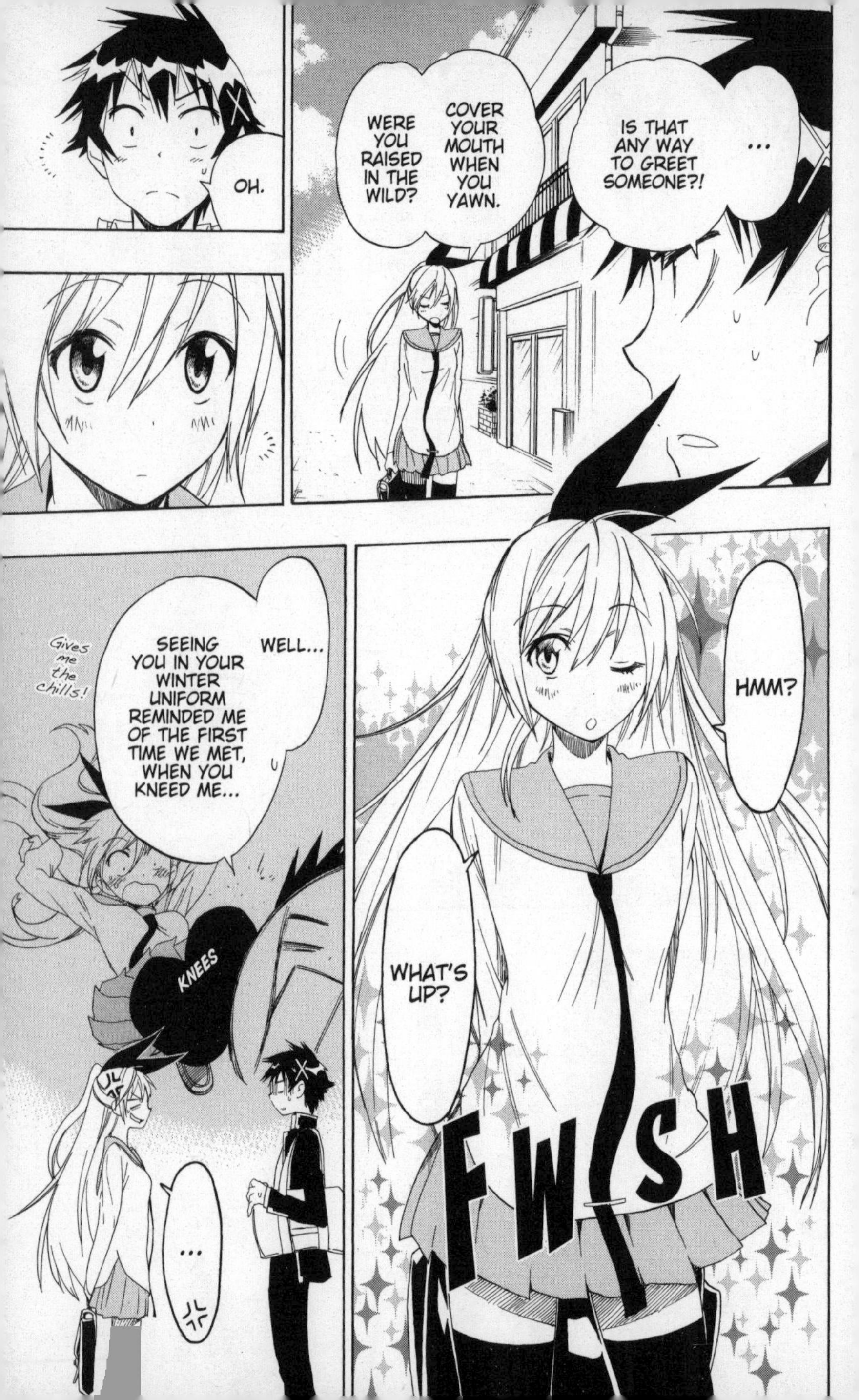
...
IS THAT ANY WAY TO GREET SOMEONE?!
COVER YOUR MOUTH WHEN YOU YAWN.
WERE YOU RAISED IN THE WILD?
OH.
HMM?
WHAT'S UP?
FWSH
WELL...
SEEING YOU IN YOUR WINTER UNIFORM REMINDED ME OF THE FIRST TIME WE MET, WHEN YOU KNEED ME...
Gives me the chills!
KNEES
...

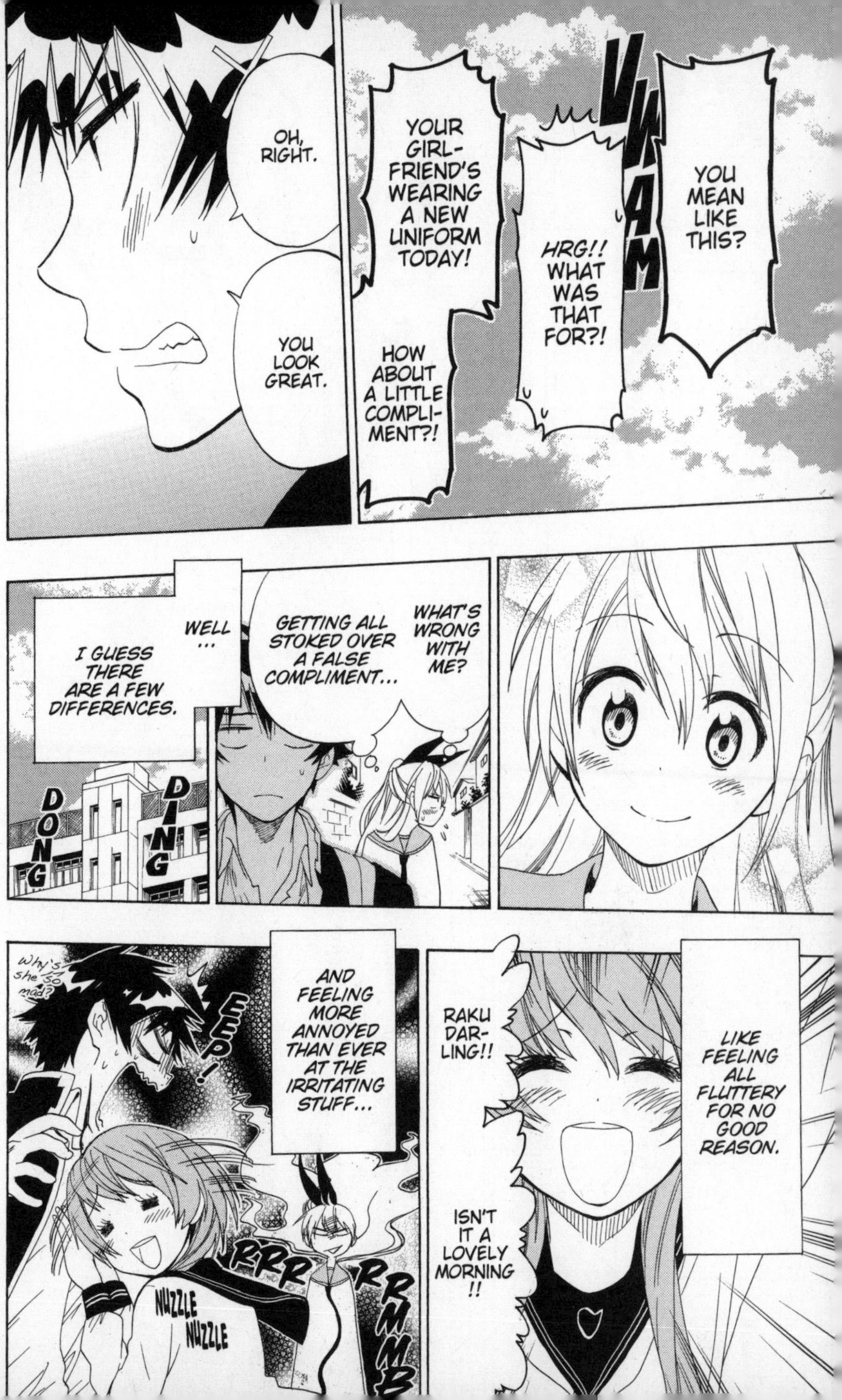
YOU MEAN LIKE THIS?
VWAM
HRG!! WHAT WAS THAT FOR?!
YOUR GIRLFRIEND'S WEARING A NEW UNIFORM TODAY!
HOW ABOUT A LITTLE COMPLIMENT?!
OH, RIGHT.
YOU LOOK GREAT.
WHAT'S WRONG WITH ME?
GETTING ALL STOKED OVER A FALSE COMPLIMENT...
WELL...
I GUESS THERE ARE A FEW DIFFERENCES.
DING
DONG
LIKE FEELING ALL FLUTTERY FOR NO GOOD REASON.
RAKU DARLING!!
ISN'T IT A LOVELY MORNING!!
AND FEELING MORE ANNOYED THAN EVER AT THE IRRITATING STUFF...
EEP!
Why's she so mad?
RRRRRMMB
NUZZLE NUZZLE

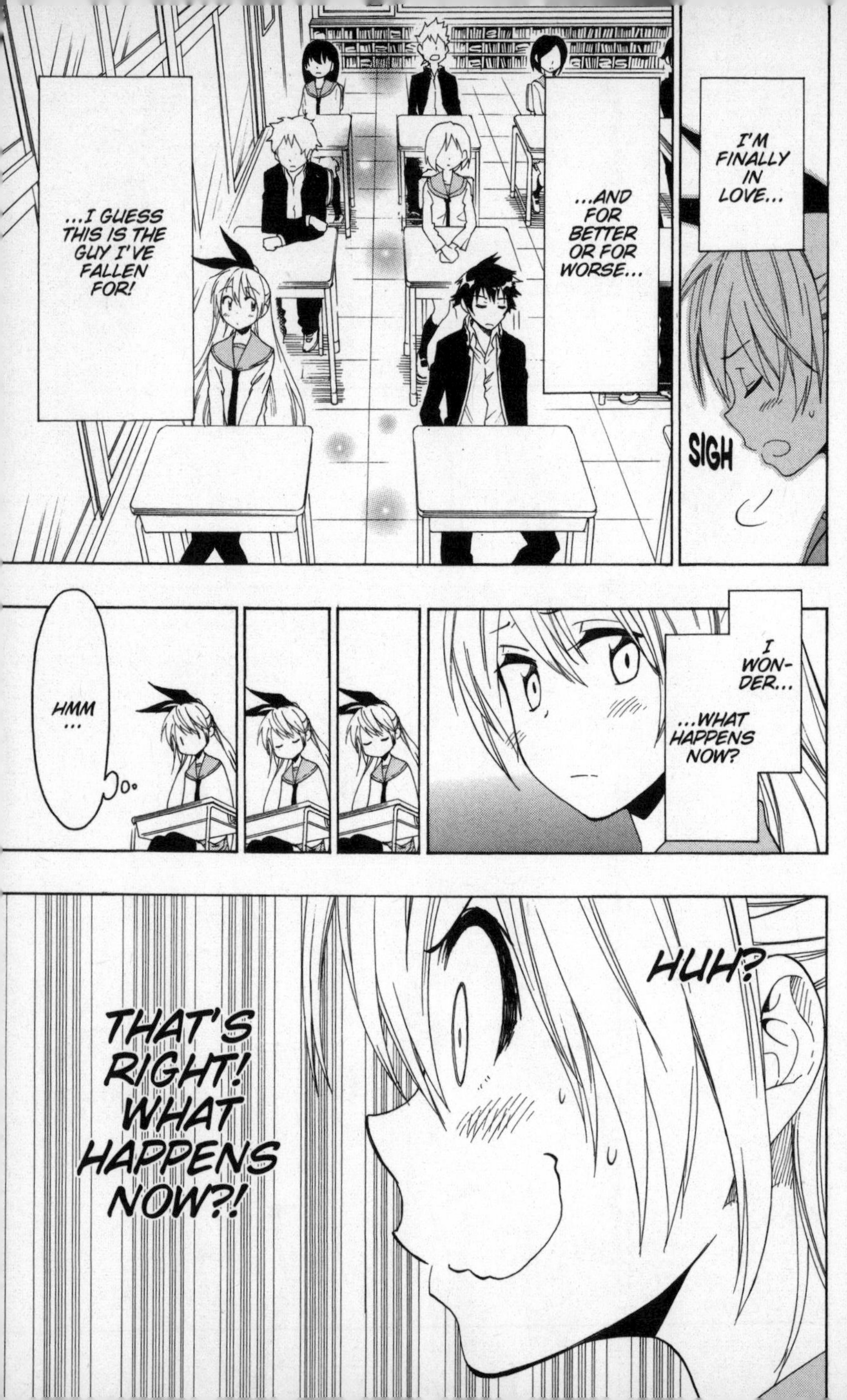
I'M FINALLY IN LOVE...
SIGH
...AND FOR BETTER OR FOR WORSE...
...I GUESS THIS IS THE GUY I'VE FALLEN FOR!
I WONDER...
...WHAT HAPPENS NOW?
HMM...
HUH?
THAT'S RIGHT! WHAT HAPPENS NOW?!

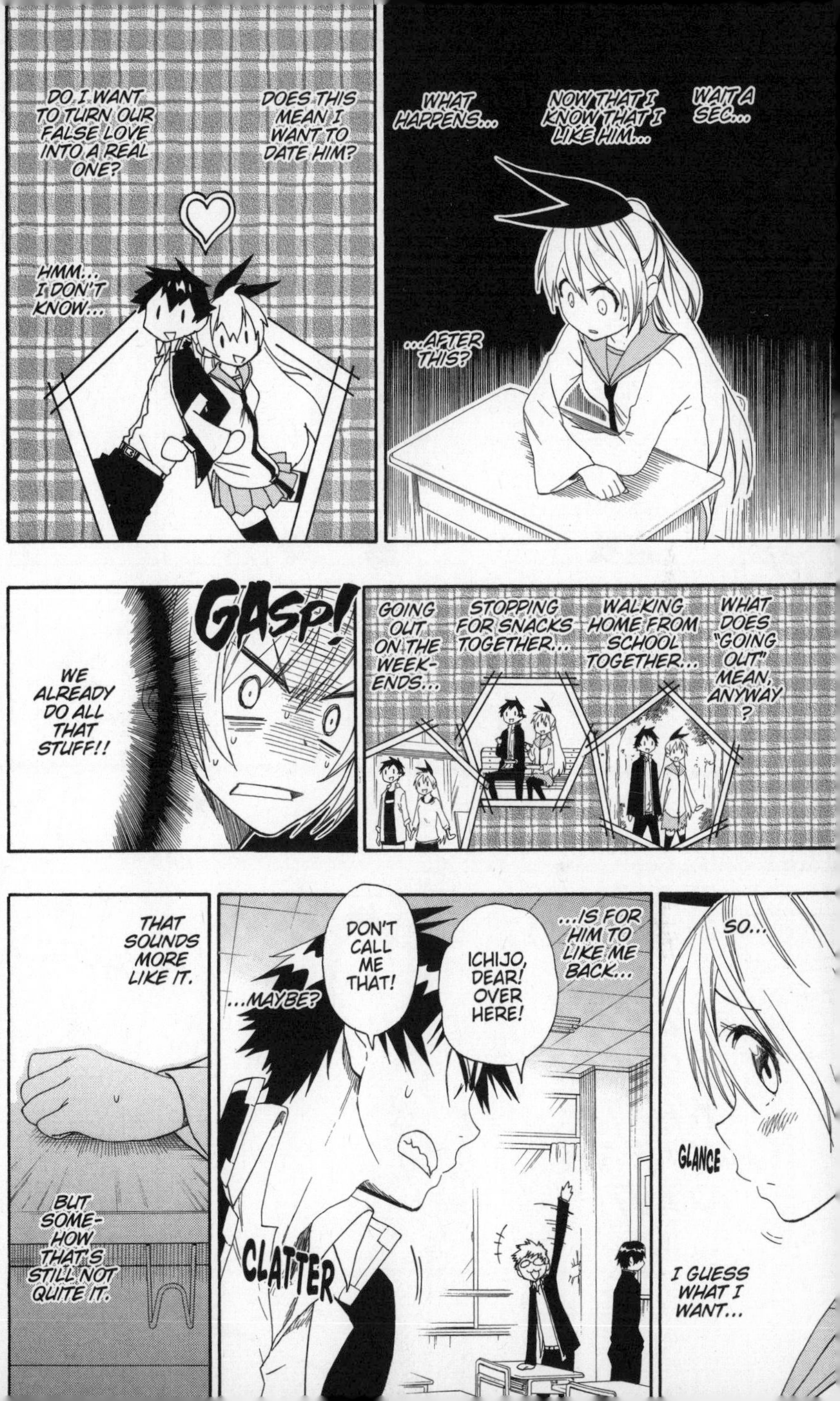
WAIT A SEC...
NOW THAT I KNOW THAT I LIKE HIM...
WHAT HAPPENS...
...AFTER THIS?
DOES THIS MEAN I WANT TO DATE HIM?
DO I WANT TO TURN OUR FALSE LOVE INTO A REAL ONE?
HMM... I DON'T KNOW...
WHAT DOES "GOING OUT" MEAN, ANYWAY?
WALKING HOME FROM SCHOOL TOGETHER...
STOPPING FOR SNACKS TOGETHER...
GOING OUT ON THE WEEK-ENDS...
GASP!
WE ALREADY DO ALL THAT STUFF!!
SO...
GLANCE
I GUESS WHAT I WANT...
...IS FOR HIM TO LIKE ME BACK...
ICHIJO, DEAR! OVER HERE!
DON'T CALL ME THAT!
...MAYBE?
CLATTER
THAT SOUNDS MORE LIKE IT.
BUT SOME-HOW THAT'S STILL NOT QUITE IT.

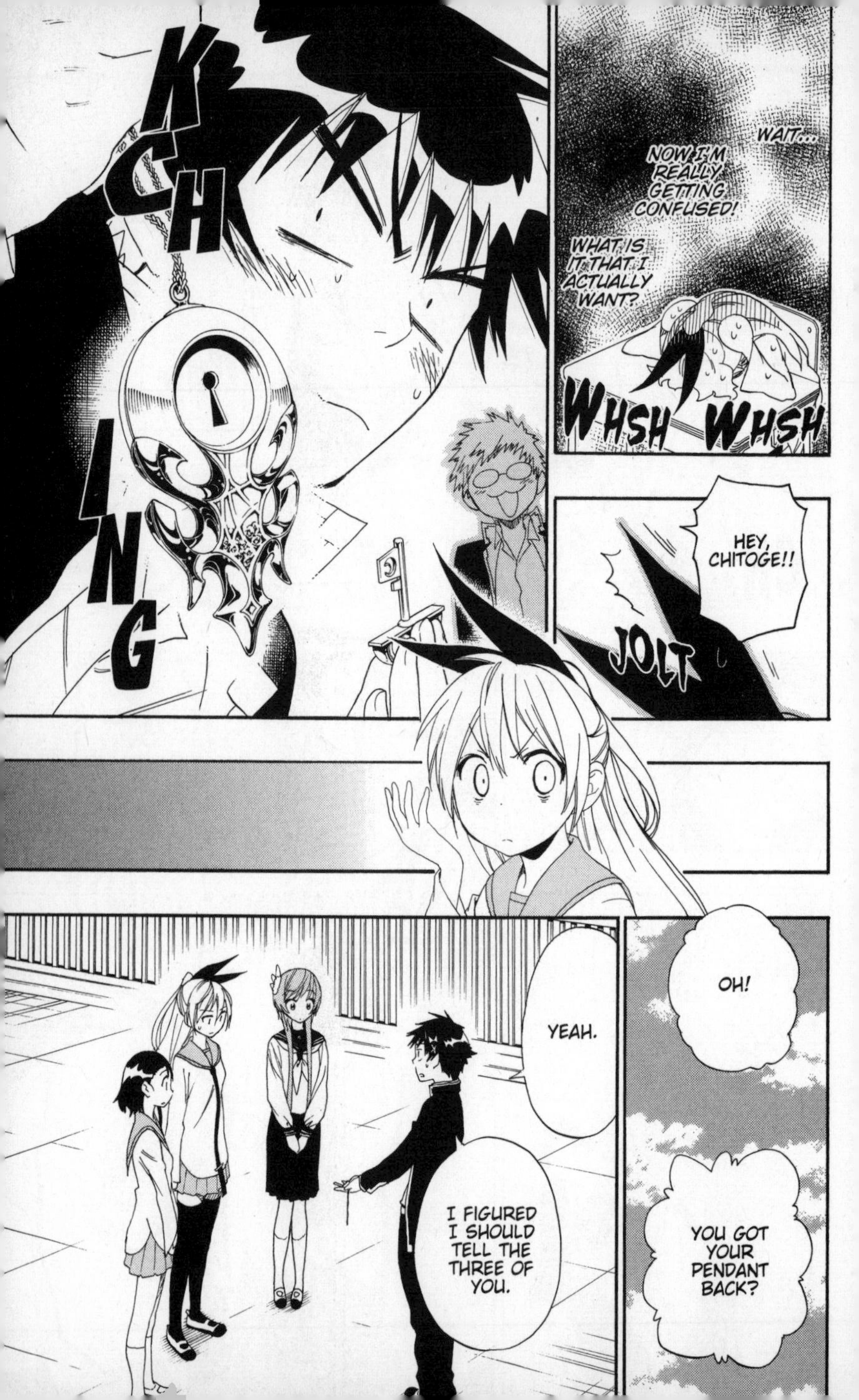
WAIT...
NOW I'M REALLY GETTING CONFUSED!
WHAT IS IT THAT I ACTUALLY WANT?
WHSH WHSH
HEY, CHITOGE!!
JOLT
KCHING
OH!
YOU GOT YOUR PENDANT BACK?
YEAH.
I FIGURED I SHOULD TELL THE THREE OF YOU.

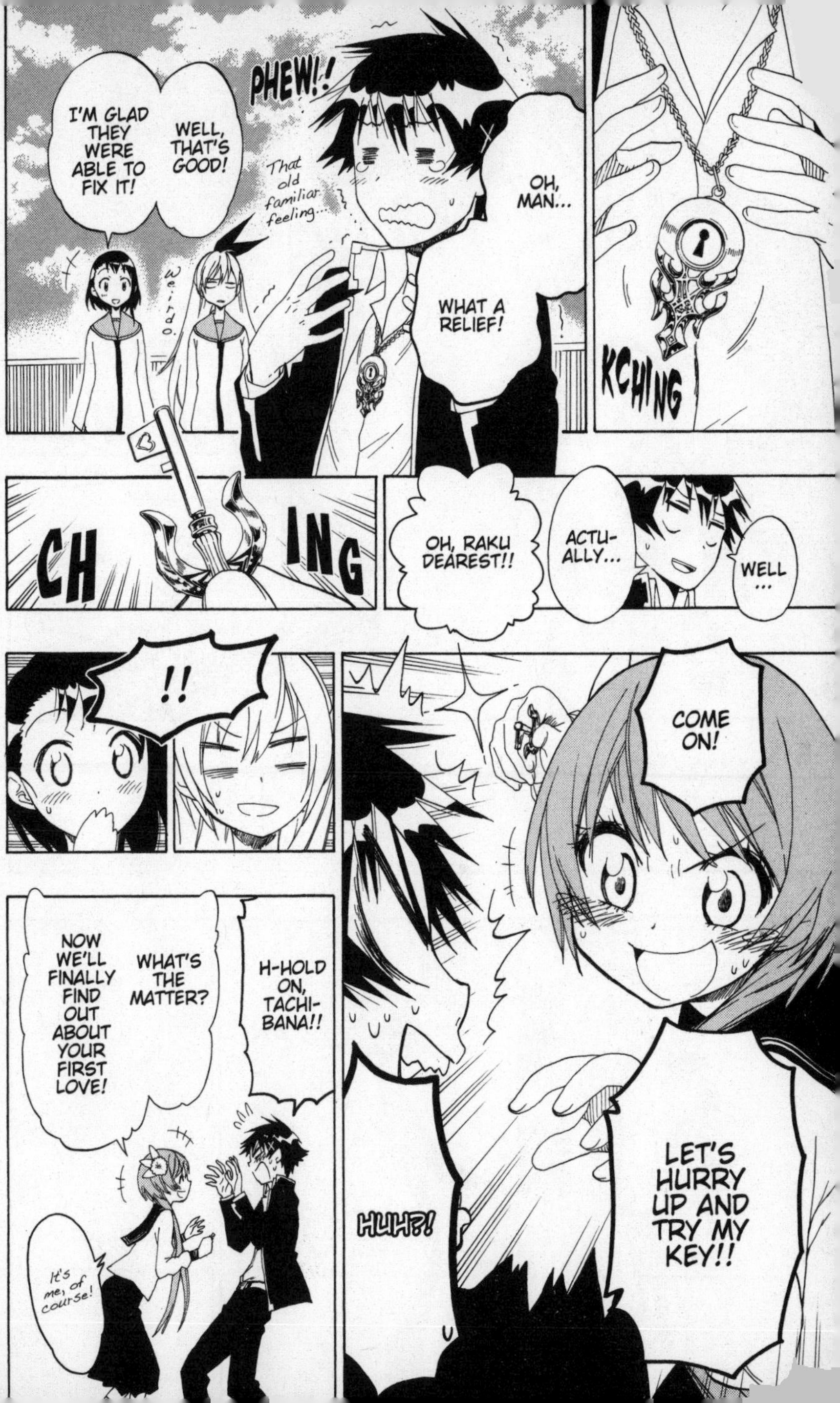
KCHING
OH, MAN...
WHAT A RELIEF!
PHEW!!
That old familiar feeling...
WELL, THAT'S GOOD!
I'M GLAD THEY WERE ABLE TO FIX IT!
Weirdo.
WELL...
ACTU-ALLY...
OH, RAKU DEAREST!!
CH ING
COME ON!
HUH?!
LET'S HURRY UP AND TRY MY KEY!!
!!
H-HOLD ON, TACHI-BANA!!
WHAT'S THE MATTER?
NOW WE'LL FINALLY FIND OUT ABOUT YOUR FIRST LOVE!
It's me, of course!

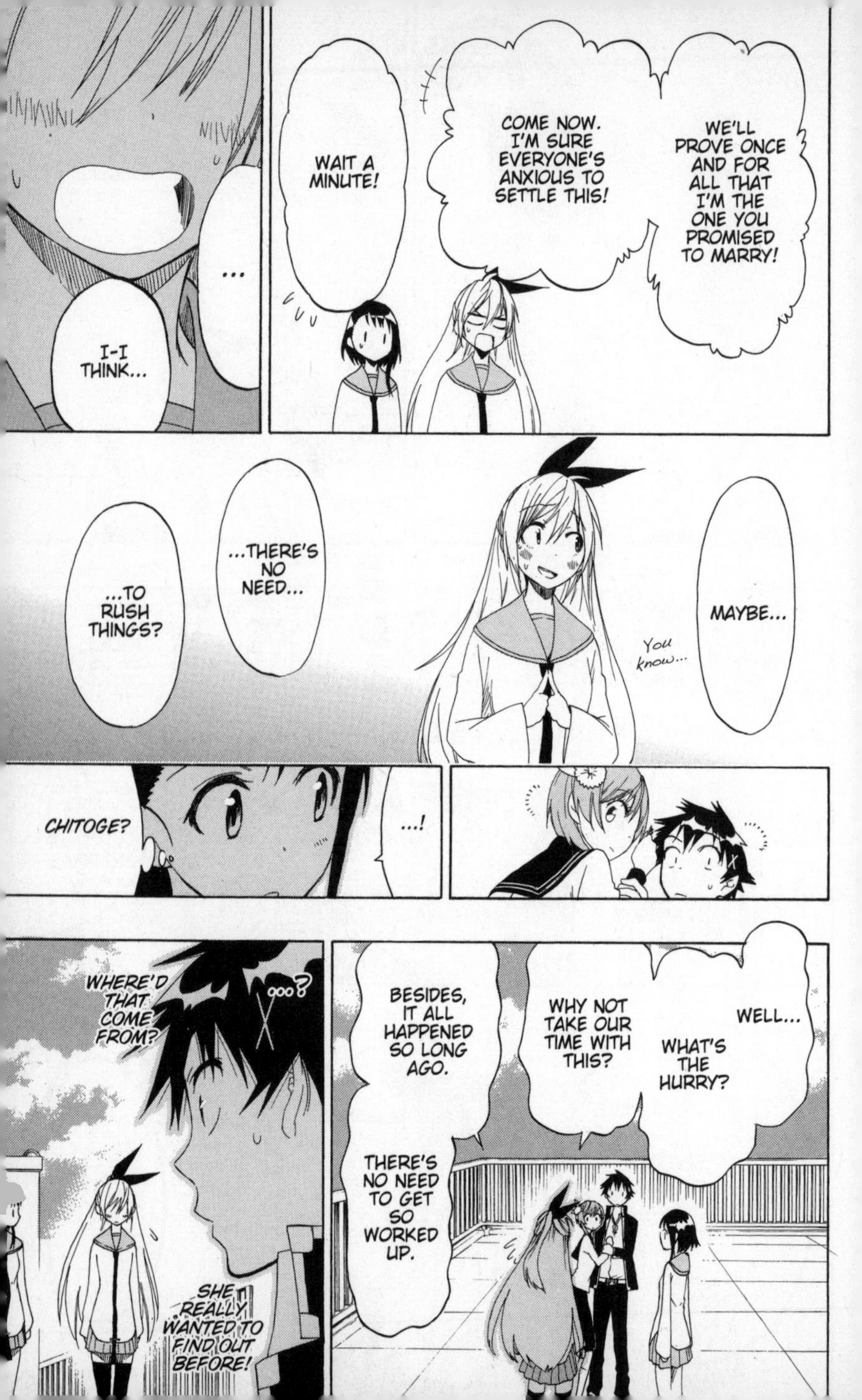
WE'LL PROVE ONCE AND FOR ALL THAT I'M THE ONE YOU PROMISED TO MARRY!
COME NOW. I'M SURE EVERYONE'S ANXIOUS TO SETTLE THIS!
WAIT A MINUTE!
...
I-I THINK...
MAYBE...
You know...
...THERE'S NO NEED...
...TO RUSH THINGS?
...!
CHITOGE?
WELL...
WHAT'S THE HURRY?
WHY NOT TAKE OUR TIME WITH THIS?
BESIDES, IT ALL HAPPENED SO LONG AGO.
THERE'S NO NEED TO GET SO WORKED UP.
WHERE'D THAT COME FROM?
SHE REALLY WANTED TO FIND OUT BEFORE!

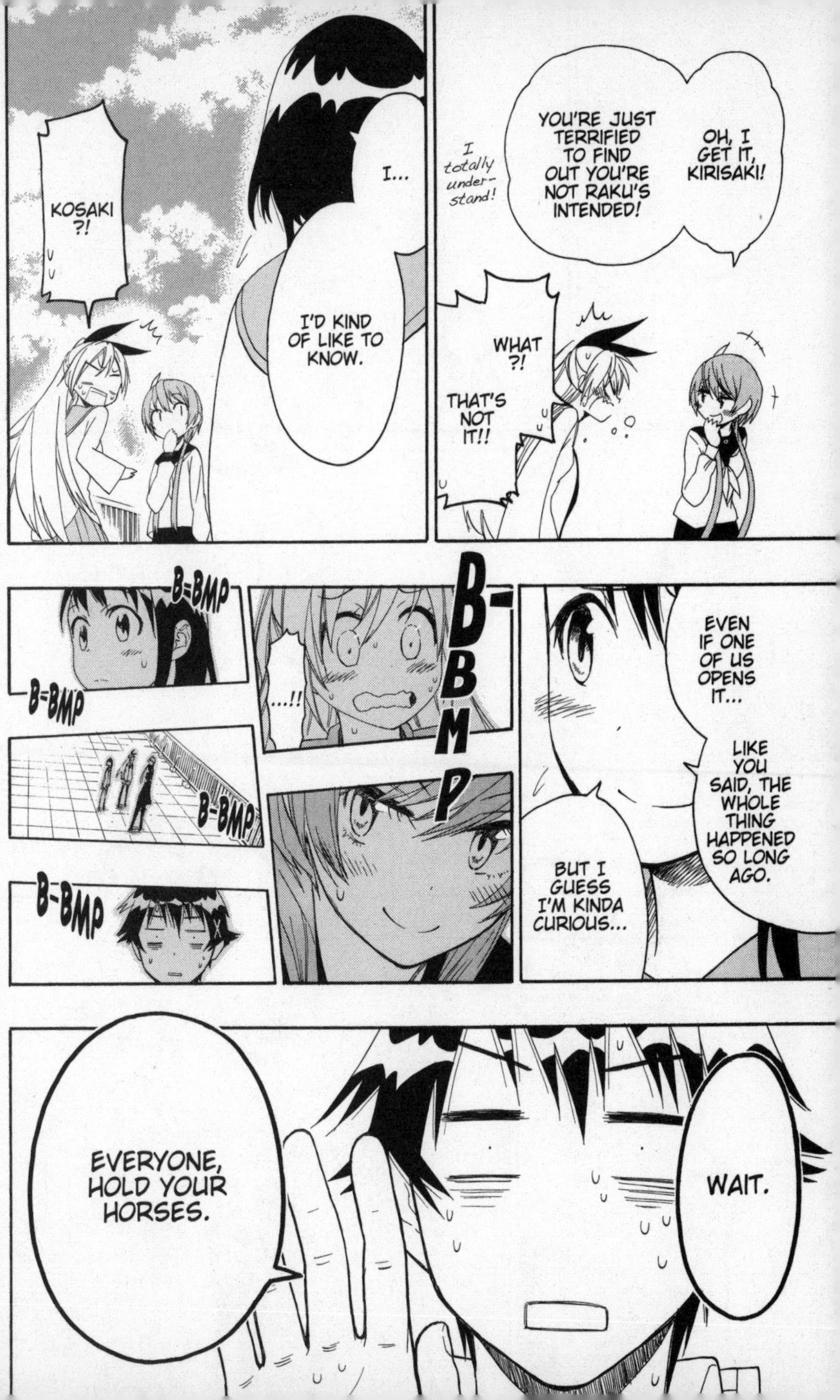
OH, I GET IT, KIRISAKI!
YOU'RE JUST TERRIFIED TO FIND OUT YOU'RE NOT RAKU'S INTENDED!
I totally under-stand!
WHAT ?!
THAT'S NOT IT!!
I...
I'D KIND OF LIKE TO KNOW.
KOSAKI ?!
EVEN IF ONE OF US OPENS IT...
LIKE YOU SAID, THE WHOLE THING HAPPENED SO LONG AGO.
BUT I GUESS I'M KINDA CURIOUS...
B-BBMP
...!!
B=BMP
B=BMP
B-BMP
B-BMP
WAIT.
EVERYONE, HOLD YOUR HORSES.

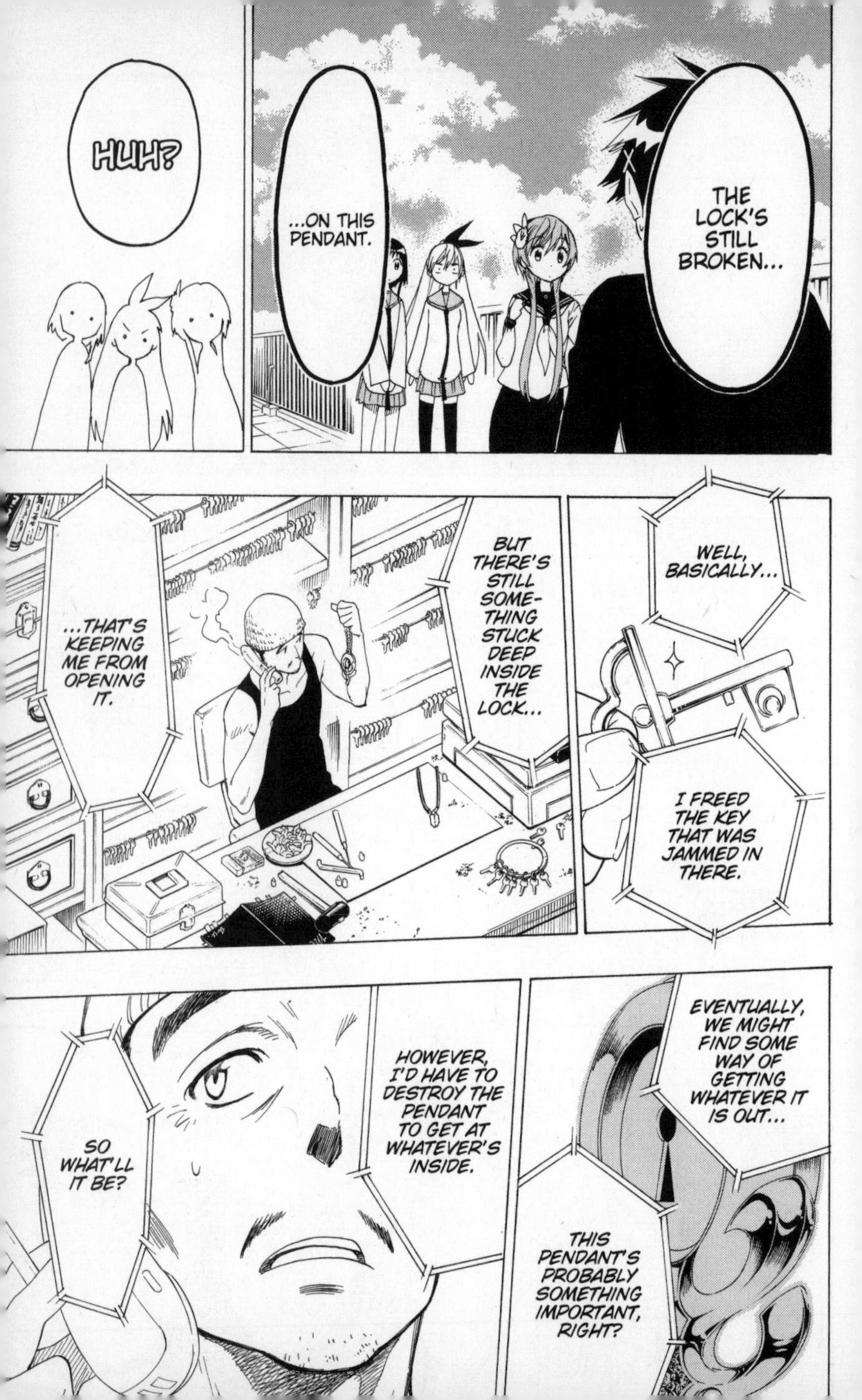
THE LOCK'S STILL BROKEN...
...ON THIS PENDANT.
HUH?
WELL, BASICALLY...
I FREED THE KEY THAT WAS JAMMED IN THERE.
BUT THERE'S STILL SOME-THING STUCK DEEP INSIDE THE LOCK...
...THAT'S KEEPING ME FROM OPENING IT.
EVENTUALLY, WE MIGHT FIND SOME WAY OF GETTING WHATEVER IT IS OUT...
THIS PENDANT'S PROBABLY SOMETHING IMPORTANT, RIGHT?
HOWEVER, I'D HAVE TO DESTROY THE PENDANT TO GET AT WHATEVER'S INSIDE.
SO WHAT'LL IT BE?

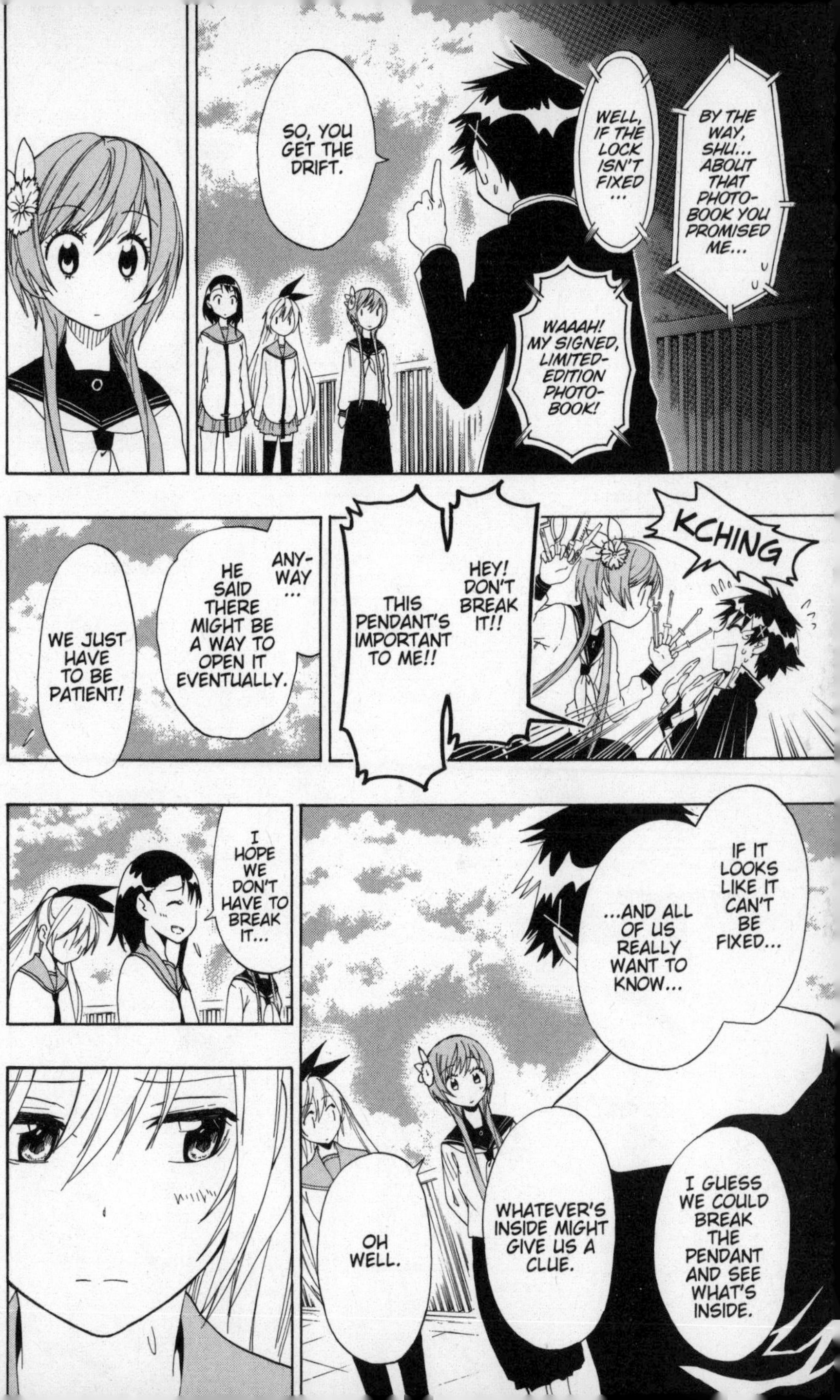
BY THE WAY, SHU... ABOUT THAT PHOTO-BOOK YOU PROMISED ME...
WELL, IF THE LOCK ISN'T FIXED...
WAAAH! MY SIGNED, LIMITED-EDITION PHOTO-BOOK!
SO, YOU GET THE DRIFT.
KCHING
HEY! DON'T BREAK IT!!
THIS PENDANT'S IMPORTANT TO ME!!
ANY-WAY...
HE SAID THERE MIGHT BE A WAY TO OPEN IT EVENTUALLY.
WE JUST HAVE TO BE PATIENT!
IF IT LOOKS LIKE IT CAN'T BE FIXED...
...AND ALL OF US REALLY WANT TO KNOW...
I GUESS WE COULD BREAK THE PENDANT AND SEE WHAT'S INSIDE.
WHATEVER'S INSIDE MIGHT GIVE US A CLUE.
OH WELL.
I HOPE WE DON'T HAVE TO BREAK IT...

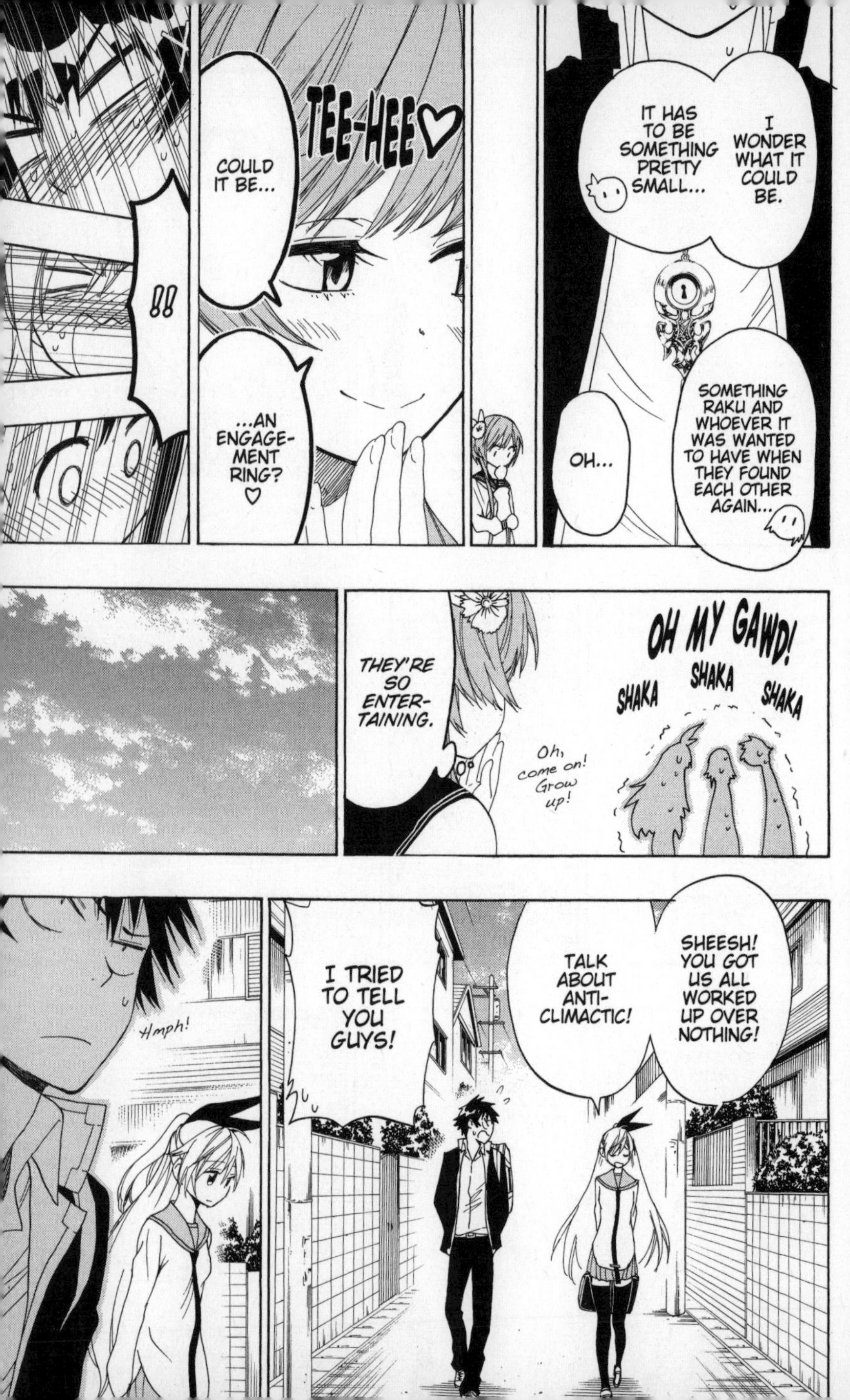
I WONDER WHAT IT COULD BE.
IT HAS TO BE SOMETHING PRETTY SMALL...
SOMETHING RAKU AND WHOEVER IT WAS WANTED TO HAVE WHEN THEY FOUND EACH OTHER AGAIN...
OH...
TEE-HEE♡
COULD IT BE...
...AN ENGAGE-MENT RING?♡
!!
OH MY GAWD!
SHAKA
SHAKA
SHAKA
THEY'RE SO ENTER-TAINING.
Oh, come on! Grow up!
SHEESH! YOU GOT US ALL WORKED UP OVER NOTHING!
TALK ABOUT ANTI-CLIMACTIC!
I TRIED TO TELL YOU GUYS!
Hmph!

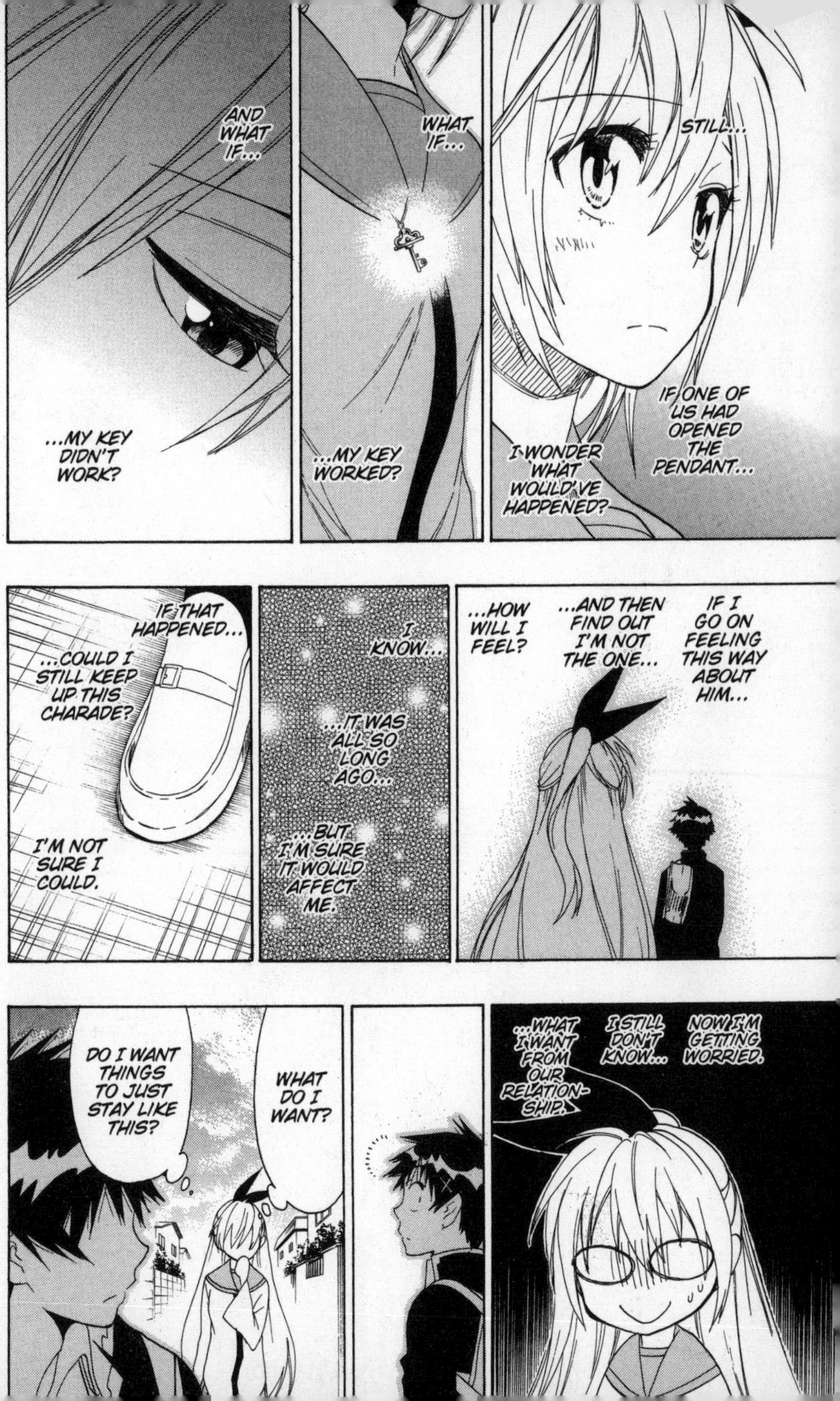
STILL...
IF ONE OF US HAD OPENED THE PENDANT...
I WONDER WHAT WOULD'VE HAPPENED?
WHAT IF...
...MY KEY WORKED?
AND WHAT IF...
...MY KEY DIDN'T WORK?
IF I GO ON FEELING THIS WAY ABOUT HIM...
...AND THEN FIND OUT I'M NOT THE ONE...
...HOW WILL I FEEL?
I KNOW...
...IT WAS ALL SO LONG AGO...
...BUT I'M SURE IT WOULD AFFECT ME.
IF THAT HAPPENED...
...COULD I STILL KEEP UP THIS CHARADE?
I'M NOT SURE I COULD.
NOW I'M GETTING WORRIED.
I STILL DON'T KNOW...
...WHAT I WANT FROM OUR RELATIONSHIP.
WHAT DO I WANT?
DO I WANT THINGS TO JUST STAY LIKE THIS?

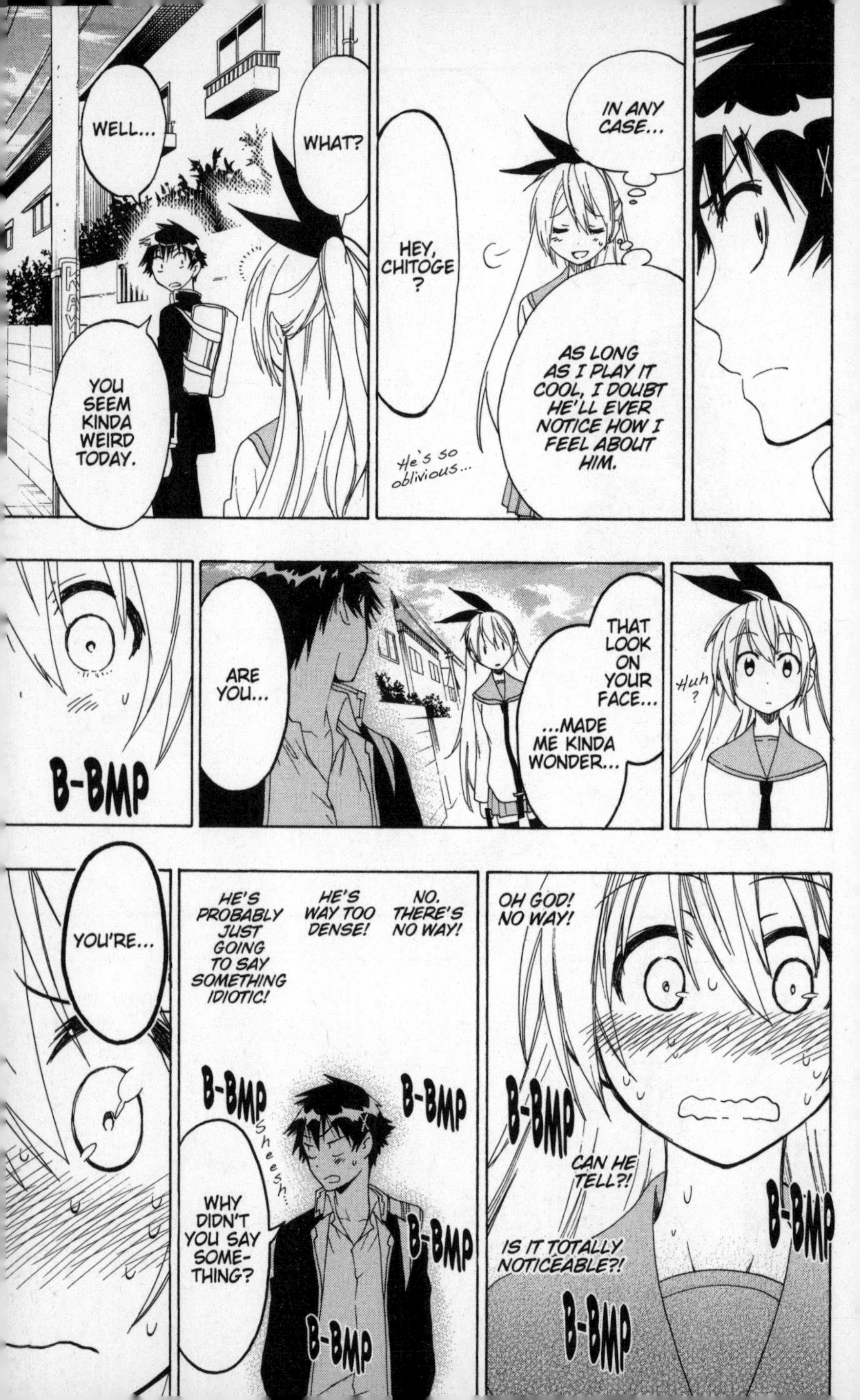
IN ANY CASE...
AS LONG AS I PLAY IT COOL, I DOUBT HE'LL EVER NOTICE HOW I FEEL ABOUT HIM.
HEY, CHITOGE?
He's so oblivious...
WHAT?
WELL...
YOU SEEM KINDA WEIRD TODAY.
Huh?
THAT LOOK ON YOUR FACE...
...MADE ME KINDA WONDER...
ARE YOU...
B-BMP
OH GOD! NO WAY!
B-BMP
CAN HE TELL?!
B-BMP
IS IT TOTALLY NOTICEABLE?!
B-BMP
NO. THERE'S NO WAY!
HE'S WAY TOO DENSE!
HE'S PROBABLY JUST GOING TO SAY SOMETHING IDIOTIC!
B-BMP
B-BMP
Sheesh...
WHY DIDN'T YOU SAY SOME-THING?
B-BMP
B-BMP
YOU'RE...

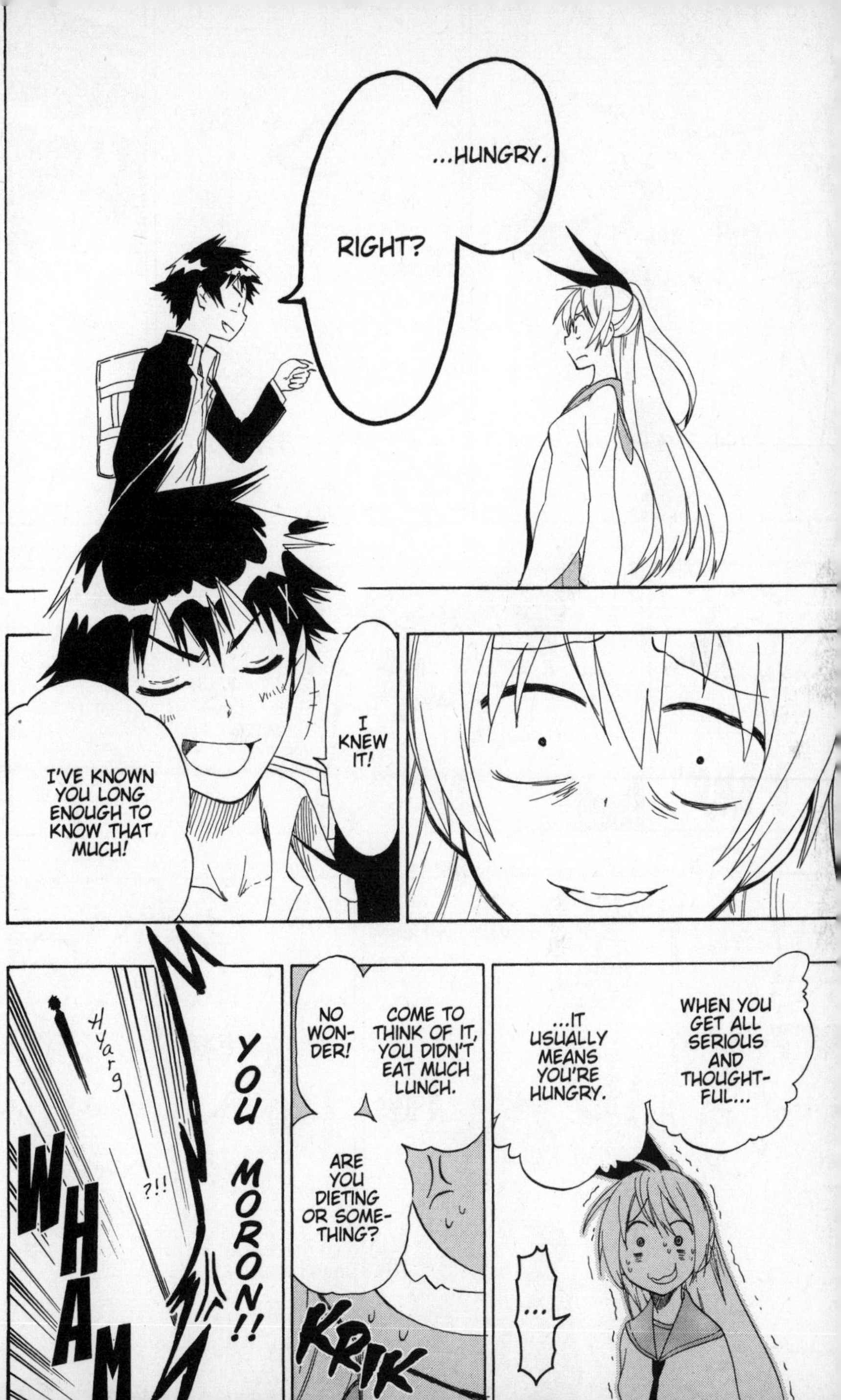
...HUNGRY.
RIGHT?
I KNEW IT!
I'VE KNOWN YOU LONG ENOUGH TO KNOW THAT MUCH!
WHEN YOU GET ALL SERIOUS AND THOUGHTFUL...
...IT USUALLY MEANS YOU'RE HUNGRY.
...
COME TO THINK OF IT, YOU DIDN'T EAT MUCH LUNCH.
NO WONDER!
ARE YOU DIETING OR SOMETHING?
KRIK
YOU MORON!!
WHAM
Hyarg
?!!

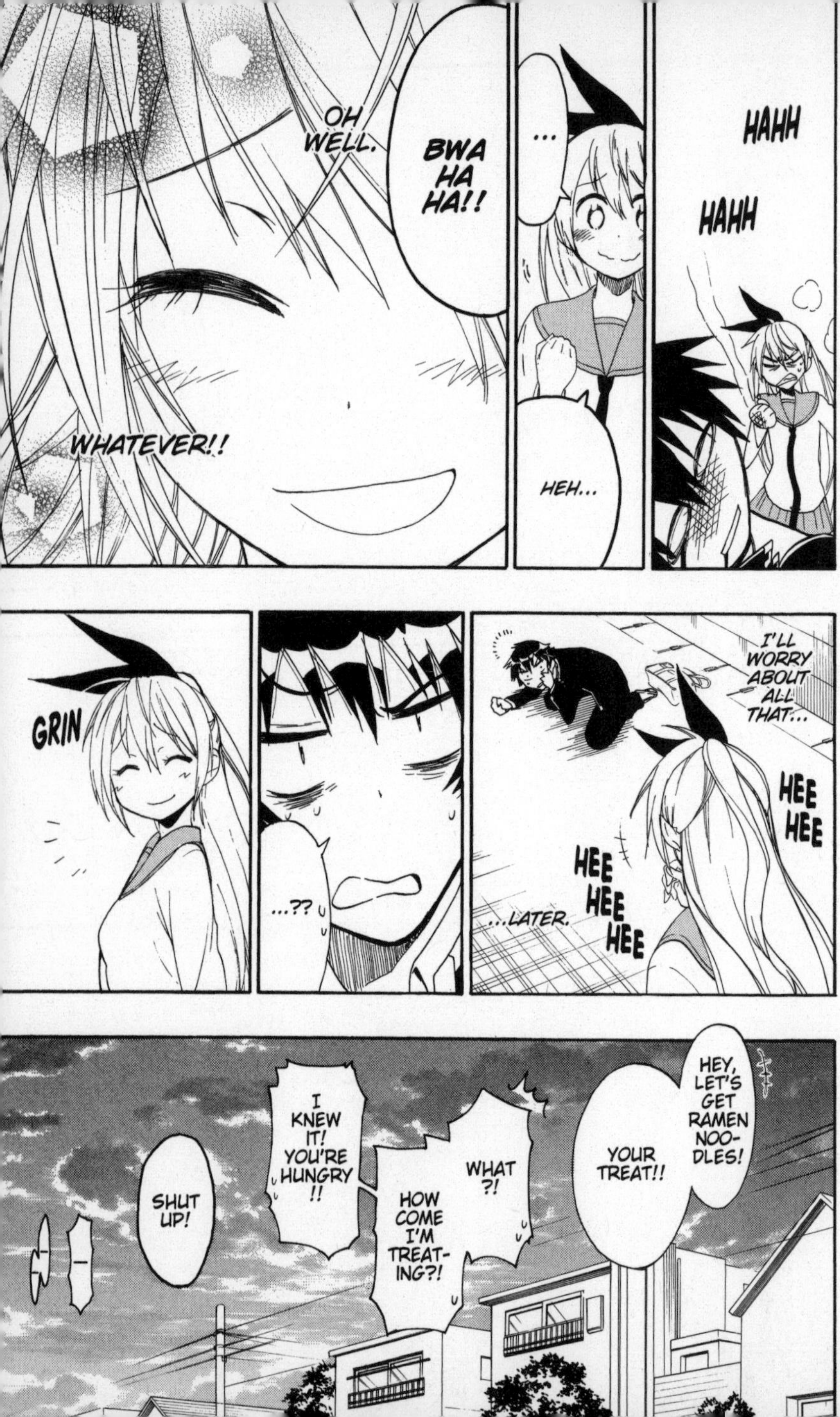
HAHH
HAHH
...
HEH...
BWA HA HA!!
OH WELL.
WHATEVER!!
I'LL WORRY ABOUT ALL THAT...
HEE HEE
HEE HEE HEE
...LATER.
...??
GRIN
HEY, LET'S GET RAMEN NOODLES!
YOUR TREAT!!
WHAT?!
HOW COME I'M TREATING?!
I KNEW IT! YOU'RE HUNGRY!!
SHUT UP!

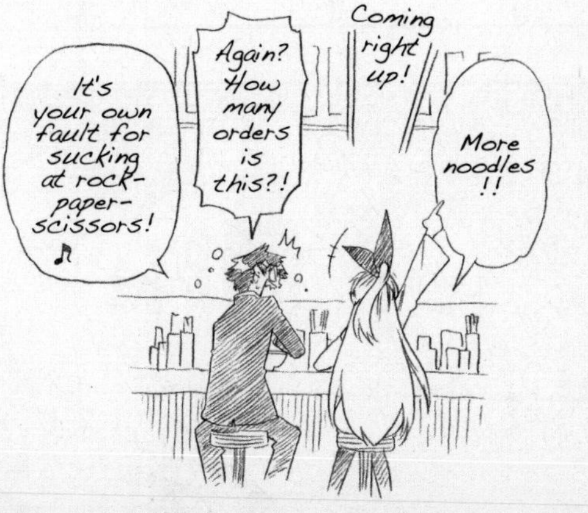
More noodles!!
Coming right up!
Again? How many orders is this?!
It's your own fault for sucking at rock-paper-scissors! ♪

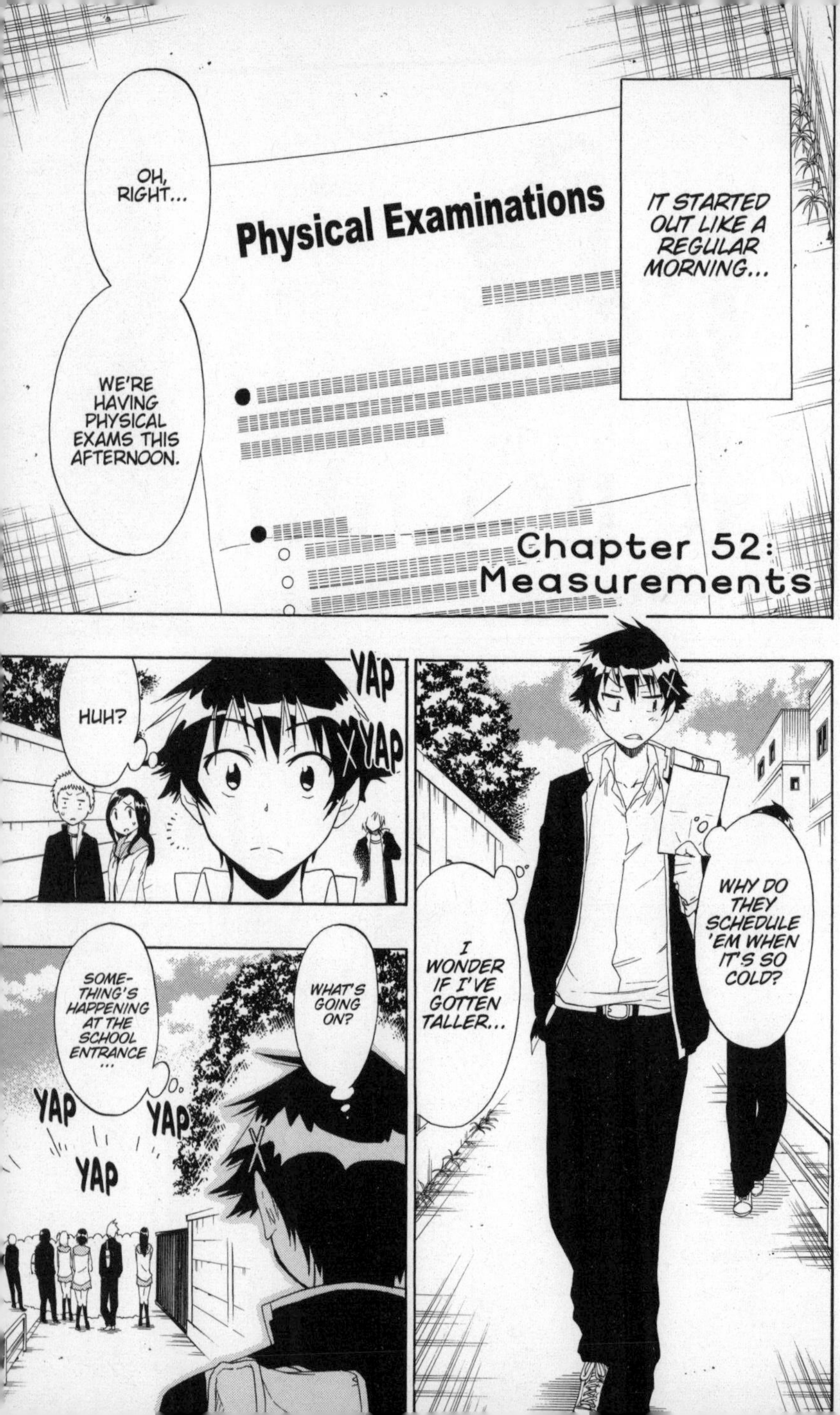

IT STARTED OUT LIKE A REGULAR MORNING...
Physical Examinations
OH, RIGHT...
WE'RE HAVING PHYSICAL EXAMS THIS AFTERNOON.
Chapter 52: Measurements
WHY DO THEY SCHEDULE 'EM WHEN IT'S SO COLD?
I WONDER IF I'VE GOTTEN TALLER...
YAP
YAP
HUH?
WHAT'S GOING ON?
SOME-THING'S HAPPENING AT THE SCHOOL ENTRANCE...
YAP
YAP
YAP

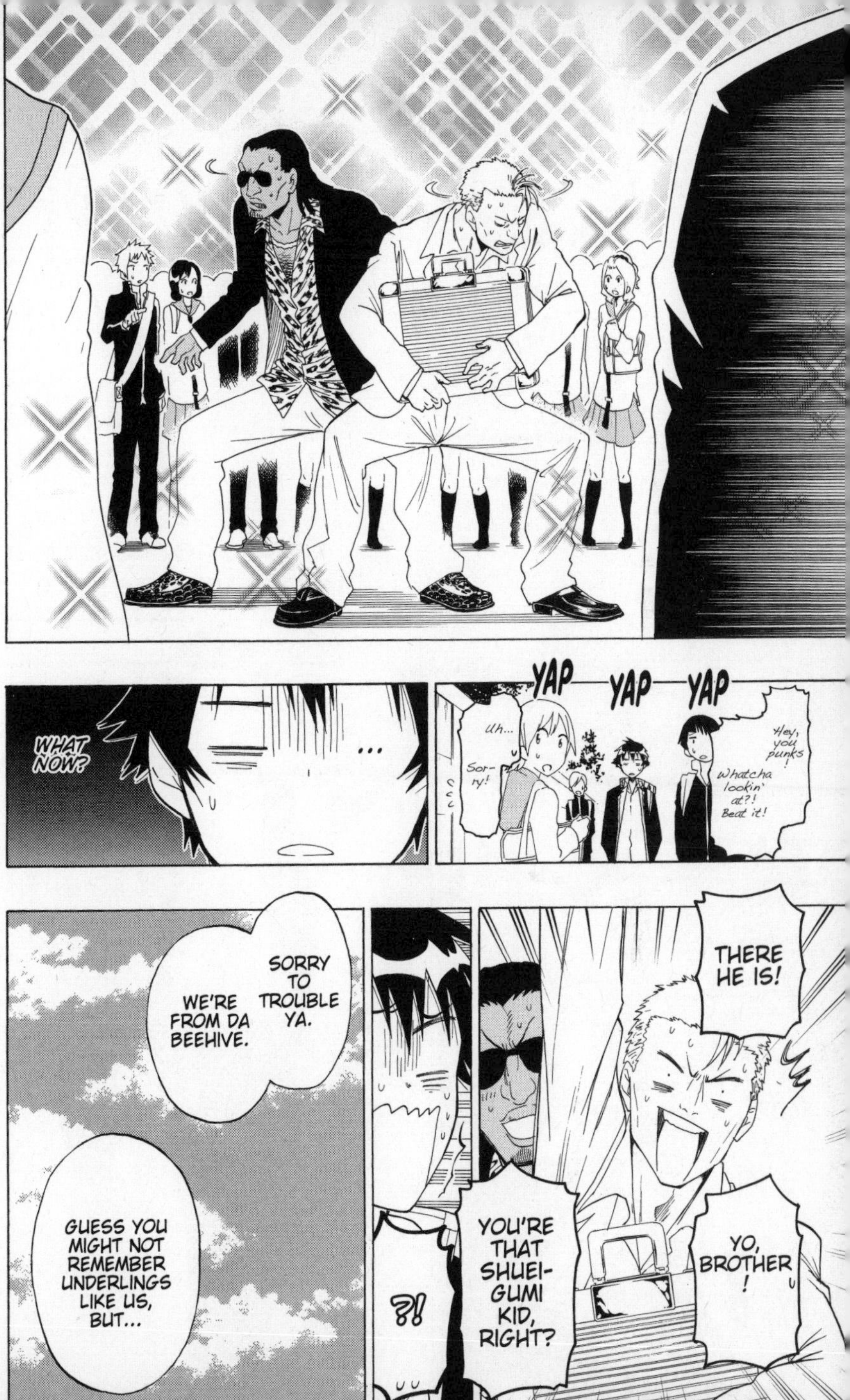
YAP YAP YAP
Hey, you punks! Whatcha lookin' at?! Beat it!
Uh... Sorry!
WHAT NOW?
...
THERE HE IS!
YO, BROTHER!
YOU'RE THAT SHUEI-GUMI KID, RIGHT?
?!
SORRY TO TROUBLE YA.
WE'RE FROM DA BEEHIVE.
GUESS YOU MIGHT NOT REMEMBER UNDERLINGS LIKE US, BUT...

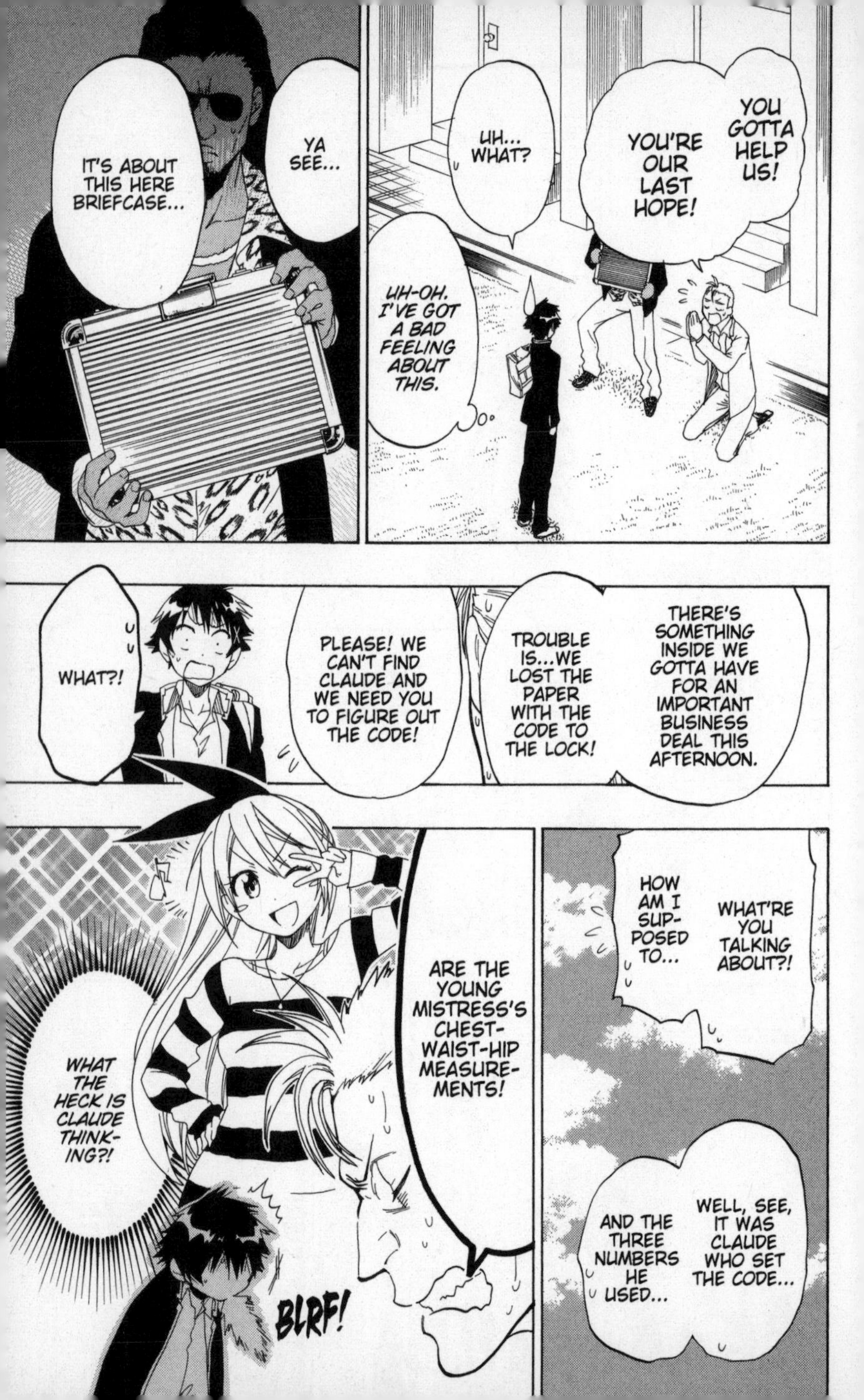
YOU GOTTA HELP US!
YOU'RE OUR LAST HOPE!
UH... WHAT?
UH-OH. I'VE GOT A BAD FEELING ABOUT THIS.
YA SEE...
IT'S ABOUT THIS HERE BRIEFCASE...
THERE'S SOMETHING INSIDE WE GOTTA HAVE FOR AN IMPORTANT BUSINESS DEAL THIS AFTERNOON.
TROUBLE IS...WE LOST THE PAPER WITH THE CODE TO THE LOCK!
PLEASE! WE CAN'T FIND CLAUDE AND WE NEED YOU TO FIGURE OUT THE CODE!
WHAT?!
WHAT'RE YOU TALKING ABOUT?!
HOW AM I SUP-POSED TO...
WELL, SEE, IT WAS CLAUDE WHO SET THE CODE...
AND THE THREE NUMBERS HE USED...
ARE THE YOUNG MISTRESS'S CHEST-WAIST-HIP MEASURE-MENTS!
WHAT THE HECK IS CLAUDE THINK-ING?!
BLRF!

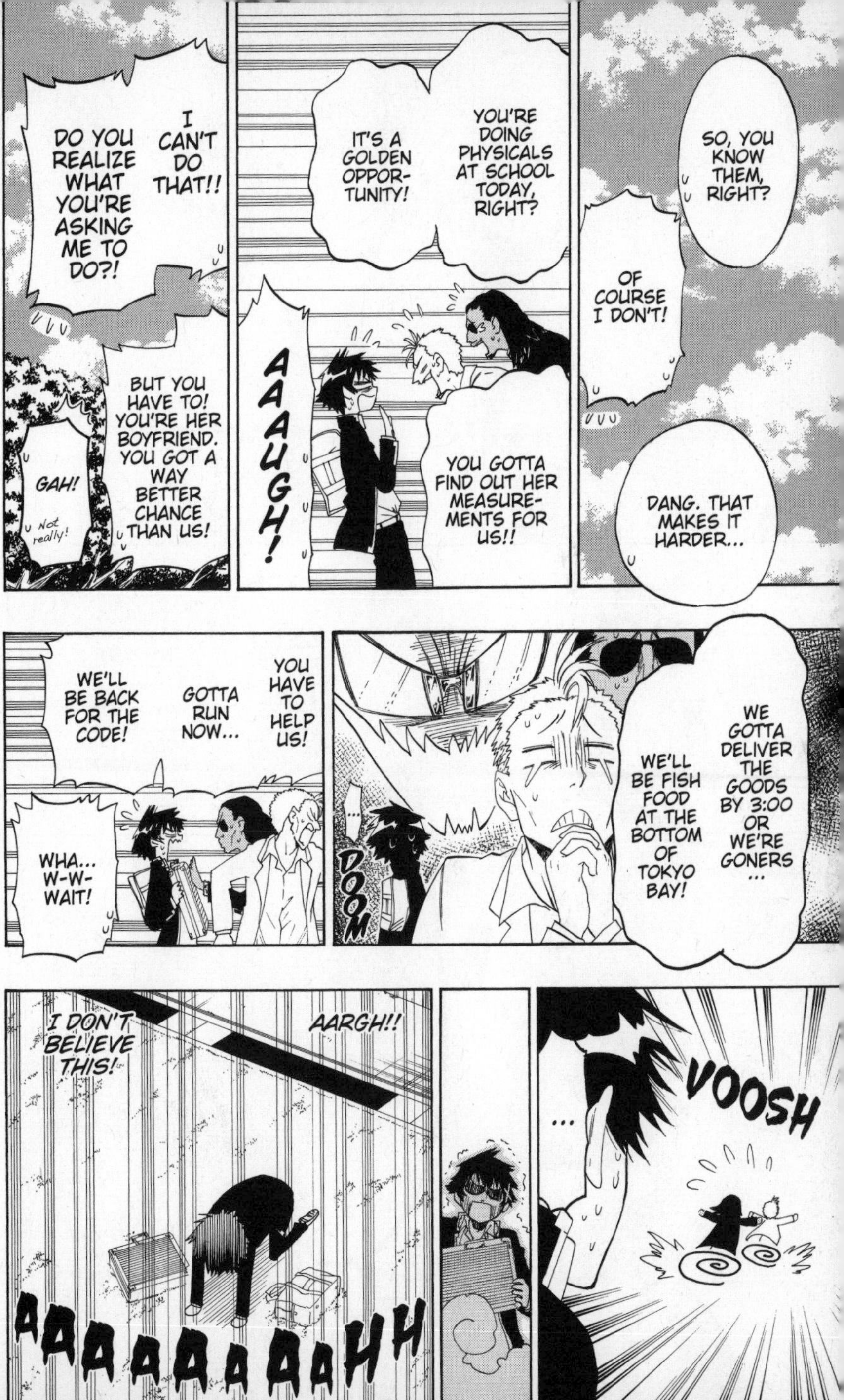
SO, YOU KNOW THEM, RIGHT?
OF COURSE I DON'T!
DANG. THAT MAKES IT HARDER...
YOU'RE DOING PHYSICALS AT SCHOOL TODAY, RIGHT?
IT'S A GOLDEN OPPOR-TUNITY!
YOU GOTTA FIND OUT HER MEASURE-MENTS FOR US!!
AAAAUGH!
I CAN'T DO THAT!!
DO YOU REALIZE WHAT YOU'RE ASKING ME TO DO?!
BUT YOU HAVE TO! YOU'RE HER BOYFRIEND. YOU GOT A WAY BETTER CHANCE THAN US!
GAH!
Not really!
WE GOTTA DELIVER THE GOODS BY 3:00 OR WE'RE GONERS...
WE'LL BE FISH FOOD AT THE BOTTOM OF TOKYO BAY!
...
DOOM
YOU HAVE TO HELP US!
GOTTA RUN NOW...
WE'LL BE BACK FOR THE CODE!
WHA... W-W-WAIT!
VOOSH
...
AARGH!!
I DON'T BELIEVE THIS!
AAAAAAAAHH

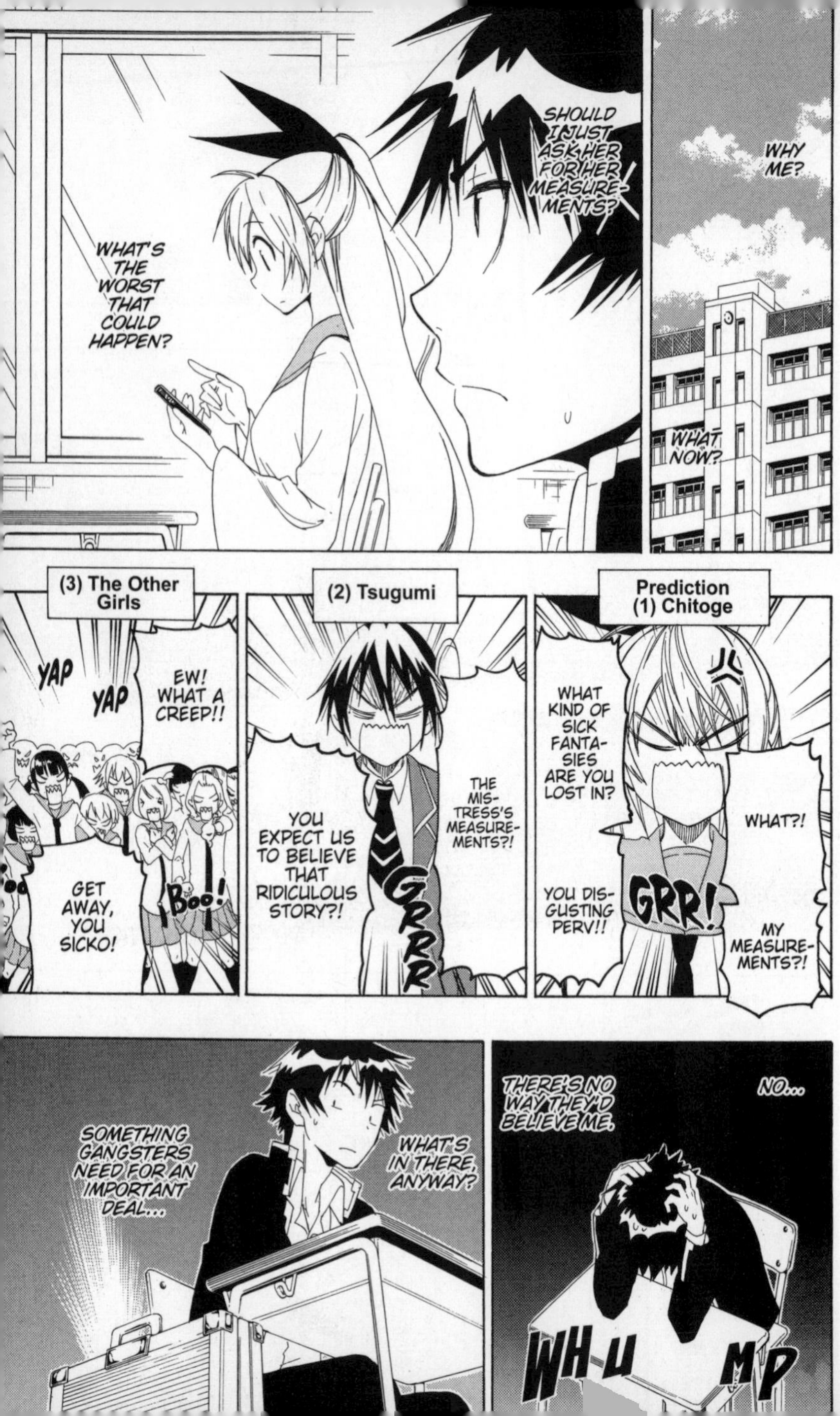
WHY ME?
WHAT NOW?
SHOULD I JUST ASK HER FOR HER MEASUREMENTS?
WHAT'S THE WORST THAT COULD HAPPEN?
Prediction (1) Chitoge
WHAT?!
MY MEASUREMENTS?!
WHAT KIND OF SICK FANTASIES ARE YOU LOST IN?
GRR!
YOU DISGUSTING PERV!!
(2) Tsugumi
THE MISTRESS'S MEASUREMENTS?!
YOU EXPECT US TO BELIEVE THAT RIDICULOUS STORY?!
GRRR
(3) The Other Girls
EW! WHAT A CREEP!!
YAP
YAP
GET AWAY, YOU SICKO!
BOO!
NO...
THERE'S NO WAY THEY'D BELIEVE ME.
WHUMP
WHAT'S IN THERE, ANYWAY?
SOMETHING GANGSTERS NEED FOR AN IMPORTANT DEAL...

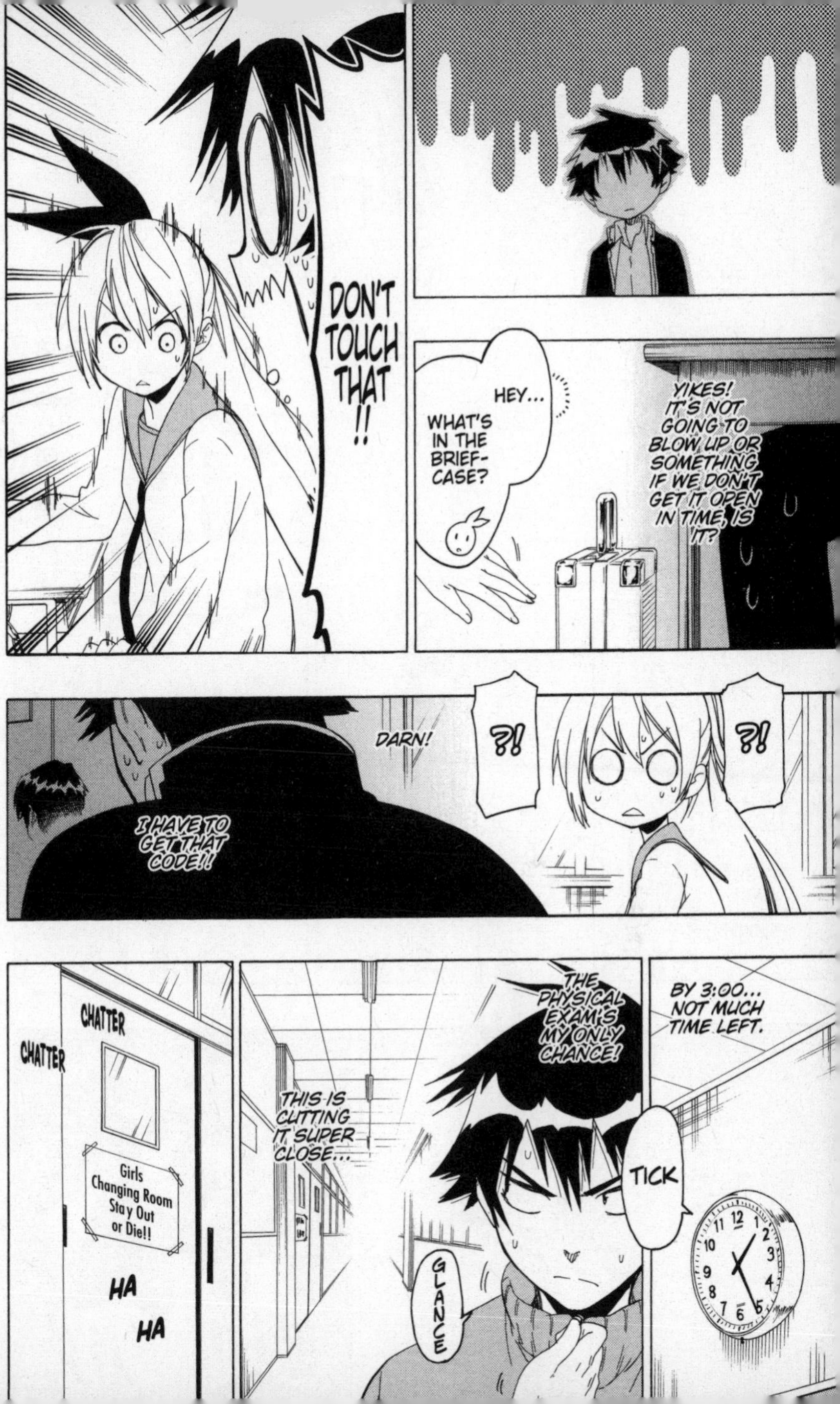
YIKES! IT'S NOT GOING TO BLOW UP OR SOMETHING IF WE DON'T GET IT OPEN IN TIME, IS IT?
HEY...
WHAT'S IN THE BRIEF-CASE?
DON'T TOUCH THAT!!
?!
?!
DARN!
I HAVE TO GET THAT CODE!!
BY 3:00... NOT MUCH TIME LEFT.
TICK
THE PHYSICAL EXAM'S MY ONLY CHANCE!
THIS IS CUTTING IT SUPER CLOSE...
GLANCE
CHATTER
CHATTER
Girls Changing Room Stay Out or Die!!
HA
HA

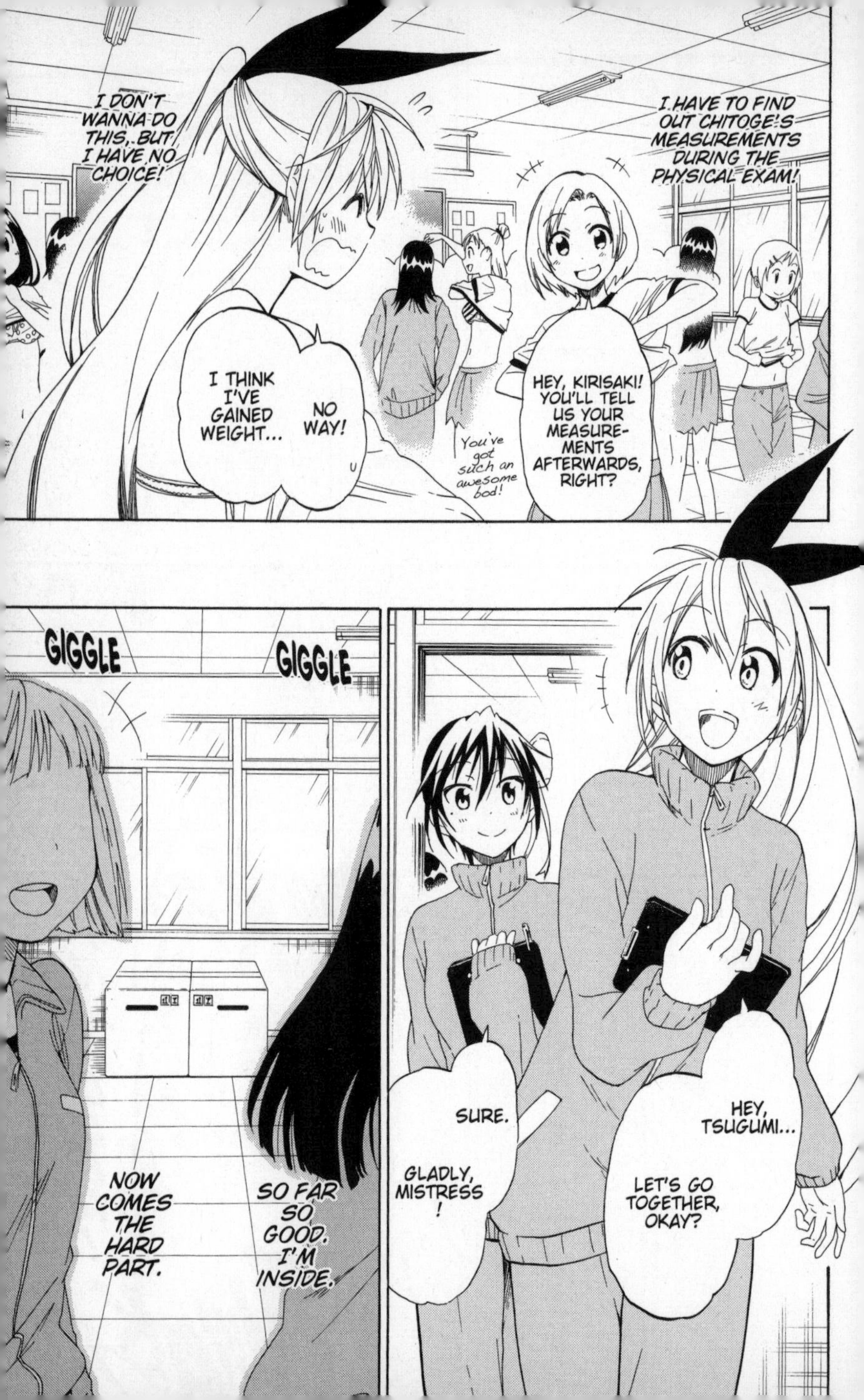
I HAVE TO FIND OUT CHITOGE'S MEASUREMENTS DURING THE PHYSICAL EXAM!
HEY, KIRISAKI! YOU'LL TELL US YOUR MEASUREMENTS AFTERWARDS, RIGHT?
You've got such an awesome bod!
NO WAY!
I THINK I'VE GAINED WEIGHT...
I DON'T WANNA DO THIS, BUT I HAVE NO CHOICE!
HEY, TSUGUMI...
LET'S GO TOGETHER, OKAY?
SURE.
GLADLY, MISTRESS!
GIGGLE
GIGGLE
SO FAR SO GOOD. I'M INSIDE.
NOW COMES THE HARD PART.

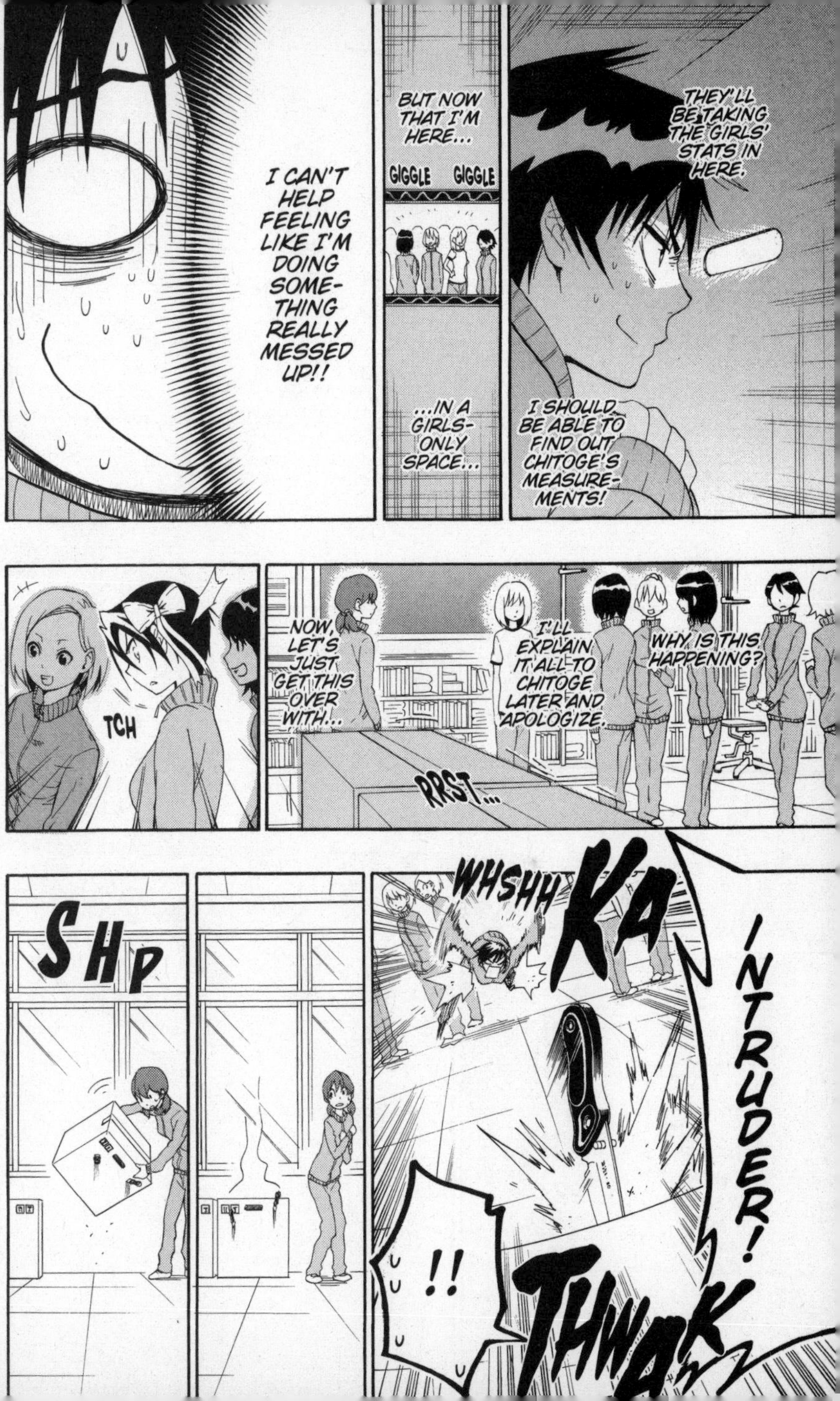
THEY'LL BE TAKING THE GIRLS' STATS IN HERE.
I SHOULD BE ABLE TO FIND OUT CHITOGE'S MEASUREMENTS!
BUT NOW THAT I'M HERE...
GIGGLE GIGGLE
...IN A GIRLS-ONLY SPACE...
I CAN'T HELP FEELING LIKE I'M DOING SOME-THING REALLY MESSED UP!!
WHY IS THIS HAPPENING?
I'LL EXPLAIN IT ALL TO CHITOGE LATER AND APOLOGIZE.
NOW, LET'S JUST GET THIS OVER WITH...
RRST...
TCH
INTRUDER!
WHSHH
KA
!!
THWAK
SHP

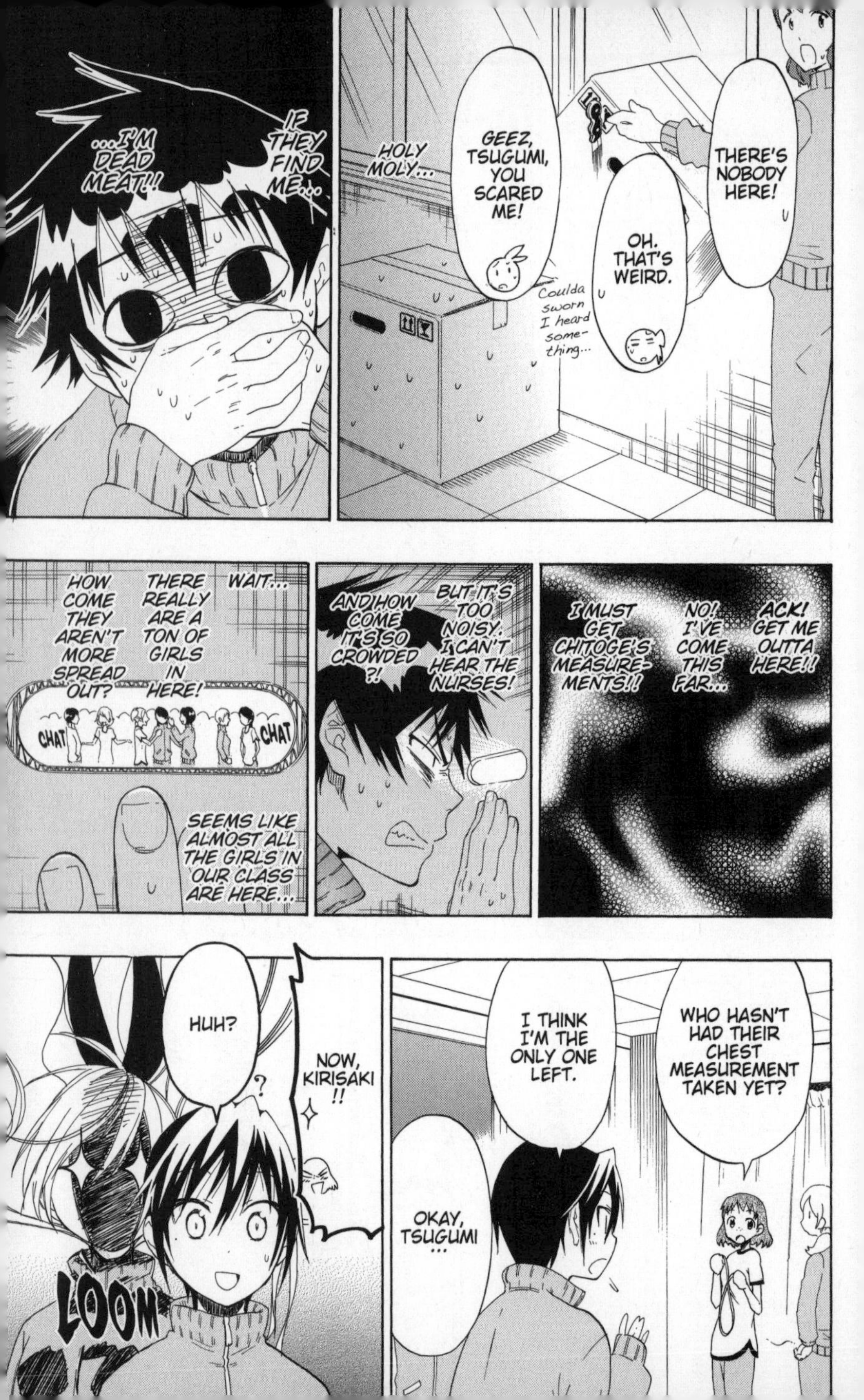
THERE'S NOBODY HERE!
OH. THAT'S WEIRD.
Coulda sworn I heard something...
GEEZ, TSUGUMI, YOU SCARED ME!
HOLY MOLY...
IF THEY FIND ME...
...I'M DEAD MEAT!!
ACK! GET ME OUTTA HERE!!
NO! I'VE COME THIS FAR...
I MUST GET CHITOGE'S MEASUREMENTS!!
BUT IT'S TOO NOISY. I CAN'T HEAR THE NURSES!
AND HOW COME IT'S SO CROWDED?!
WAIT...
THERE REALLY ARE A TON OF GIRLS IN HERE!
HOW COME THEY AREN'T MORE SPREAD OUT?
CHAT
CHAT
SEEMS LIKE ALMOST ALL THE GIRLS IN OUR CLASS ARE HERE...
WHO HASN'T HAD THEIR CHEST MEASUREMENT TAKEN YET?
I THINK I'M THE ONLY ONE LEFT.
OKAY, TSUGUMI...
NOW, KIRISAKI!!
HUH?
LOOM

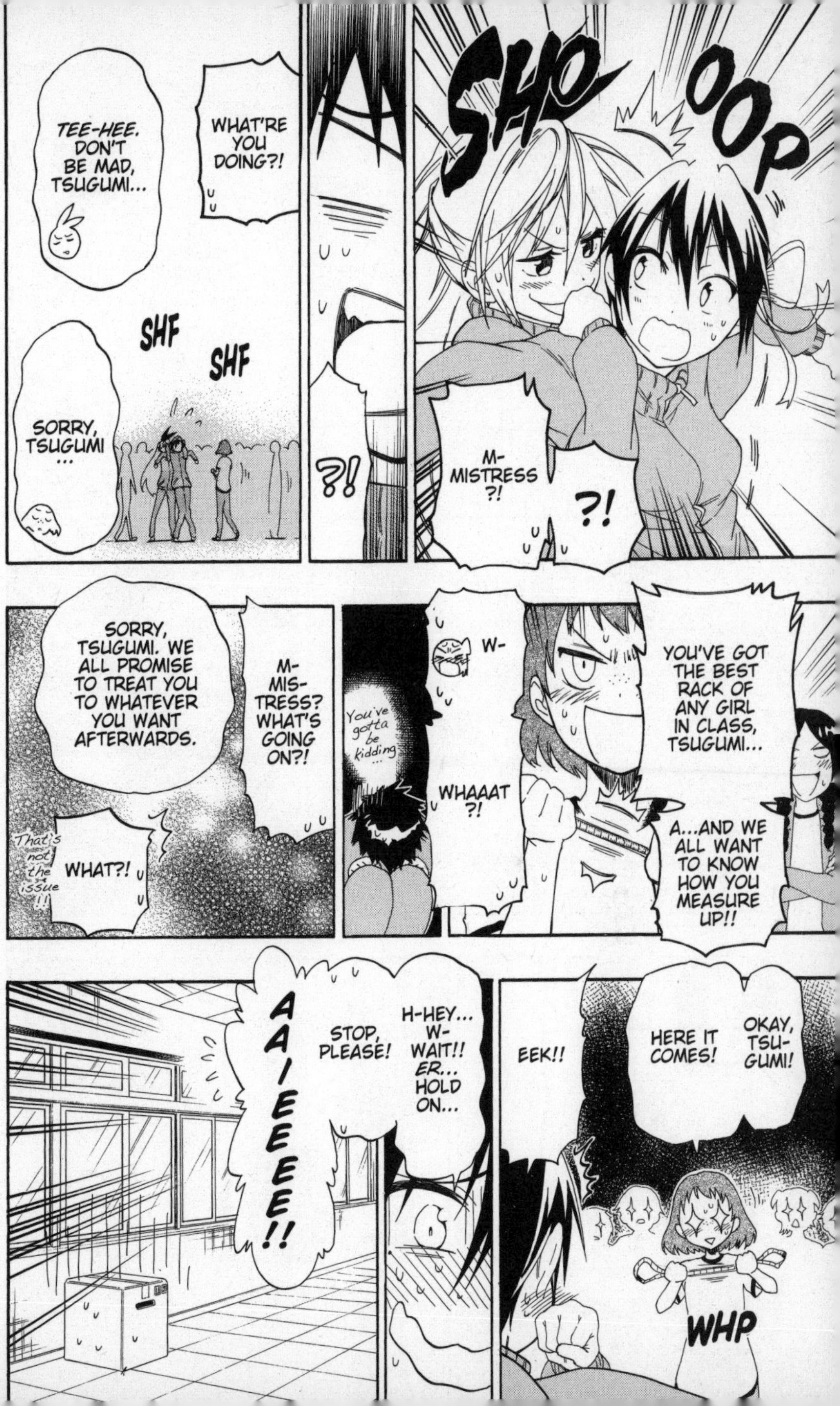
SHOOOP
M-MISTRESS?!
?!
?!
WHAT'RE YOU DOING?!
TEE-HEE. DON'T BE MAD, TSUGUMI...
SHF
SHF
SORRY, TSUGUMI...
YOU'VE GOT THE BEST RACK OF ANY GIRL IN CLASS, TSUGUMI...
A...AND WE ALL WANT TO KNOW HOW YOU MEASURE UP!!
W-
WHAAAT?!
You've gotta be kidding...
M-MIS-TRESS? WHAT'S GOING ON?!
SORRY, TSUGUMI. WE ALL PROMISE TO TREAT YOU TO WHATEVER YOU WANT AFTERWARDS.
WHAT?!
That's not the issue!!
OKAY, TSU-GUMI!
HERE IT COMES!
EEK!!
WHP
H-HEY... W-WAIT!! ER... HOLD ON...
STOP, PLEASE!
AAIEEEEEE!!

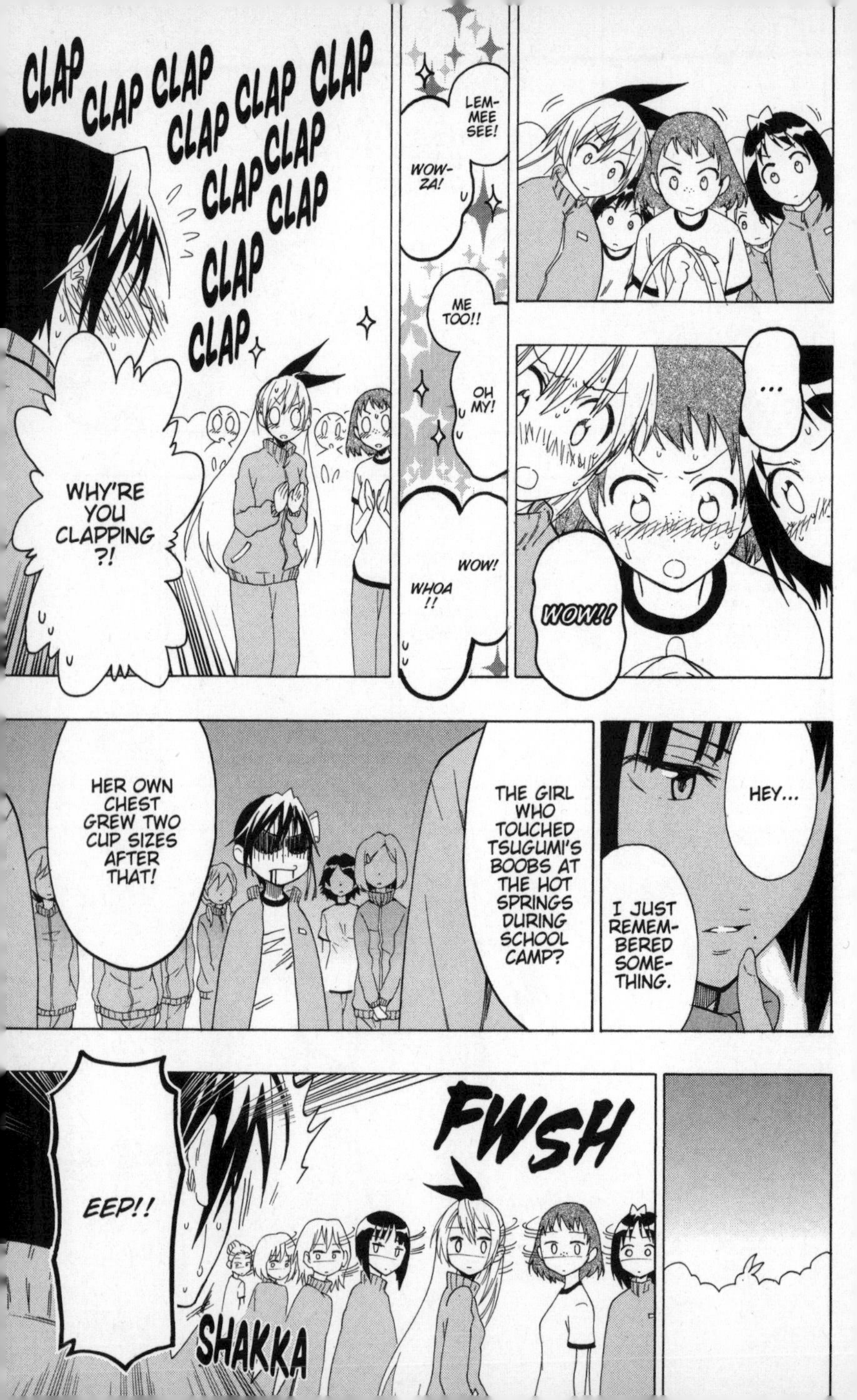
...
WOW!!
LEMMEE SEE!
WOWZA!
ME TOO!!
OH MY!
WOW!
WHOA!!
CLAP CLAP CLAP CLAP CLAP CLAP CLAP CLAP CLAP CLAP CLAP
WHY'RE YOU CLAPPING?!
HEY...
I JUST REMEMBERED SOMETHING.
THE GIRL WHO TOUCHED TSUGUMI'S BOOBS AT THE HOT SPRINGS DURING SCHOOL CAMP?
HER OWN CHEST GREW TWO CUP SIZES AFTER THAT!
FWSH
EEP!!
SHAKKA

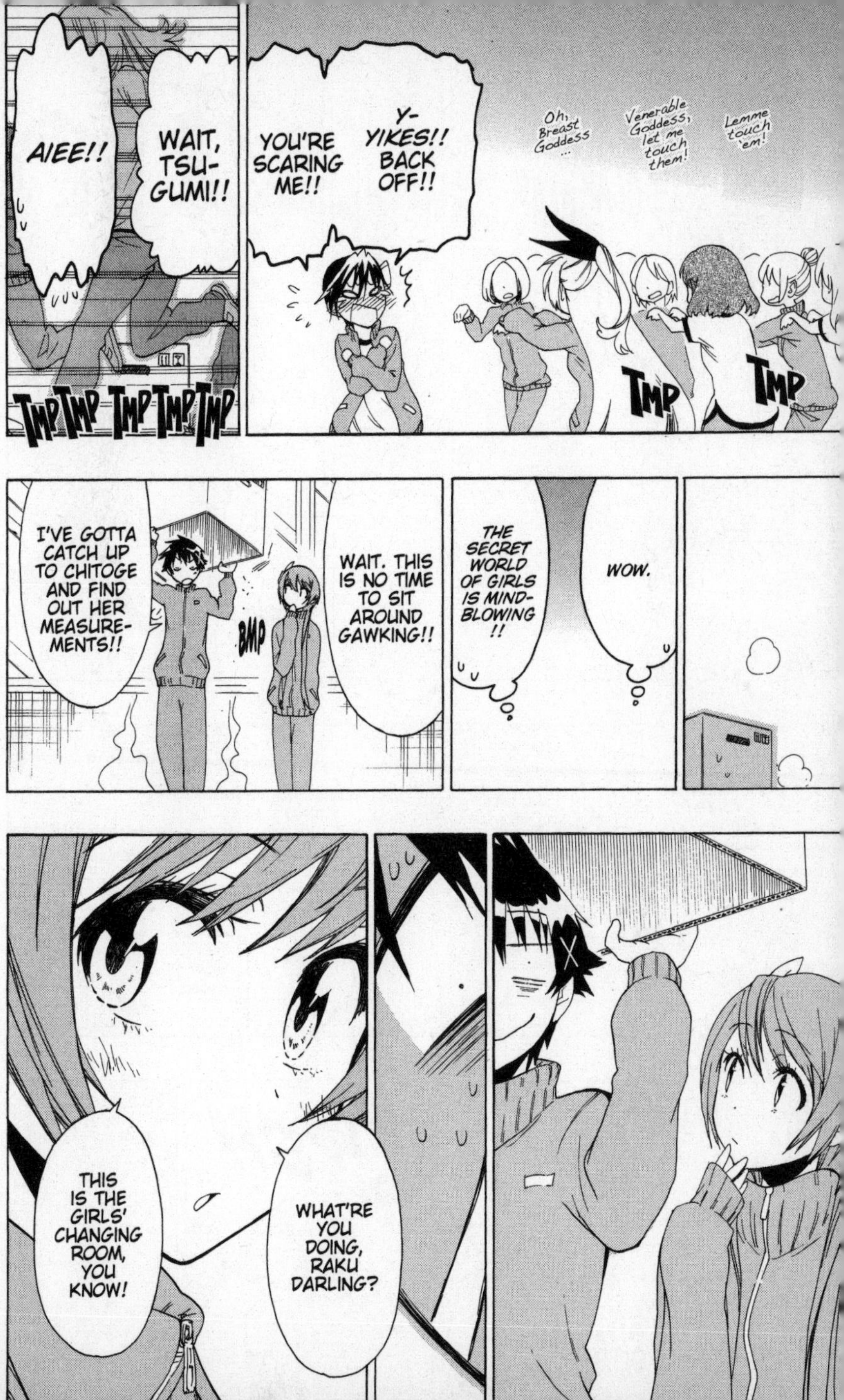
Lemme touch 'em!
Venerable Goddess, let me touch them!
Oh, Breast Goddess ...
Y-YIKES!! BACK OFF!!
YOU'RE SCARING ME!!
TMP
TMP
WAIT, TSUGUMI!!
AIEE!!
TMP TMP TMP TMP TMP
WOW.
THE SECRET WORLD OF GIRLS IS MIND-BLOWING!!
WAIT. THIS IS NO TIME TO SIT AROUND GAWKING!!
BMP
I'VE GOTTA CATCH UP TO CHITOGE AND FIND OUT HER MEASUREMENTS!!
WHAT'RE YOU DOING, RAKU DARLING?
THIS IS THE GIRLS' CHANGING ROOM, YOU KNOW!

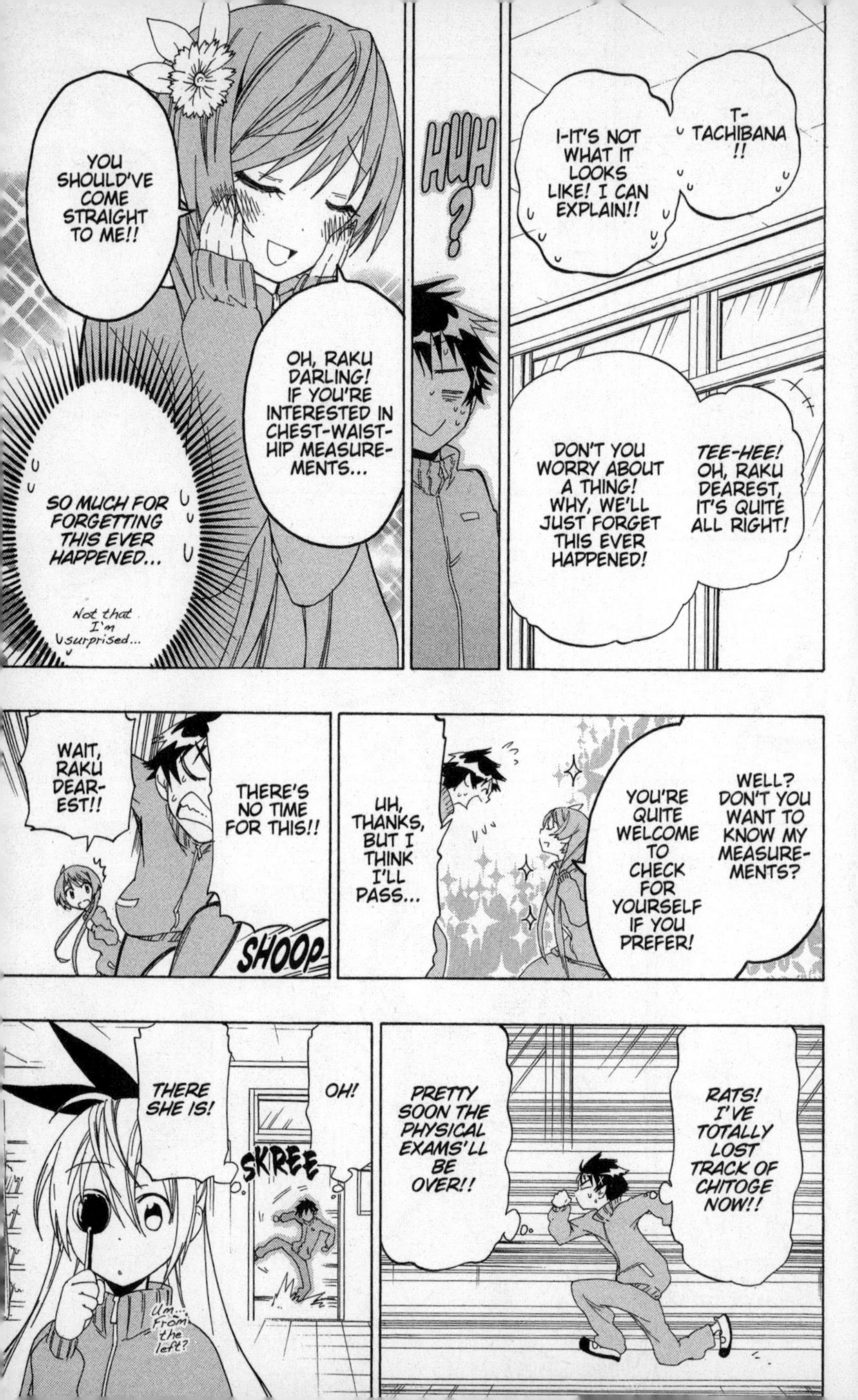
T-TACHIBANA!!
I-IT'S NOT WHAT IT LOOKS LIKE! I CAN EXPLAIN!!
TEE-HEE! OH, RAKU DEAREST, IT'S QUITE ALL RIGHT!
DON'T YOU WORRY ABOUT A THING! WHY, WE'LL JUST FORGET THIS EVER HAPPENED!
HUH ?
OH, RAKU DARLING! IF YOU'RE INTERESTED IN CHEST-WAIST-HIP MEASUREMENTS...
YOU SHOULD'VE COME STRAIGHT TO ME!!
SO MUCH FOR FORGETTING THIS EVER HAPPENED...
Not that I'm surprised...
WELL? DON'T YOU WANT TO KNOW MY MEASUREMENTS?
YOU'RE QUITE WELCOME TO CHECK FOR YOURSELF IF YOU PREFER!
UH, THANKS, BUT I THINK I'LL PASS...
THERE'S NO TIME FOR THIS!!
WAIT, RAKU DEAREST!!
SHOOP
RATS! I'VE TOTALLY LOST TRACK OF CHITOGE NOW!!
PRETTY SOON THE PHYSICAL EXAMS'LL BE OVER!!
OH!
THERE SHE IS!
SKREE
Um... From the left?

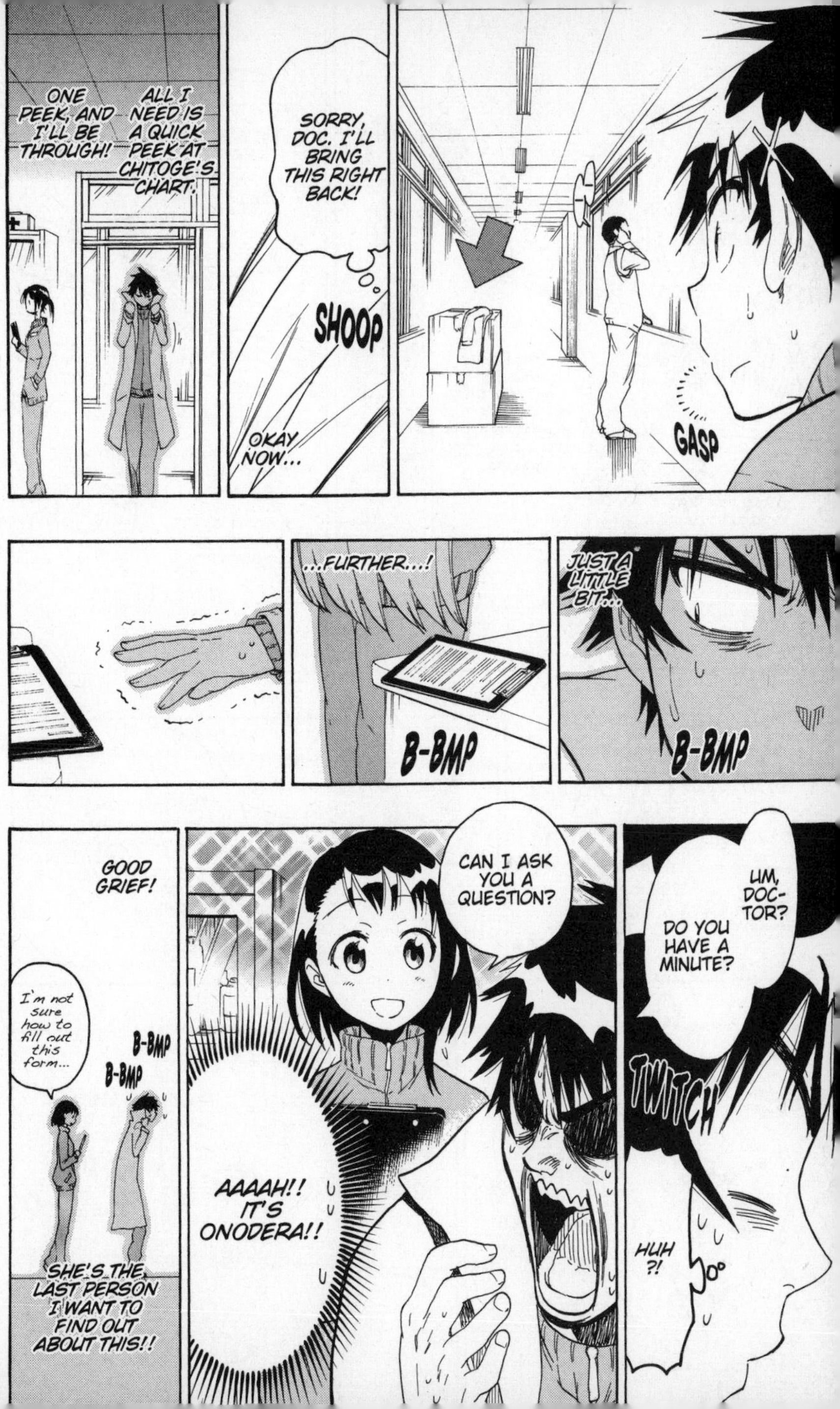
GASP
SORRY, DOC. I'LL BRING THIS RIGHT BACK!
SHOOP
OKAY NOW...
ALL I NEED IS A QUICK PEEK AT CHITOGE'S CHART.
ONE PEEK, AND I'LL BE THROUGH!
JUST A LITTLE BIT...
B-BMP
...FURTHER...!
B-BMP
UM, DOCTOR?
DO YOU HAVE A MINUTE?
TWITCH
HUH?!
CAN I ASK YOU A QUESTION?
AAAAH!! IT'S ONODERA!!
GOOD GRIEF!
I'm not sure how to fill out this form...
B-BMP
B-BMP
SHE'S THE LAST PERSON I WANT TO FIND OUT ABOUT THIS!!

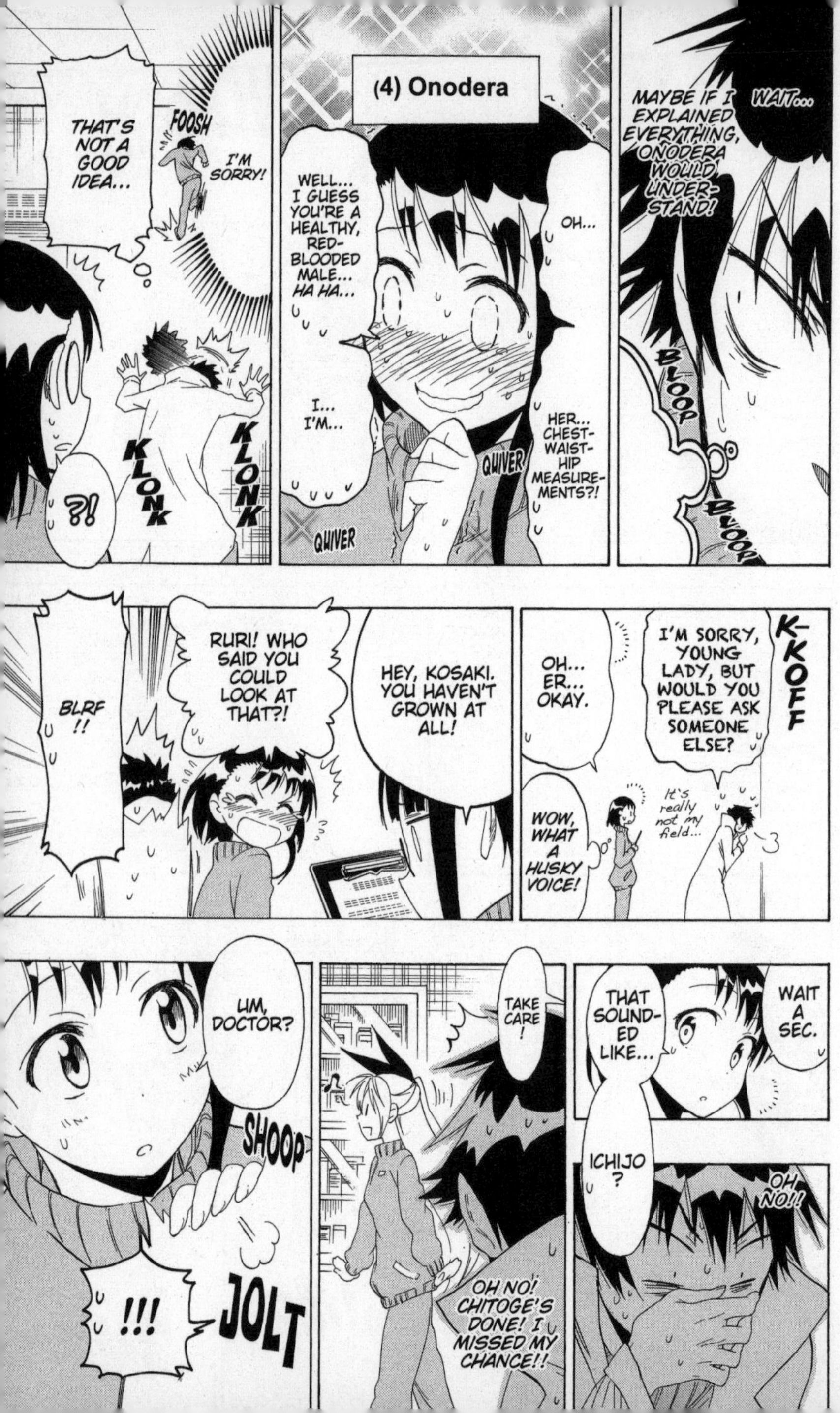
WAIT...
MAYBE IF I EXPLAINED EVERYTHING, ONODERA WOULD UNDERSTAND!
BLOOP
BLOOP
(4) Onodera
OH...
HER... CHEST-WAIST-HIP MEASUREMENTS?!
WELL... I GUESS YOU'RE A HEALTHY, RED-BLOODED MALE... HA HA...
I... I'M...
QUIVER
QUIVER
I'M SORRY!
FOOSH
THAT'S NOT A GOOD IDEA...
KLONK
KLONK
?!
K-KOFF
I'M SORRY, YOUNG LADY, BUT WOULD YOU PLEASE ASK SOMEONE ELSE?
It's really not my field...
OH... ER... OKAY.
WOW, WHAT A HUSKY VOICE!
HEY, KOSAKI. YOU HAVEN'T GROWN AT ALL!
RURI! WHO SAID YOU COULD LOOK AT THAT?!
BLRF !!
WAIT A SEC.
THAT SOUND-ED LIKE...
ICHIJO ?
OH NO!!
TAKE CARE !
OH NO! CHITOGE'S DONE! I MISSED MY CHANCE!!
UM, DOCTOR?
SHOOP
!!!
JOLT

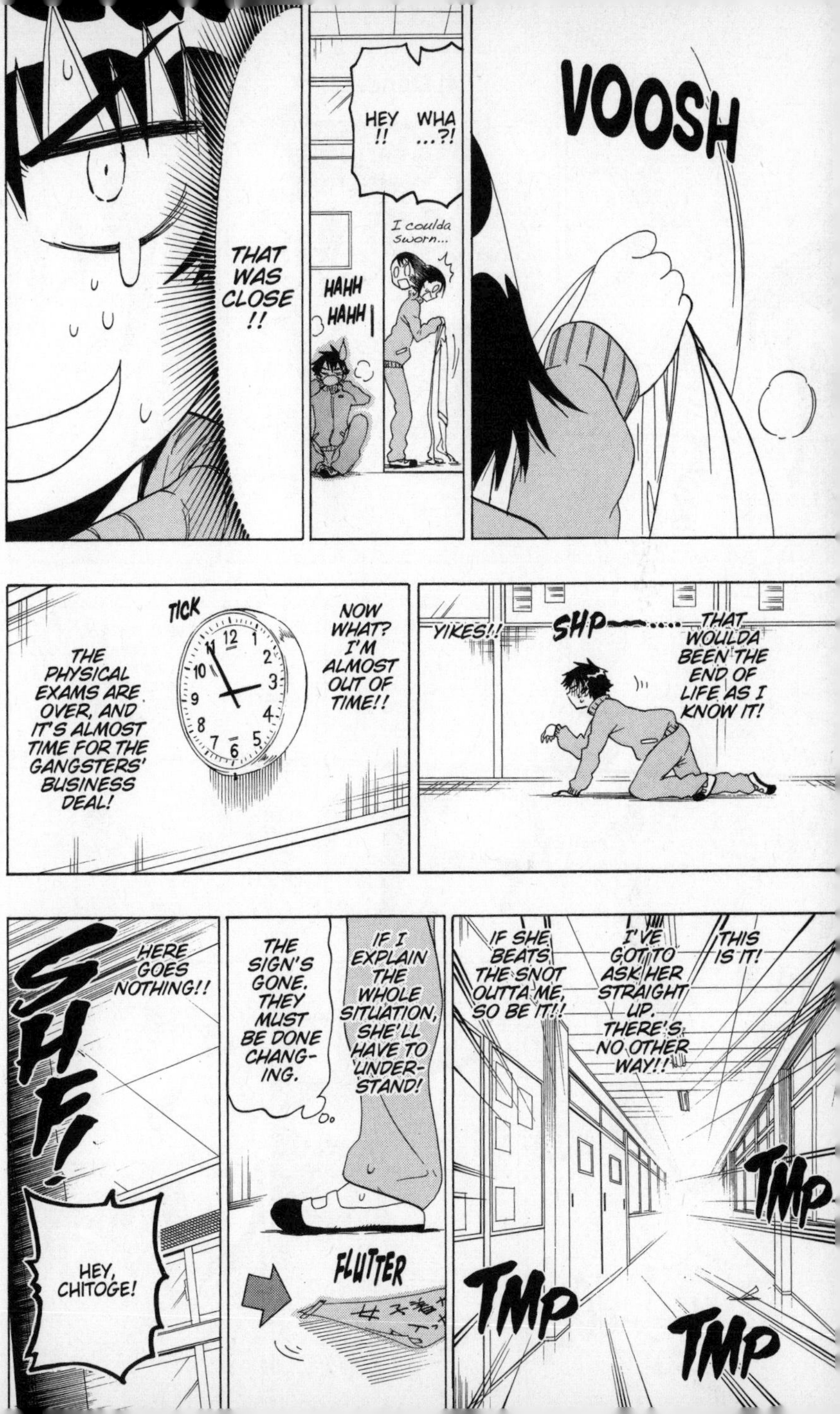
VOOSH
HEY!! WHA...?!
I coulda sworn...
HAHH HAHH
THAT WAS CLOSE!!
YIKES!!
SHP——....
THAT WOULDA BEEN THE END OF LIFE AS I KNOW IT!
NOW WHAT? I'M ALMOST OUT OF TIME!!
TICK
THE PHYSICAL EXAMS ARE OVER, AND IT'S ALMOST TIME FOR THE GANGSTERS' BUSINESS DEAL!
THIS IS IT!
I'VE GOT TO ASK HER STRAIGHT UP. THERE'S NO OTHER WAY!!
IF SHE BEATS THE SNOT OUTTA ME, SO BE IT!!
TMP
TMP
TMP
IF I EXPLAIN THE WHOLE SITUATION, SHE'LL HAVE TO UNDER-STAND!
THE SIGN'S GONE. THEY MUST BE DONE CHANG-ING.
FLUTTER
HERE GOES NOTHING!!
SHF!
HEY, CHITOGE!

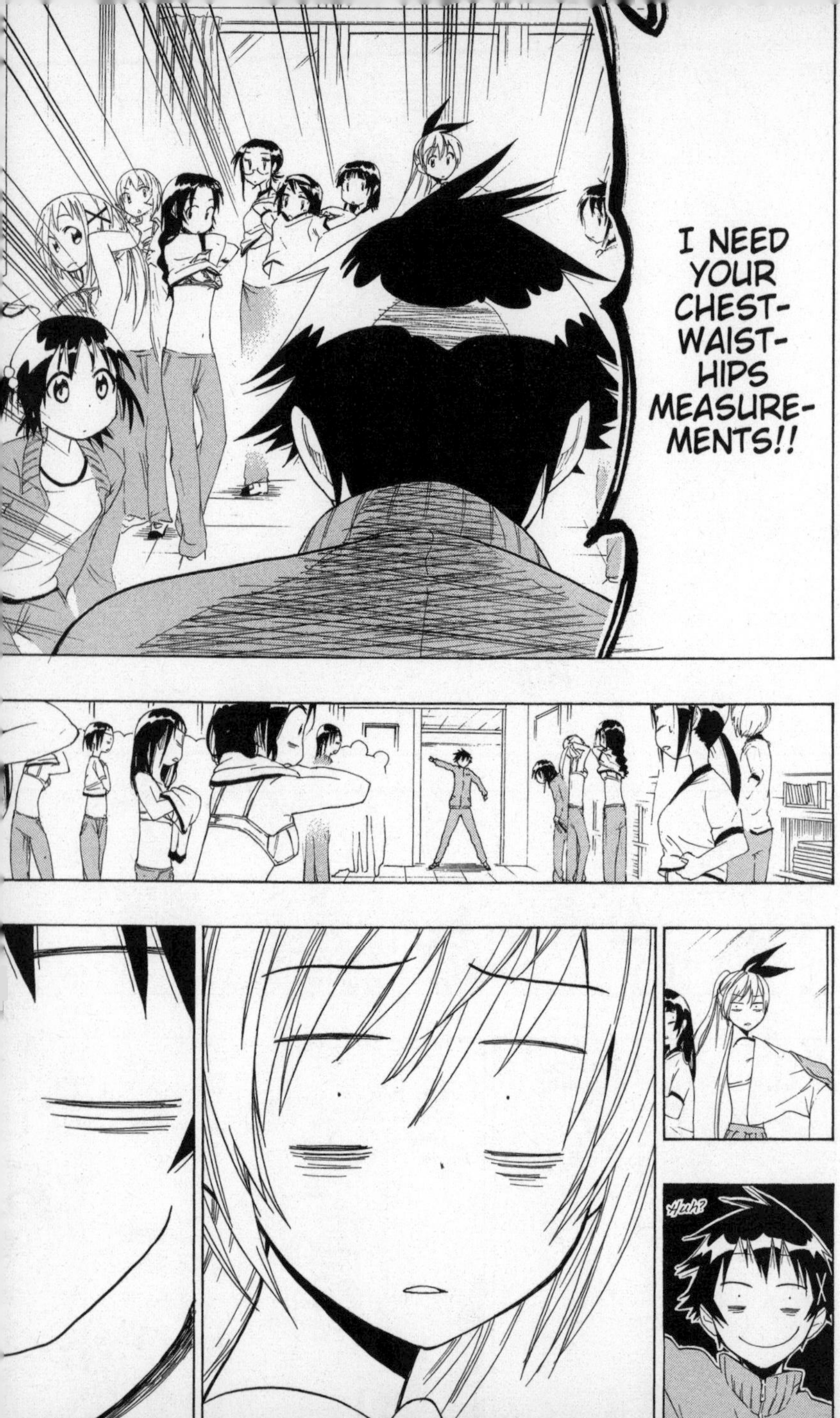
I NEED YOUR CHEST-WAIST-HIPS MEASUREMENTS!!
Huh?

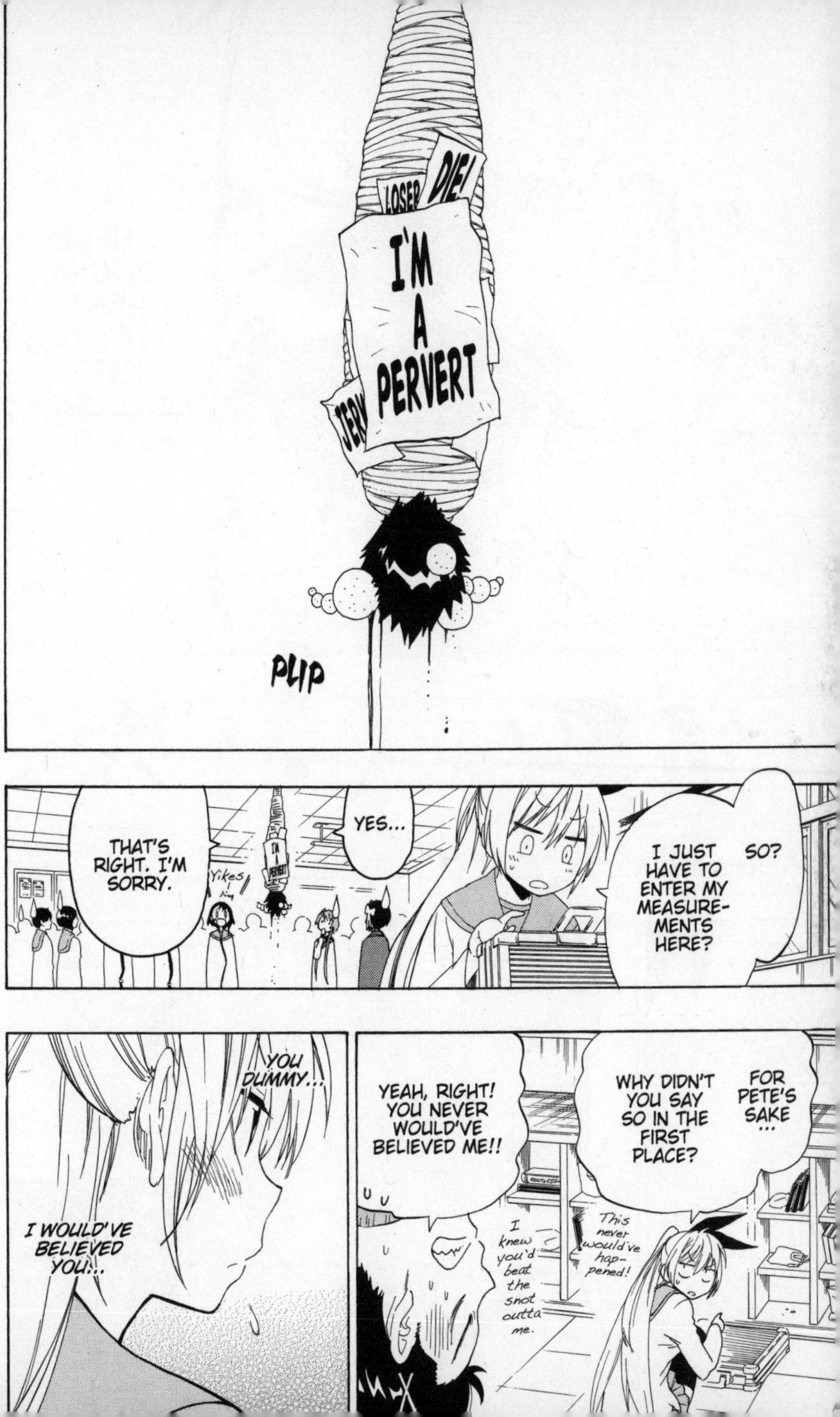
LOSER
DIE!
I'M A PERVERT
PLIP
SO?
I JUST HAVE TO ENTER MY MEASUREMENTS HERE?
YES...
I'M A PERVERT
Yikes
THAT'S RIGHT. I'M SORRY.
FOR PETE'S SAKE...
WHY DIDN'T YOU SAY SO IN THE FIRST PLACE?
This never would've happened!
YEAH, RIGHT! YOU NEVER WOULD'VE BELIEVED ME!!
I knew you'd beat the snot outta me.
YOU DUMMY...
I WOULD'VE BELIEVED YOU...

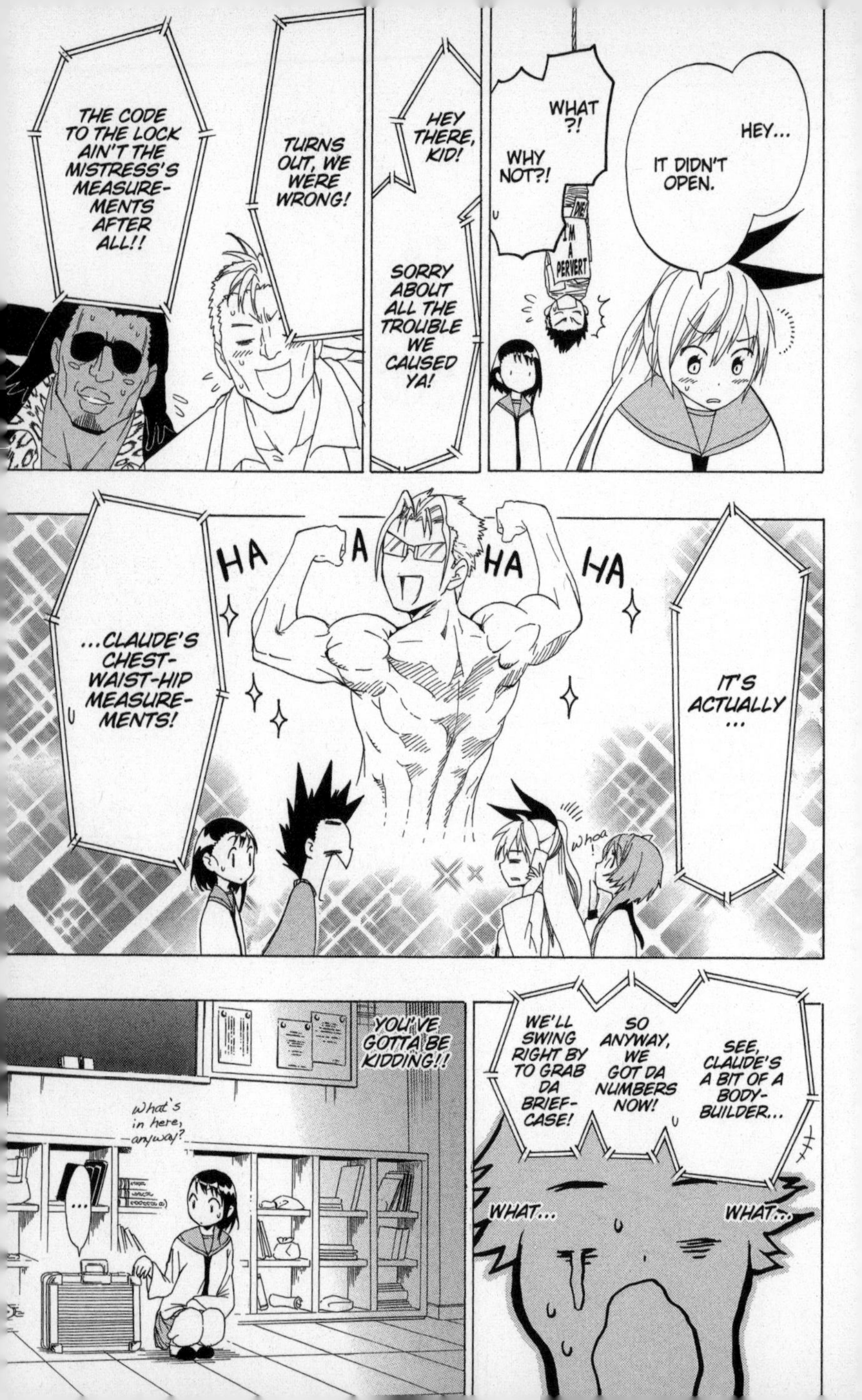
HEY...
IT DIDN'T OPEN.
WHAT?!
WHY NOT?!
DIE!
I'M A PERVERT
HEY THERE, KID!
SORRY ABOUT ALL THE TROUBLE WE CAUSED YA!
TURNS OUT, WE WERE WRONG!
THE CODE TO THE LOCK AIN'T THE MISTRESS'S MEASUREMENTS AFTER ALL!!
IT'S ACTUALLY...
HA HA HA HA
...CLAUDE'S CHEST-WAIST-HIP MEASUREMENTS!
Whoa
SEE, CLAUDE'S A BIT OF A BODY-BUILDER...
SO ANYWAY, WE GOT DA NUMBERS NOW!
WE'LL SWING RIGHT BY TO GRAB DA BRIEFCASE!
WHAT... WHAT...
YOU'VE GOTTA BE KIDDING!!
What's in here, anyway?
...

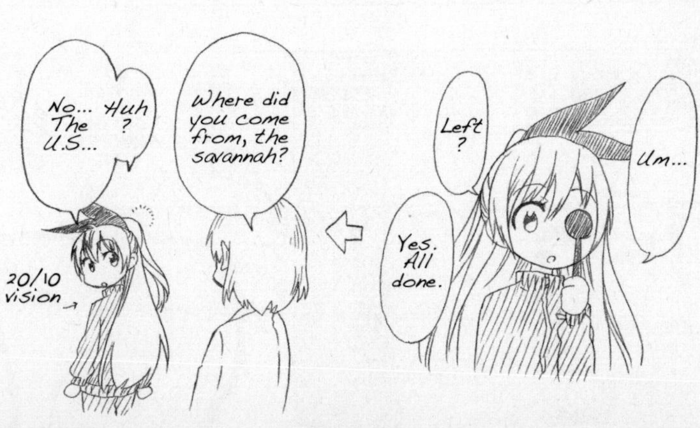
Um...
Left?
Yes. All done.
Where did you come from, the savannah?
Huh?
No... The U.S...
20/10 vision

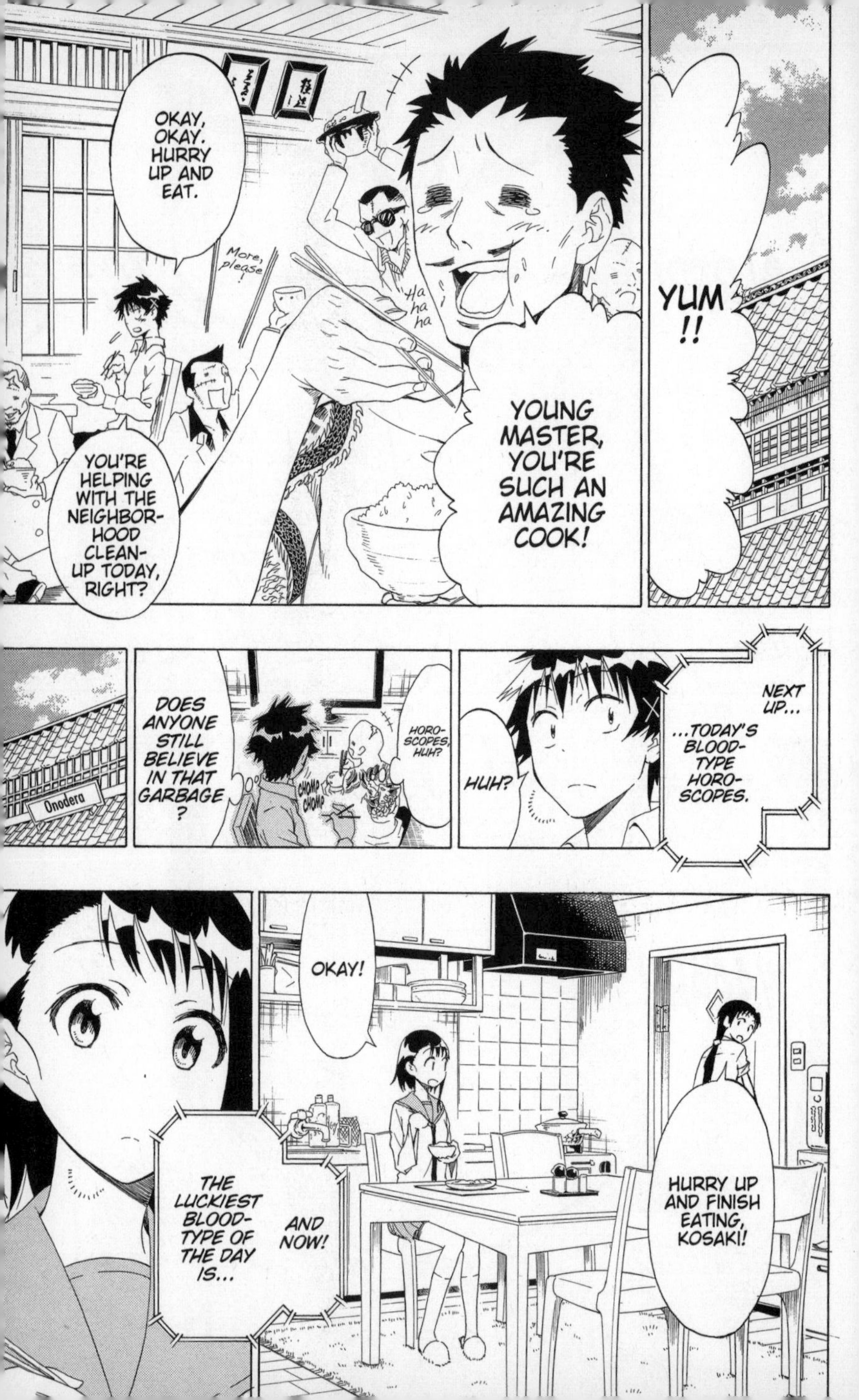
YUM!!
YOUNG MASTER, YOU'RE SUCH AN AMAZING COOK!
Ha ha ha
More, please!
OKAY, OKAY. HURRY UP AND EAT.
YOU'RE HELPING WITH THE NEIGHBORHOOD CLEAN-UP TODAY, RIGHT?
NEXT UP...
...TODAY'S BLOOD-TYPE HOROSCOPES.
HUH?
HOROSCOPES, HUH?
CHOMP CHOMP
DOES ANYONE STILL BELIEVE IN THAT GARBAGE?
Onodera
HURRY UP AND FINISH EATING, KOSAKI!
OKAY!
AND NOW!
THE LUCKIEST BLOOD-TYPE OF THE DAY IS...

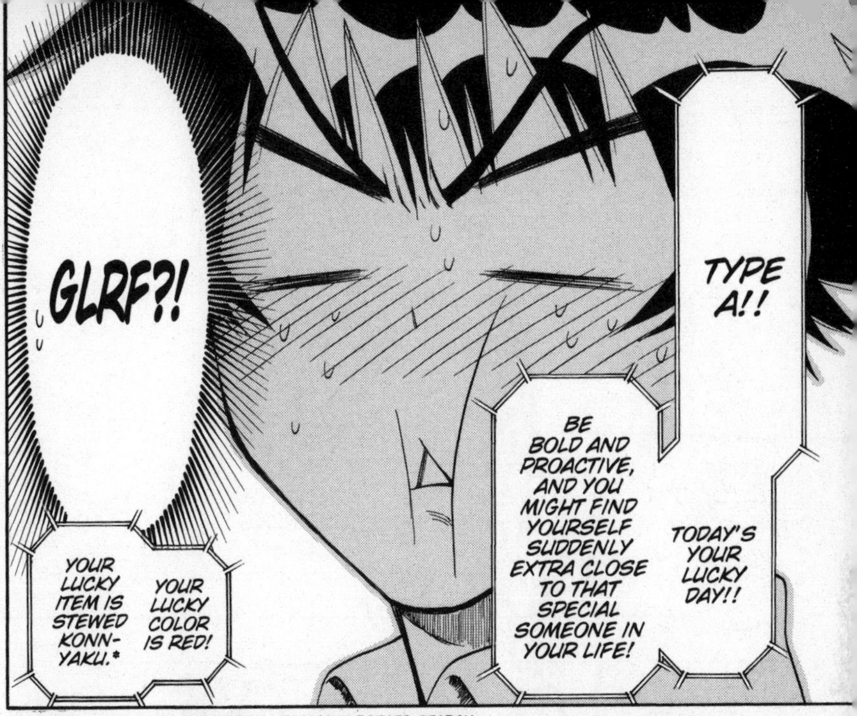
TYPE A!!
TODAY'S YOUR LUCKY DAY!!
BE BOLD AND PROACTIVE, AND YOU MIGHT FIND YOURSELF SUDDENLY EXTRA CLOSE TO THAT SPECIAL SOMEONE IN YOUR LIFE!
YOUR LUCKY COLOR IS RED!
YOUR LUCKY ITEM IS STEWED KONN-YAKU.*
GLRF?!

*A JELLY-LIKE FOOD MADE FROM KONNYAKU POTATO STARCH.

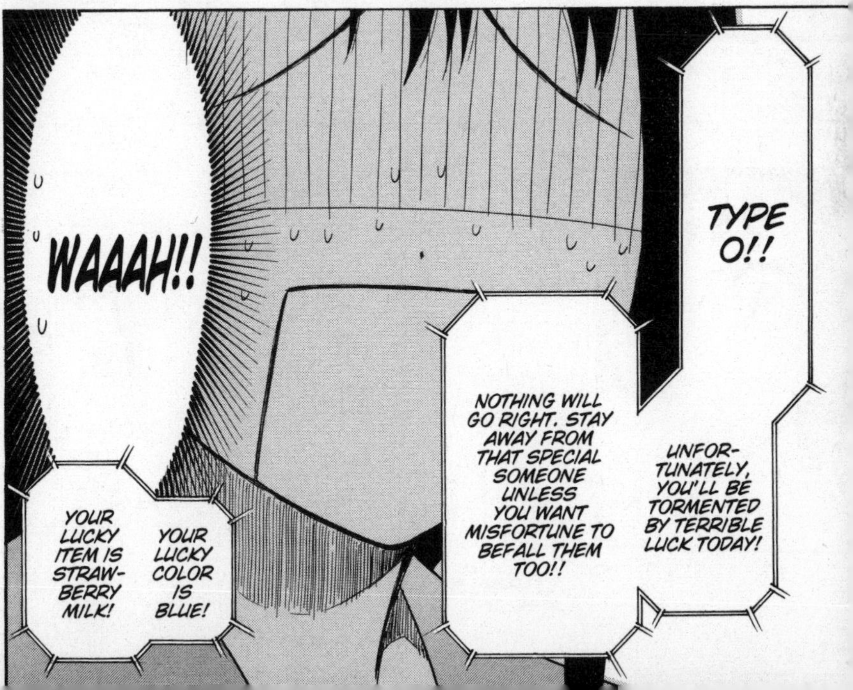
TYPE O!!
UNFOR-TUNATELY, YOU'LL BE TORMENTED BY TERRIBLE LUCK TODAY!
NOTHING WILL GO RIGHT. STAY AWAY FROM THAT SPECIAL SOMEONE UNLESS YOU WANT MISFORTUNE TO BEFALL THEM TOO!!
YOUR LUCKY COLOR IS BLUE!
YOUR LUCKY ITEM IS STRAW-BERRY MILK!
WAAAH!!

Chapter 53: Horoscope

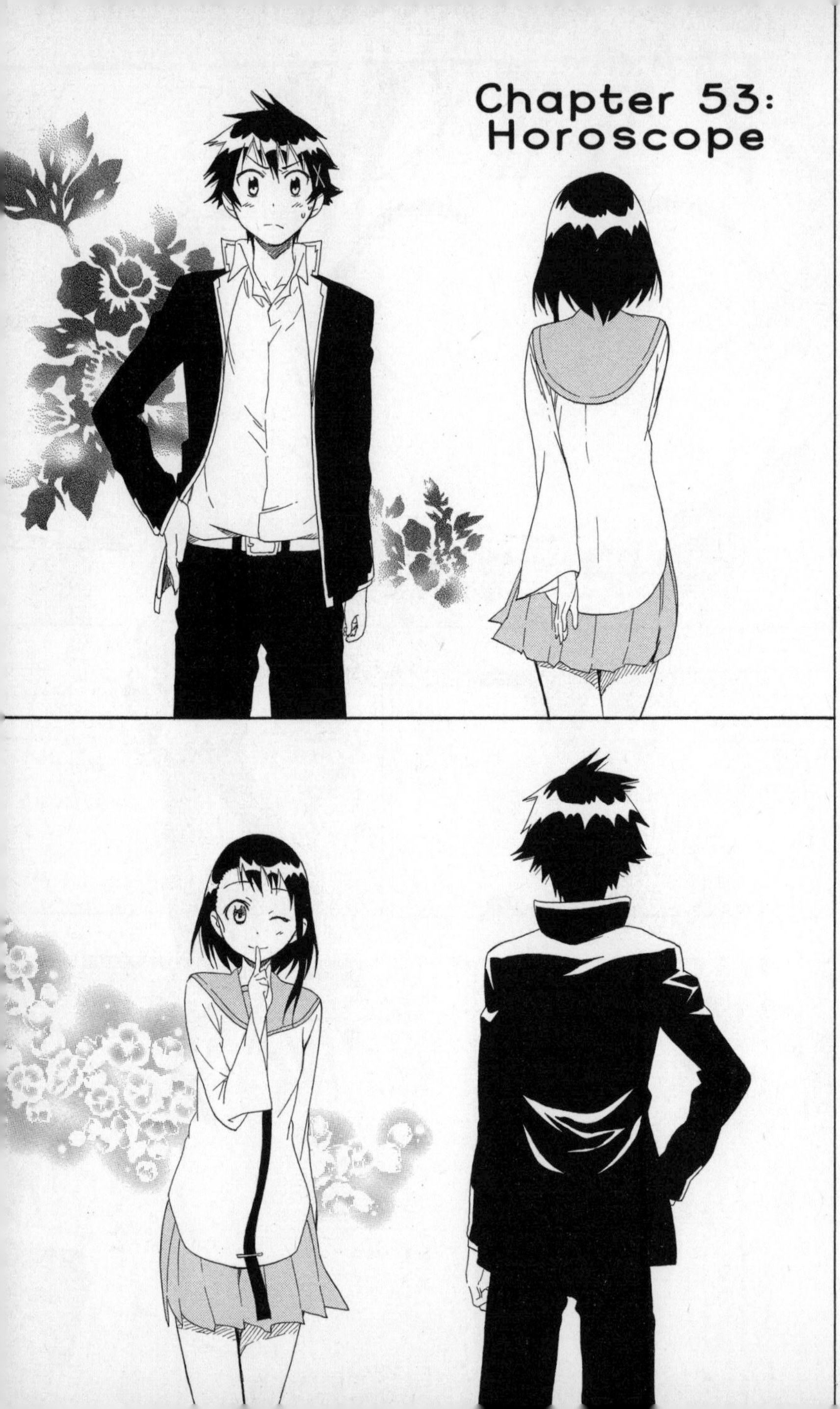

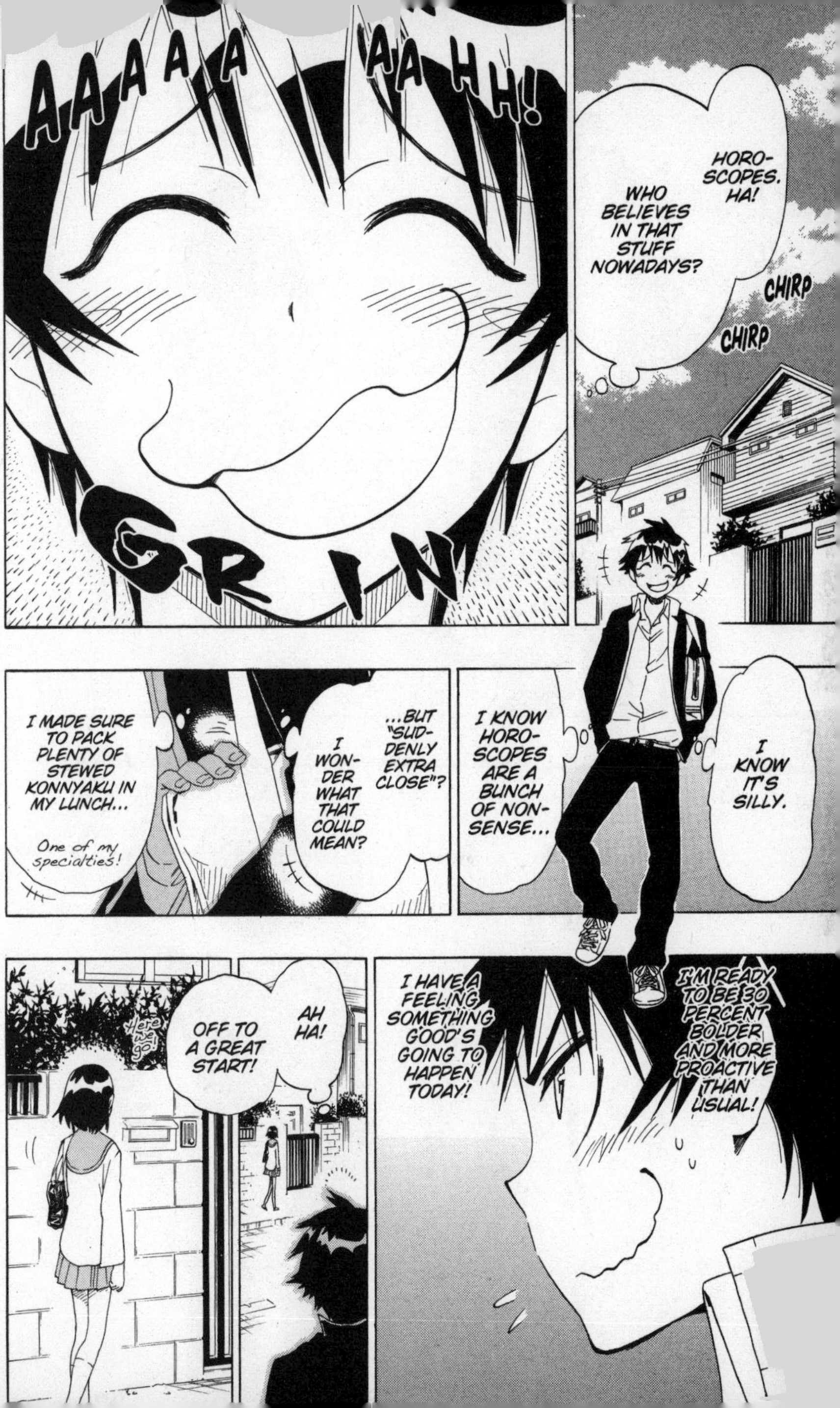
HOROSCOPES. HA!
WHO BELIEVES IN THAT STUFF NOWADAYS?
CHIRP
CHIRP
AAAAAAAHH!
GRIN
I KNOW IT'S SILLY.
I KNOW HOROSCOPES ARE A BUNCH OF NONSENSE...
...BUT "SUDDENLY EXTRA CLOSE"?
I WONDER WHAT THAT COULD MEAN?
I MADE SURE TO PACK PLENTY OF STEWED KONNYAKU IN MY LUNCH...
One of my specialties!
I'M READY TO BE 30 PERCENT BOLDER AND MORE PROACTIVE THAN USUAL!
I HAVE A FEELING SOMETHING GOOD'S GOING TO HAPPEN TODAY!
AH HA!
OFF TO A GREAT START!
Here we go!

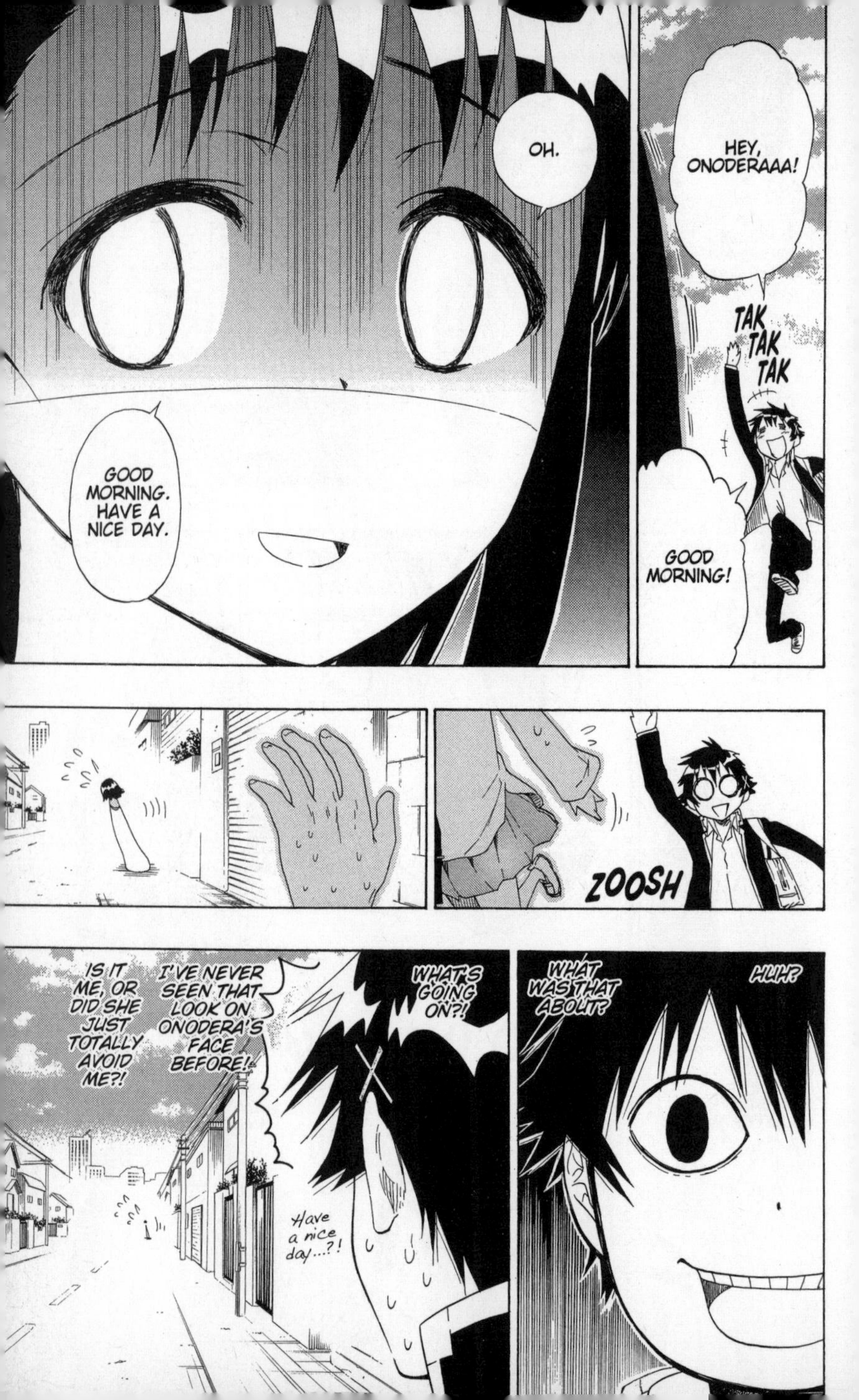
HEY, ONODERAAA!
TAK TAK TAK
GOOD MORNING!
OH.
GOOD MORNING. HAVE A NICE DAY.
ZOOSH
HUH?
WHAT WAS THAT ABOUT?
WHAT'S GOING ON?!
I'VE NEVER SEEN THAT LOOK ON ONODERA'S FACE BEFORE!
IS IT ME, OR DID SHE JUST TOTALLY AVOID ME?!
Have a nice day...?!

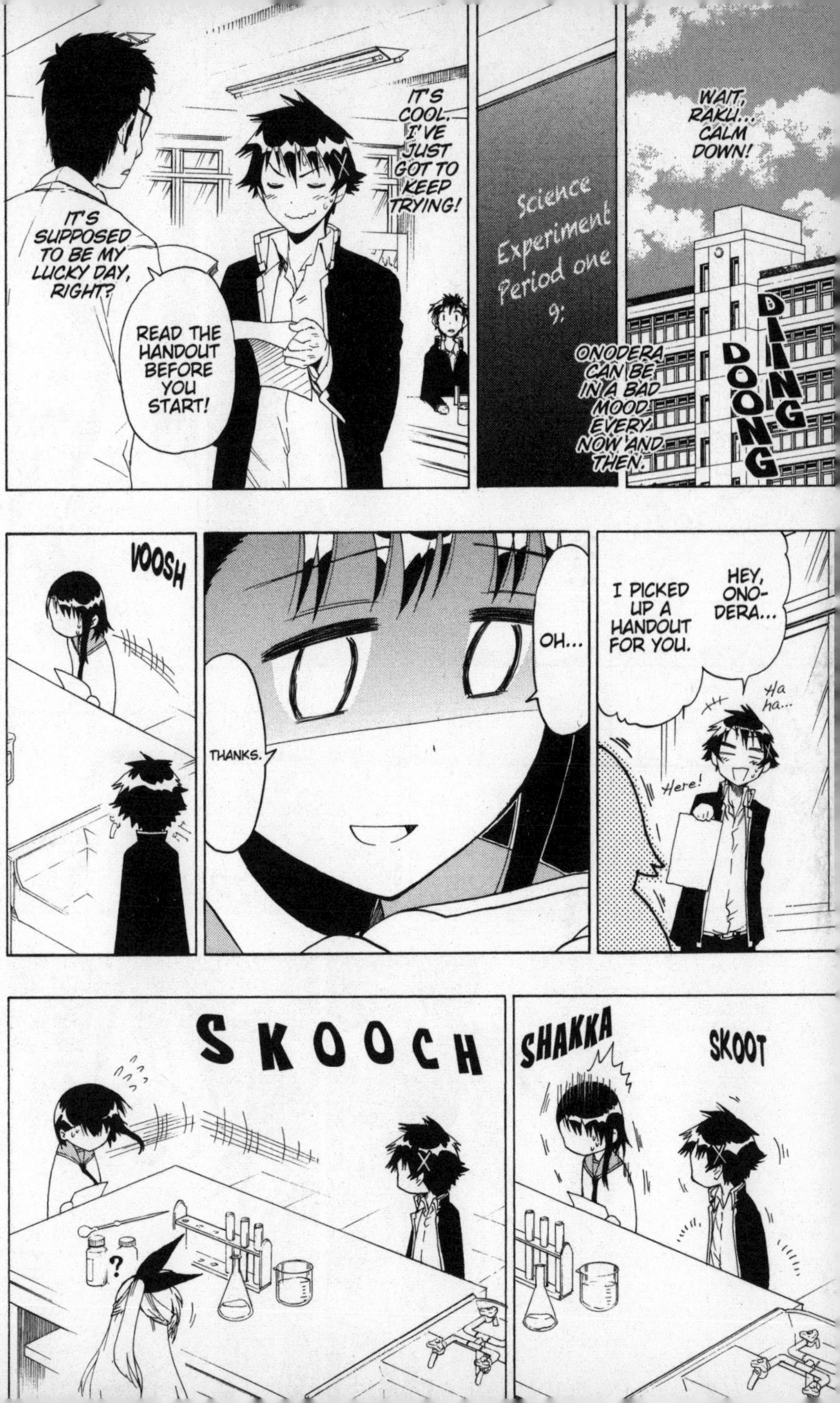
WAIT, RAKU... CALM DOWN!
DING
DONG
ONODERA CAN BE IN A BAD MOOD EVERY NOW AND THEN.
Science Experiment Period one 9:
IT'S COOL. I'VE JUST GOT TO KEEP TRYING!
IT'S SUPPOSED TO BE MY LUCKY DAY, RIGHT?
READ THE HANDOUT BEFORE YOU START!
HEY, ONO-DERA...
I PICKED UP A HANDOUT FOR YOU.
Ha ha...
Here!
OH...
THANKS.
VOOSH
SKOOT
SHAKKA
SKOOCH

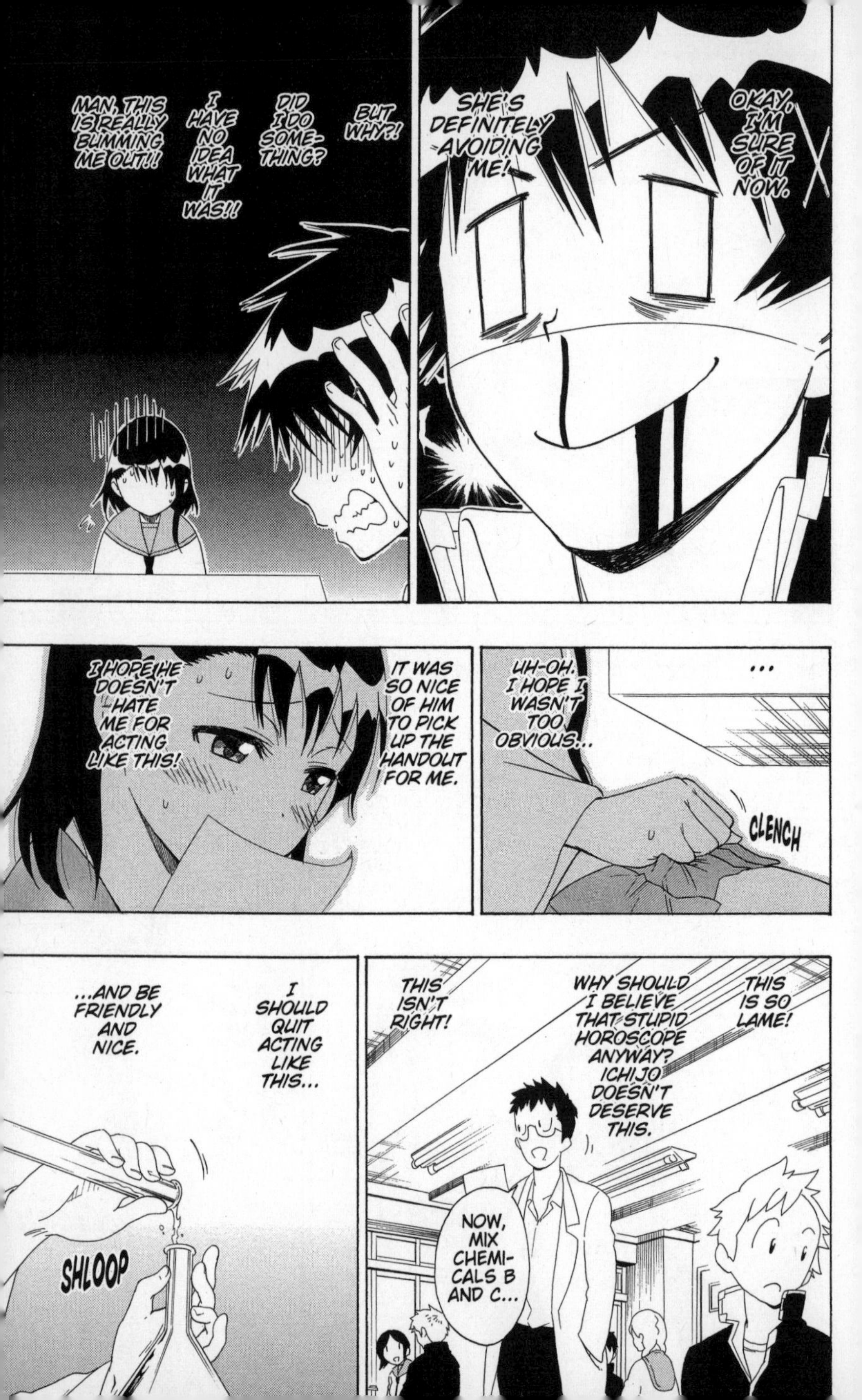
OKAY, I'M SURE OF IT NOW.
SHE'S DEFINITELY AVOIDING ME!
BUT WHY?!
DID I DO SOMETHING?
I HAVE NO IDEA WHAT IT WAS!!
MAN, THIS IS REALLY BUMMING ME OUT!!
...
UH-OH. I HOPE I WASN'T TOO OBVIOUS...
CLENCH
IT WAS SO NICE OF HIM TO PICK UP THE HANDOUT FOR ME.
I HOPE HE DOESN'T HATE ME FOR ACTING LIKE THIS!
THIS IS SO LAME!
WHY SHOULD I BELIEVE THAT STUPID HOROSCOPE ANYWAY? ICHIJO DOESN'T DESERVE THIS.
THIS ISN'T RIGHT!
NOW, MIX CHEMICALS B AND C...
I SHOULD QUIT ACTING LIKE THIS...
...AND BE FRIENDLY AND NICE.
SHLOOP

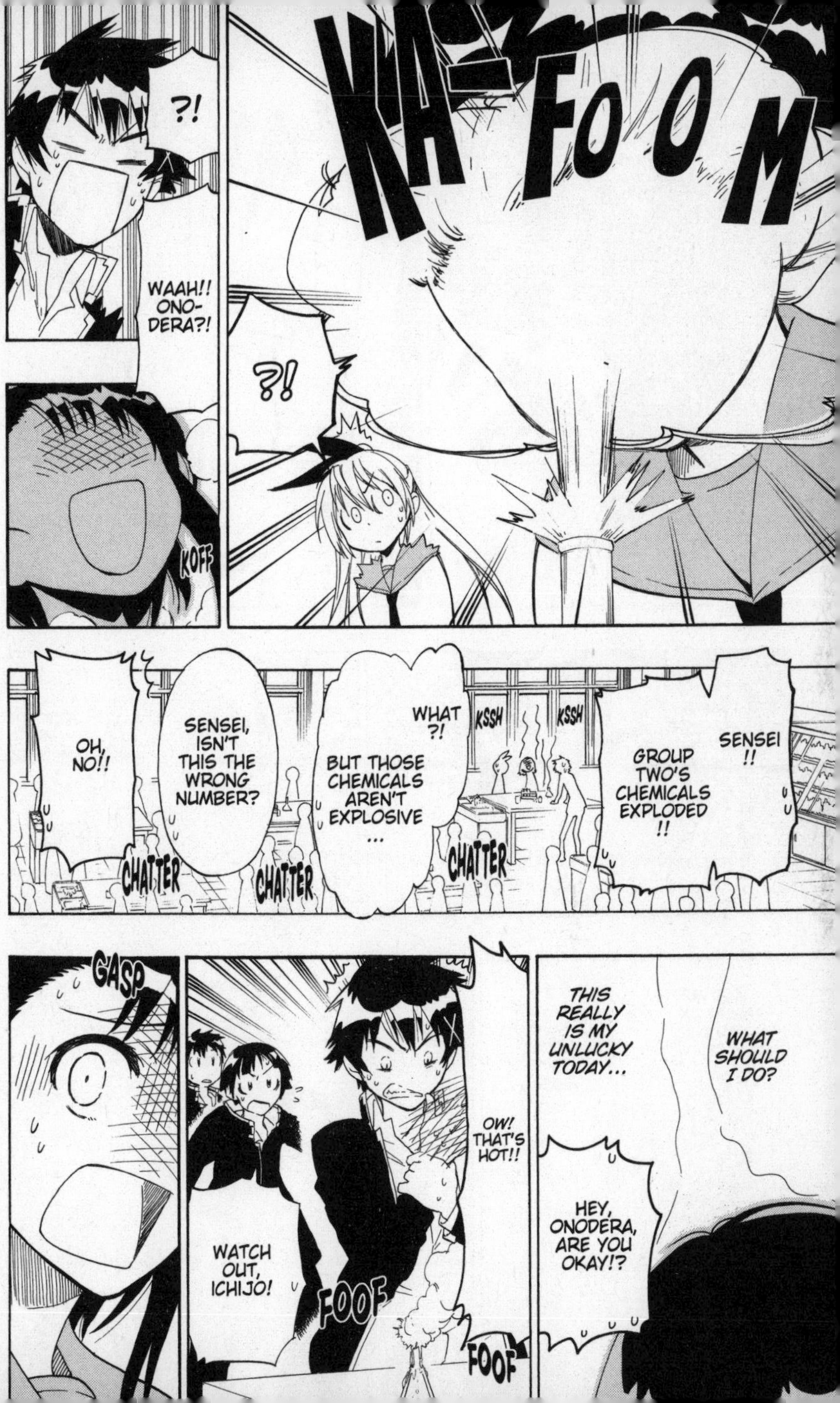
KA-FOOM
?!
?!
WAAH!! ONO-DERA?!
KOFF
SENSEI!!
GROUP TWO'S CHEMICALS EXPLODED!!
KSSH
KSSH
CHATTER
WHAT?!
BUT THOSE CHEMICALS AREN'T EXPLOSIVE...
CHATTER
SENSEI, ISN'T THIS THE WRONG NUMBER?
CHATTER
OH, NO!!
WHAT SHOULD I DO?
THIS REALLY IS MY UNLUCKY TODAY...
HEY, ONODERA, ARE YOU OKAY!?
OW! THAT'S HOT!!
WATCH OUT, ICHIJO!
FOOF
FOOF
GASP

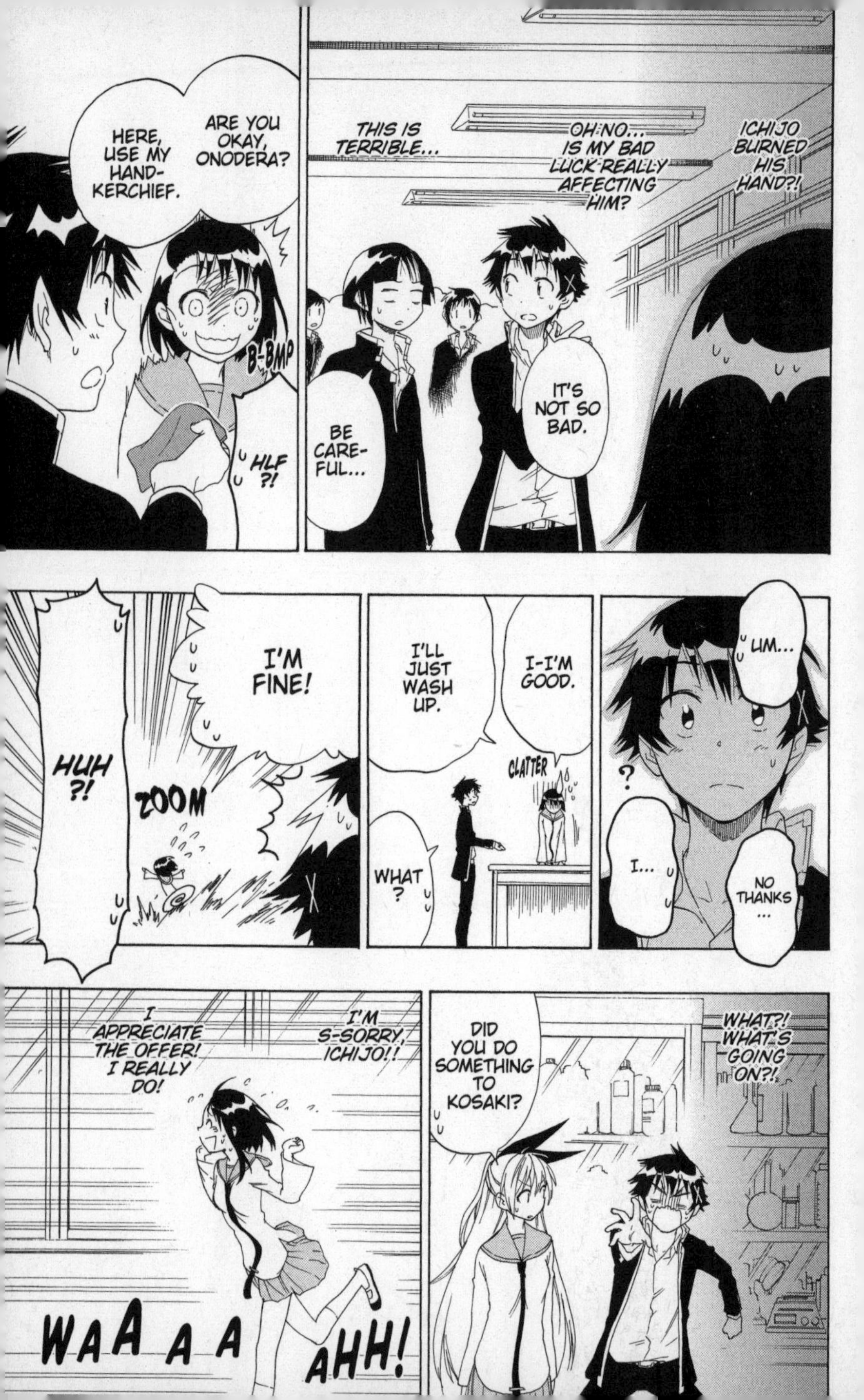
ICHIJO BURNED HIS HAND?!
OH NO... IS MY BAD LUCK REALLY AFFECTING HIM?
THIS IS TERRIBLE...
IT'S NOT SO BAD.
BE CAREFUL...
ARE YOU OKAY, ONODERA?
HERE, USE MY HANDKERCHIEF.
B-BMP
HLF ?!
UM...
?
I...
NO THANKS...
I-I'M GOOD.
I'LL JUST WASH UP.
CLATTER
WHAT?
I'M FINE!
HUH?!
ZOOM
WHAT?! WHAT'S GOING ON?!
DID YOU DO SOMETHING TO KOSAKI?
I'M S-SORRY, ICHIJO!!
I APPRECIATE THE OFFER! I REALLY DO!
WAAAAAHH!

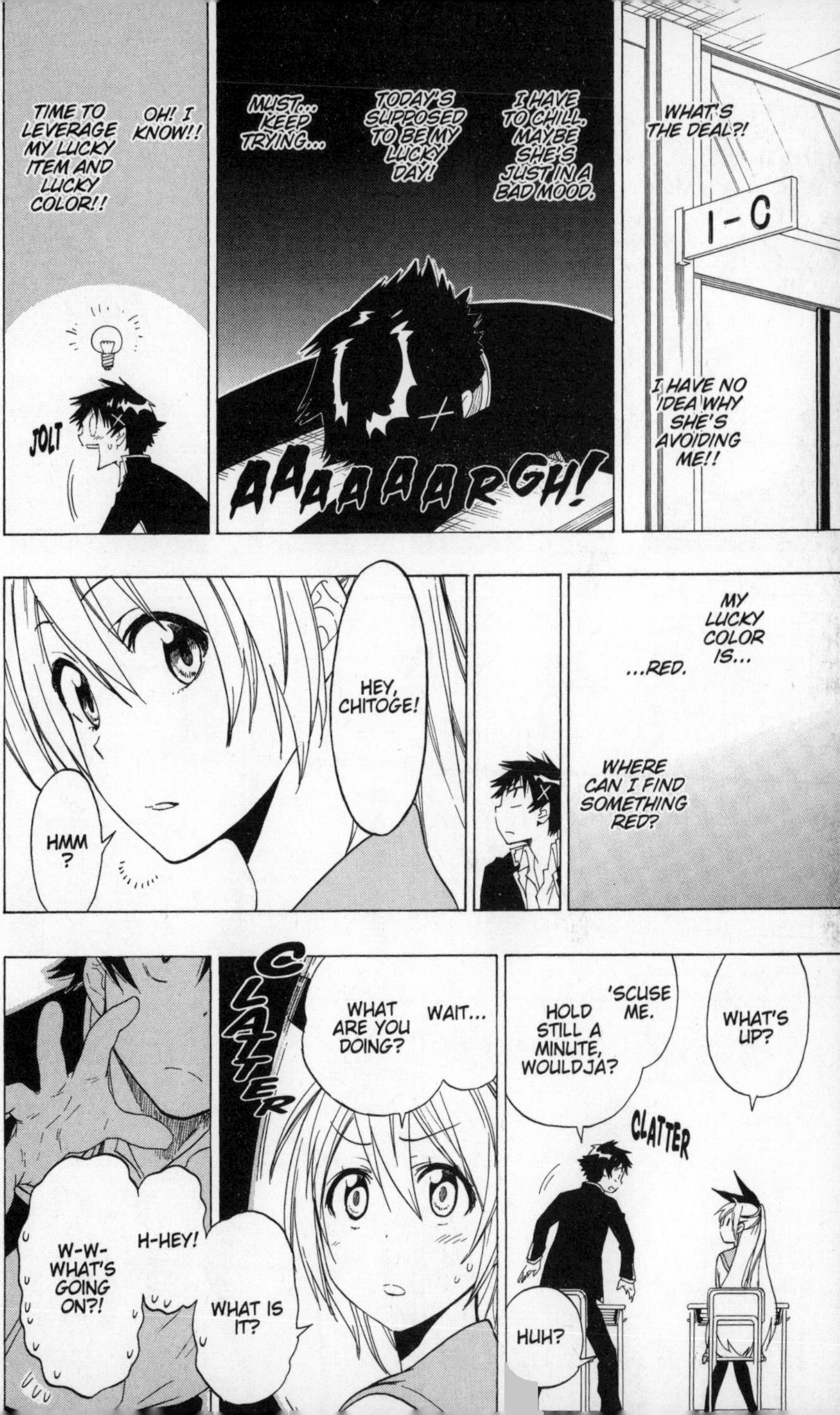
WHAT'S THE DEAL?!
I HAVE NO IDEA WHY SHE'S AVOIDING ME!!
I HAVE TO CHILL. MAYBE SHE'S JUST IN A BAD MOOD.
TODAY'S SUPPOSED TO BE MY LUCKY DAY!
MUST... KEEP TRYING...
AAAAAAARGH!
OH! I KNOW!!
TIME TO LEVERAGE MY LUCKY ITEM AND LUCKY COLOR!!
JOLT
MY LUCKY COLOR IS...
...RED.
WHERE CAN I FIND SOMETHING RED?
HEY, CHITOGE!
HMM?
WHAT'S UP?
'SCUSE ME.
HOLD STILL A MINUTE, WOULDJA?
CLATTER
HUH?
WAIT...
WHAT ARE YOU DOING?
CLATTER
WHAT IS IT?
H-HEY!
W-W-WHAT'S GOING ON?!

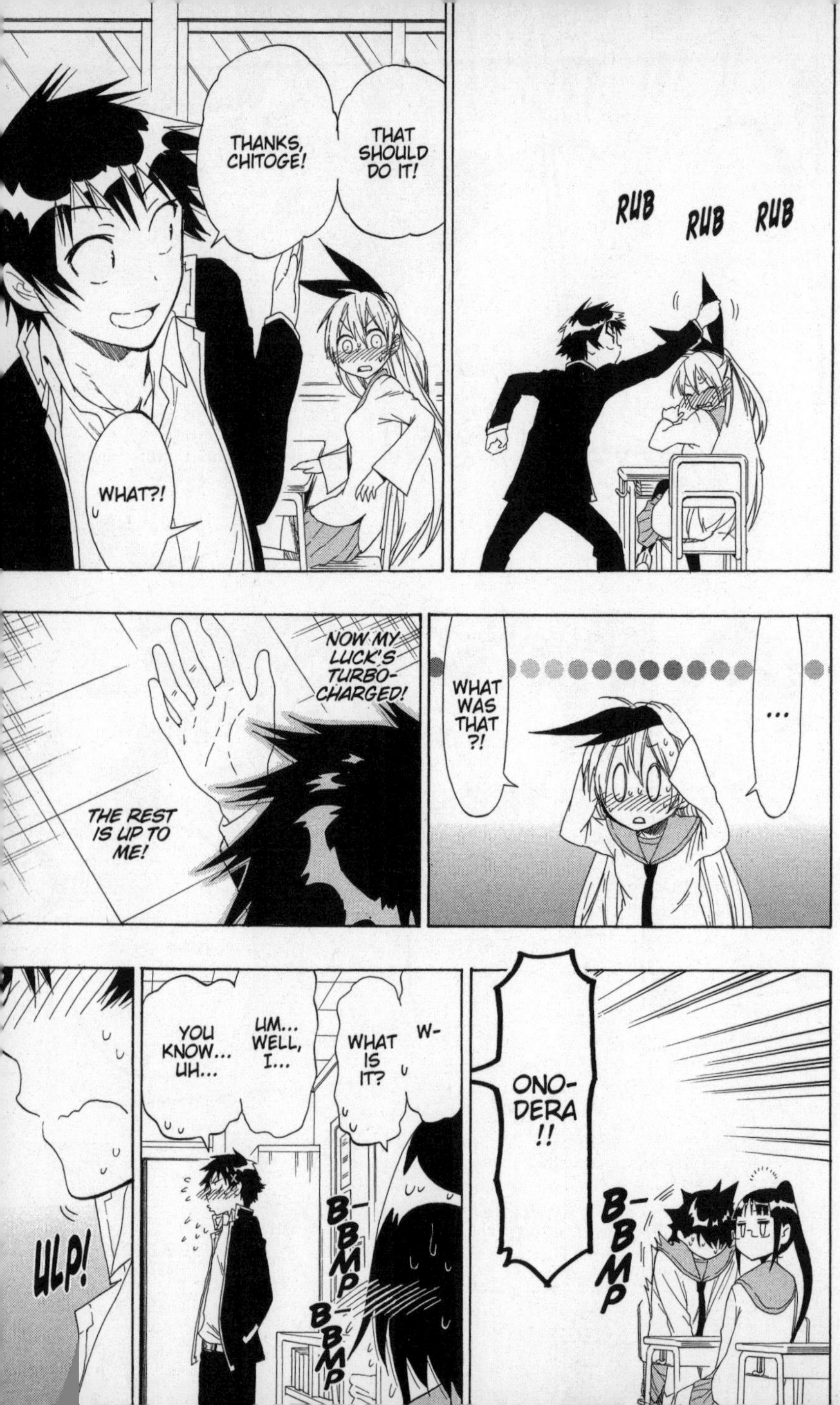
RUB
RUB
RUB
THAT SHOULD DO IT!
THANKS, CHITOGE!
WHAT?!
...
WHAT WAS THAT?!
NOW MY LUCK'S TURBO-CHARGED!
THE REST IS UP TO ME!
ONO-DERA!!
B-BBMP
W-
WHAT IS IT?
UM... WELL, I...
YOU KNOW... UH...
B-BBMP
B-BBMP
ULP!

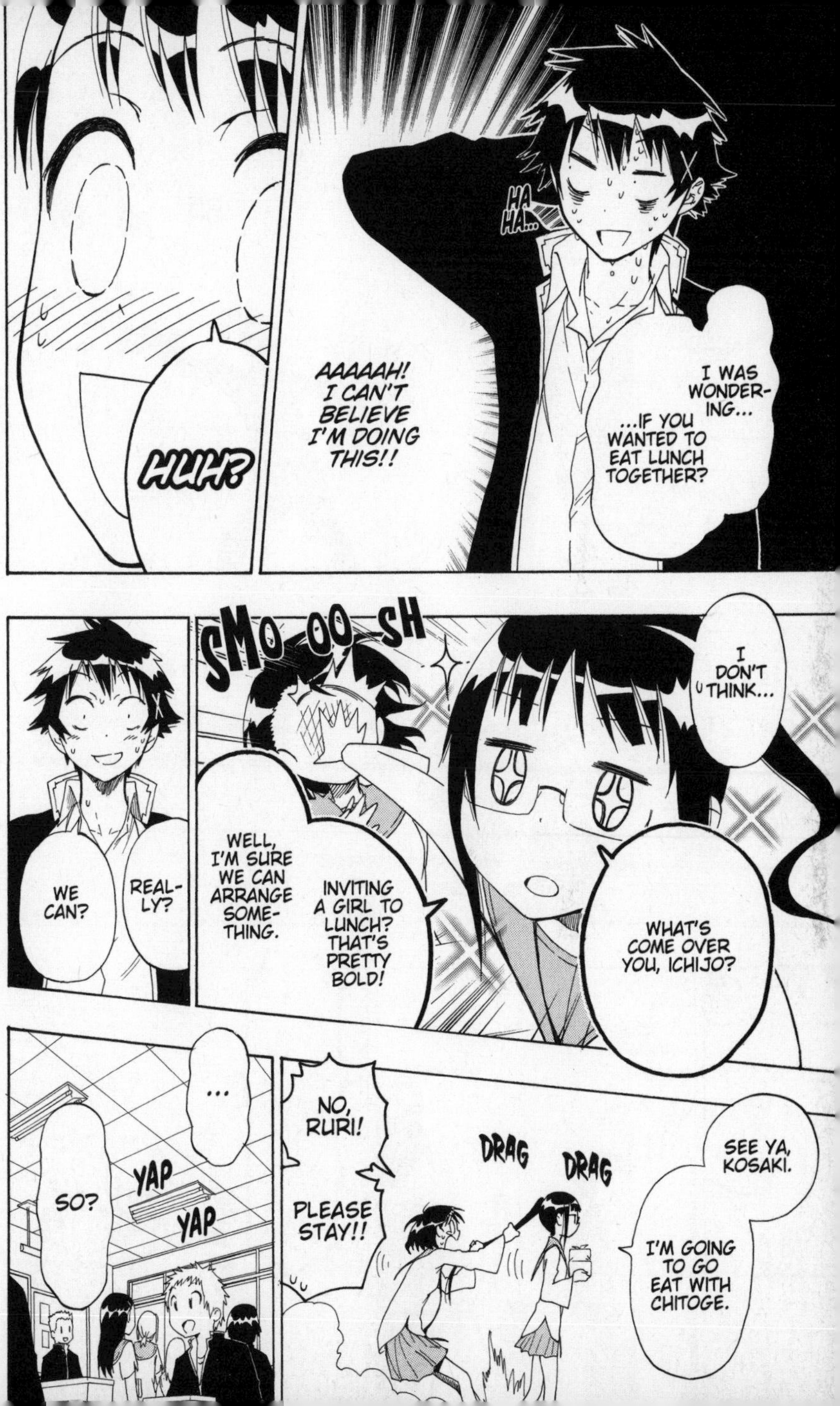
HA HA...
I WAS WONDERING...
...IF YOU WANTED TO EAT LUNCH TOGETHER?
AAAAAH! I CAN'T BELIEVE I'M DOING THIS!!
HUH?
I DON'T THINK...
WHAT'S COME OVER YOU, ICHIJO?
SMO-OO-SH
INVITING A GIRL TO LUNCH? THAT'S PRETTY BOLD!
WELL, I'M SURE WE CAN ARRANGE SOMETHING.
REAL-LY?
WE CAN?
SEE YA, KOSAKI.
I'M GOING TO GO EAT WITH CHITOGE.
DRAG
DRAG
NO, RURI!
PLEASE STAY!!
...
SO?
YAP
YAP

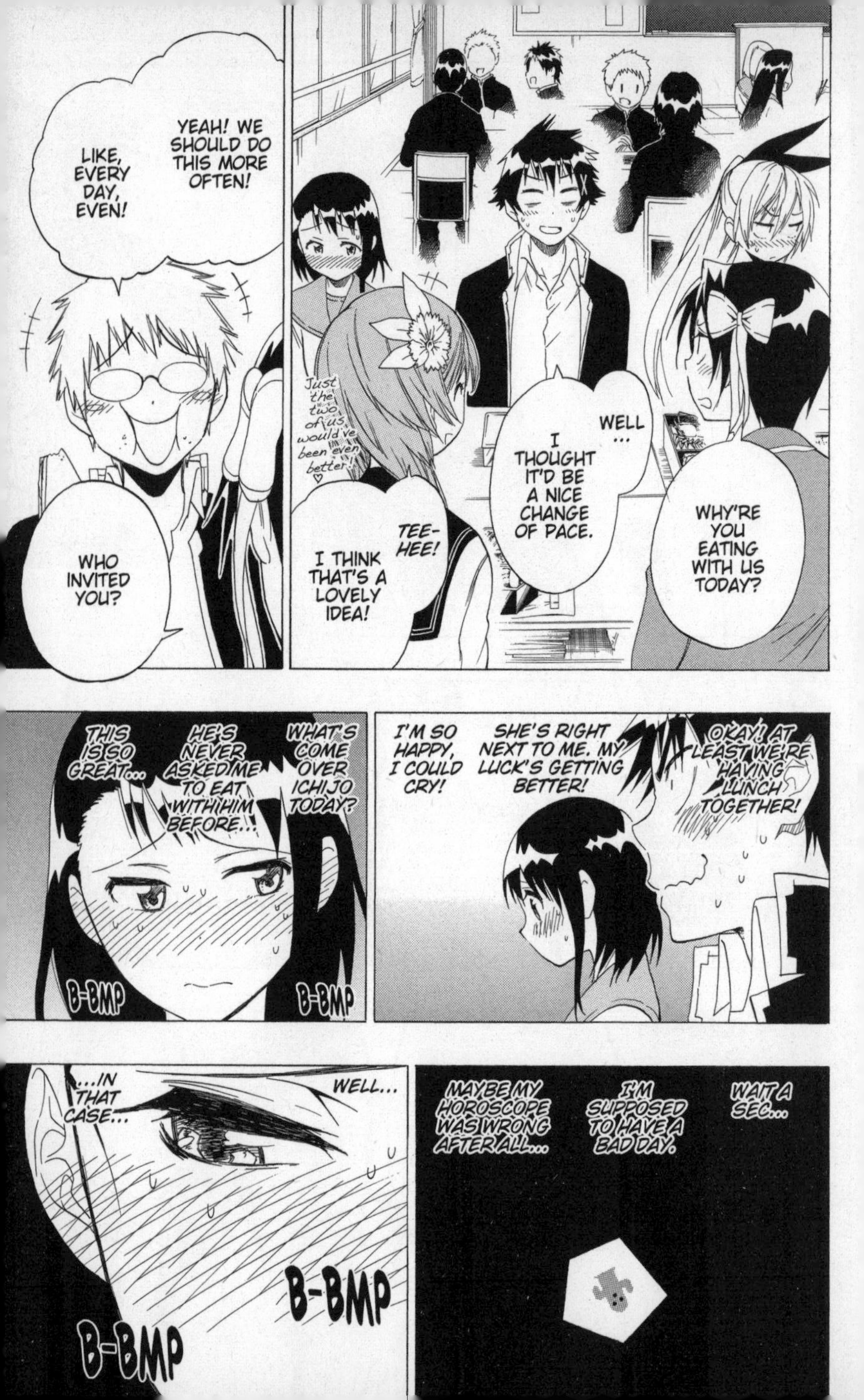
WHY'RE YOU EATING WITH US TODAY?
WELL ... I THOUGHT IT'D BE A NICE CHANGE OF PACE.
TEE-HEE! I THINK THAT'S A LOVELY IDEA!
Just the two of us would've been even better ♥
YEAH! WE SHOULD DO THIS MORE OFTEN!
LIKE, EVERY DAY, EVEN!
WHO INVITED YOU?
OKAY! AT LEAST WE'RE HAVING LUNCH TOGETHER!
SHE'S RIGHT NEXT TO ME. MY LUCK'S GETTING BETTER!
I'M SO HAPPY, I COULD CRY!
WHAT'S COME OVER ICHIJO TODAY?
HE'S NEVER ASKED ME TO EAT WITH HIM BEFORE...
THIS IS SO GREAT...
B-BMP
B-BMP
WAIT A SEC...
I'M SUPPOSED TO HAVE A BAD DAY.
MAYBE MY HOROSCOPE WAS WRONG AFTER ALL...
WELL...
...IN THAT CASE...
B-BMP
B-BMP

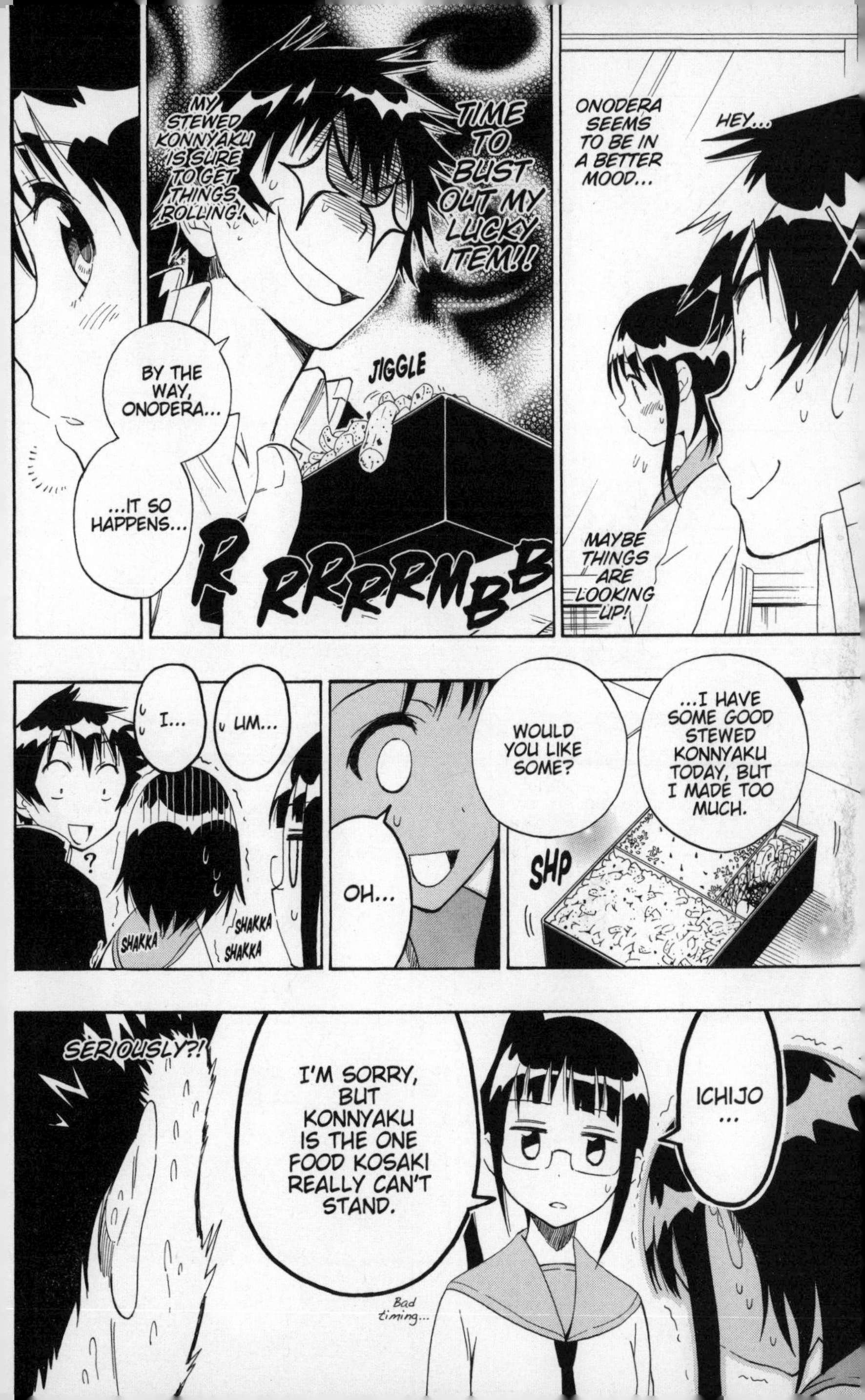
HEY...
ONODERA SEEMS TO BE IN A BETTER MOOD...
MAYBE THINGS ARE LOOKING UP!
TIME TO BUST OUT MY LUCKY ITEM!!
MY STEWED KONNYAKU IS SURE TO GET THINGS ROLLING!
JIGGLE
BY THE WAY, ONODERA...
...IT SO HAPPENS...
R RRRRMBB
SHP
...I HAVE SOME GOOD STEWED KONNYAKU TODAY, BUT I MADE TOO MUCH.
WOULD YOU LIKE SOME?
OH...
UM...
I...
?
SHAKKA
SHAKKA
SHAKKA
ICHIJO...
I'M SORRY, BUT KONNYAKU IS THE ONE FOOD KOSAKI REALLY CAN'T STAND.
Bad timing...
SERIOUSLY?!

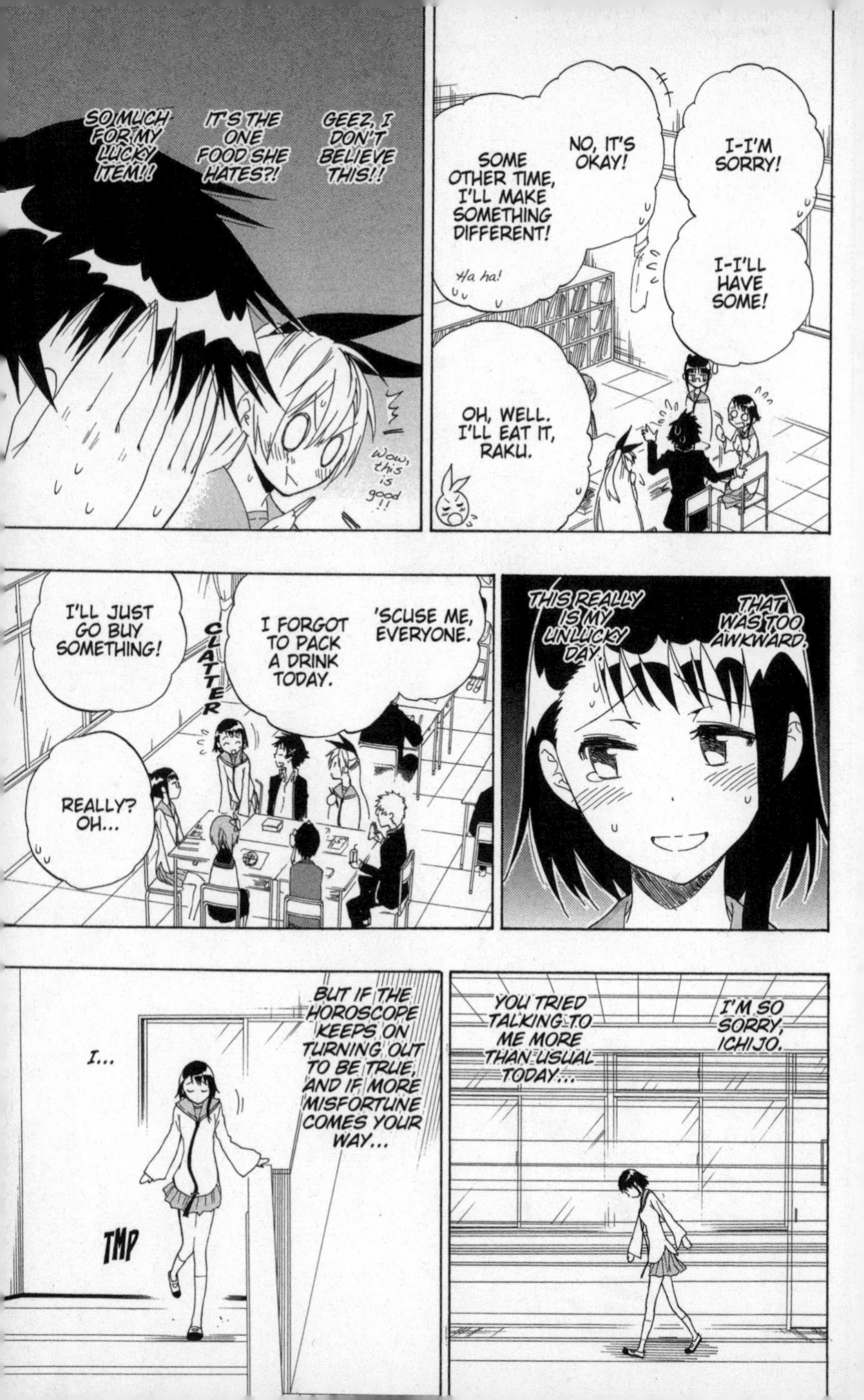
I-I'M SORRY!
I-I'LL HAVE SOME!
NO, IT'S OKAY!
SOME OTHER TIME, I'LL MAKE SOMETHING DIFFERENT!
Ha ha!
OH, WELL. I'LL EAT IT, RAKU.
GEEZ, I DON'T BELIEVE THIS!!
IT'S THE ONE FOOD SHE HATES?!
SO MUCH FOR MY LUCKY ITEM!!
Wow, this is good!!
THAT WAS TOO AWKWARD.
THIS REALLY IS MY UNLUCKY DAY.
'SCUSE ME, EVERYONE.
I FORGOT TO PACK A DRINK TODAY.
CLATTER
I'LL JUST GO BUY SOMETHING!
REALLY? OH...
I'M SO SORRY, ICHIJO.
YOU TRIED TALKING TO ME MORE THAN USUAL TODAY...
BUT IF THE HOROSCOPE KEEPS ON TURNING OUT TO BE TRUE, AND IF MORE MISFORTUNE COMES YOUR WAY...
I...
TMP

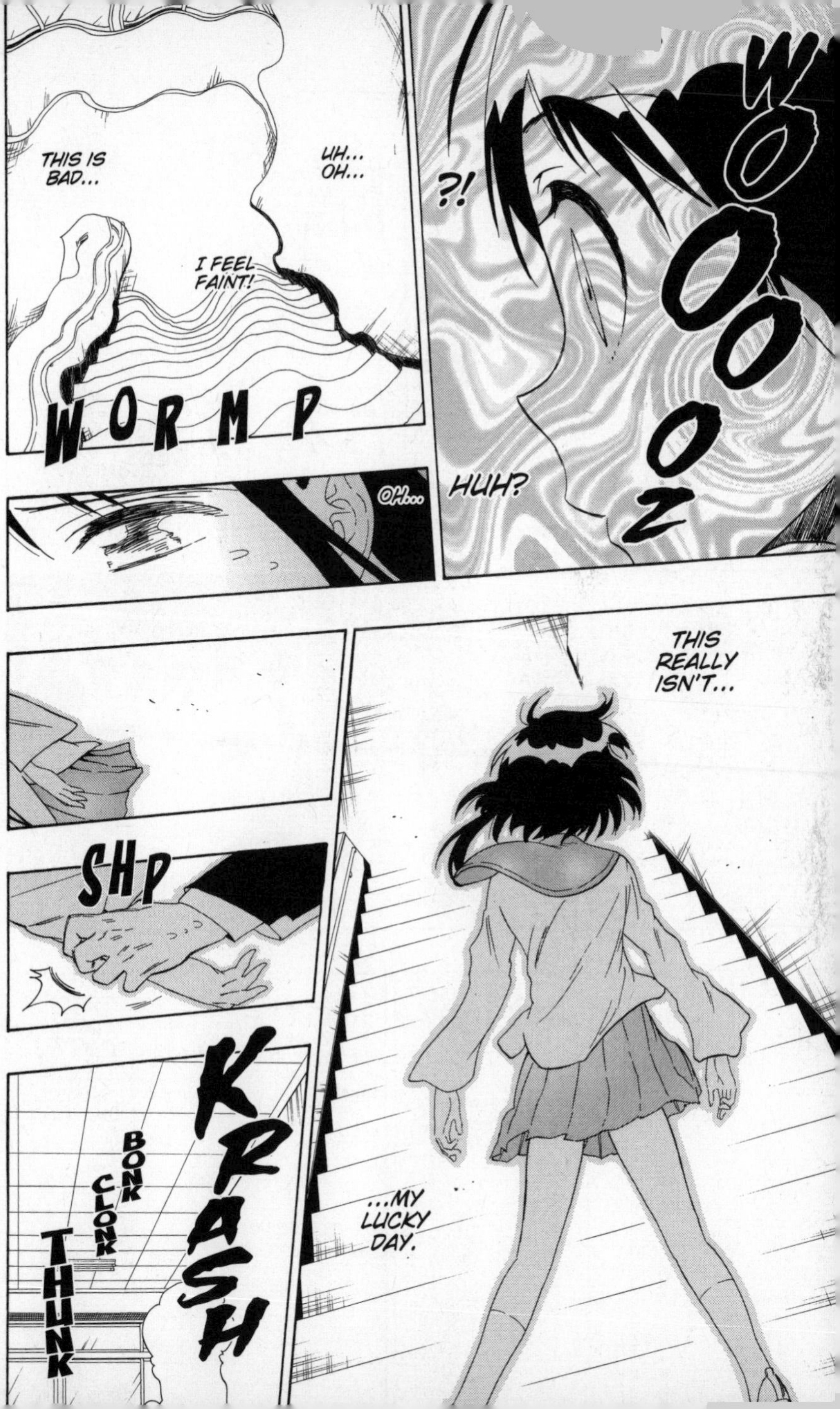
WOOOOOZ
?!
HUH?
UH... OH...
THIS IS BAD...
I FEEL FAINT!
WORMP
OH...
THIS REALLY ISN'T...
...MY LUCKY DAY.
SHP
KRASH
BONK
CLONK
THUNK

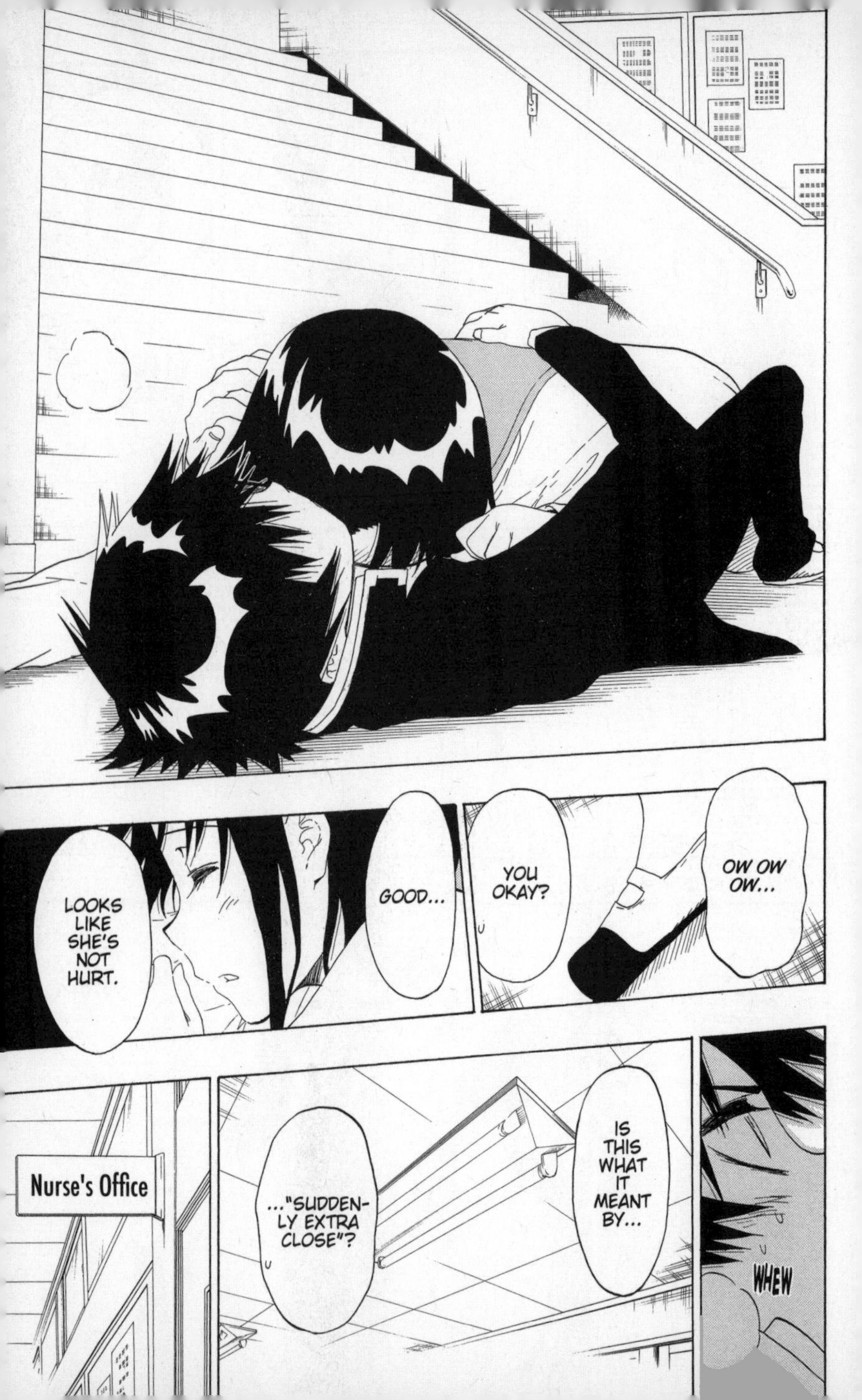
OW OW OW...
YOU OKAY?
GOOD...
LOOKS LIKE SHE'S NOT HURT.
WHEW
IS THIS WHAT IT MEANT BY...
..."SUDDENLY EXTRA CLOSE"?
Nurse's Office

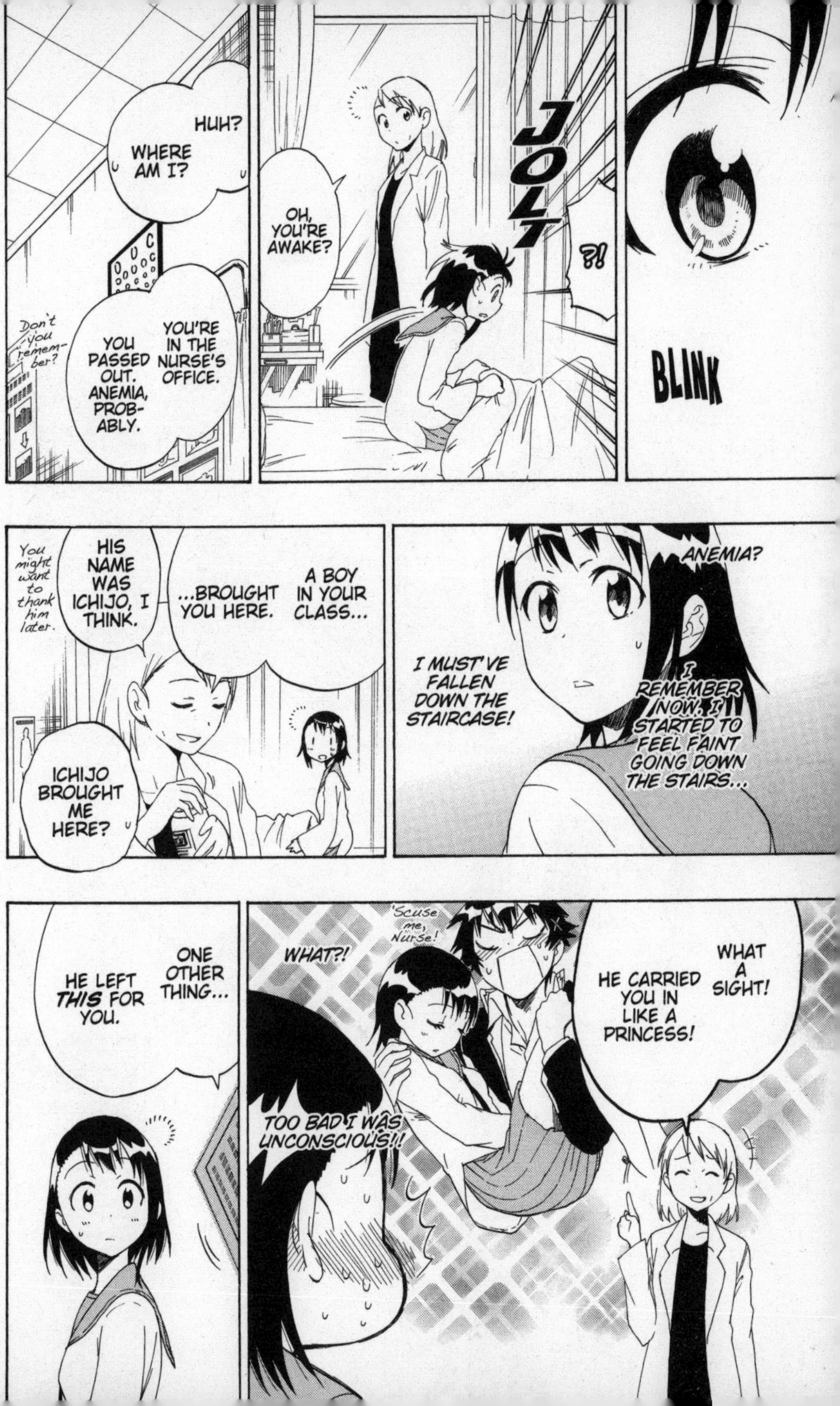
BLINK
JOLT
?!
OH, YOU'RE AWAKE?
HUH?
WHERE AM I?
YOU'RE IN THE NURSE'S OFFICE.
YOU PASSED OUT. ANEMIA, PROBABLY.
Don't you remember?
ANEMIA?
I REMEMBER NOW. I STARTED TO FEEL FAINT GOING DOWN THE STAIRS...
I MUST'VE FALLEN DOWN THE STAIRCASE!
A BOY IN YOUR CLASS...
...BROUGHT YOU HERE.
HIS NAME WAS ICHIJO, I THINK.
You might want to thank him later.
ICHIJO BROUGHT ME HERE?
WHAT A SIGHT!
HE CARRIED YOU IN LIKE A PRINCESS!
'Scuse me, Nurse!
WHAT?!
TOO BAD I WAS UNCONSCIOUS!!
ONE OTHER THING...
HE LEFT *THIS* FOR YOU.

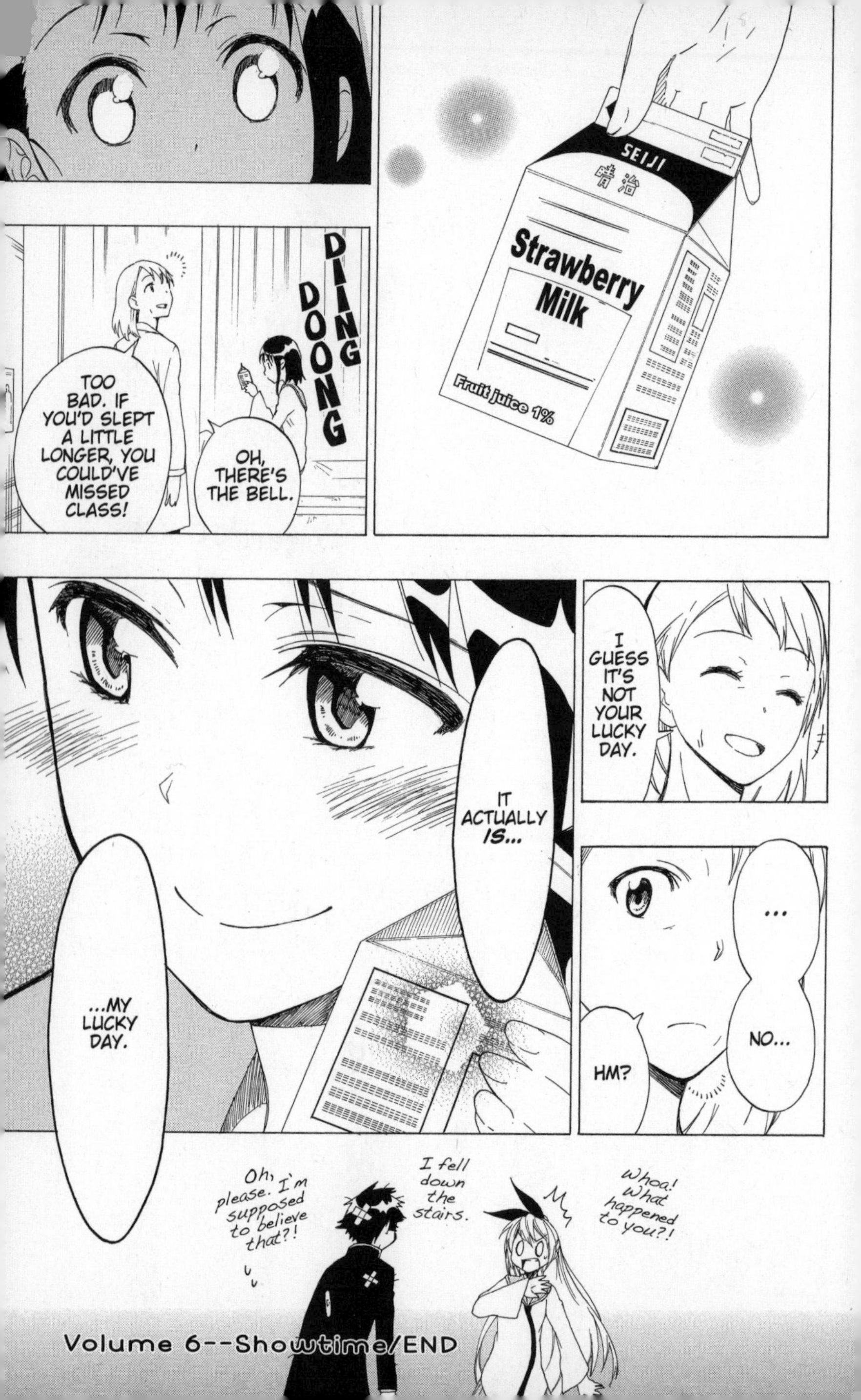

SEIJI
Strawberry Milk
Fruit juice 1%
DING DOONG DONG
OH, THERE'S THE BELL.
TOO BAD. IF YOU'D SLEPT A LITTLE LONGER, YOU COULD'VE MISSED CLASS!
I GUESS IT'S NOT YOUR LUCKY DAY.
...
NO...
HM?
IT ACTUALLY *IS*...
...MY LUCKY DAY.
Whoa! What happened to you?!
I fell down the stairs.
Oh, please. I'm supposed to believe that?!
Volume 6--Showtime/END

Bonus Manga

☆ Meanwhile... ☆

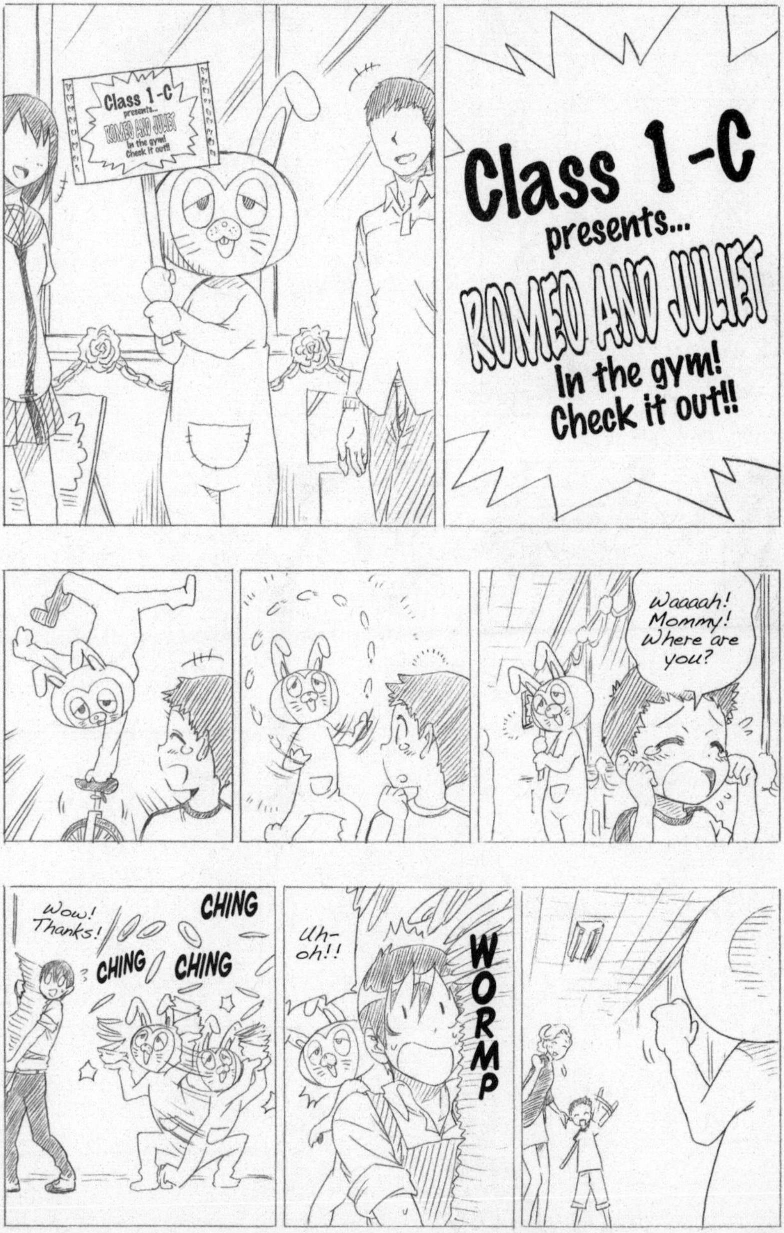
Class 1-C
presents...
ROMEO AND JULIET
In the gym!
Check it out!!
Class 1-C
presents...
ROMEO AND JULIET
In the gym!
Check it out!!
Waaaah! Mommy! Where are you?
WORMP
Uh-oh!!
CHING
Wow! Thanks!
CHING
CHING

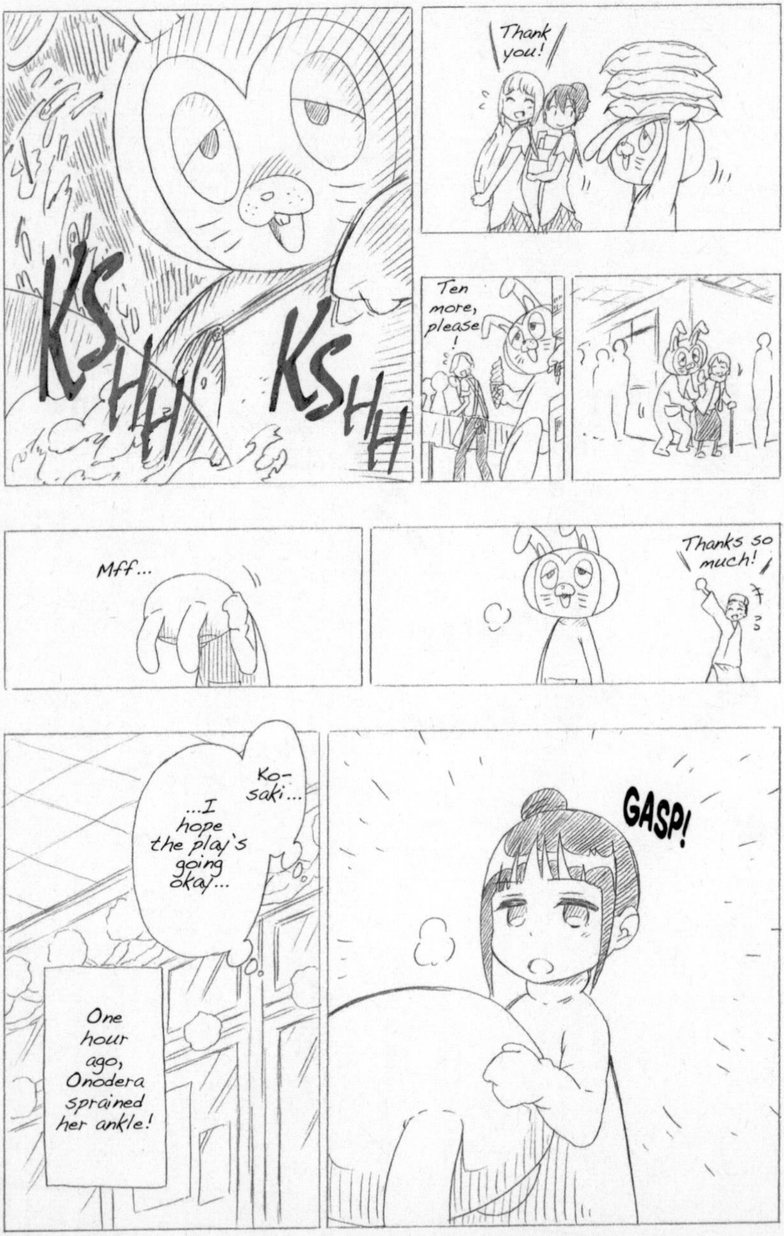
Thank you!
Ten more, please!
KSHH
KSHH
Thanks so much!
Mff...
GASP!
Ko-saki... ...I hope the play's going okay...
One hour ago, Onodera sprained her ankle!
☆ END ☆

Bonus Manga

☆A day in the life of Tachibana☆

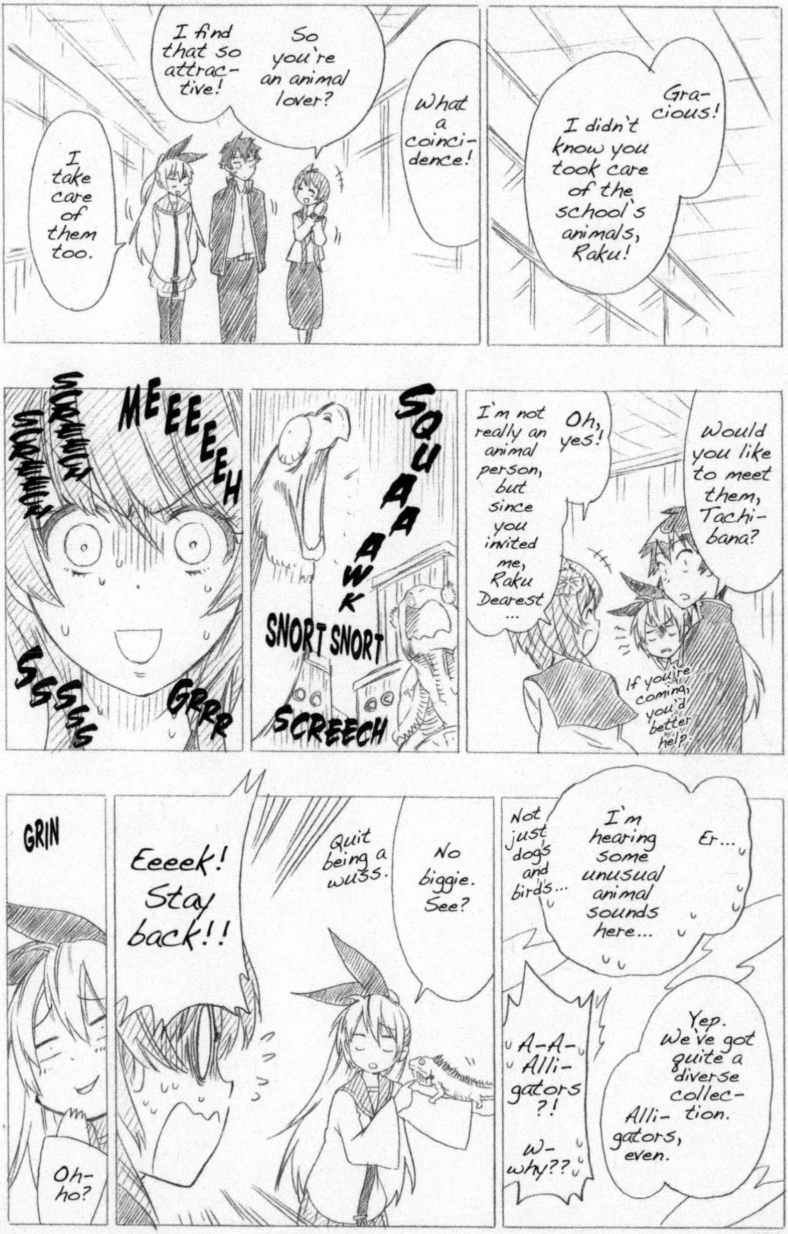

Gracious!
I didn't know you took care of the school's animals, Raku!
What a coincidence!
So you're an animal lover?
I find that so attractive!
I take care of them too.
Would you like to meet them, Tachibana?
Oh, yes!
I'm not really an animal person, but since you invited me, Raku Dearest...
If you're coming, you'd better help.
SQUAAAAWK
SNORT SNORT
SCREECH
MEEEEEH
SCREECH
SCREECH
GRRR
SSSSS
Er...
I'm hearing some unusual animal sounds here...
Not just dogs and birds...
Yep. We've got quite a diverse collection. Alligators, even.
A-A-Alligators?!
W-why??
No biggie. See?
Quit being a wuss.
Eeeek! Stay back!!
GRIN
Oh-ho?

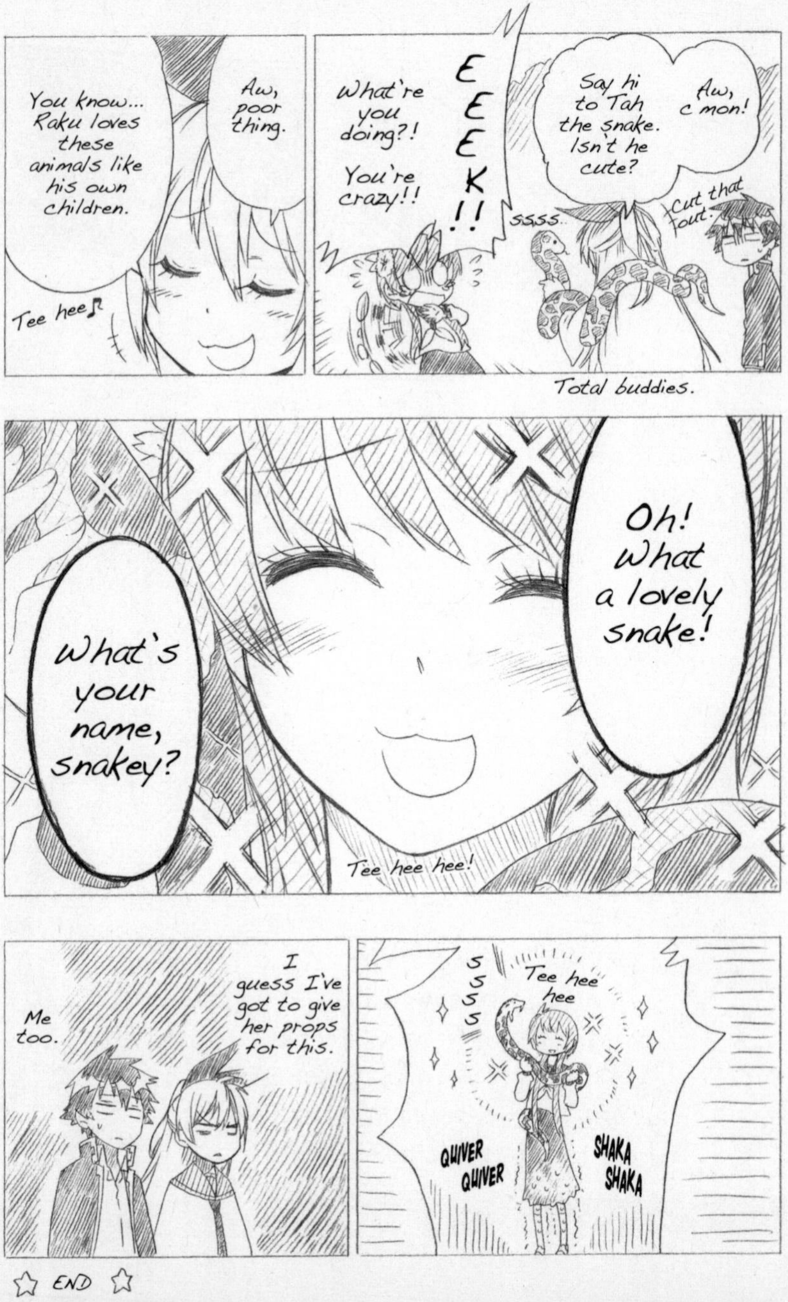
Aw, c'mon!
Say hi to Tah the snake. Isn't he cute?
Cut that out.
ssss..
EEEK!!
What're you doing?!
You're crazy!!
Total buddies.
Aw, poor thing.
You know... Raku loves these animals like his own children.
Tee hee♪
Oh! What a lovely snake!
What's your name, snakey?
Tee hee hee!
SSSS
Tee hee hee
QUIVER QUIVER
SHAKA SHAKA
I guess I've got to give her props for this.
Me too.

☆ END ☆

You're Reading the WRONG WAY!

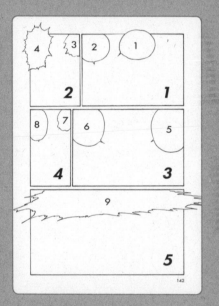

NISEKOI reads from right to left, starting in the upper-right corner. Japanese is read from right to left, meaning that action, sound effects, and word-balloon order are completely reversed from English order.